FRANKLIN PARK PUBLIC LIBRARY

3 1316 00343 4376

W9-DDF-041

5/07

WITHDRAWN

FRANKLIN PARK PUBLIC LIBRARY
FRANKLIN PARK, ILL.

Each borrower is held responsible for all library material drawn on his card and for fines accruing on the same. No material will be issued until such fine has been paid.

All injuries to library material beyond reasonable wear and all losses shall be made good to the satisfaction of the librarian.

Replacement costs will be billed after 42 days overdue.

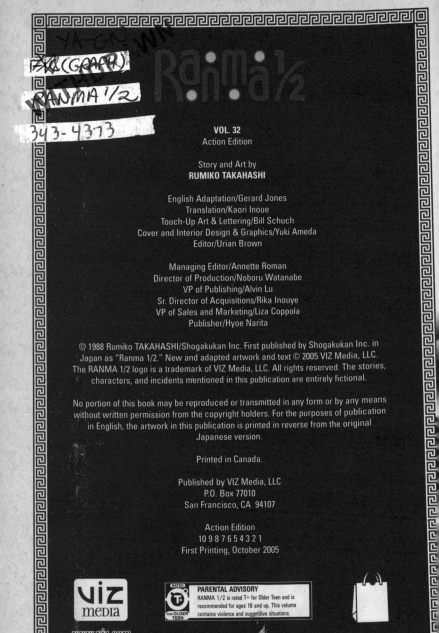

Ranma ½

VOL. 32
Action Edition

Story and Art by
RUMIKO TAKAHASHI

English Adaptation/Gerard Jones
Translation/Kaori Inoue
Touch-Up Art & Lettering/Bill Schuch
Cover and Interior Design & Graphics/Yuki Ameda
Editor/Urian Brown

Managing Editor/Annette Roman
Director of Production/Noboru Watanabe
VP of Publishing/Alvin Lu
Sr. Director of Acquisitions/Rika Inouye
VP of Sales and Marketing/Liza Coppola
Publisher/Hyoe Narita

© 1988 Rumiko TAKAHASHI/Shogakukan Inc. First published by Shogakukan Inc. in
Japan as "Ranma 1/2." New and adapted artwork and text © 2005 VIZ Media, LLC.
The RANMA 1/2 logo is a trademark of VIZ Media, LLC. All rights reserved. The stories,
characters, and incidents mentioned in this publication are entirely fictional.

No portion of this book may be reproduced or transmitted in any form or by any means
without written permission from the copyright holders. For the purposes of publication
in English, the artwork in this publication is printed in reverse from the original
Japanese version.

Printed in Canada.

Published by VIZ Media, LLC
P.O. Box 77010
San Francisco, CA 94107

Action Edition
10 9 8 7 6 5 4 3 2 1
First Printing, October 2005

www.viz.com

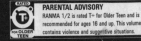

PARENTAL ADVISORY
RANMA 1/2 is rated T+ for Older Teen and is
recommended for ages 16 and up. This volume
contains violence and suggestive situations.

Ranma 1/2

VOL. 32
Action Edition

WITHDRAWN
FRANKLIN PARK LIBRARY
FRANKLIN PARK, IL

STORY & ART BY
RUMIKO TAKAHASHI

STORY THUS FAR

The Tendos are an average, run-of-the-mill Japanese family—on the surface, that is. Soun Tendo is the owner and proprietor of the Tendo Dojo, where "Anything Goes Martial Arts" is practiced. Like the name says, anything goes, and usually does.

When Soun's old friend Genma Saotome comes to visit, Soun's three lovely young daughters—Akane, Nabiki and Kasumi—are told that it's time for one of them to become the fiancée of Genma's teenage son, as per an agreement made between the two fathers years ago. Youngest daughter Akane—who says she hates boys—is quickly nominated for bridal duty by her sisters.

Unfortunately, Ranma and his father have suffered a strange accident. While training in China, both plunged into one of many "cursed" springs at the legendary martial arts training ground of Jusenkyo. These springs transform the unlucky dunkee into whomever—or whatever—drowned there hundreds of years ago.

From then on, a splash of cold water turns Ranma's father into a giant panda, and Ranma becomes a beautiful, busty young woman. Hot water reverses the effect...but only until next time. As it turns out, Ranma and Genma aren't the only ones who have taken the Jusenkyo plunge—and it isn't long before they meet several other members of the Jusenkyo "cursed."

Although their parents are still determined to see Ranma and Akane marry and assume ownership of the training hall, Ranma seems to have a strange talent for accumulating surplus fiancées...and Akane has a few stubbornly determined suitors of her own. Will the two ever work out their differences, get rid of all these "extra" people, or will they just call the whole thing off? What's a half-boy, half-girl (not to mention all-girl, angry girl) to do...?

CAST OF CHARACTERS

THE AOTOMES

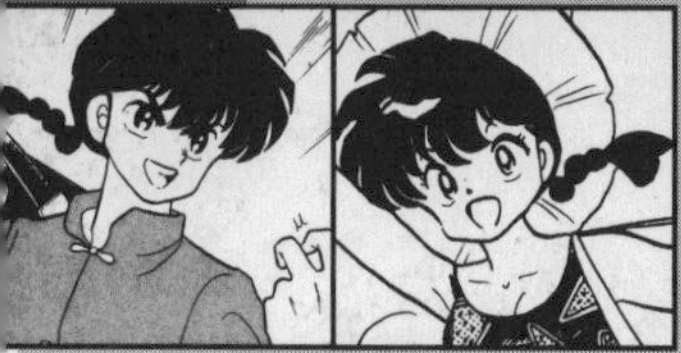

RANMA SAOTOME
Martial artist with far too many fiancées, and an ego that won't let him take defeat. Changes into a girl when splashed with cold water.

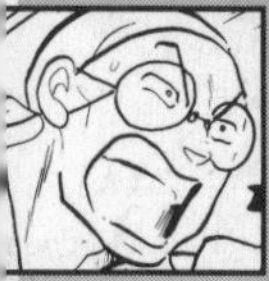

GENMA SAOTOME
Ranma's lazy father, who left his wife and home years ago with his young son (Ranma), to train in the martial arts. Changes into a panda.

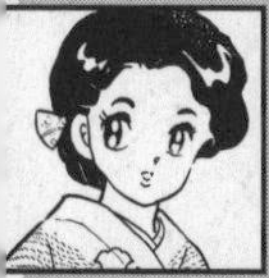

NODOKA SAOTOME
The wife of Genma and mother of Ranma, who doesn't know of their curse or where they are, as they always disguise themselves in their panda and girl forms whenever she is around...

THE MASTER

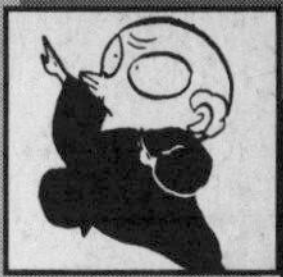

HAPPOSAI
Happosai is the founding father of Anything Goes Martial Arts, and is a dirty old man with a penchant for stealing girls underwear.

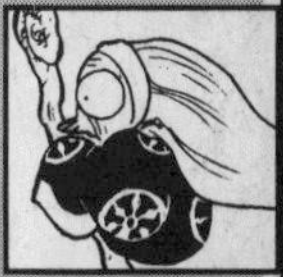

COLOGNE
Grumpy old granny of Shampoo who wants to see her dear granddaughter do well. Is she a better martial arts coach than Genma and Soun?

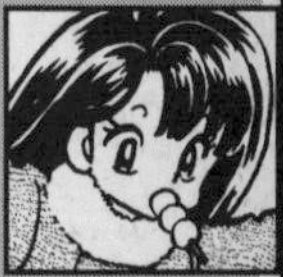

HINAKO NINOMIYA
An English teacher at Furinkan High who switches between the form of a child and an adult woman (by draining an opponent's energy).

THE TENDOS

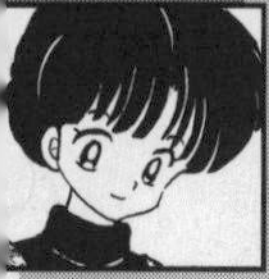

AKANE TENDO
Martial artist, tomboy, and Ranma's reluctant fiancée. Has no clue how much Ryoga likes her, or what relation he might have to her pet black pig, P-chan.

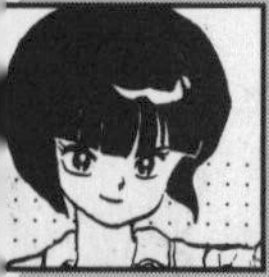

NABIKI TENDO
Always ready to "make a buck" off the suffering of others, cold-hearted capitalist Nabiki is the middle Tendo daughter.

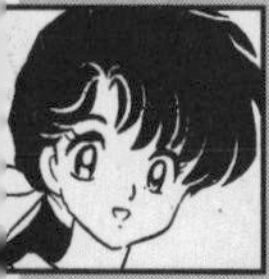

KASUMI TENDO
Sweet-natured eldest Tendo daughter and substitute mother figure for the Tendo family.

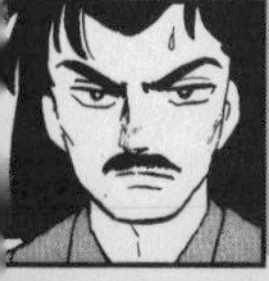

SOUN TENDO
Head of the Tendo household and owner of the Tendo Dojo. Father of three daughters.

THE SUITORS

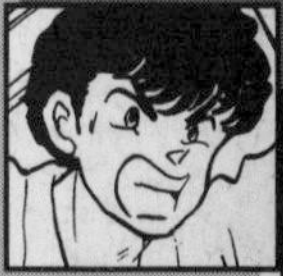

TATEWAKI KUNO
Poetry spouting Tatewaki is the school's Kendo captain and is one of Ranma's major rivals. He is in love with both girl-type Ranma and Akane...

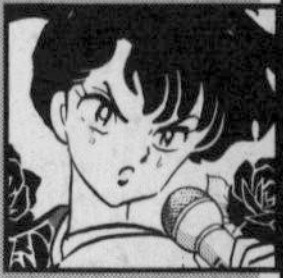

KODACHI KUNO
Twisted sister of Tatewaki. An expert in Martial Arts Rhythmic Gymnastics, she's determined to use her ribbon-whipping skills to tame Ranma.

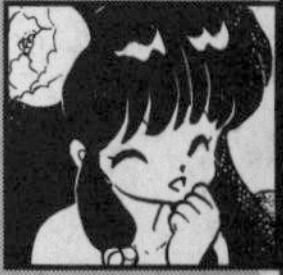

SHAMPOO
Works at the Cat Care and fell into one of the accursed springs. Has a thing for Ranma, and definitely doesn't have a thing for Mousse or Akane. Mee-yow!

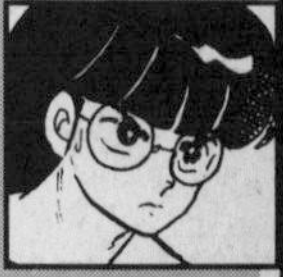

MOUSSE
Nearsighted quacker who fell into one of the accursed springs and has a thing for Shampoo.

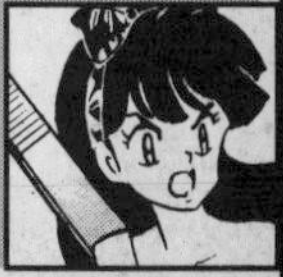

UKYO KUONJI
Okonomiyaki chef Ukyo's grudge against Ranma goes way back to when their fathers agreed to have them become engaged to each other as little children, but stole their okonomiyaki cart and left her behind.

CONTENTS

PART 1

SHOTGUN BEANS!!

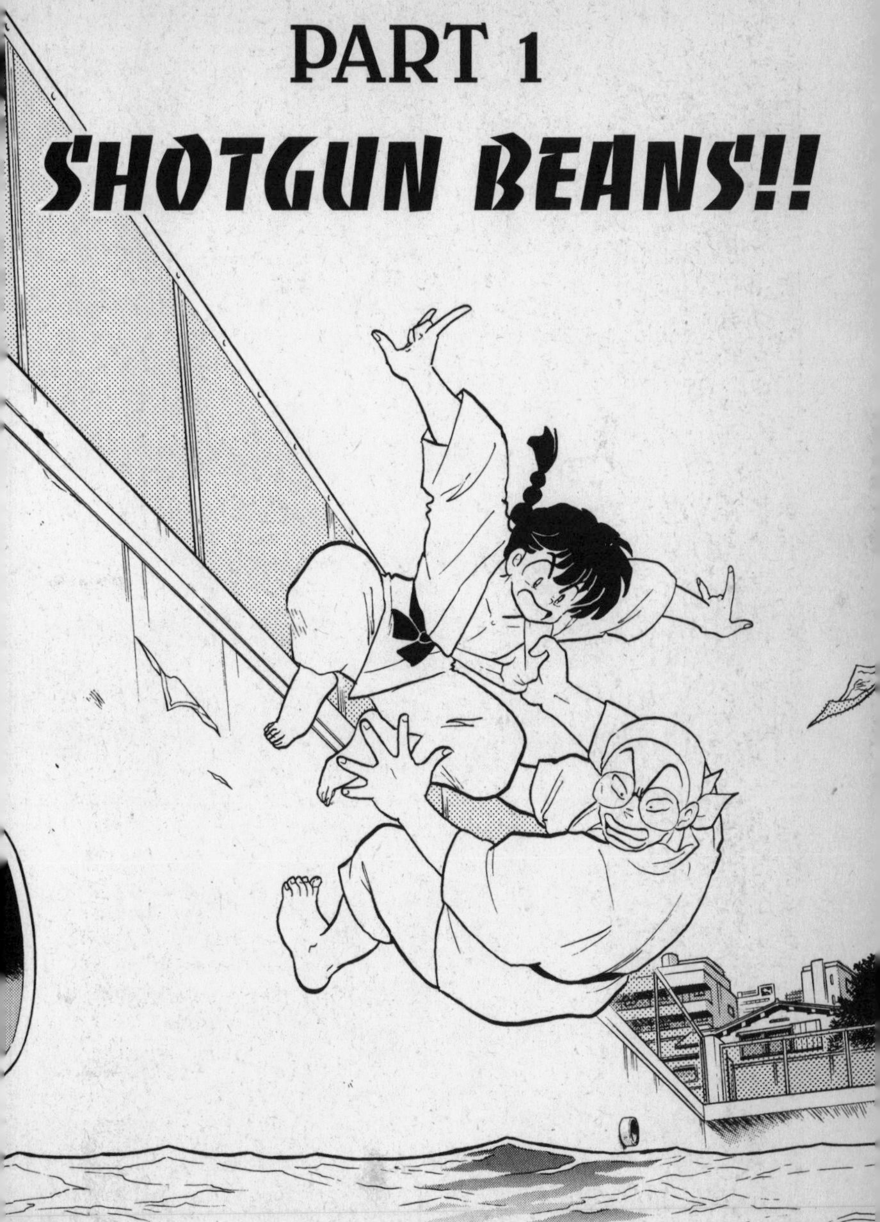

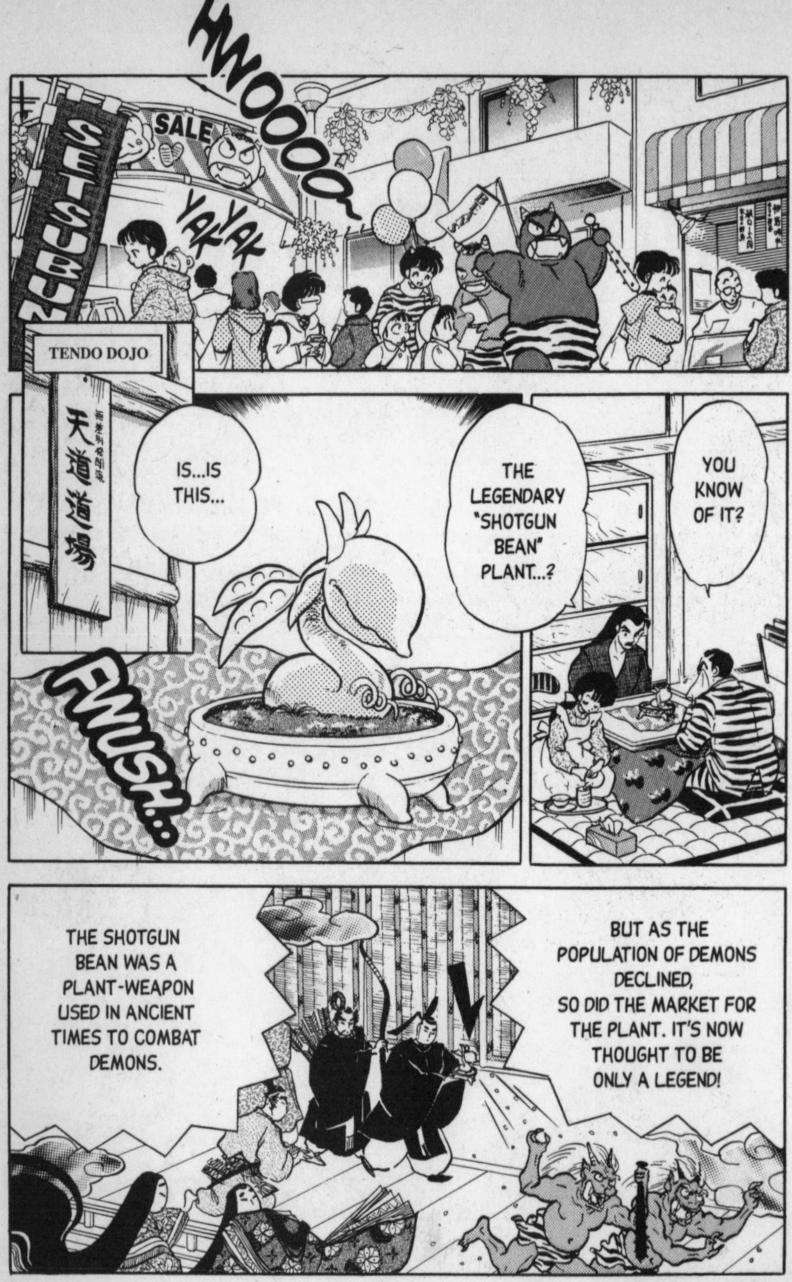
HWOOOO
SETSUBUN
SALE
YAK YAK
TENDO DOJO
天道道場
IS...IS THIS...
FWUSH...
THE LEGENDARY "SHOTGUN BEAN" PLANT...?
YOU KNOW OF IT?
THE SHOTGUN BEAN WAS A PLANT-WEAPON USED IN ANCIENT TIMES TO COMBAT DEMONS.
BUT AS THE POPULATION OF DEMONS DECLINED, SO DID THE MARKET FOR THE PLANT. IT'S NOW THOUGHT TO BE ONLY A LEGEND!

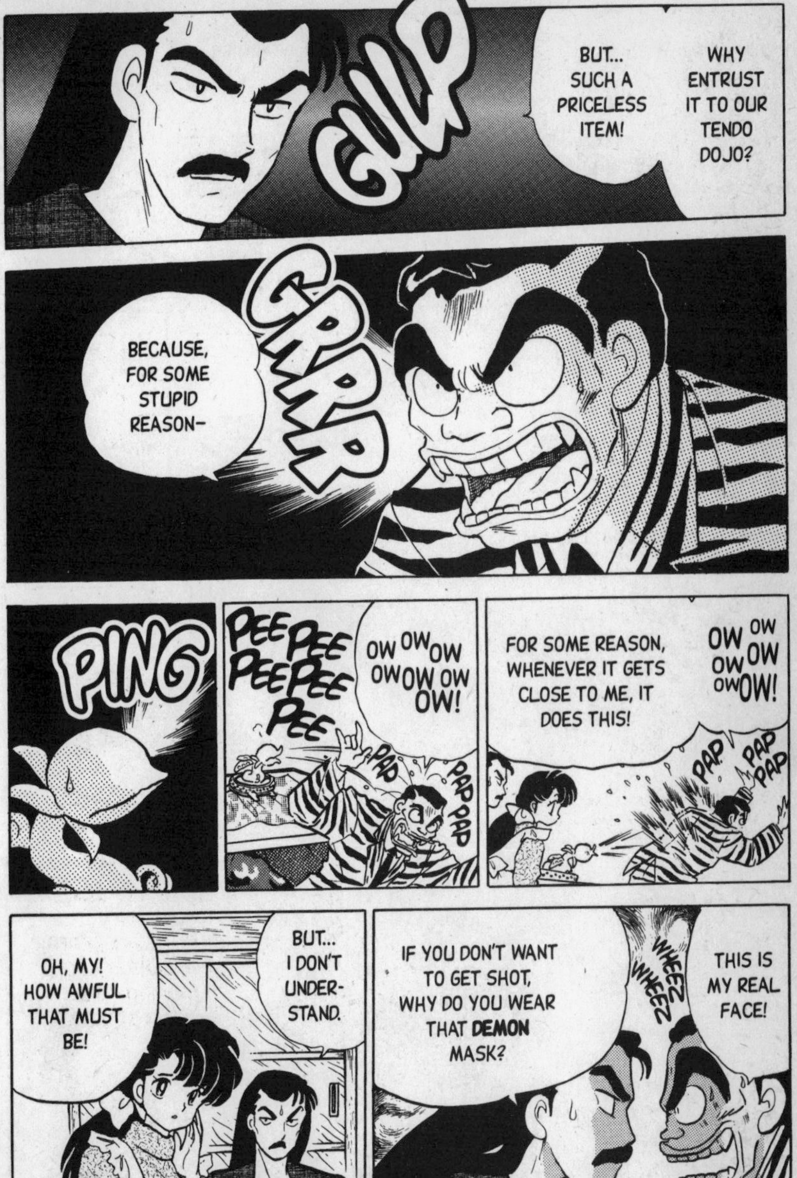
GULP
BUT... SUCH A PRICELESS ITEM!
WHY ENTRUST IT TO OUR TENDO DOJO?
BECAUSE, FOR SOME STUPID REASON–
GRRR
PING
PEE PEE PEE PEE PEE PEE PEE
OW OW OW OW OW OW OW!
PAP PAP PAP PAP
FOR SOME REASON, WHENEVER IT GETS CLOSE TO ME, IT DOES THIS!
OW OW OW OW OW OW!
PAP PAP PAP
OH, MY! HOW AWFUL THAT MUST BE!
BUT... I DON'T UNDER-STAND.
IF YOU DON'T WANT TO GET SHOT, WHY DO YOU WEAR THAT **DEMON** MASK?
WHEEZ WHEEZ
THIS IS MY REAL FACE!

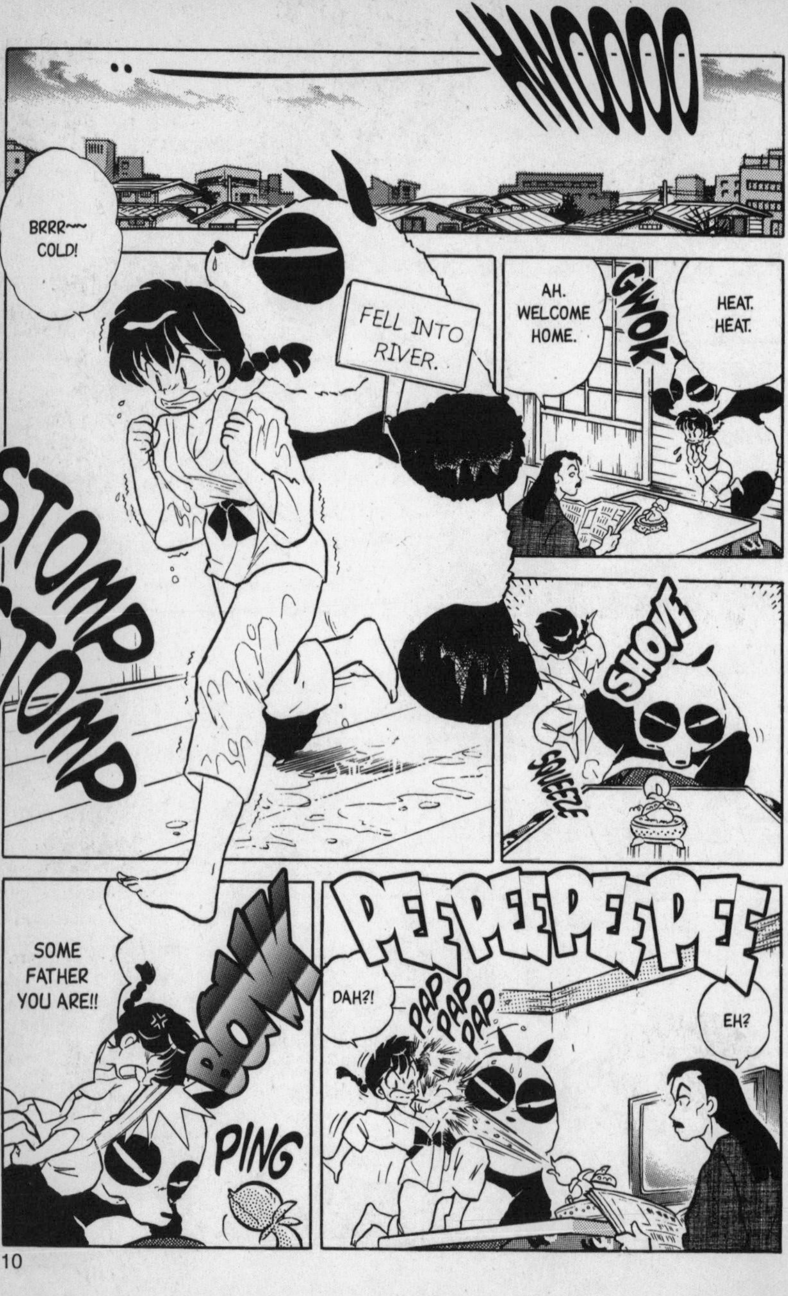
..
WHOOOO
BRRR~~ COLD!
FELL INTO RIVER.
STOMP STOMP
AH. WELCOME HOME.
GWOK
HEAT. HEAT.
SHOVE
SQUEEZE
SOME FATHER YOU ARE!!
BONK
PING
PEE PEE PEE PEE
DAH?!
PAP PAP PAP
EH?

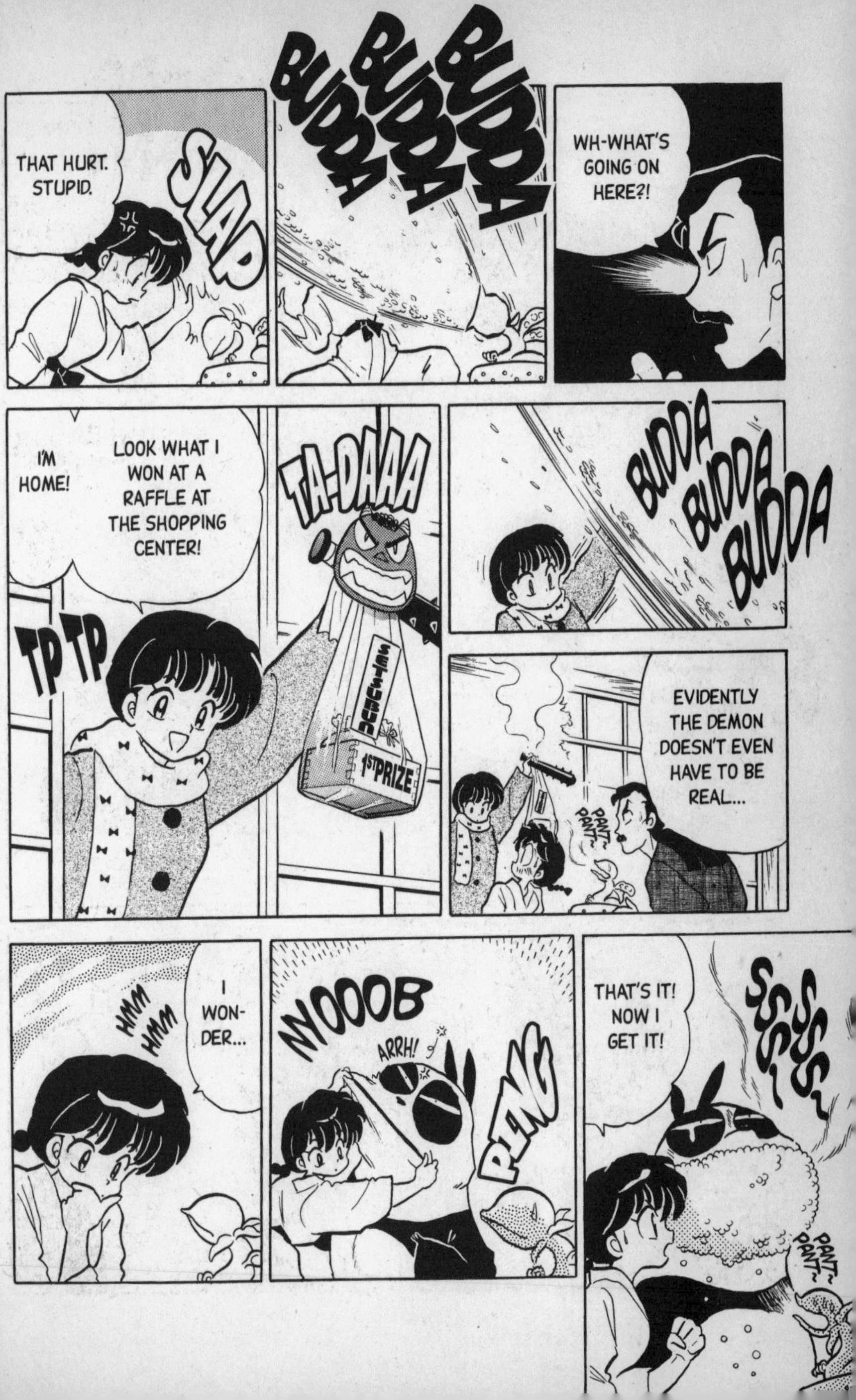
THAT HURT. STUPID.
SLAP
BUDDA BUDDA BUDDA
WH-WHAT'S GOING ON HERE?!
I'M HOME!
LOOK WHAT I WON AT A RAFFLE AT THE SHOPPING CENTER!
TA-DAAA
TP TP
SETSUBUN
1ST PRIZE
BUDDA BUDDA BUDDA
EVIDENTLY THE DEMON DOESN'T EVEN HAVE TO BE REAL...
PANT PANT~
HMM HMM
I WON-DER...
NYOOOB
ARRH!
PING
THAT'S IT! NOW I GET IT!
SSSS~ SSSS~
PANT PANT~

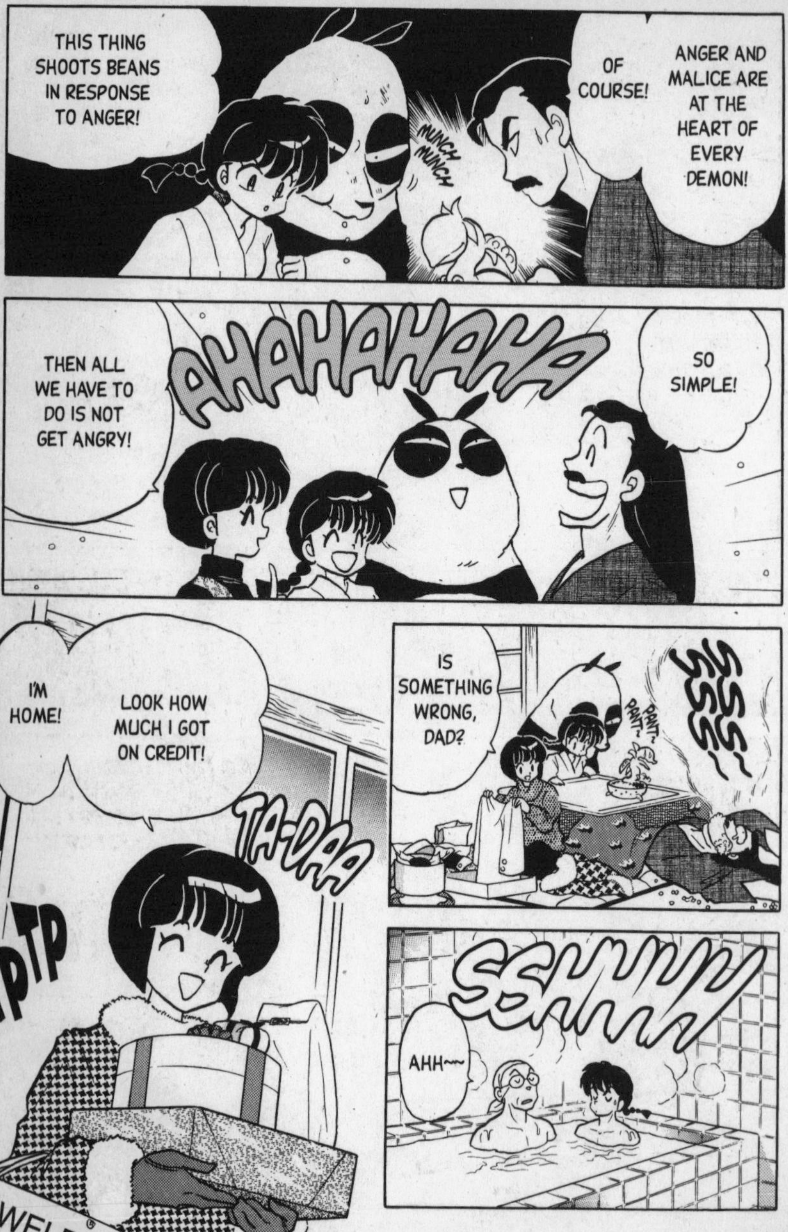
THIS THING SHOOTS BEANS IN RESPONSE TO ANGER!
MUNCH MUNCH
OF COURSE!
ANGER AND MALICE ARE AT THE HEART OF EVERY DEMON!
THEN ALL WE HAVE TO DO IS NOT GET ANGRY!
AHAHAHAHA
SO SIMPLE!
I'M HOME!
LOOK HOW MUCH I GOT ON CREDIT!
TA-DAA
TP TP
JEWELRY
IS SOMETHING WRONG, DAD?
PANT~ PANT~
SSS~ SSS~
AHH~~

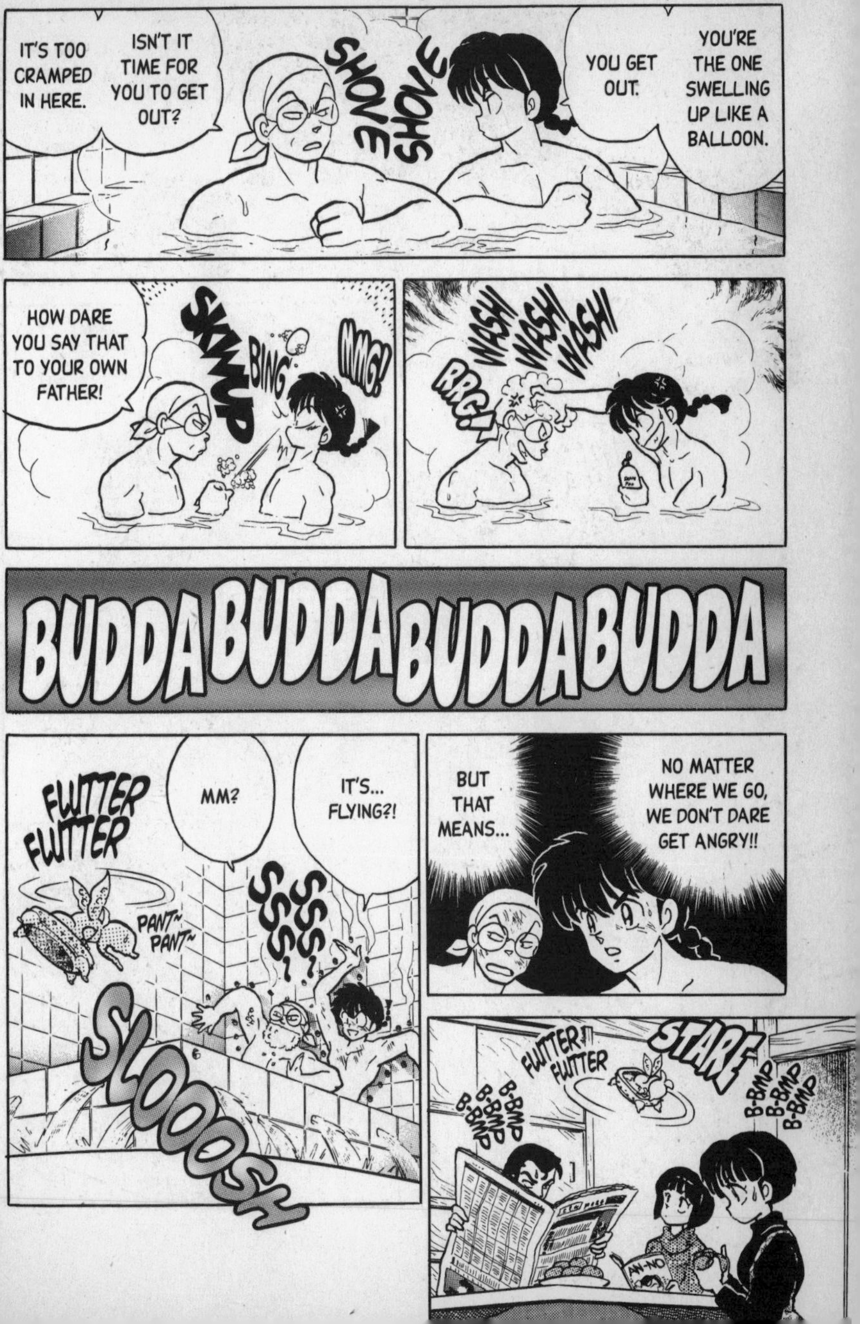
IT'S TOO CRAMPED IN HERE.
ISN'T IT TIME FOR YOU TO GET OUT?
SHOVE
SHOVE
YOU GET OUT.
YOU'RE THE ONE SWELLING UP LIKE A BALLOON.
HOW DARE YOU SAY THAT TO YOUR OWN FATHER!
SKWUP
BING
MMG!
RRG!!
WASH
WASH
WASH
BUDDA BUDDA BUDDA BUDDA
FLUTTER FLUTTER
MM?
IT'S... FLYING?!
PANT~ PANT~
SSSS SSSS
SLOOOSH
BUT THAT MEANS...
NO MATTER WHERE WE GO, WE DON'T DARE GET ANGRY!!
FLUTTER FLUTTER
STARE
B-BMP B-BMP B-BMP
B-BMP B-BMP B-BMP
AN-NO

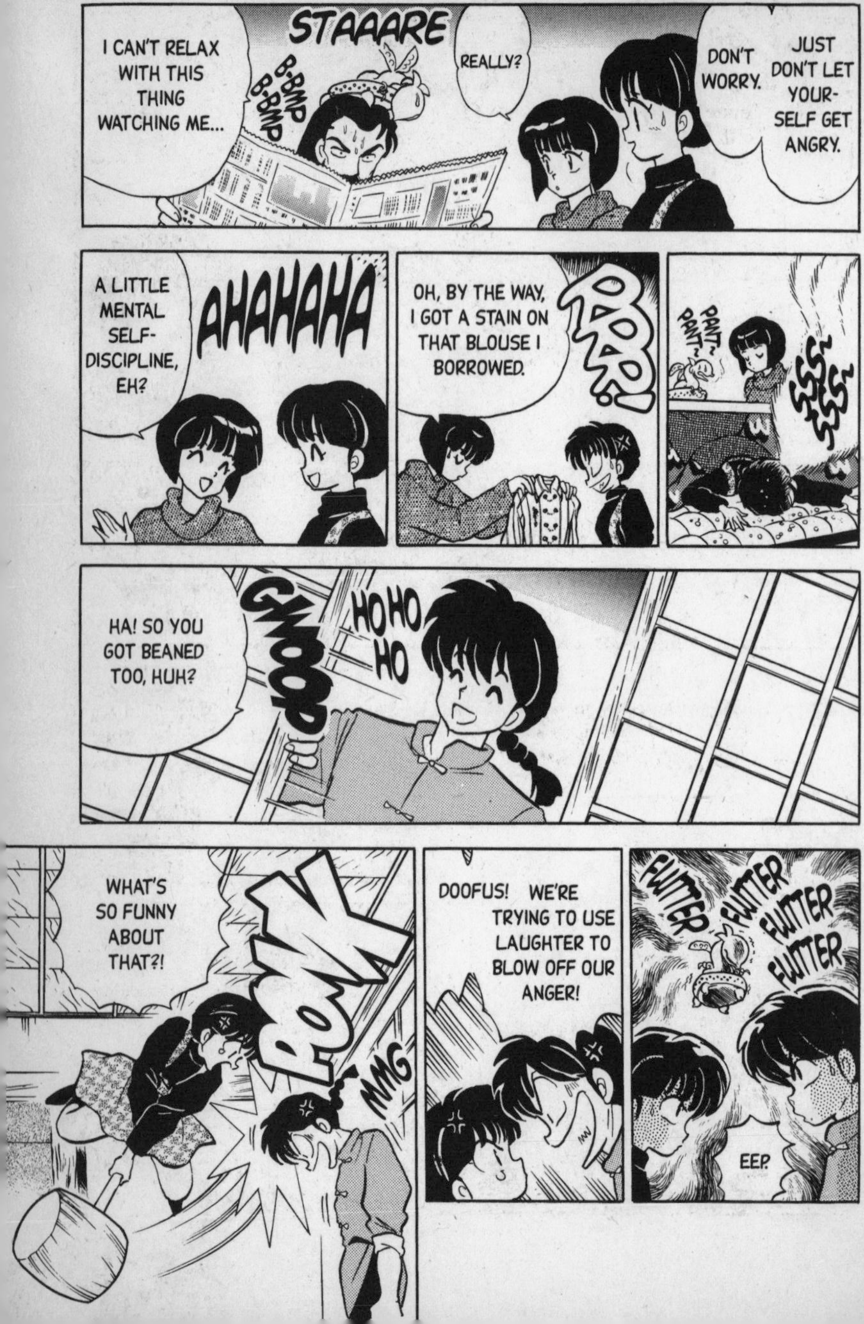
I CAN'T RELAX WITH THIS THING WATCHING ME...
STAAARE
B-BMP B-BMP
REALLY?
DON'T WORRY.
JUST DON'T LET YOURSELF GET ANGRY.
A LITTLE MENTAL SELF-DISCIPLINE, EH?
AHAHAHA
OH, BY THE WAY, I GOT A STAIN ON THAT BLOUSE I BORROWED.
PANT PANT
HA! SO YOU GOT BEANED TOO, HUH?
GWOOP
HO HO HO
WHAT'S SO FUNNY ABOUT THAT?!
BONK
MMG
DOOFUS! WE'RE TRYING TO USE LAUGHTER TO BLOW OFF OUR ANGER!
FLUTTER FLUTTER FLUTTER FLUTTER
EEP.

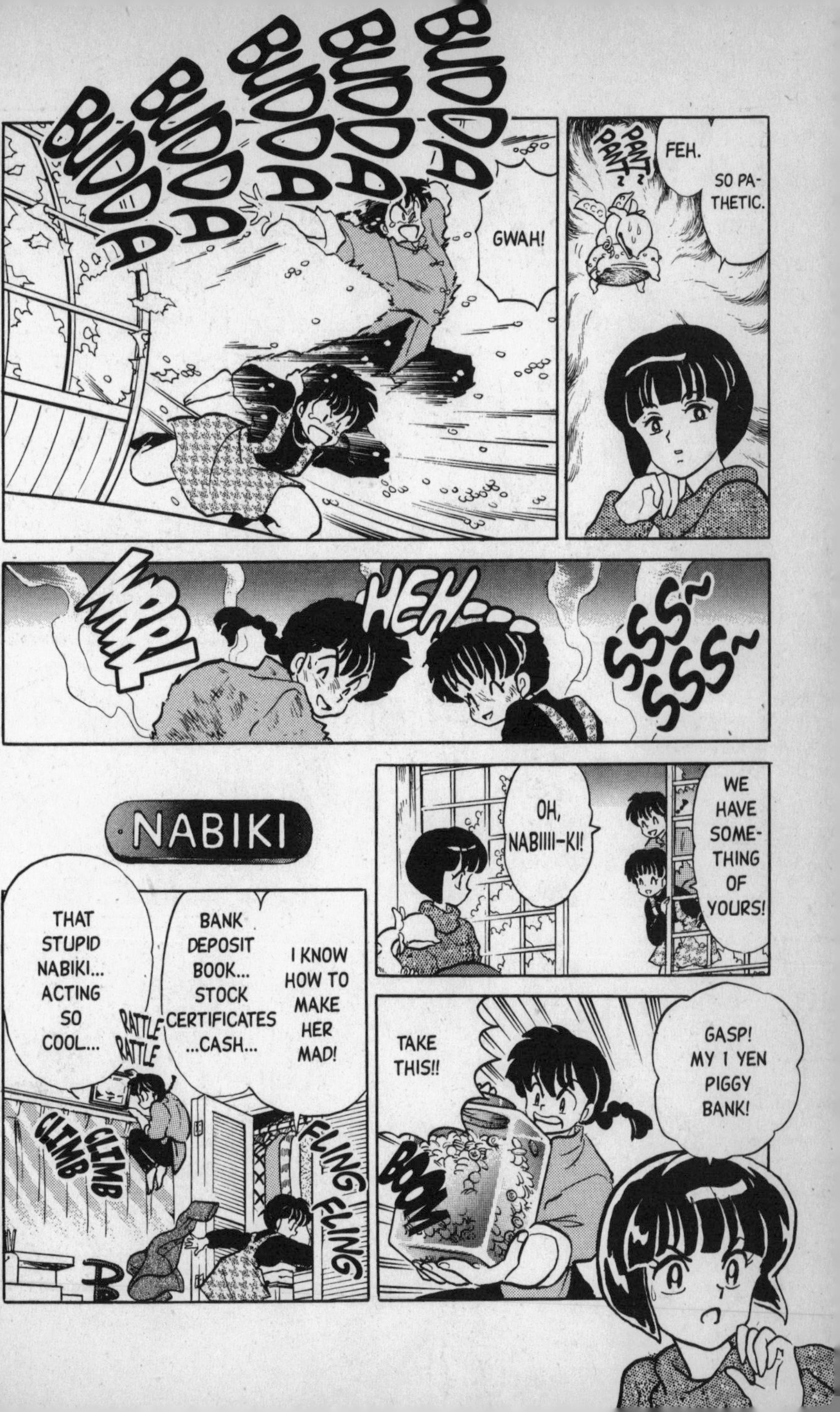
BUDDA BUDDA BUDDA BUDDA BUDDA
GWAH!
PANT PANT
FEH.
SO PATHETIC.
WRRL
HEH...
SSS~ SSS~
NABIKI
THAT STUPID NABIKI... ACTING SO COOL...
RATTLE RATTLE
BANK DEPOSIT BOOK... STOCK CERTIFICATES ...CASH...
I KNOW HOW TO MAKE HER MAD!
CLIMB CLIMB
FLING FLING
OH, NABIIII-KI!
WE HAVE SOMETHING OF YOURS!
TAKE THIS!!
BOOM
GASP! MY 1 YEN PIGGY BANK!

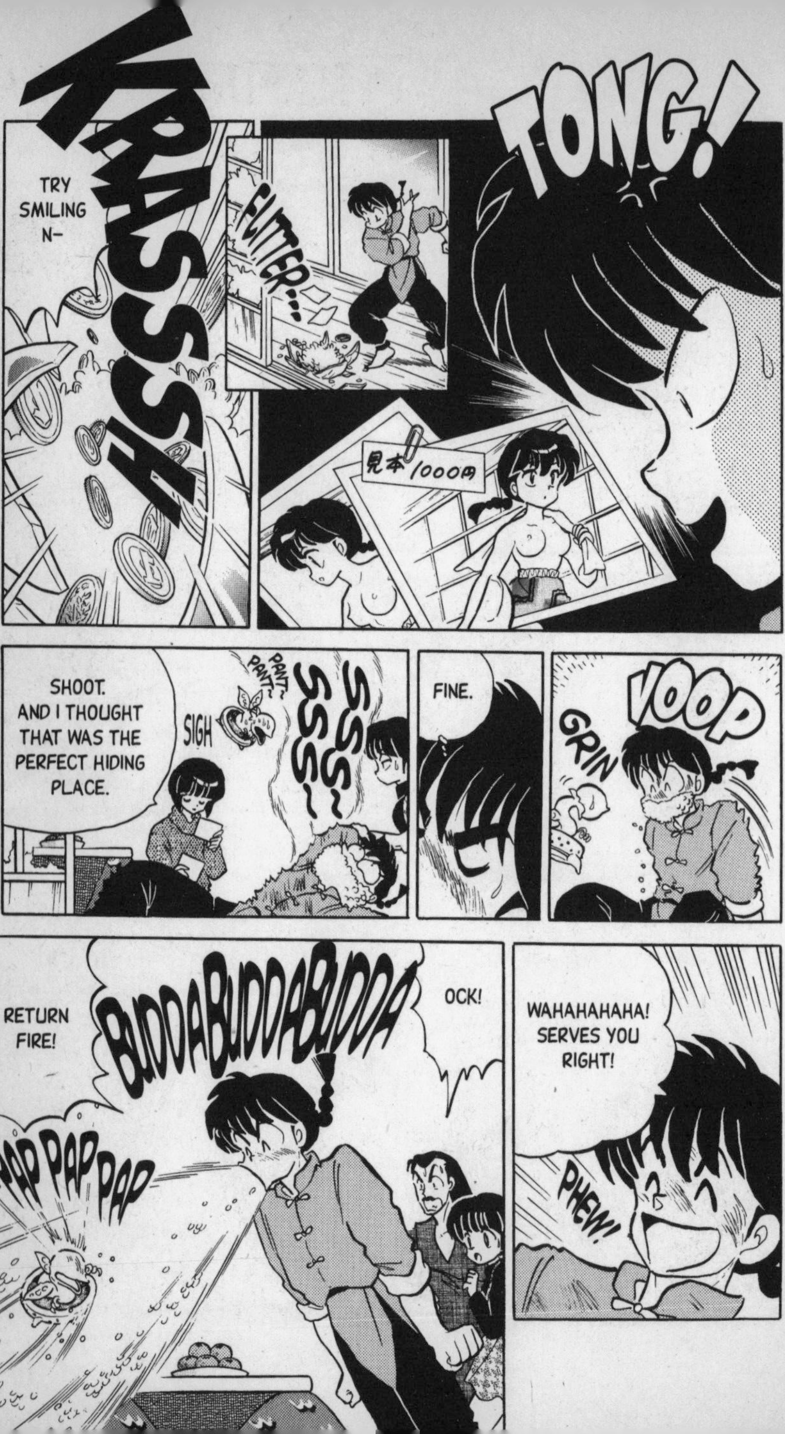
TRY SMILING N–
KRASSSH
FLUTTER...
TONG!
見本 1000円
SHOOT. AND I THOUGHT THAT WAS THE PERFECT HIDING PLACE.
SIGH
PANT PANT
SSSS~ SSSS~
FINE.
VOOP
GRIN
RETURN FIRE!
BUDDABUDDABUDDA
OCK!
PAP PAP PAP
WAHAHAHAHA! SERVES YOU RIGHT!
PHEW!

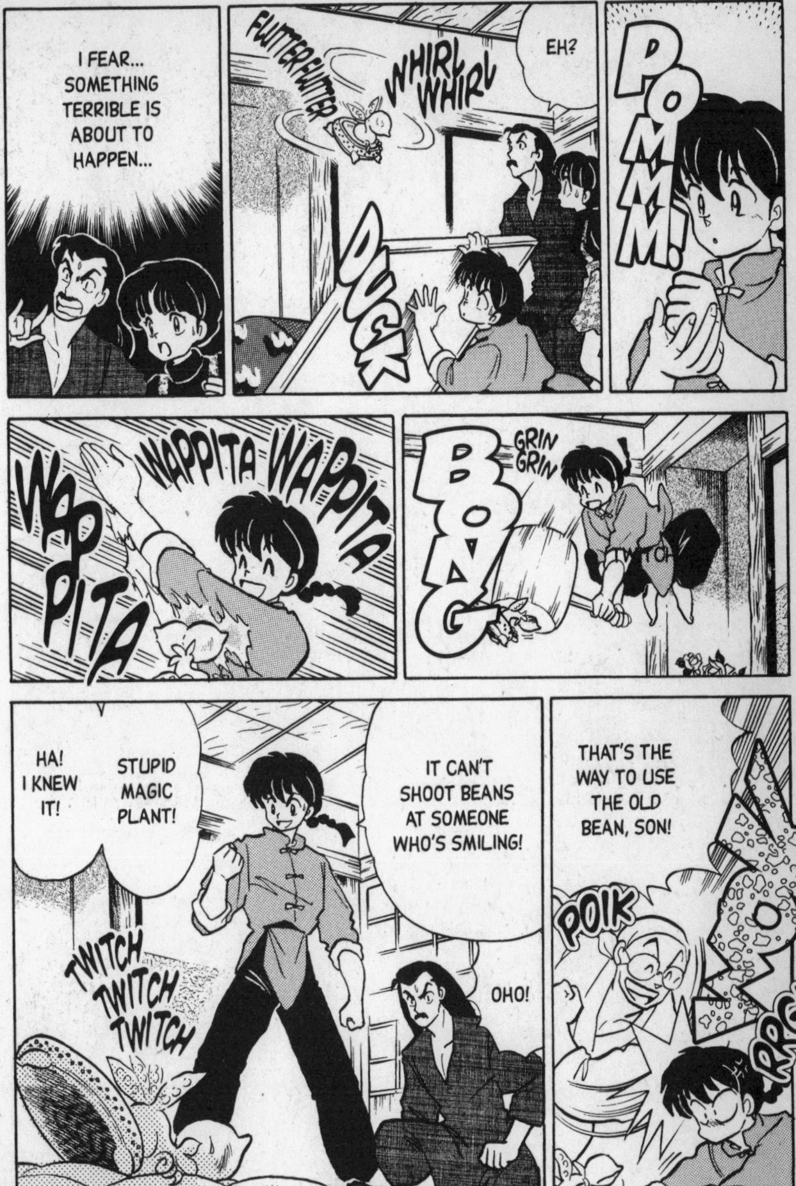
I FEAR... SOMETHING TERRIBLE IS ABOUT TO HAPPEN...
FLUTTERFLUTTER
WHIRL WHIRL
EH?
DUCK
POMMM!
WAPPITA WAPPITA
WAP PITA
GRIN GRIN
BONG
TWITCH
HA! I KNEW IT!
STUPID MAGIC PLANT!
IT CAN'T SHOOT BEANS AT SOMEONE WHO'S SMILING!
TWITCH TWITCH TWITCH
OHO!
THAT'S THE WAY TO USE THE OLD BEAN, SON!
POIK
RRG!

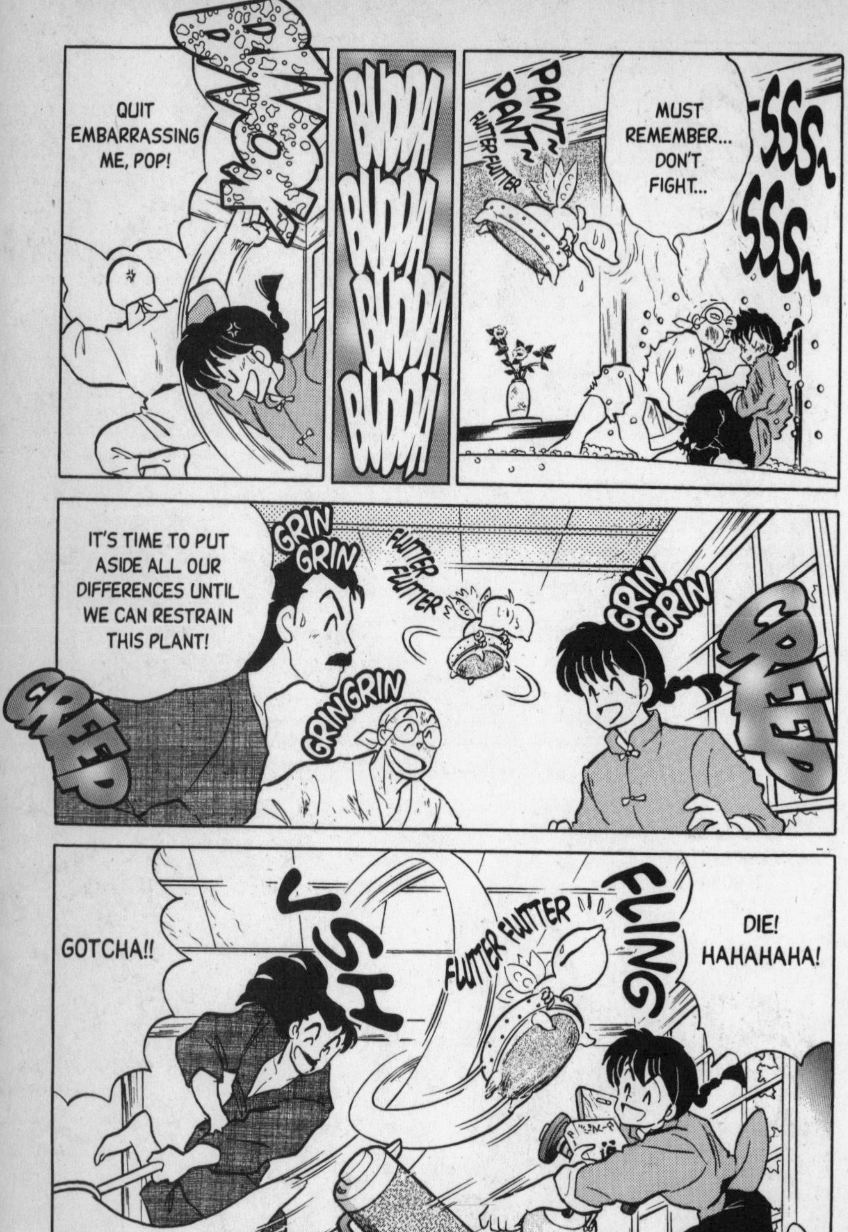
QUIT EMBARRASSING ME, POP!
WOK
BUDDA BUDDA BUDDA BUDDA
PANT~ PANT~
FLUTTER FLUTTER
MUST REMEMBER... DON'T FIGHT...
SSS~ SSS~
IT'S TIME TO PUT ASIDE ALL OUR DIFFERENCES UNTIL WE CAN RESTRAIN THIS PLANT!
GRIN GRIN
CREEP
FLUTTER FLUTTER
GRINGRIN
GRIN GRIN
CREEP
GOTCHA!!
VSH
FLUTTER FLUTTER
FLING
DIE! HAHAHAHA!

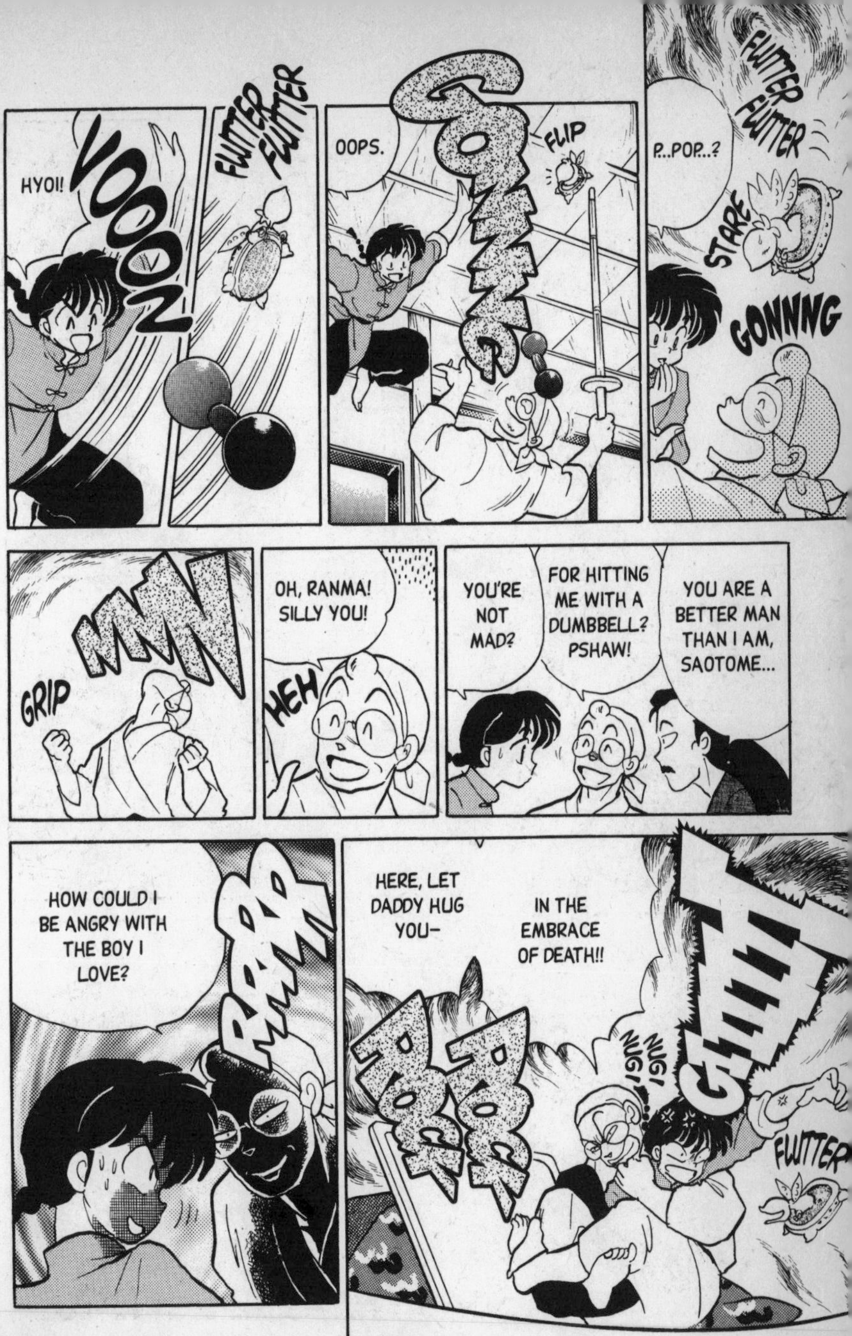
HYOI!
VOOON
FLUTTER FLUTTER
OOPS.
GONNNG
FLIP
P...POP...?
FLUTTER FLUTTER
STARE
GONNNG
MMN
GRIP
OH, RANMA! SILLY YOU!
HEH
YOU'RE NOT MAD?
FOR HITTING ME WITH A DUMBBELL? PSHAW!
YOU ARE A BETTER MAN THAN I AM, SAOTOME...
HOW COULD I BE ANGRY WITH THE BOY I LOVE?
HERE, LET DADDY HUG YOU—
IN THE EMBRACE OF DEATH!!
NUGI NUGI
FLUTTER

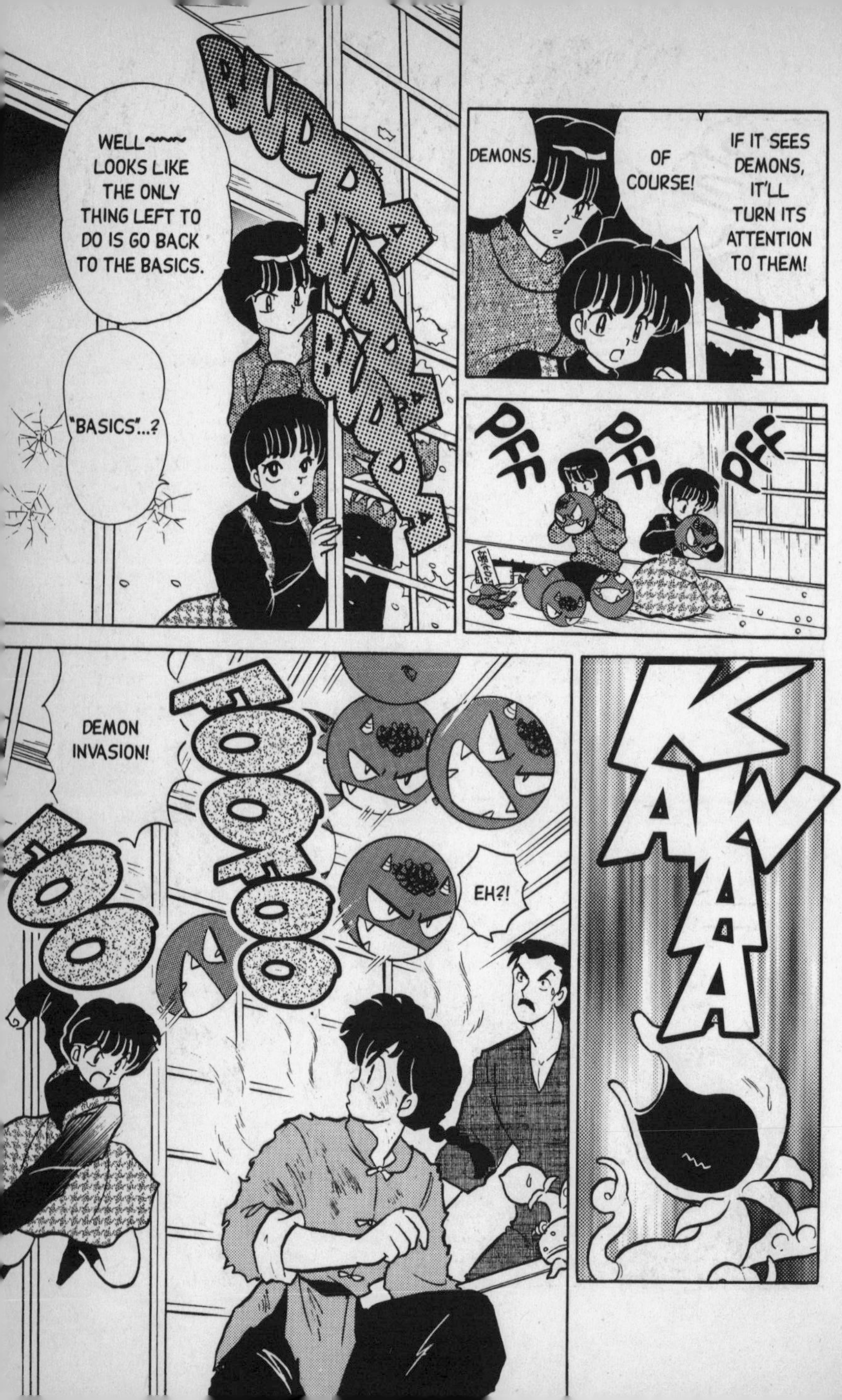
WELL~~~~ LOOKS LIKE THE ONLY THING LEFT TO DO IS GO BACK TO THE BASICS.
"BASICS"...?
DEMONS.
OF COURSE!
IF IT SEES DEMONS, IT'LL TURN ITS ATTENTION TO THEM!
PFF
PFF
PFF
DEMON INVASION!
FOOO
FOOFOO
EH?!
KAWAAA

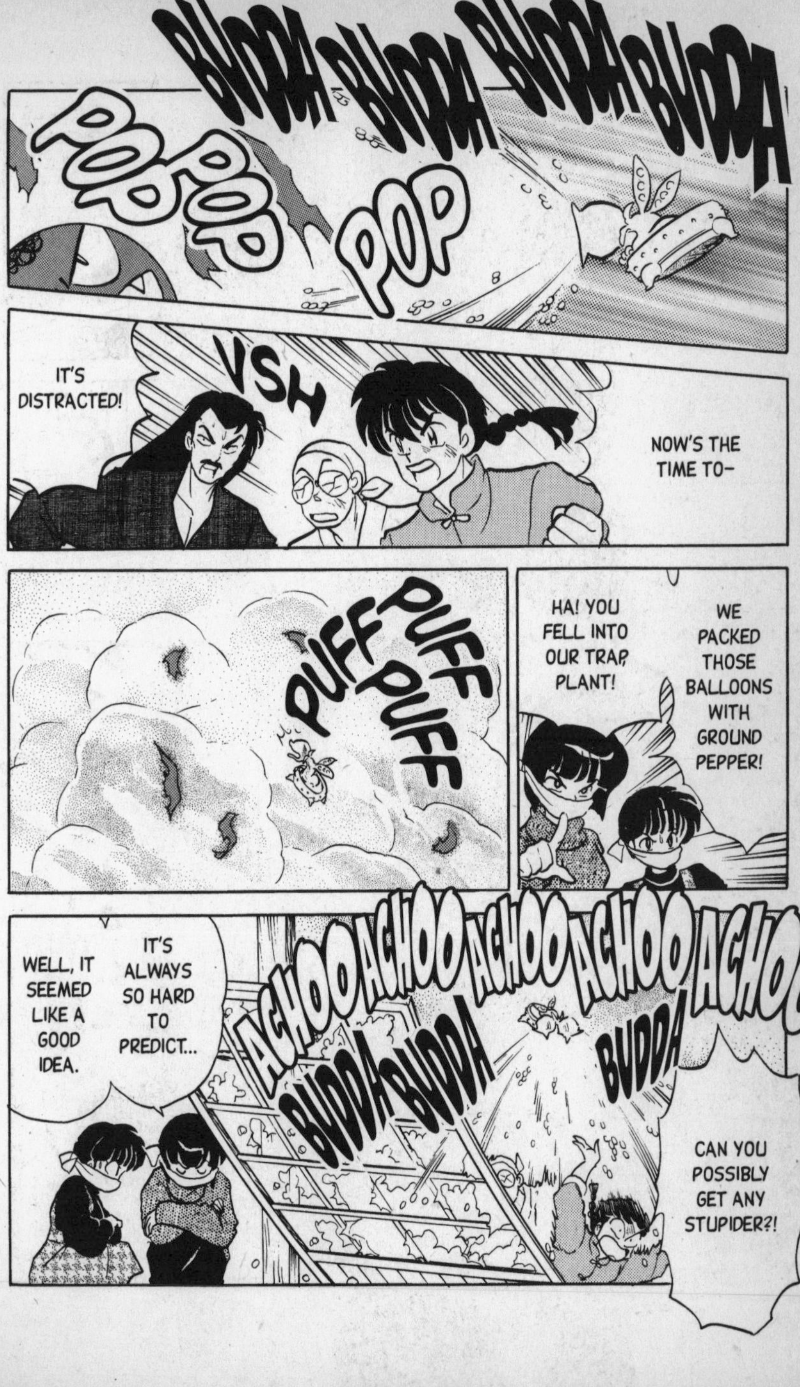
BUDDA BUDDA BUDDA BUDDA
POP POP
POP
VSH
IT'S DISTRACTED!
NOW'S THE TIME TO–
PUFF PUFF PUFF PUFF
HA! YOU FELL INTO OUR TRAP, PLANT!
WE PACKED THOSE BALLOONS WITH GROUND PEPPER!
ACHOO ACHOO ACHOO ACHOO ACHOO
BUDDA BUDDA
BUDDA
WELL, IT SEEMED LIKE A GOOD IDEA.
IT'S ALWAYS SO HARD TO PREDICT...
CAN YOU POSSIBLY GET ANY STUPIDER?!

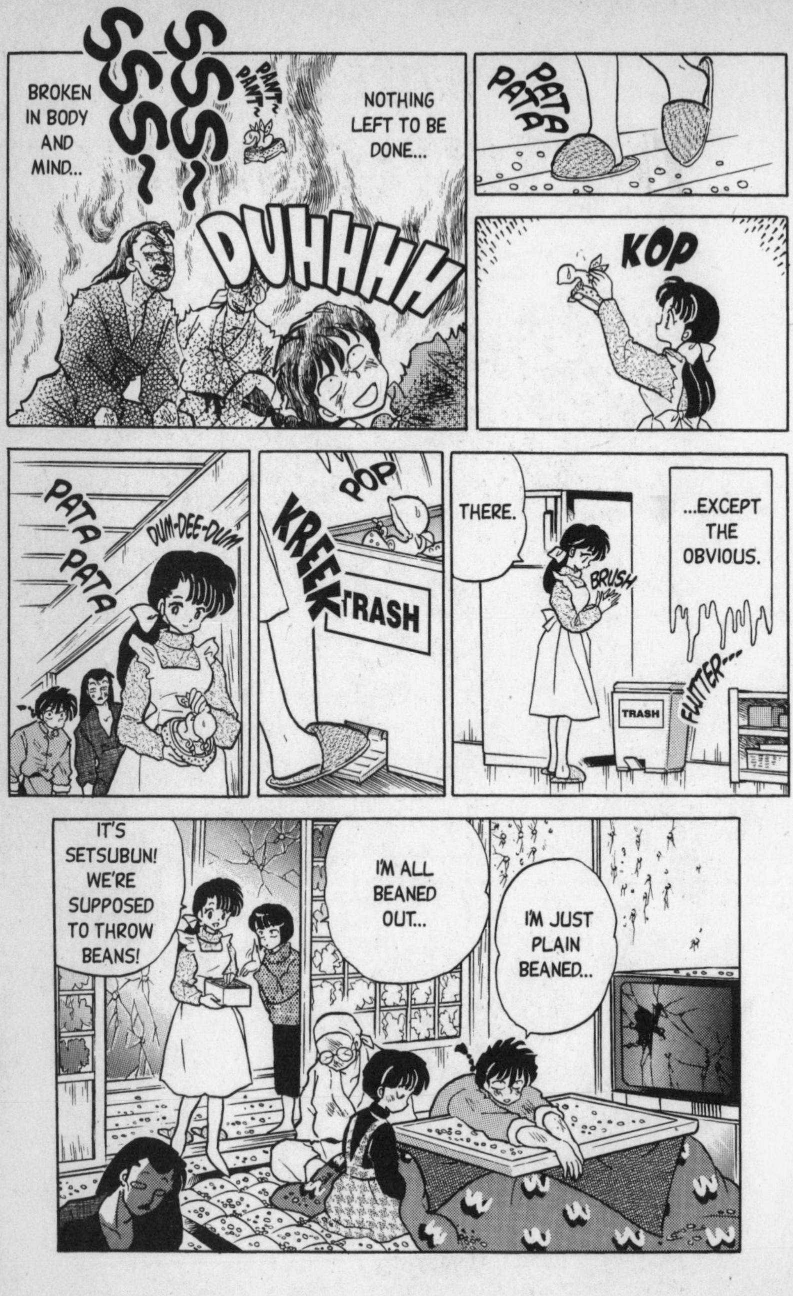
SSS~
SSS~
BROKEN IN BODY AND MIND...
PANT~ PANT~
NOTHING LEFT TO BE DONE...
DUHHHH
PATA PATA
KOP
PATA PATA
DUM-DEE-DUM
POP
KREEK
TRASH
THERE.
BRUSH
TRASH
...EXCEPT THE OBVIOUS.
FLUTTER---
IT'S SETSUBUN! WE'RE SUPPOSED TO THROW BEANS!
I'M ALL BEANED OUT...
I'M JUST PLAIN BEANED...

PART 2

THE LITTLE HEART

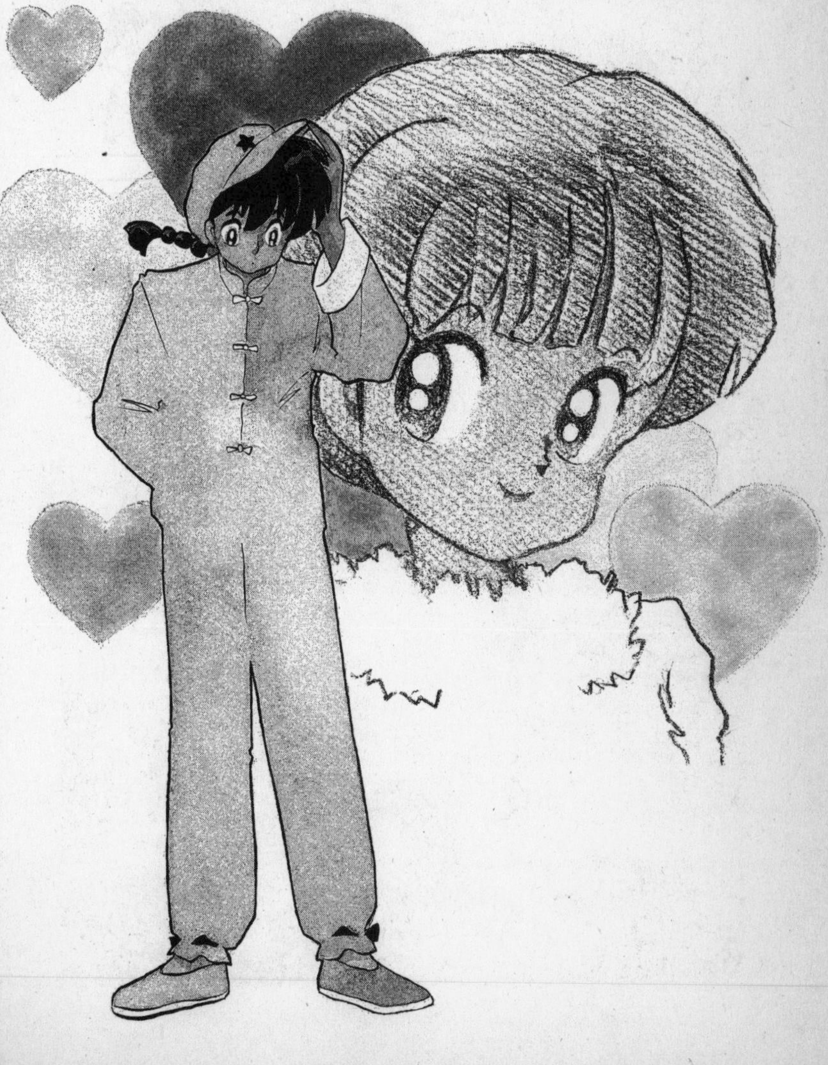

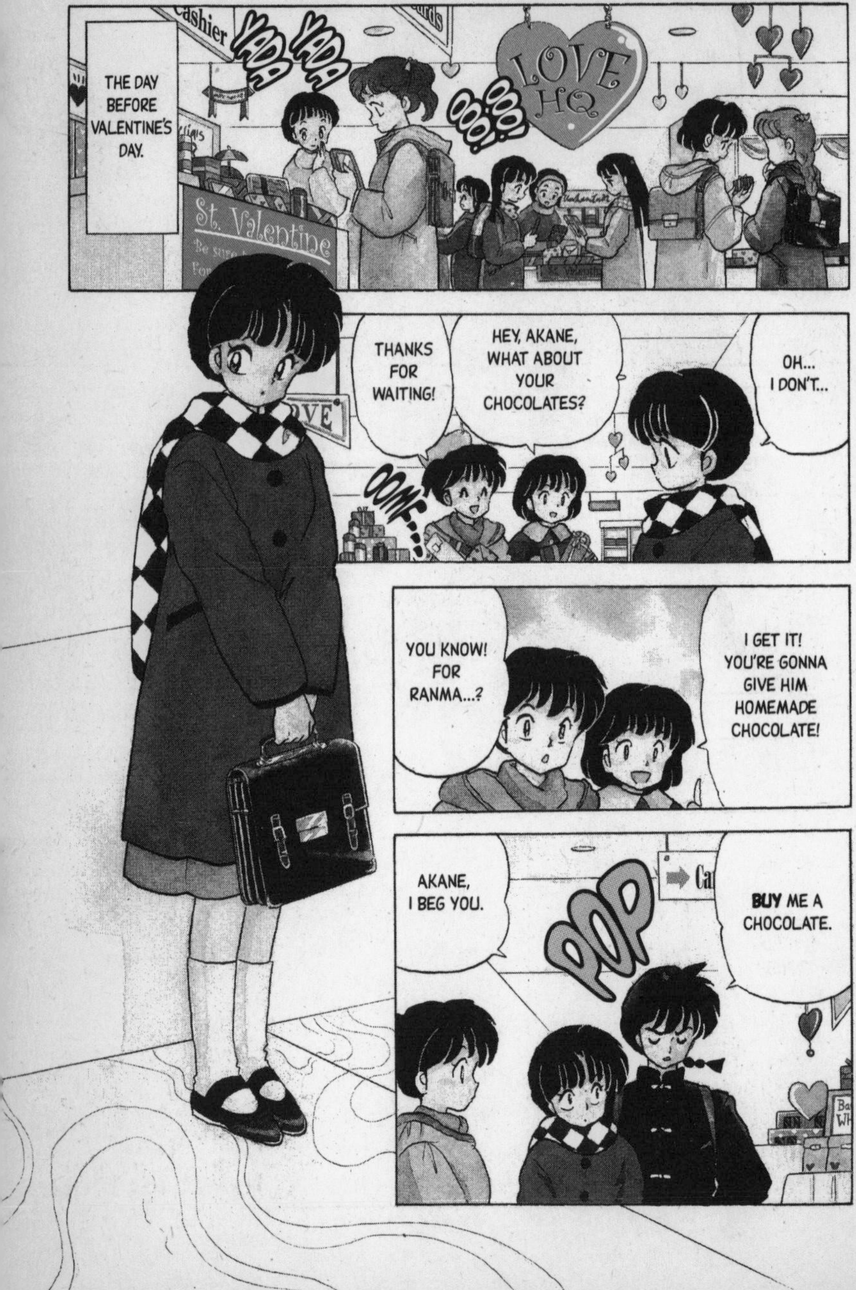
THE DAY BEFORE VALENTINE'S DAY.
Cashier
YADA YADA
OOO! OOO!
LOVE HQ
St. Valentine
THANKS FOR WAITING!
HEY, AKANE, WHAT ABOUT YOUR CHOCOLATES?
OOMF...
OH... I DON'T...
YOU KNOW! FOR RANMA...?
I GET IT! YOU'RE GONNA GIVE HIM HOMEMADE CHOCOLATE!
AKANE, I BEG YOU.
POP
BUY ME A CHOCOLATE.

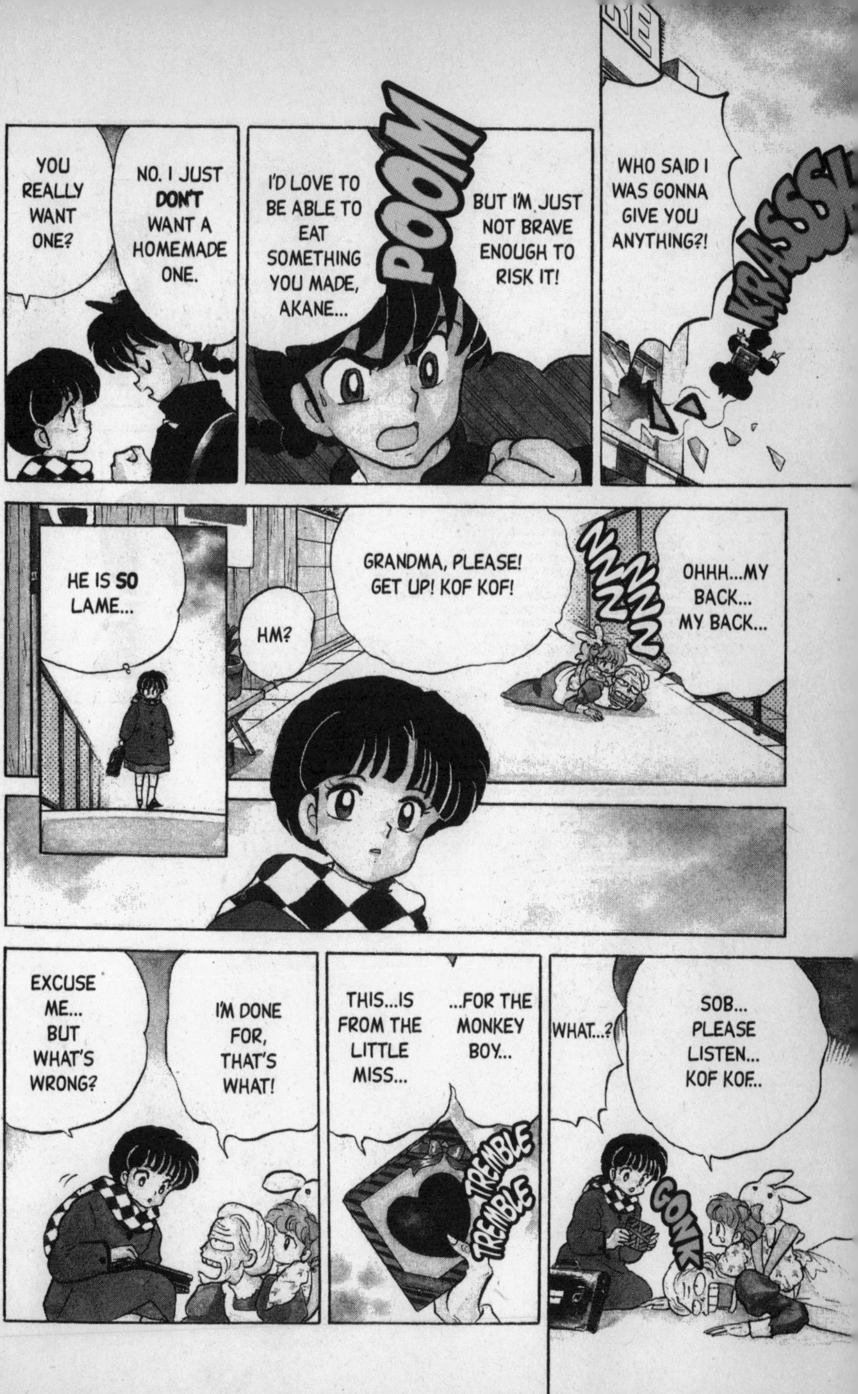
YOU REALLY WANT ONE?
NO. I JUST DON'T WANT A HOMEMADE ONE.
I'D LOVE TO BE ABLE TO EAT SOMETHING YOU MADE, AKANE...
POOM
BUT I'M JUST NOT BRAVE ENOUGH TO RISK IT!
WHO SAID I WAS GONNA GIVE YOU ANYTHING?!
KRASSSH
HE IS SO LAME...
HM?
GRANDMA, PLEASE! GET UP! KOF KOF!
NNNNN
OHHH...MY BACK... MY BACK...
EXCUSE ME... BUT WHAT'S WRONG?
I'M DONE FOR, THAT'S WHAT!
THIS...IS FROM THE LITTLE MISS...
...FOR THE MONKEY BOY...
TREMBLE TREMBLE
WHAT...?
SOB... PLEASE LISTEN... KOF KOF...
GONK

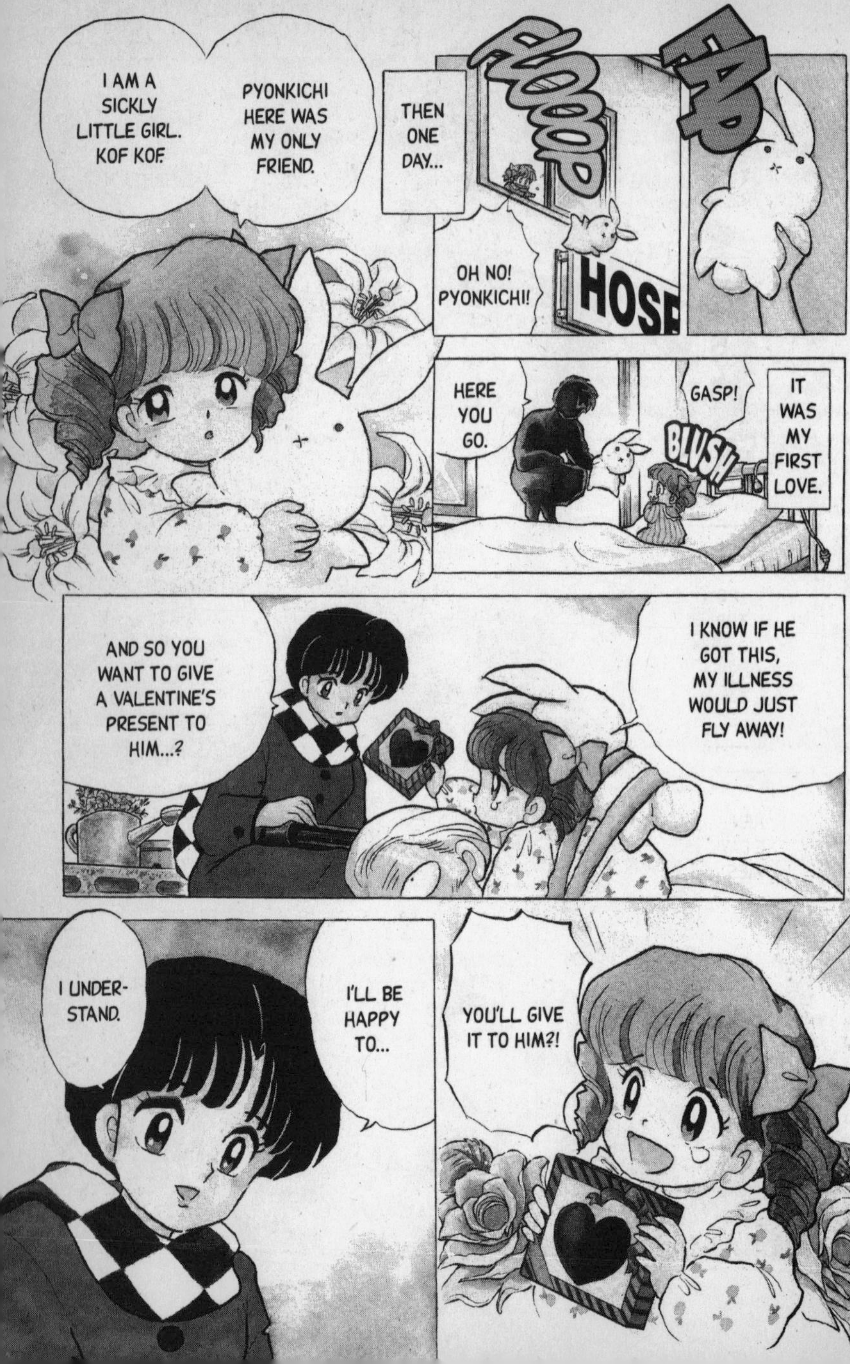
I AM A SICKLY LITTLE GIRL. KOF KOF.
PYONKICHI HERE WAS MY ONLY FRIEND.
THEN ONE DAY...
FLOOOP
FAP
OH NO! PYONKICHI!
HOSP
HERE YOU GO.
GASP!
BLUSH
IT WAS MY FIRST LOVE.
AND SO YOU WANT TO GIVE A VALENTINE'S PRESENT TO HIM...?
I KNOW IF HE GOT THIS, MY ILLNESS WOULD JUST FLY AWAY!
I UNDER-STAND.
I'LL BE HAPPY TO...
YOU'LL GIVE IT TO HIM?!

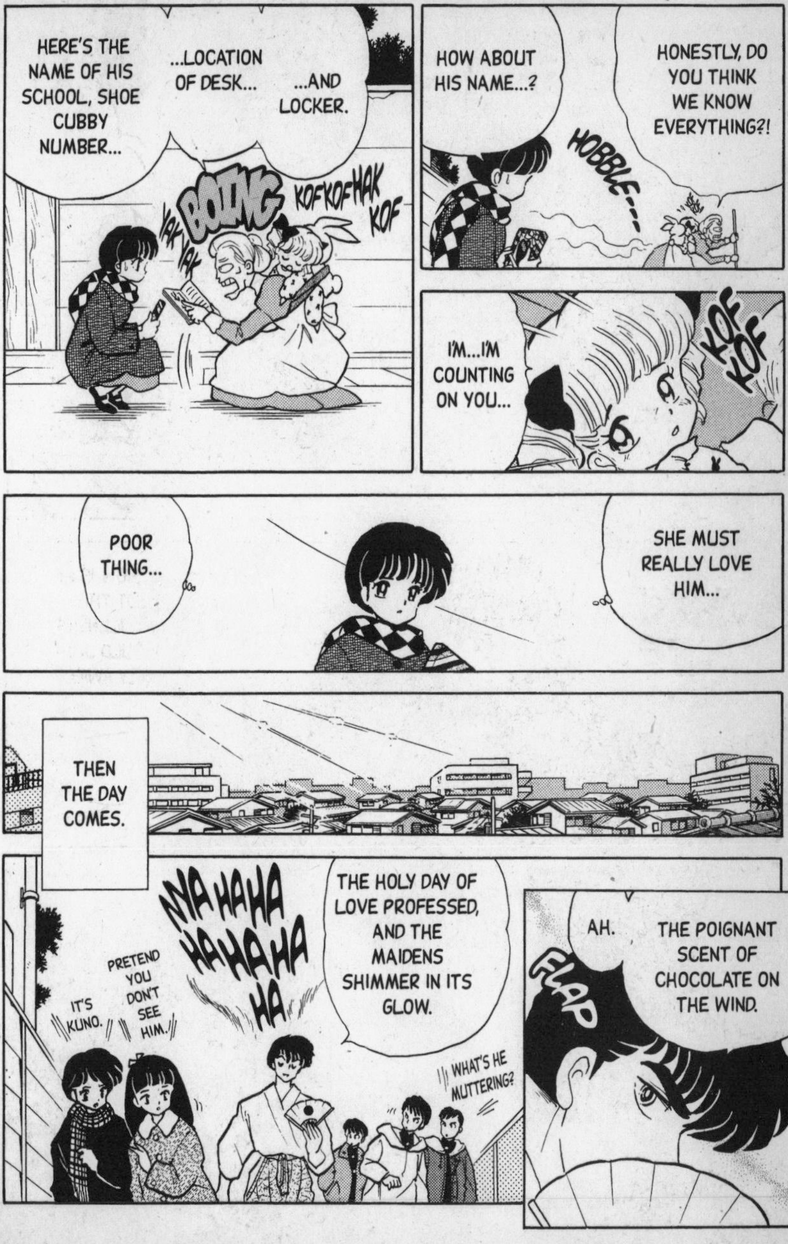
HERE'S THE NAME OF HIS SCHOOL, SHOE CUBBY NUMBER...
...LOCATION OF DESK...
...AND LOCKER.
BOING
YAK YAK
KOFKOFHAK KOF
HOW ABOUT HIS NAME...?
HONESTLY, DO YOU THINK WE KNOW EVERYTHING?!
HOBBLE...
I'M...I'M COUNTING ON YOU...
KOF KOF
POOR THING...
SHE MUST REALLY LOVE HIM...
THEN THE DAY COMES.
IT'S KUNO.
PRETEND YOU DON'T SEE HIM.
NYAHAHA HAHAHA HA
THE HOLY DAY OF LOVE PROFESSED, AND THE MAIDENS SHIMMER IN ITS GLOW.
WHAT'S HE MUTTERING?
AH.
THE POIGNANT SCENT OF CHOCOLATE ON THE WIND.
FLAP

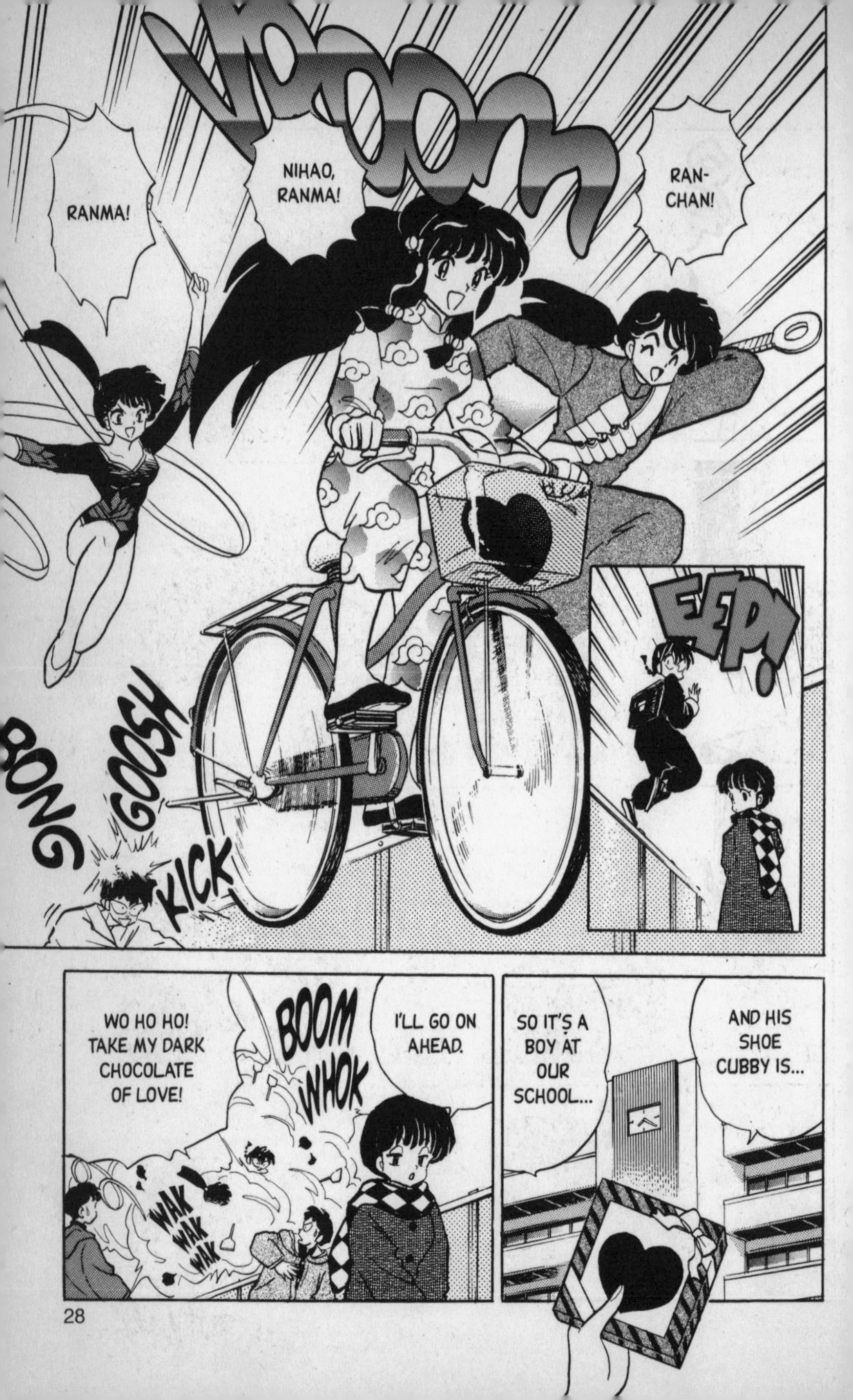
RANMA!
NIHAO, RANMA!
VROOOM
RAN-CHAN!
BONG
GOOSH
KICK
EEP!
WO HO HO! TAKE MY DARK CHOCOLATE OF LOVE!
BOOM
WHOK
WAK WAK WAK
I'LL GO ON AHEAD.
SO IT'S A BOY AT OUR SCHOOL...
AND HIS SHOE CUBBY IS...

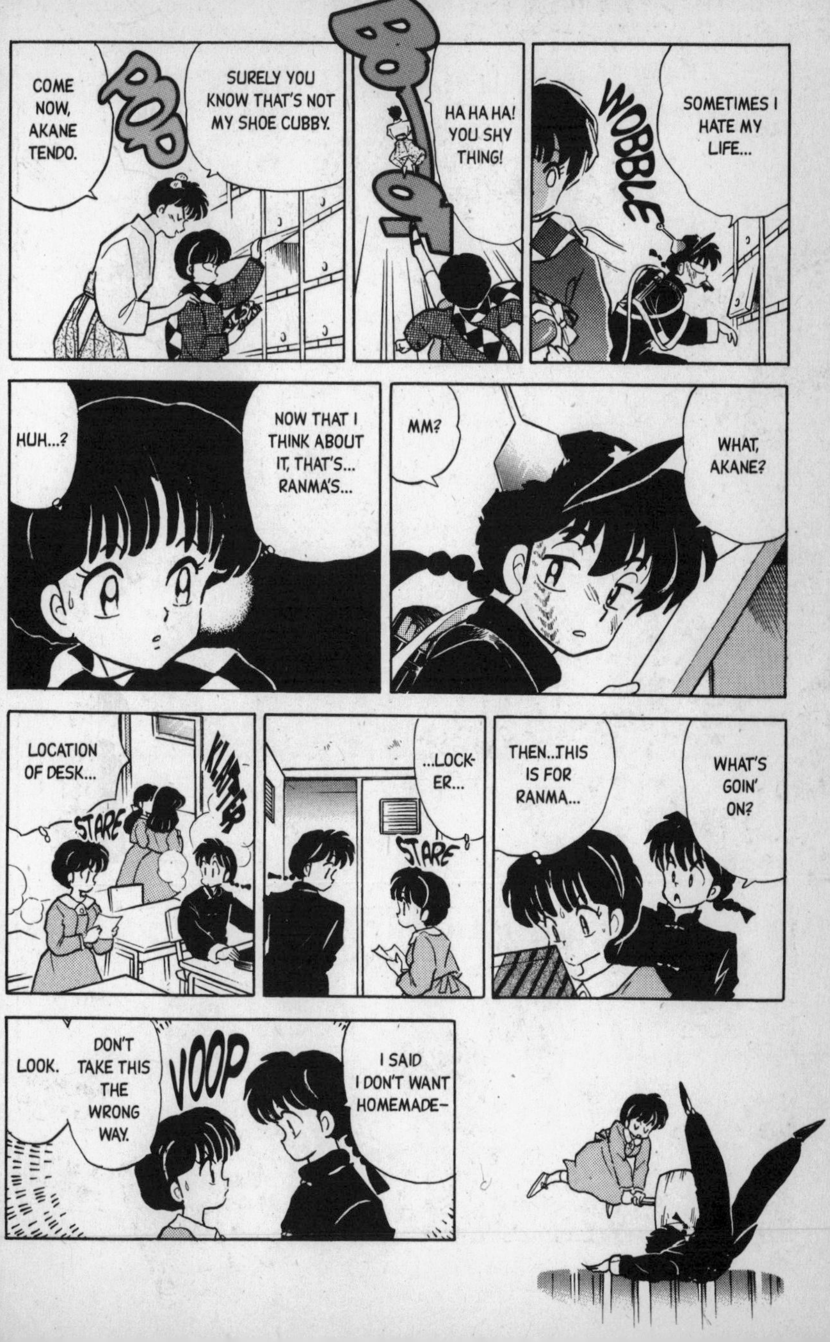
COME NOW, AKANE TENDO.
POP
SURELY YOU KNOW THAT'S NOT MY SHOE CUBBY.
BOOM
HA HA HA! YOU SHY THING!
WOBBLE
SOMETIMES I HATE MY LIFE...
HUH...?
NOW THAT I THINK ABOUT IT, THAT'S... RANMA'S...
MM?
WHAT, AKANE?
LOCATION OF DESK...
STARE
KLATTER
...LOCK-ER...
STARE
THEN...THIS IS FOR RANMA...
WHAT'S GOIN' ON?
LOOK.
DON'T TAKE THIS THE WRONG WAY.
VOOP
I SAID I DON'T WANT HOMEMADE-

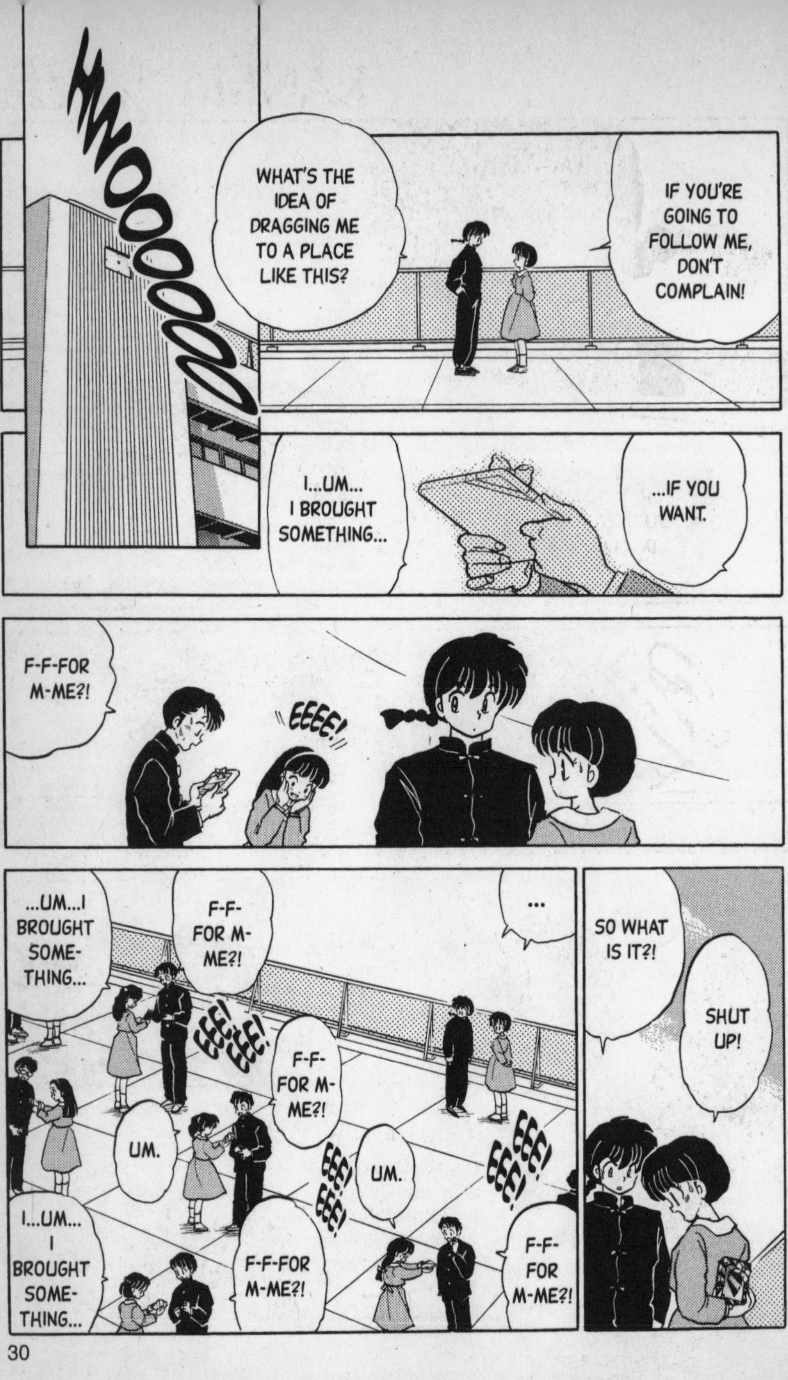
HWOOOOOO
WHAT'S THE IDEA OF DRAGGING ME TO A PLACE LIKE THIS?
IF YOU'RE GOING TO FOLLOW ME, DON'T COMPLAIN!
I...UM... I BROUGHT SOMETHING...
...IF YOU WANT.
F-F-FOR M-ME?!
EEEE!
...UM...I BROUGHT SOME-THING...
F-F-FOR M-ME?!
...
EEE! EEE!
F-F-FOR M-ME?!
UM.
EEE! EEE!
UM.
EEE! EEE!
I...UM... I BROUGHT SOME-THING...
F-F-FOR M-ME?!
F-F-FOR M-ME?!
SO WHAT IS IT?!
SHUT UP!

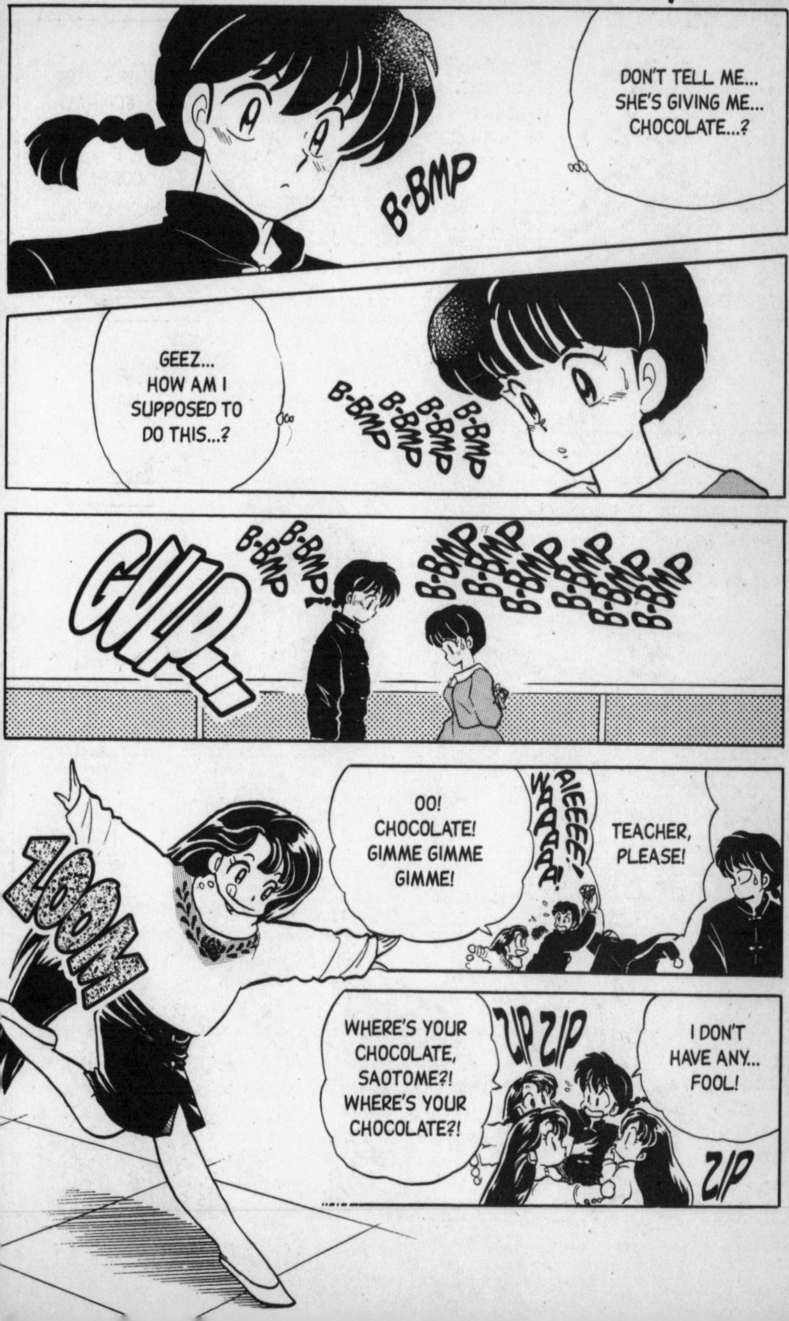
B-BMP
DON'T TELL ME... SHE'S GIVING ME... CHOCOLATE...?
GEEZ... HOW AM I SUPPOSED TO DO THIS...?
B-BMP B-BMP B-BMP B-BMP
GULP...
B-BMP B-BMP
B-BMP B-BMP B-BMP B-BMP B-BMP B-BMP B-BMP B-BMP
ZOOM
OO! CHOCOLATE! GIMME GIMME GIMME!
AIEEEE! WAAAAA!
TEACHER, PLEASE!
WHERE'S YOUR CHOCOLATE, SAOTOME?! WHERE'S YOUR CHOCOLATE?!
ZIP ZIP
I DON'T HAVE ANY... FOOL!
ZIP

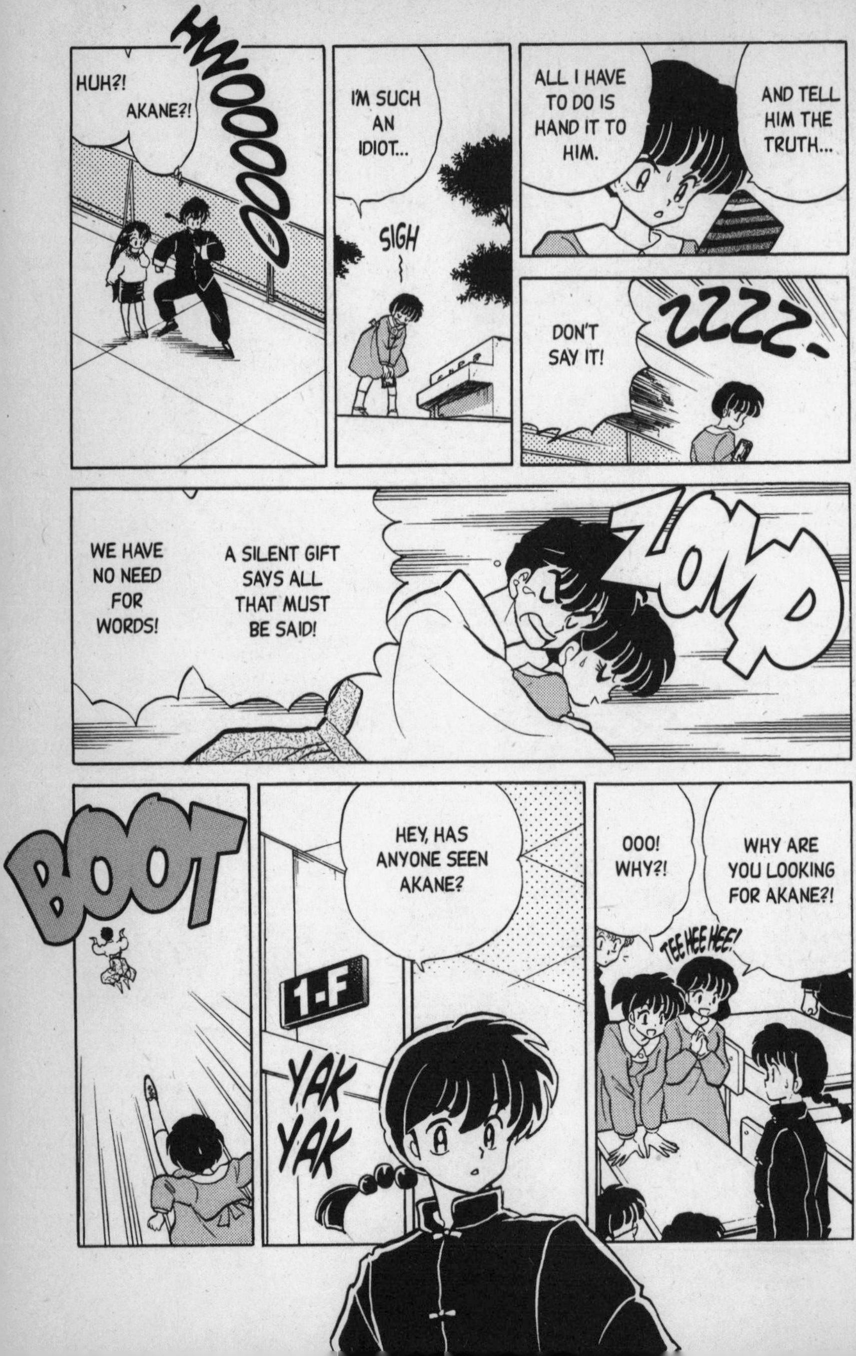
HUH?! AKANE?!
HWOOOOO
I'M SUCH AN IDIOT...
SIGH
ALL I HAVE TO DO IS HAND IT TO HIM.
AND TELL HIM THE TRUTH...
DON'T SAY IT!
ZZZZ
WE HAVE NO NEED FOR WORDS!
A SILENT GIFT SAYS ALL THAT MUST BE SAID!
ZOMP
BOOT
HEY, HAS ANYONE SEEN AKANE?
1-F
YAK YAK
OOO! WHY?!
WHY ARE YOU LOOKING FOR AKANE?!
TEE HEE HEE!

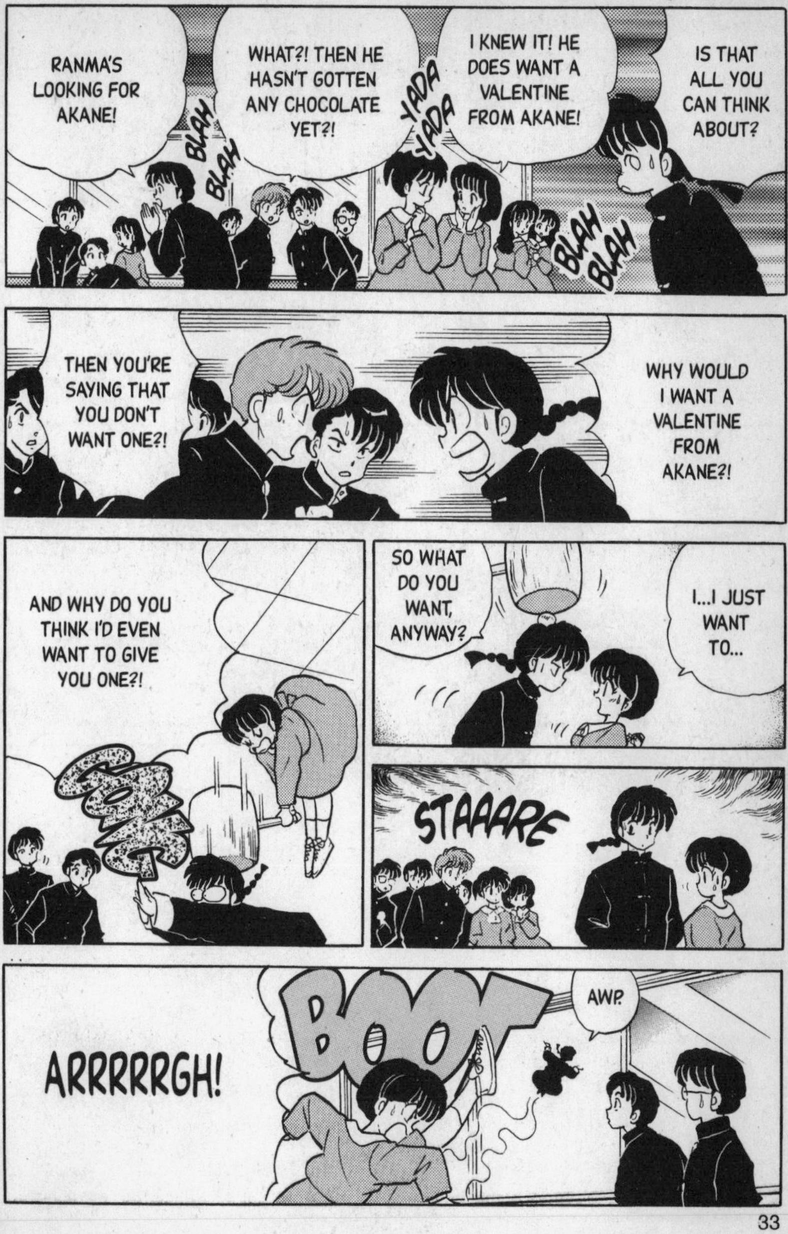
RANMA'S LOOKING FOR AKANE!
BLAH BLAH
WHAT?! THEN HE HASN'T GOTTEN ANY CHOCOLATE YET?!
YADA YADA
I KNEW IT! HE DOES WANT A VALENTINE FROM AKANE!
IS THAT ALL YOU CAN THINK ABOUT?
BLAH BLAH
THEN YOU'RE SAYING THAT YOU DON'T WANT ONE?!
WHY WOULD I WANT A VALENTINE FROM AKANE?!
AND WHY DO YOU THINK I'D EVEN WANT TO GIVE YOU ONE?!
SO WHAT DO YOU WANT, ANYWAY?
I...I JUST WANT TO...
STAAARE
ARRRRRGH!
BOOT
AWP?

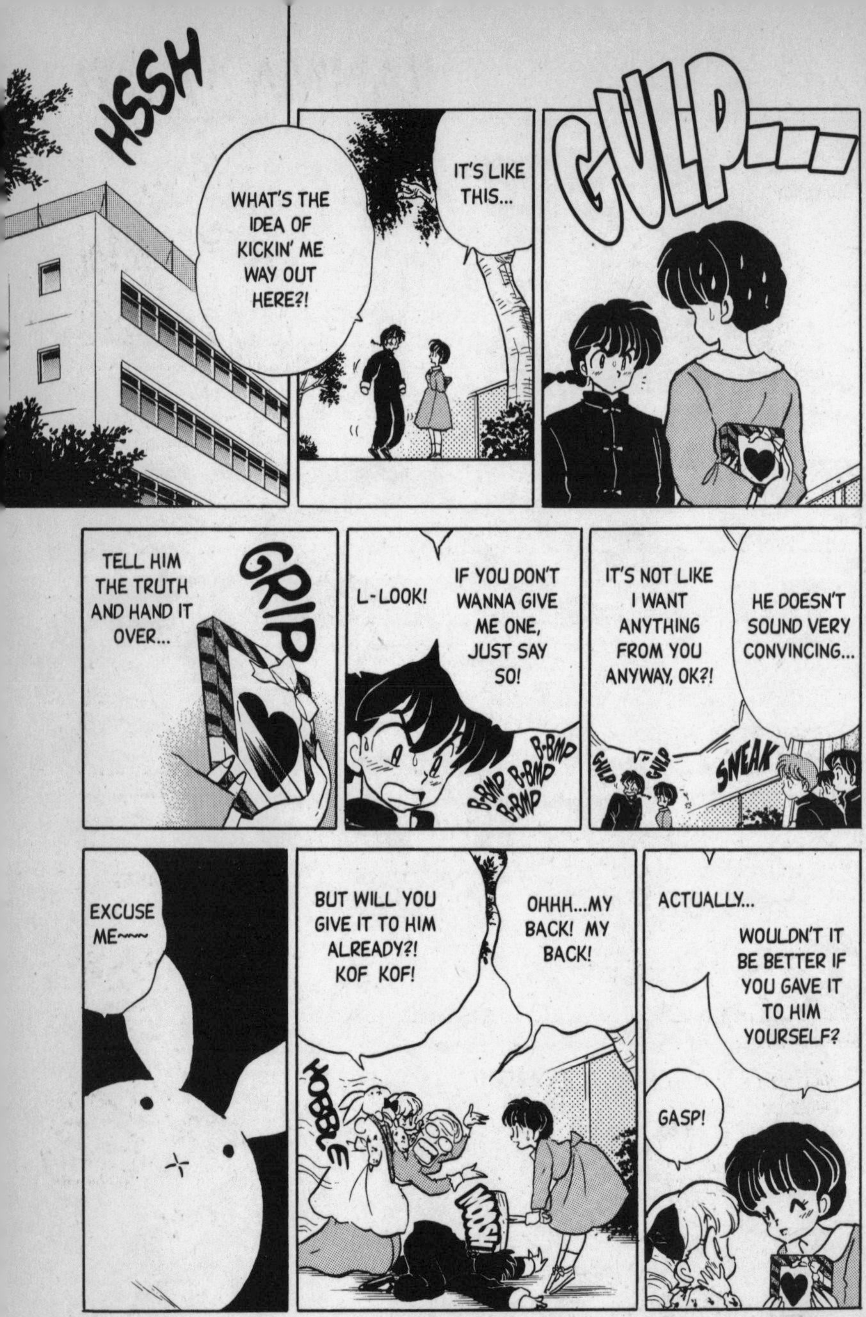
HSSH
WHAT'S THE IDEA OF KICKIN' ME WAY OUT HERE?!
IT'S LIKE THIS...
GULP...
TELL HIM THE TRUTH AND HAND IT OVER...
GRIP
L-LOOK!
IF YOU DON'T WANNA GIVE ME ONE, JUST SAY SO!
B-BMP B-BMP B-BMP B-BMP
IT'S NOT LIKE I WANT ANYTHING FROM YOU ANYWAY, OK?!
HE DOESN'T SOUND VERY CONVINCING...
GULP GULP
SNEAK
EXCUSE ME~~~
BUT WILL YOU GIVE IT TO HIM ALREADY?! KOF KOF!
OHHH...MY BACK! MY BACK!
HOBBLE
WOOSH
ACTUALLY...
WOULDN'T IT BE BETTER IF YOU GAVE IT TO HIM YOURSELF?
GASP!

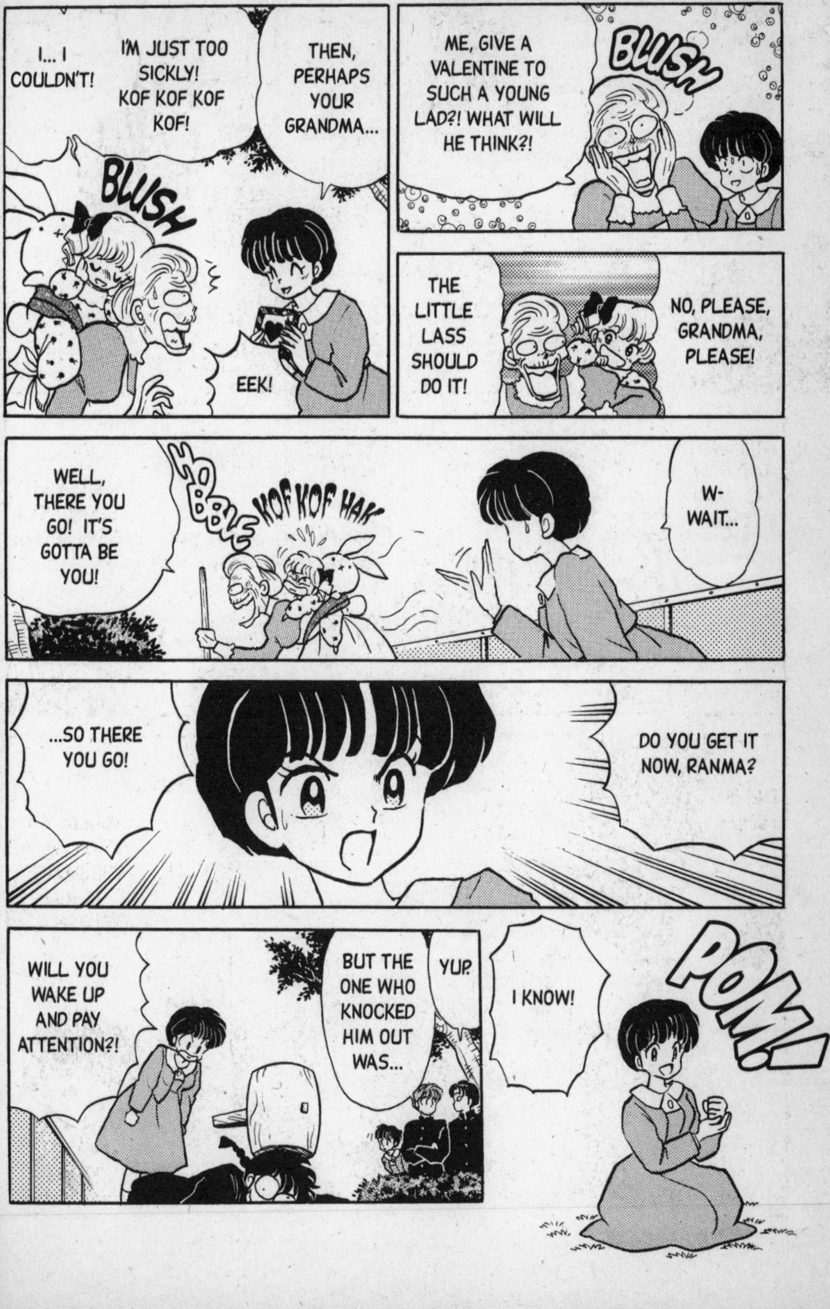
I... I COULDN'T!
I'M JUST TOO SICKLY! KOF KOF KOF KOF!
THEN, PERHAPS YOUR GRANDMA...
BLUSH
EEK!
ME, GIVE A VALENTINE TO SUCH A YOUNG LAD?! WHAT WILL HE THINK?!
BLUSH
THE LITTLE LASS SHOULD DO IT!
NO, PLEASE, GRANDMA, PLEASE!
WELL, THERE YOU GO! IT'S GOTTA BE YOU!
HOBBLE
KOF KOF HAK
W-WAIT...
...SO THERE YOU GO!
DO YOU GET IT NOW, RANMA?
WILL YOU WAKE UP AND PAY ATTENTION?!
BUT THE ONE WHO KNOCKED HIM OUT WAS...
YUP.
I KNOW!
POM!

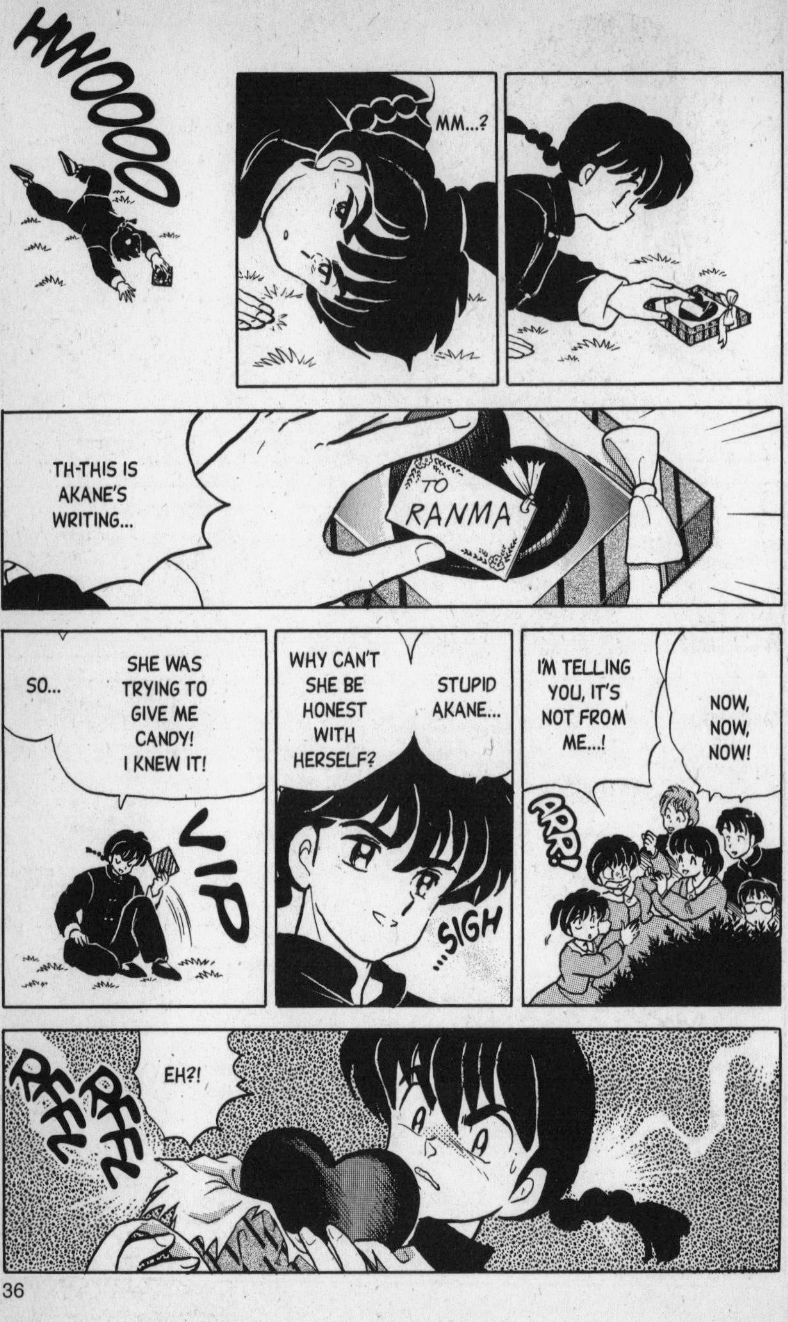

HWOOOO
MM...?
TH-THIS IS AKANE'S WRITING...
TO RANMA
SO...
SHE WAS TRYING TO GIVE ME CANDY! I KNEW IT!
VIP
WHY CAN'T SHE BE HONEST WITH HERSELF?
STUPID AKANE...
...SIGH
I'M TELLING YOU, IT'S NOT FROM ME...!
NOW, NOW, NOW!
ARR!
RFFFL RFFFL
EH?!

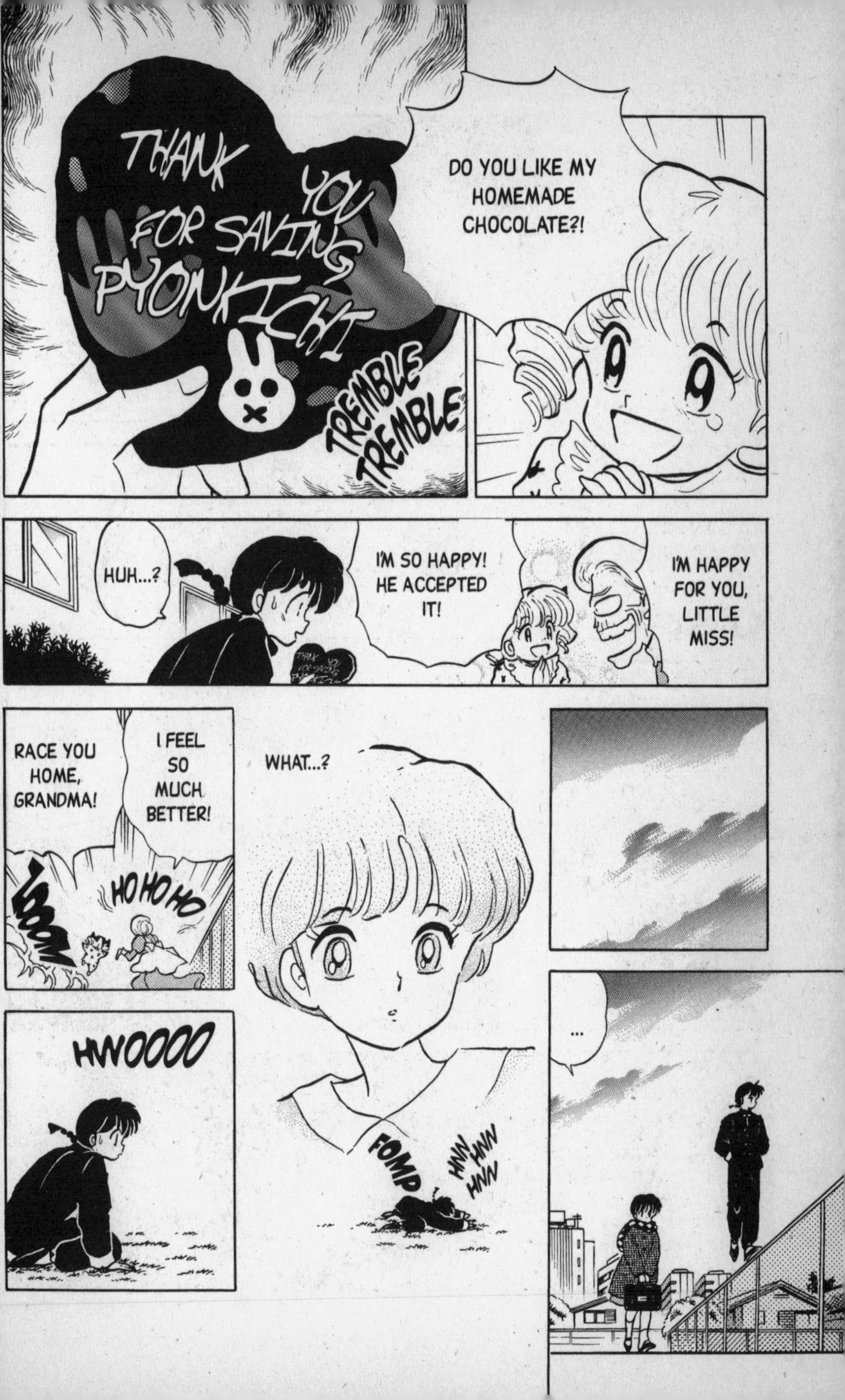
THANK YOU FOR SAVING PYONKICHI
TREMBLE TREMBLE
DO YOU LIKE MY HOMEMADE CHOCOLATE?!
HUH...?
I'M SO HAPPY! HE ACCEPTED IT!
I'M HAPPY FOR YOU, LITTLE MISS!
RACE YOU HOME, GRANDMA!
I FEEL SO MUCH BETTER!
ZOOOM
HO HO HO
WHAT...?
HWOOOO
FOMP
HNN HNN HNN
...

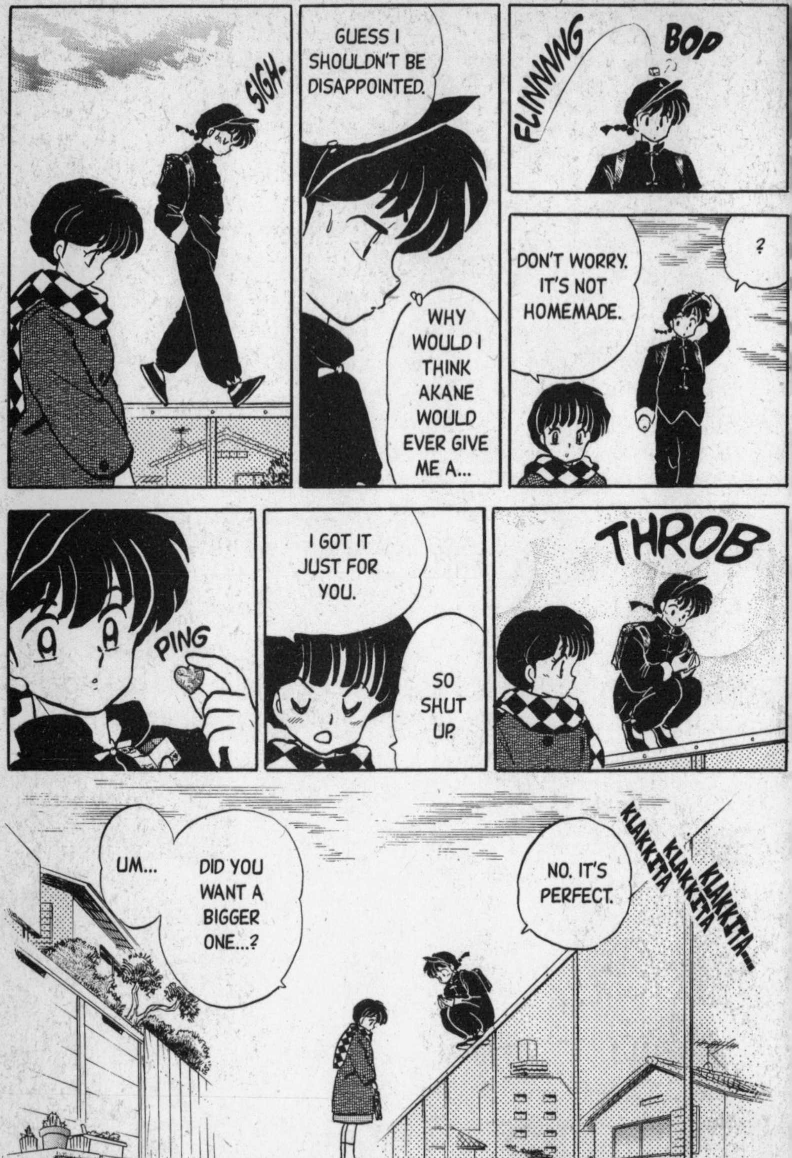
SIGH
GUESS I SHOULDN'T BE DISAPPOINTED.
WHY WOULD I THINK AKANE WOULD EVER GIVE ME A...
FLINNNNG
BOP
DON'T WORRY. IT'S NOT HOMEMADE.
?
PING
I GOT IT JUST FOR YOU.
SO SHUT UP.
THROB
UM...
DID YOU WANT A BIGGER ONE...?
NO. IT'S PERFECT.
KLAKKITA KLAKKITA KLAKKITA...

PART 37

WHACK THE PRINCIPAL!

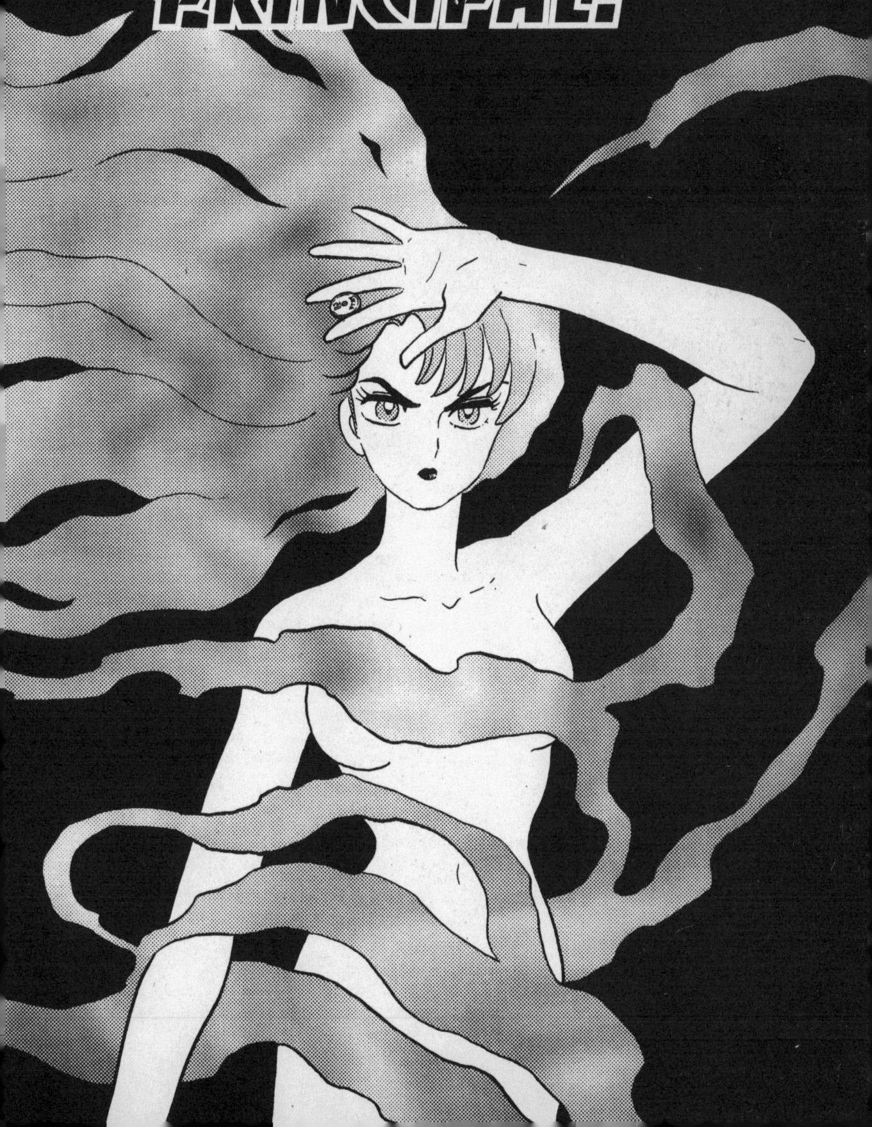

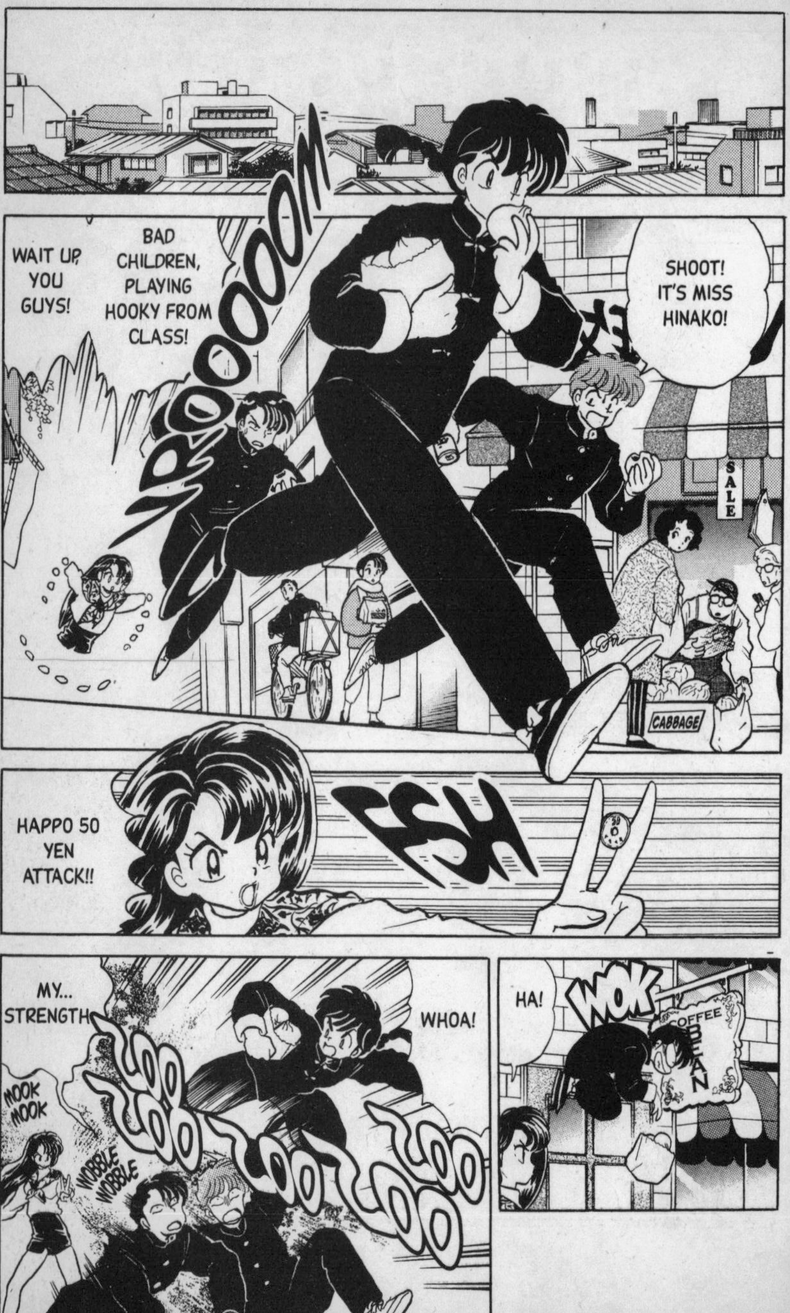
WAIT UP, YOU GUYS!
BAD CHILDREN, PLAYING HOOKY FROM CLASS!
VROOOOOOM
SHOOT! IT'S MISS HINAKO!
SALE
CABBAGE
HAPPO 50 YEN ATTACK!!
FSH
MY... STRENGTH
MOOK MOOK
WOBBLE WOBBLE
ZOO ZOO ZOO ZOO ZOO ZOO
WHOA!
HA!
WOK
COFFEE BEAN

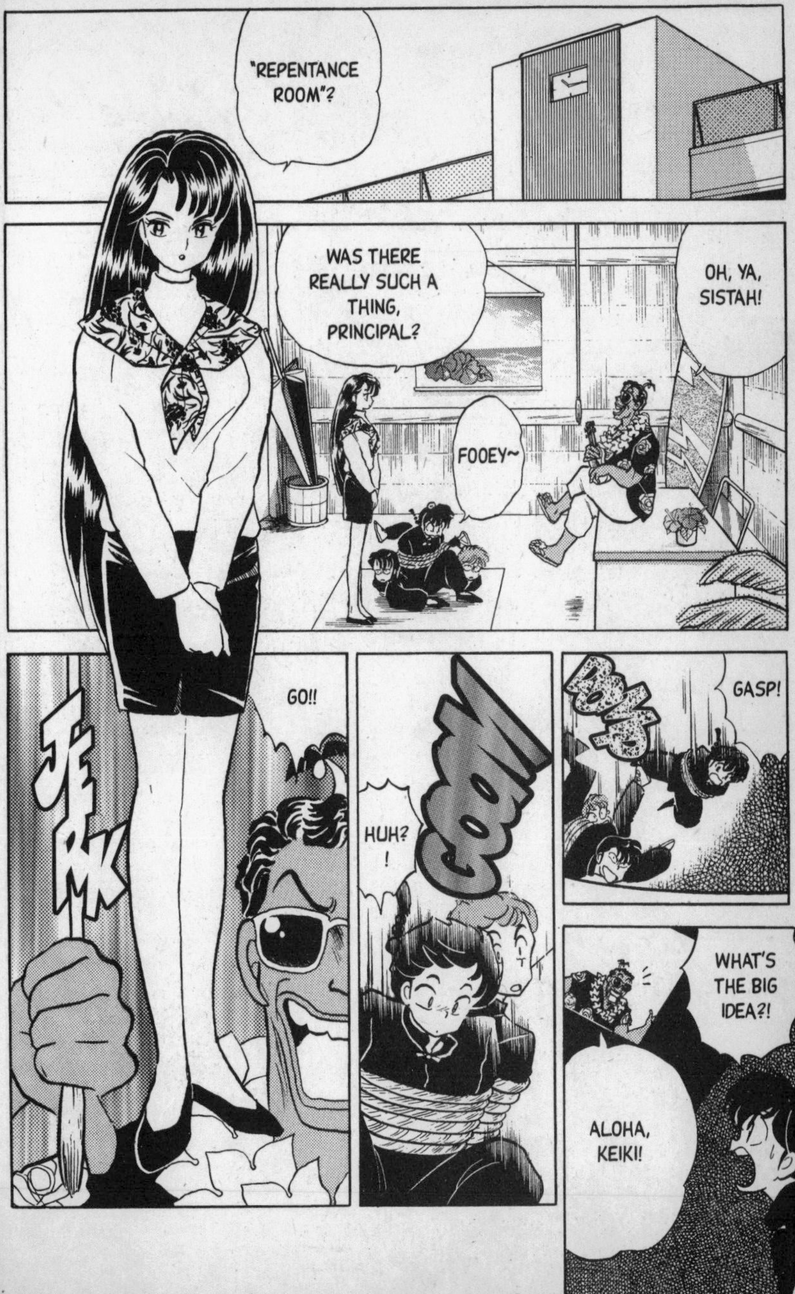
"REPENTANCE ROOM"?
WAS THERE REALLY SUCH A THING, PRINCIPAL?
FOOEY~
OH, YA, SISTAH!
JERK
GO!!
HUH? !
COOM
BOMP
GASP!
WHAT'S THE BIG IDEA?!
ALOHA, KEIKI!

EVEN DA BADDEST BUGGAH GONA BEG FO' FO'GIVENESS WHEN I DROPPIN' HIM IN DE REPENTANCE ROOM!

HA HA HA HA HA HA

B-BUT WHY?

WELL, IT MAKES ME NEVER WANT TO APOLOGIZE!

PLEASE FORGIVE ME, OH GLORIOUS PRINCIPAL.

I'M A PATHETIC LOSER

SORRY

RIP

HUH?

TM TM

HEY, THERE'S A DOOR. LET'S JUST—

GRIP

BZZZZZ

ELEC-TRICITY!!

ONLY ONE WAY TO OPEN DAT DOOR, BRAH!

HA HA HA HA HA

BOW YO' HEAD TO DE FLOOR IN FRONT OF DAT STATUE!

WHAT?!

GROVEL HERE

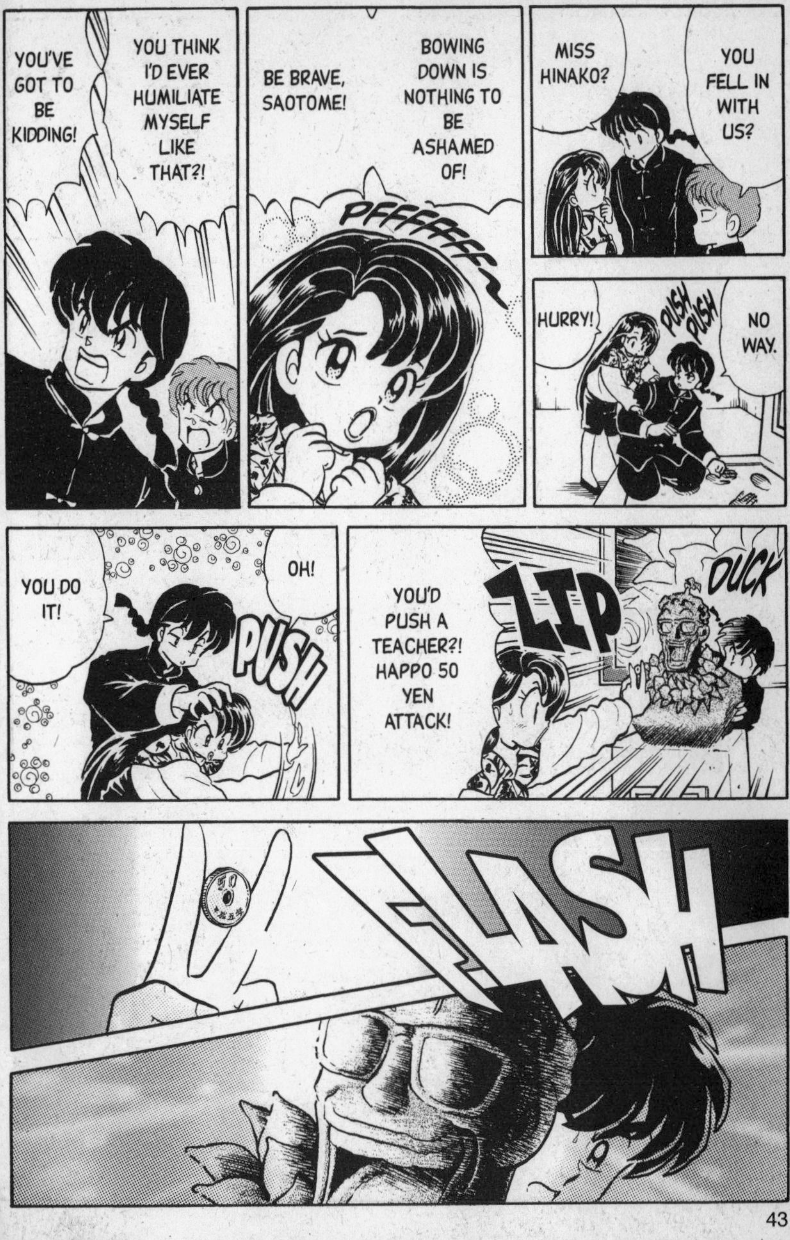
YOU'VE GOT TO BE KIDDING!
YOU THINK I'D EVER HUMILIATE MYSELF LIKE THAT?!
BE BRAVE, SAOTOME!
BOWING DOWN IS NOTHING TO BE ASHAMED OF!
PFFFFFFF
MISS HINAKO?
YOU FELL IN WITH US?
HURRY!
PUSH PUSH
NO WAY.
YOU DO IT!
OH!
PUSH
YOU'D PUSH A TEACHER?! HAPPO 50 YEN ATTACK!
ZIP
DUCK
FLASH

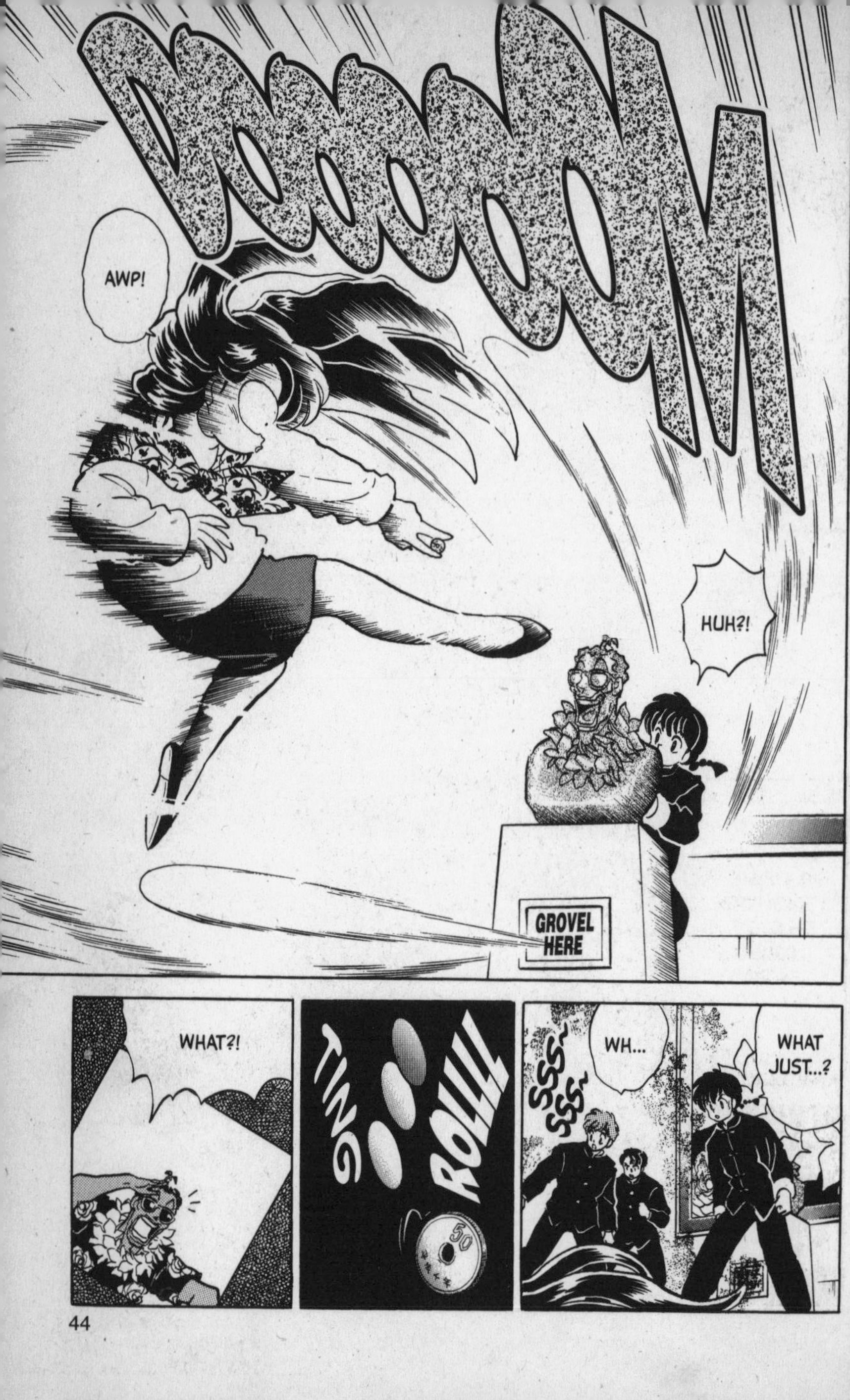
DOOOOOM
AWP!
HUH?!
GROVEL HERE
WHAT?!
TING
ROLLL
50
SSS~ SSS~
WH...
WHAT JUST...?

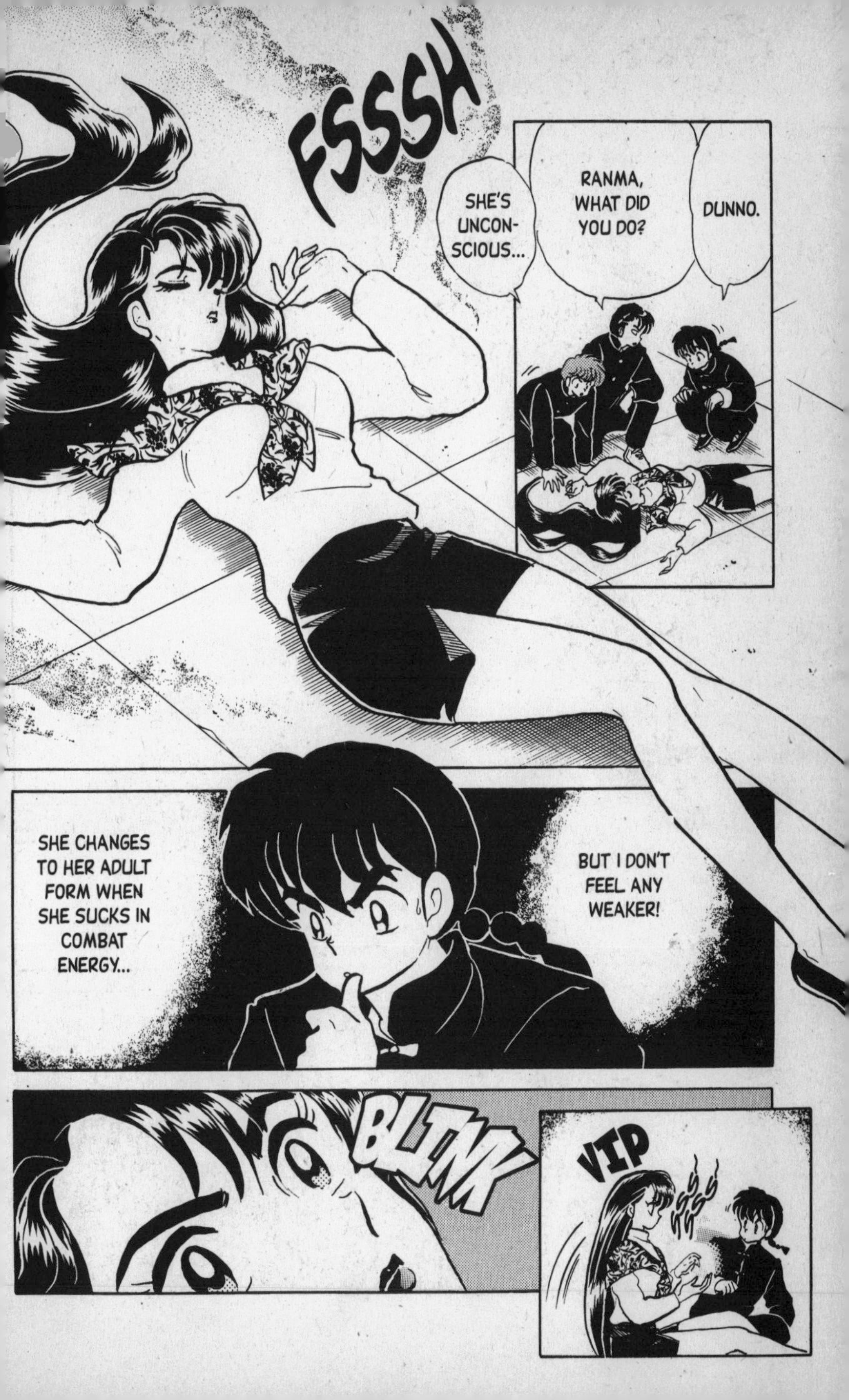
FSSSH
SHE'S UNCON-SCIOUS...
RANMA, WHAT DID YOU DO?
DUNNO.
SHE CHANGES TO HER ADULT FORM WHEN SHE SUCKS IN COMBAT ENERGY...
BUT I DON'T FEEL ANY WEAKER!
BLINK
VIP

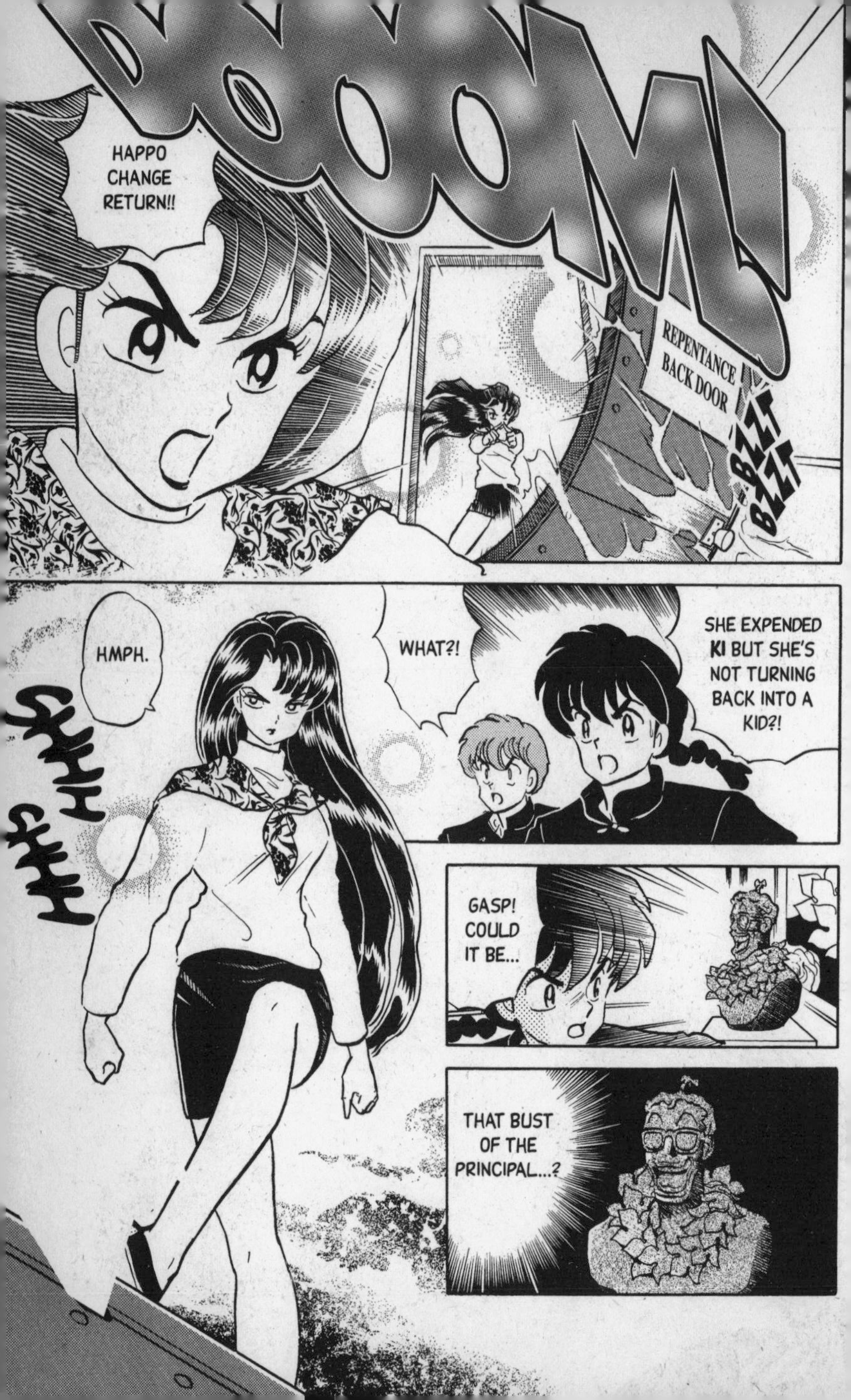

BOOOM!
HAPPO CHANGE RETURN!!
REPENTANCE BACK DOOR
BZZT BZZT
HMPH.
WHAT?!
SHE EXPENDED KI BUT SHE'S NOT TURNING BACK INTO A KID?!
GASP! COULD IT BE...
THAT BUST OF THE PRINCIPAL...?

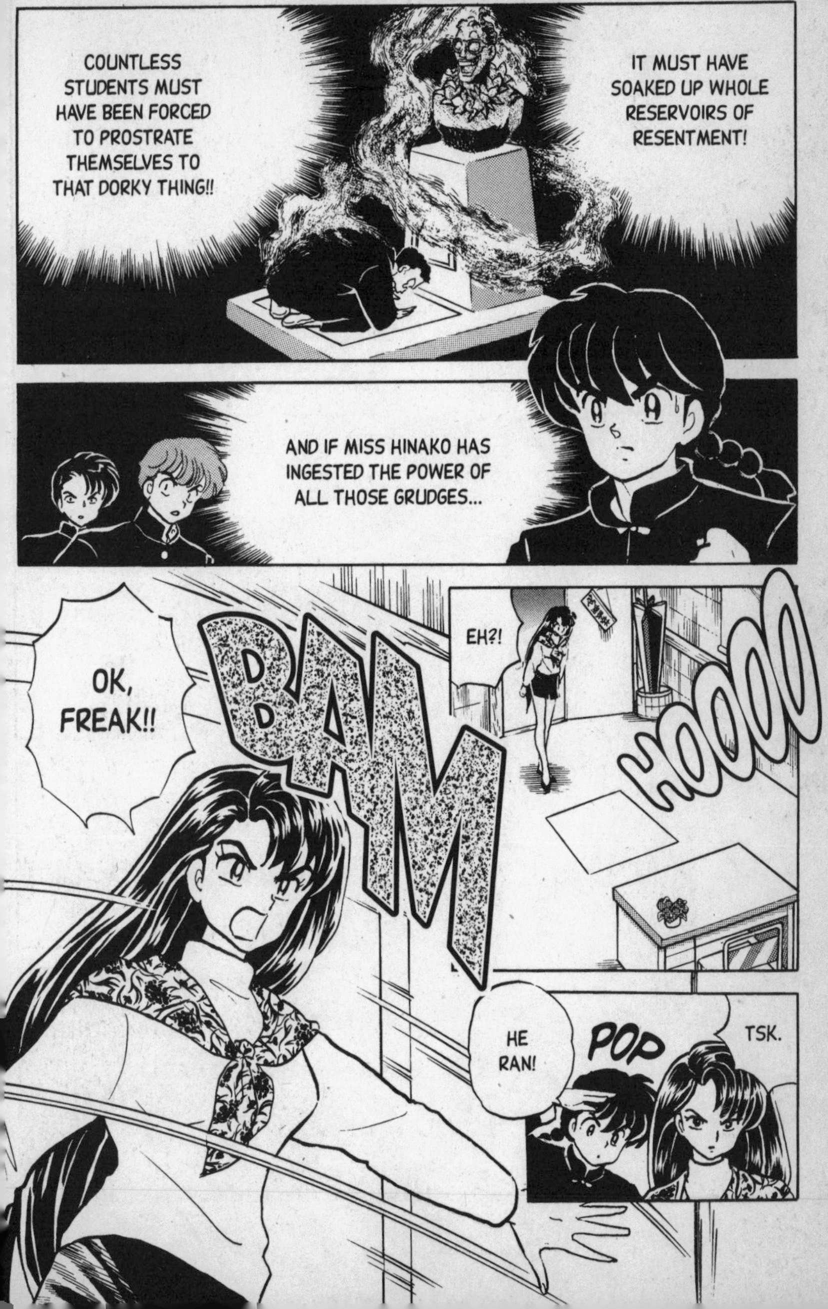
COUNTLESS STUDENTS MUST HAVE BEEN FORCED TO PROSTRATE THEMSELVES TO THAT DORKY THING!!
IT MUST HAVE SOAKED UP WHOLE RESERVOIRS OF RESENTMENT!
AND IF MISS HINAKO HAS INGESTED THE POWER OF ALL THOSE GRUDGES...
OK, FREAK!!
BAM
EH?!
HOOOO
HE RAN!
POP
TSK.

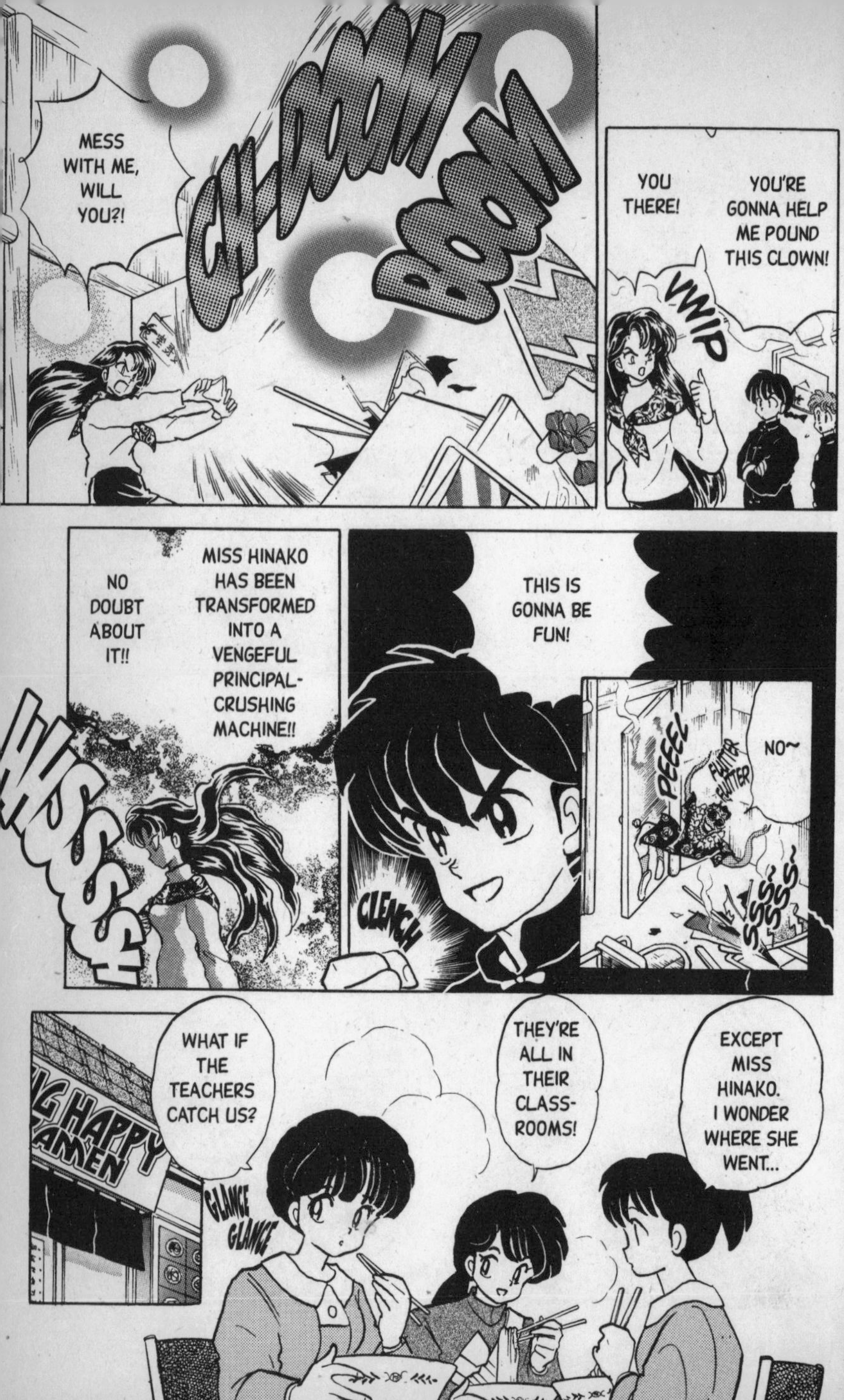
MESS WITH ME, WILL YOU?!
CH-ZOOM
BOOM
YOU THERE!
YOU'RE GONNA HELP ME POUND THIS CLOWN!
VWIP
NO DOUBT ABOUT IT!!
MISS HINAKO HAS BEEN TRANSFORMED INTO A VENGEFUL PRINCIPAL-CRUSHING MACHINE!!
HISSSH
THIS IS GONNA BE FUN!
CLENCH
PEEEL
FLUTTER FLUTTER
NO~
SSS SSS
WHAT IF THE TEACHERS CATCH US?
THEY'RE ALL IN THEIR CLASS-ROOMS!
EXCEPT MISS HINAKO. I WONDER WHERE SHE WENT...
GLANCE GLANCE

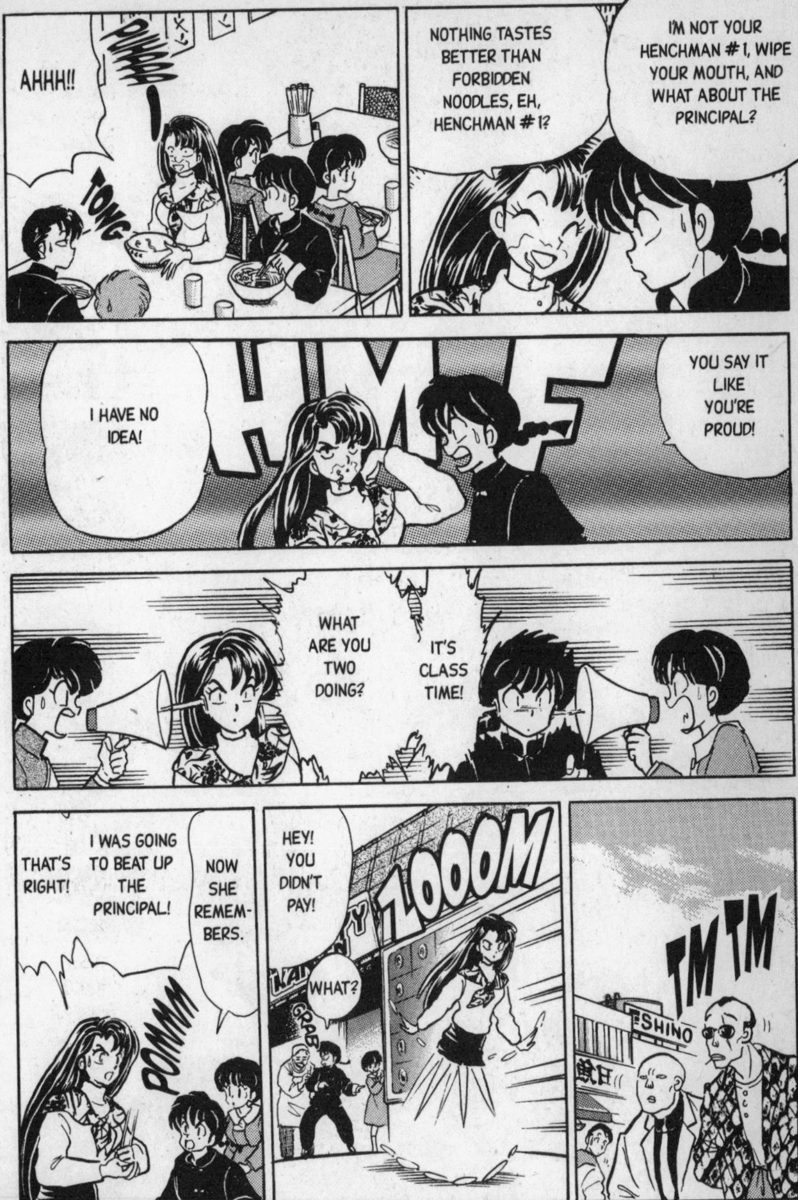
AHHH!!
TONG
NOTHING TASTES BETTER THAN FORBIDDEN NOODLES, EH, HENCHMAN #1?
I'M NOT YOUR HENCHMAN #1, WIPE YOUR MOUTH, AND WHAT ABOUT THE PRINCIPAL?
I HAVE NO IDEA!
HMF
YOU SAY IT LIKE YOU'RE PROUD!
WHAT ARE YOU TWO DOING?
IT'S CLASS TIME!
THAT'S RIGHT!
I WAS GOING TO BEAT UP THE PRINCIPAL!
NOW SHE REMEMBERS.
HEY! YOU DIDN'T PAY!
ZOOOM
WHAT?
GRAB
TM TM
SHINO

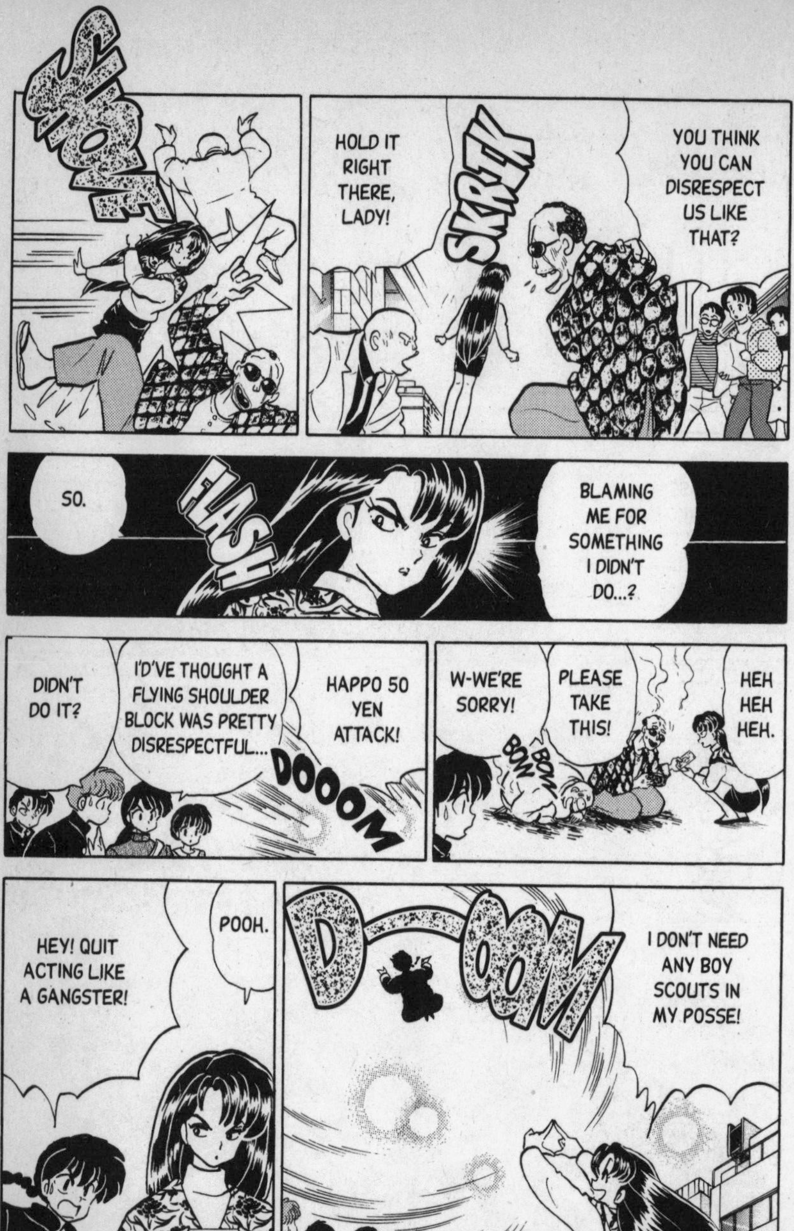
SHOVE!
HOLD IT RIGHT THERE, LADY!
YOU THINK YOU CAN DISRESPECT US LIKE THAT?
SO.
FLASH
BLAMING ME FOR SOMETHING I DIDN'T DO...?
DIDN'T DO IT?
I'D'VE THOUGHT A FLYING SHOULDER BLOCK WAS PRETTY DISRESPECTFUL...
HAPPO 50 YEN ATTACK!
DOOOM
W-WE'RE SORRY!
BOW BOW
PLEASE TAKE THIS!
HEH HEH HEH.
HEY! QUIT ACTING LIKE A GANGSTER!
POOH.
D-OOM
I DON'T NEED ANY BOY SCOUTS IN MY POSSE!

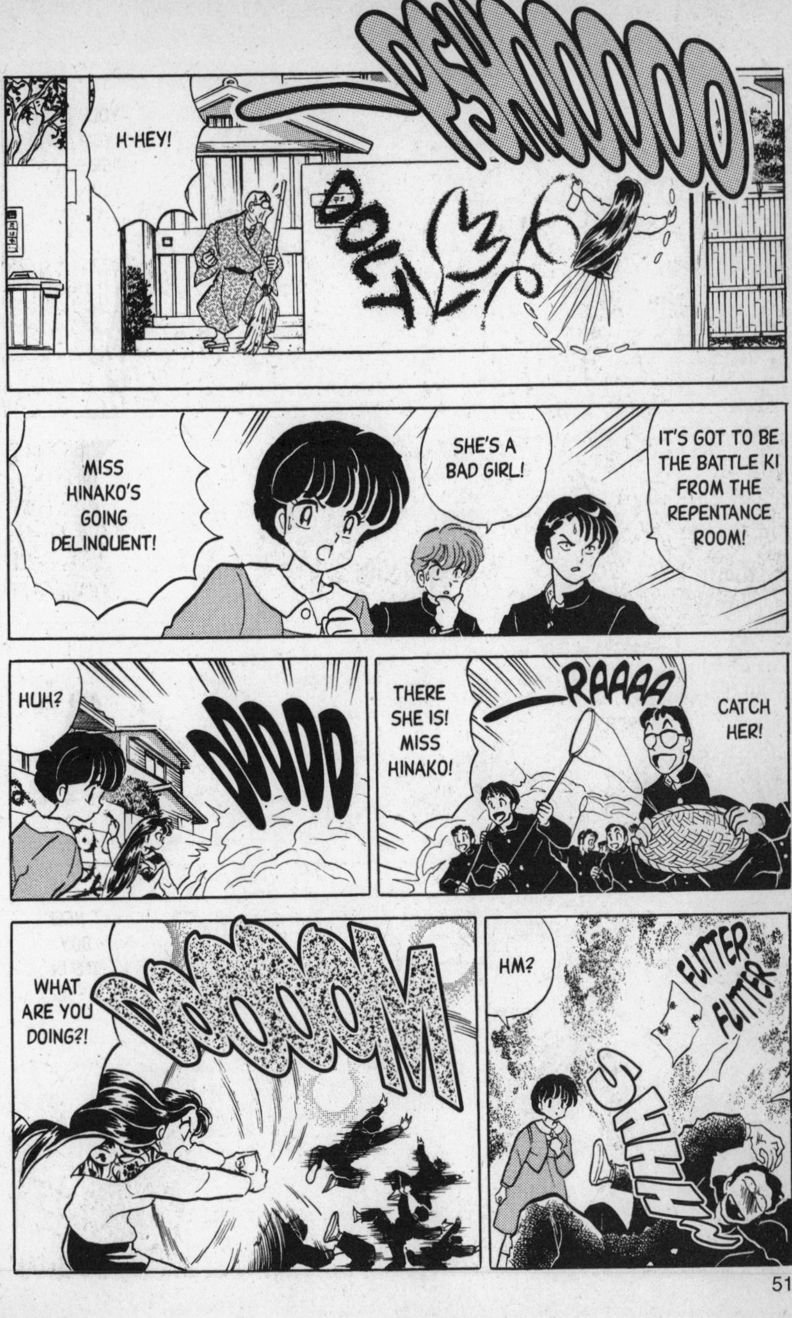
PSHOOOOO
H-HEY!
DOLT
MISS HINAKO'S GOING DELINQUENT!
SHE'S A BAD GIRL!
IT'S GOT TO BE THE BATTLE KI FROM THE REPENTANCE ROOM!
HUH?
DDDDD
—RAAAA
THERE SHE IS! MISS HINAKO!
CATCH HER!
WHAT ARE YOU DOING?!
DOOOOM
HM?
FLUTTER FLUTTER
SHHH

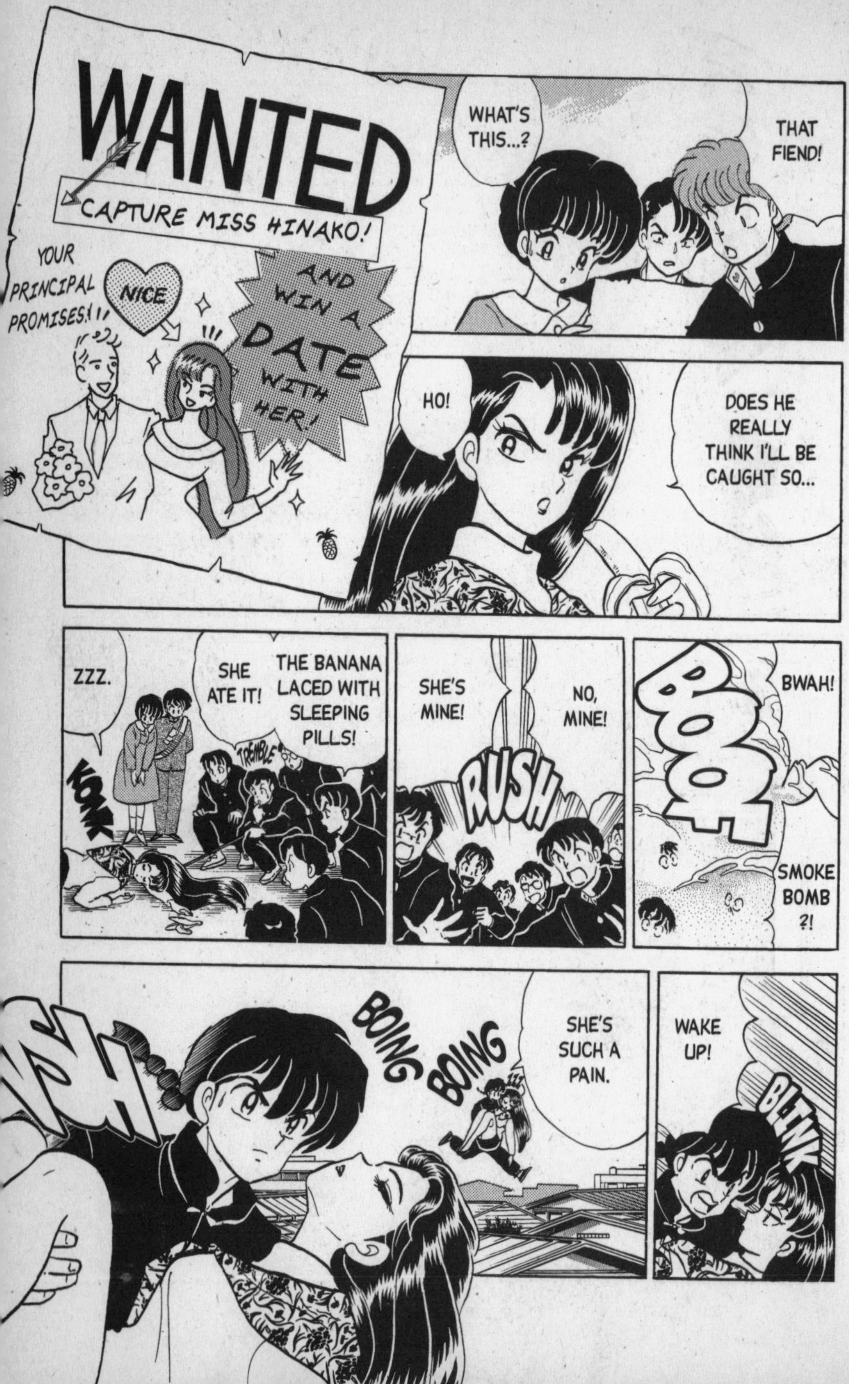
WANTED
CAPTURE MISS HINAKO!
YOUR PRINCIPAL PROMISES!
NICE
AND WIN A DATE WITH HER!
WHAT'S THIS...?
THAT FIEND!
HO!
DOES HE REALLY THINK I'LL BE CAUGHT SO...
ZZZ.
KONK
SHE ATE IT!
THE BANANA LACED WITH SLEEPING PILLS!
TREMBLE
SHE'S MINE!
NO, MINE!
RUSH
BOOF
BWAH!
SMOKE BOMB ?!
BOING
BOING
SHE'S SUCH A PAIN.
WAKE UP!
BLINK

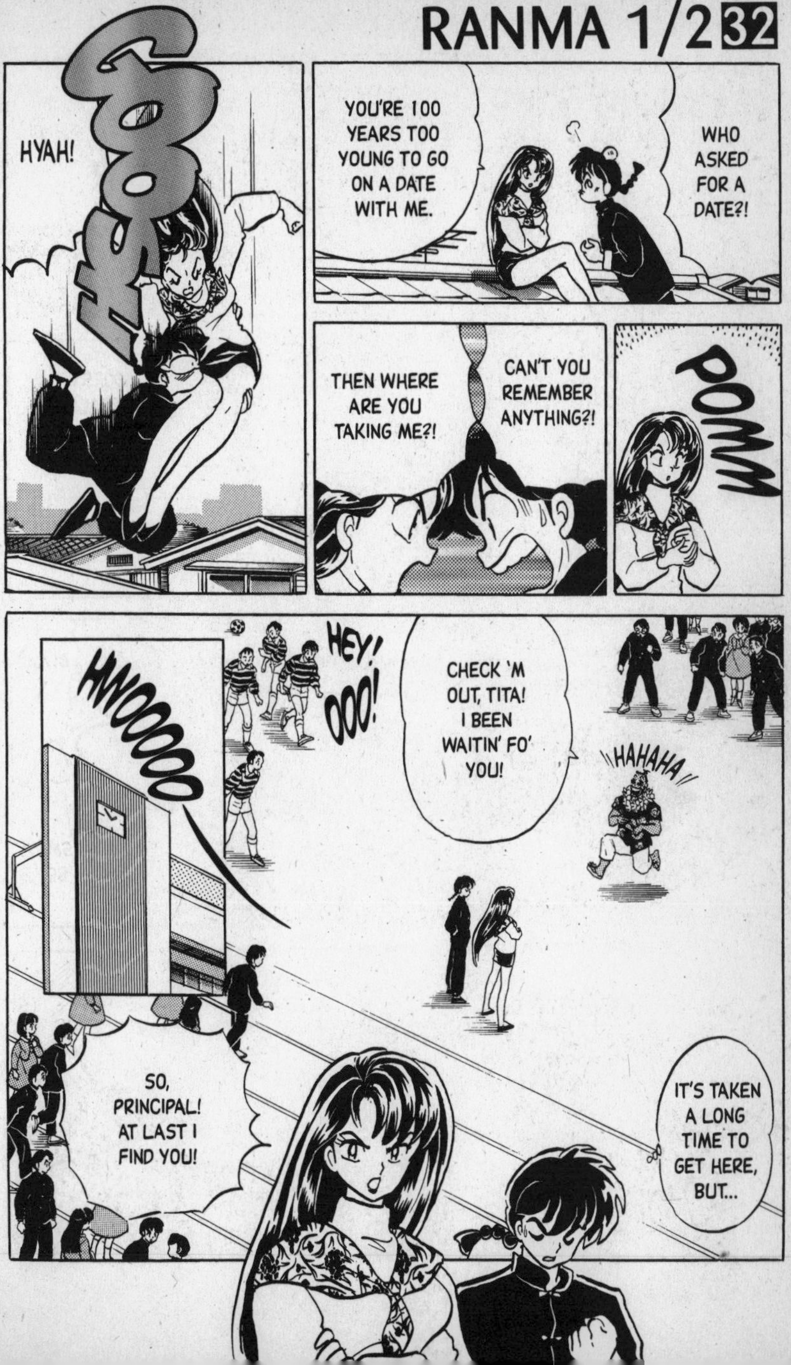
HYAH!
GOOSH
YOU'RE 100 YEARS TOO YOUNG TO GO ON A DATE WITH ME.
WHO ASKED FOR A DATE?!
THEN WHERE ARE YOU TAKING ME?!
CAN'T YOU REMEMBER ANYTHING?!
POMM
HWOOOOOO
HEY! OOO!
CHECK 'M OUT, TITA! I BEEN WAITIN' FO' YOU!
HAHAHA
SO, PRINCIPAL! AT LAST I FIND YOU!
IT'S TAKEN A LONG TIME TO GET HERE, BUT...

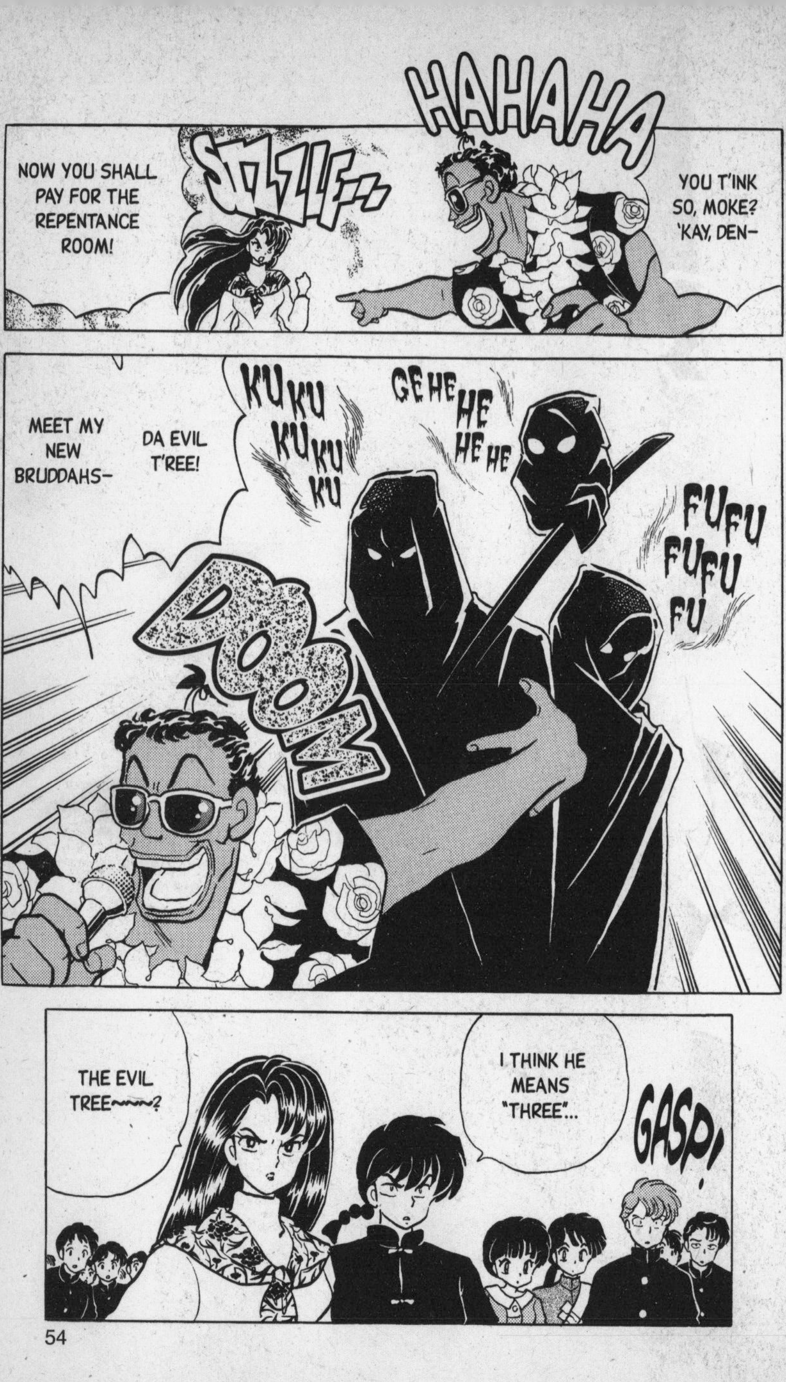
HAHAHA
NOW YOU SHALL PAY FOR THE REPENTANCE ROOM!
YOU T'INK SO, MOKE? 'KAY, DEN—
MEET MY NEW BRUDDAHS—
DA EVIL T'REE!
KU KU KU KU KU KU
GE HE HE HE HE HE
FUFU FUFU FU
DOOOM!
THE EVIL TREE~~~?
I THINK HE MEANS "THREE"...
GASP!

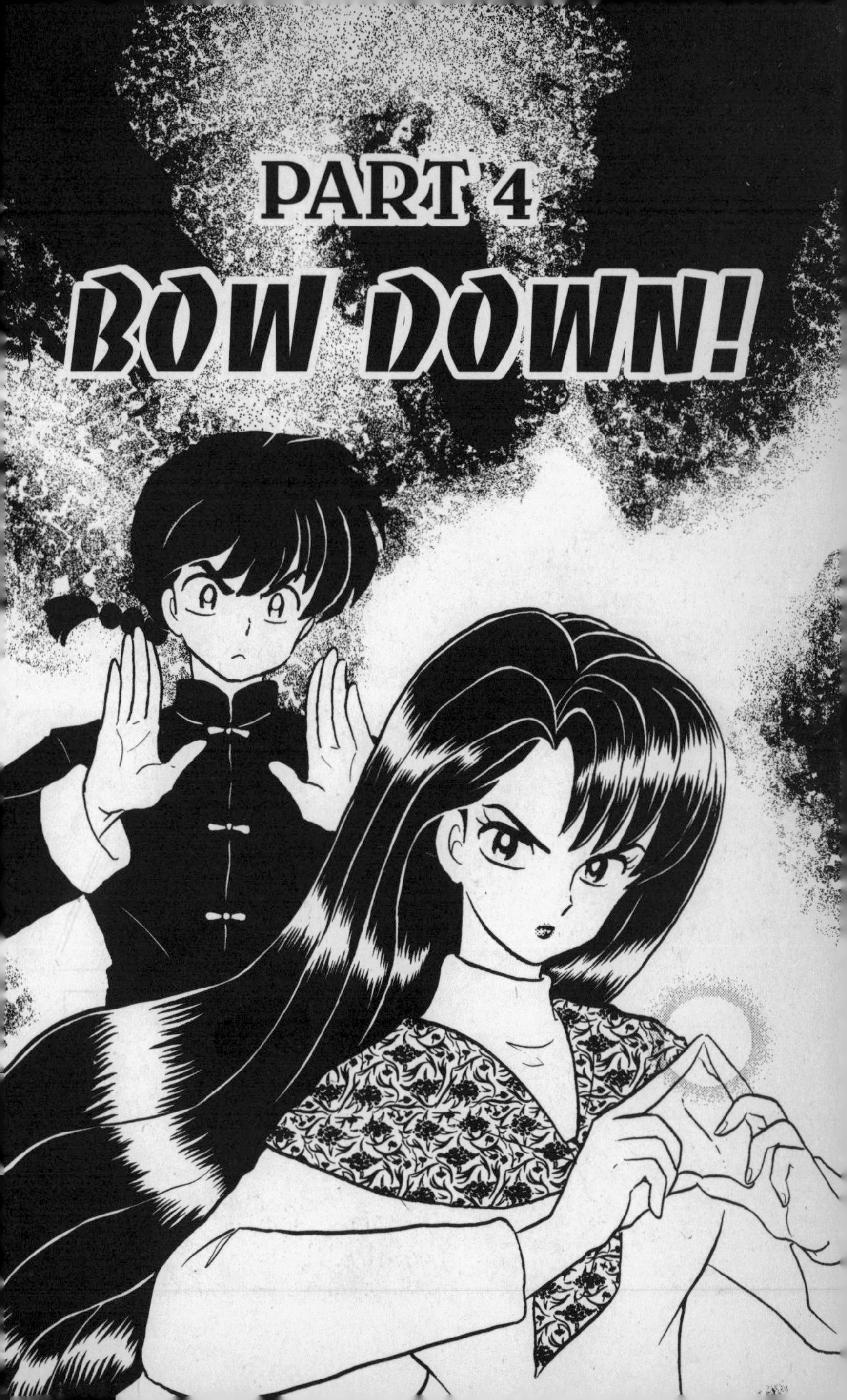
PART 4
BOW DOWN!

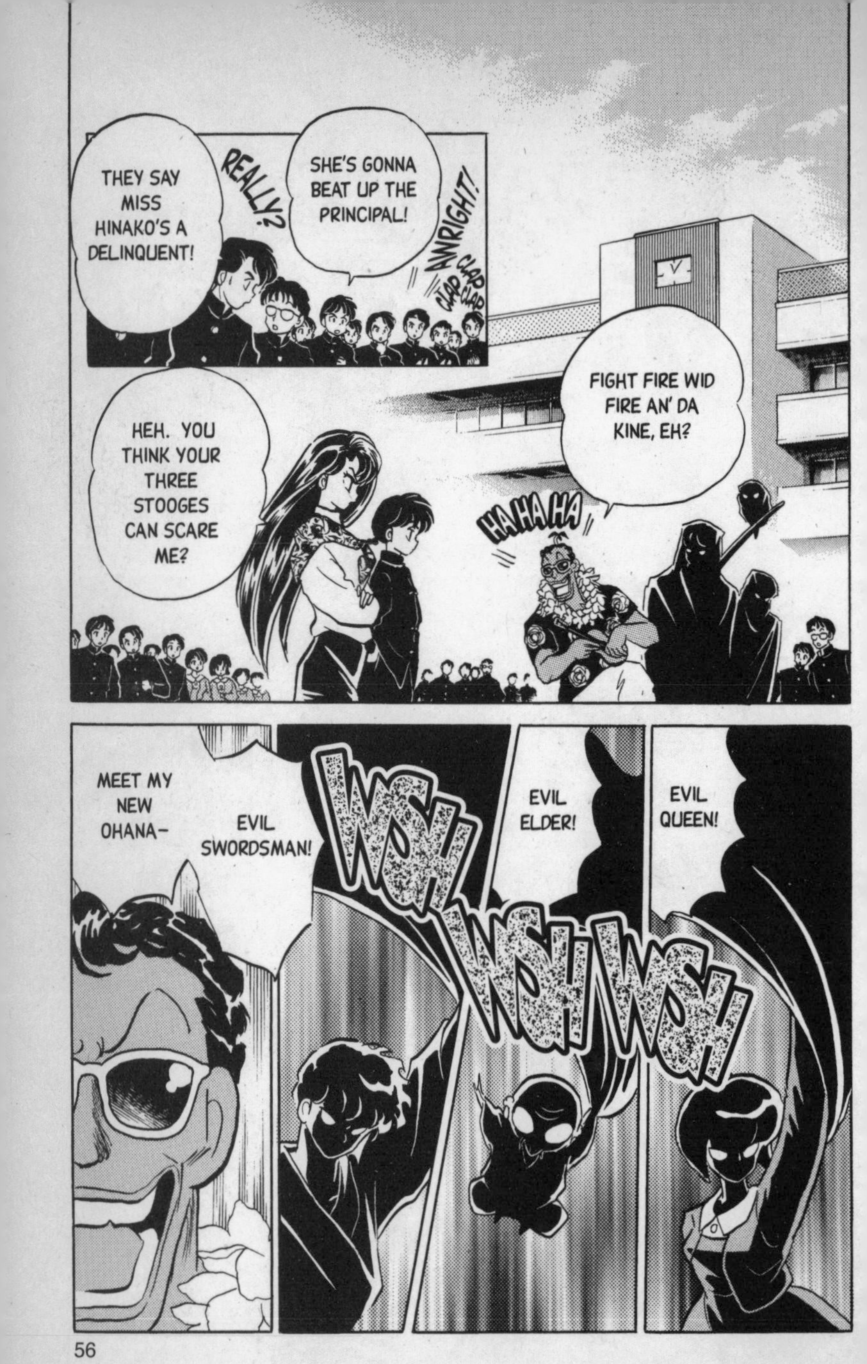
THEY SAY MISS HINAKO'S A DELINQUENT!
REALLY?
SHE'S GONNA BEAT UP THE PRINCIPAL!
AWRIGHT!!
CLAP CLAP CLAP
HEH. YOU THINK YOUR THREE STOOGES CAN SCARE ME?
HA HA HA
FIGHT FIRE WID FIRE AN' DA KINE, EH?
MEET MY NEW OHANA—
EVIL SWORDSMAN!
WSH
EVIL ELDER!
WSH WSH WSH
EVIL QUEEN!

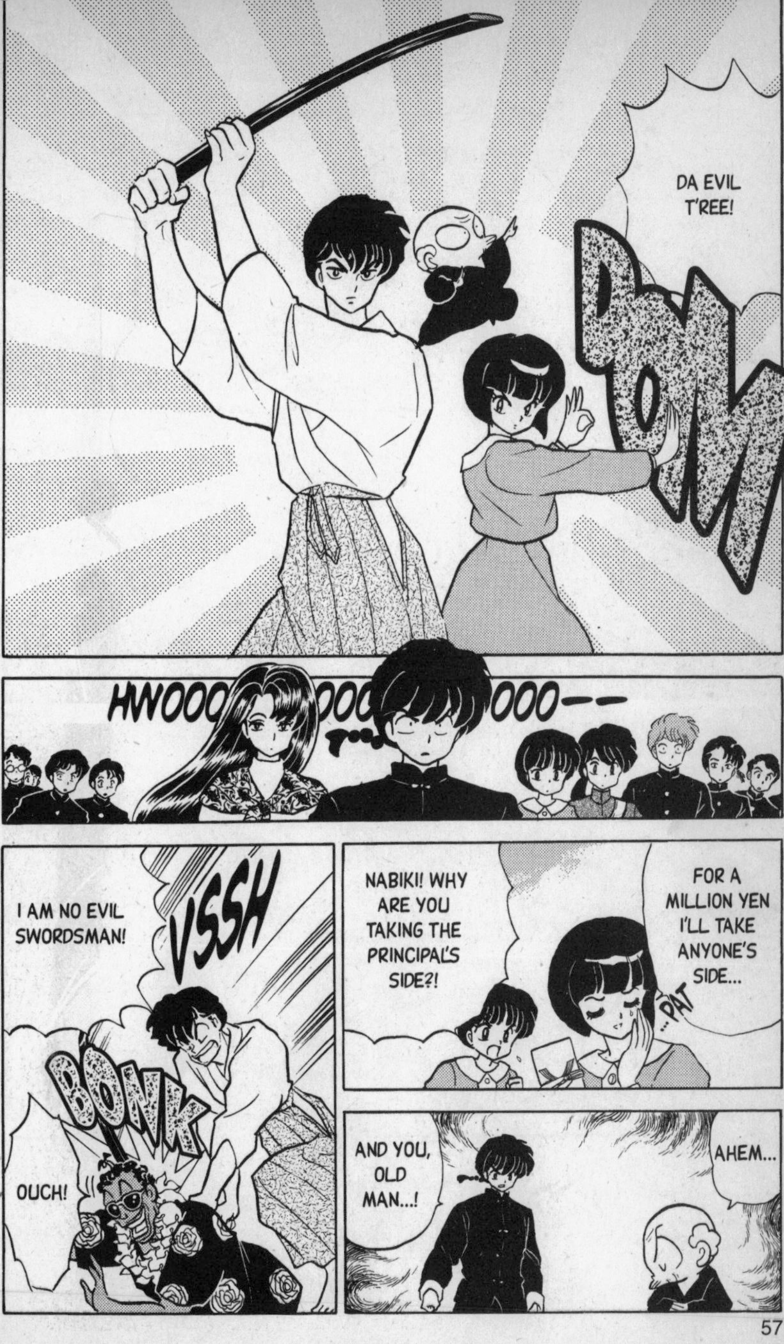
DA EVIL T'REE!
DOOM
HWOOOOOOOOOO--
I AM NO EVIL SWORDSMAN!
VSSH
BONK
OUCH!
NABIKI! WHY ARE YOU TAKING THE PRINCIPAL'S SIDE?!
FOR A MILLION YEN I'LL TAKE ANYONE'S SIDE...
...PAT
AND YOU, OLD MAN...!
AHEM...

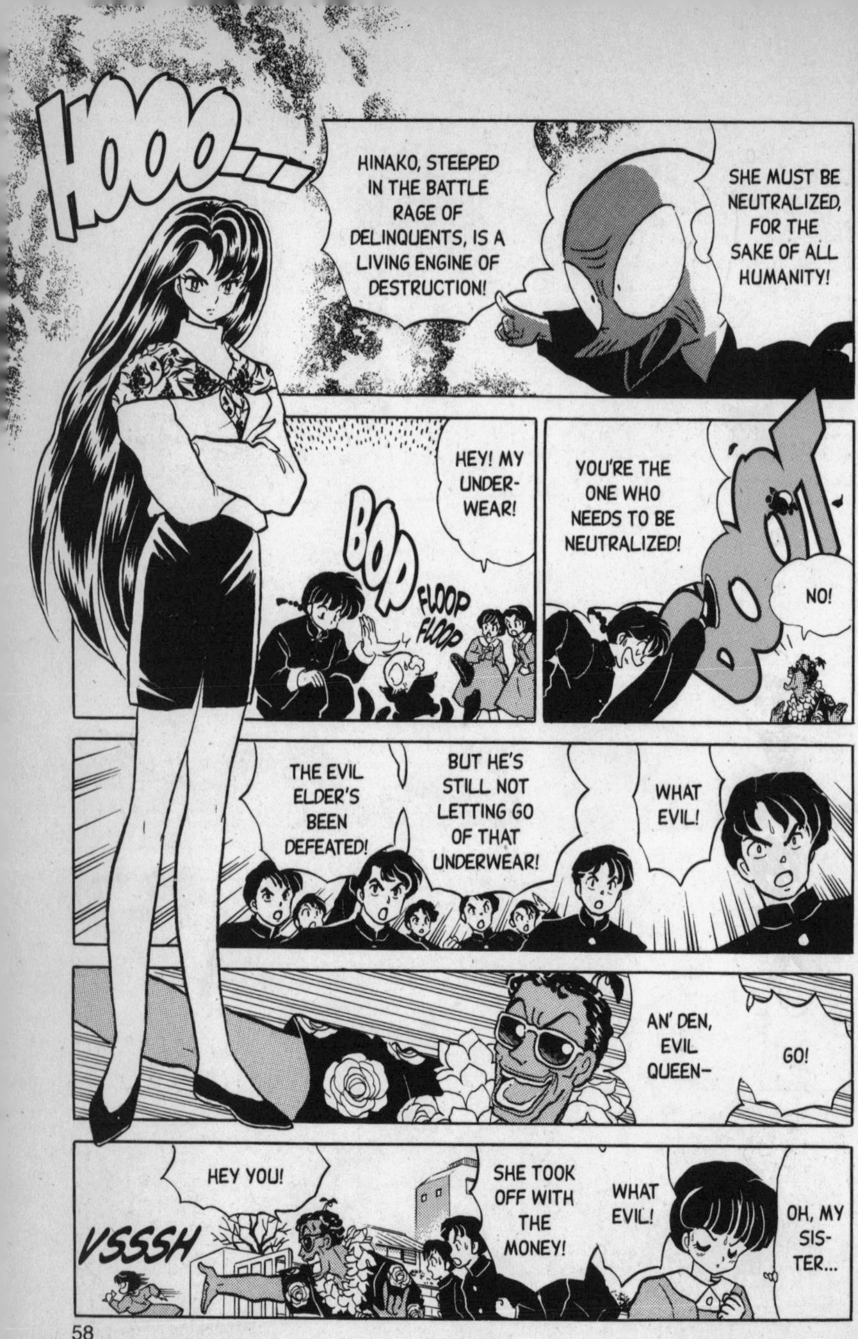
HOOO....
HINAKO, STEEPED IN THE BATTLE RAGE OF DELINQUENTS, IS A LIVING ENGINE OF DESTRUCTION!
SHE MUST BE NEUTRALIZED, FOR THE SAKE OF ALL HUMANITY!
HEY! MY UNDER-WEAR!
BOP
FLOOP
FLOOP
YOU'RE THE ONE WHO NEEDS TO BE NEUTRALIZED!
NO!
THE EVIL ELDER'S BEEN DEFEATED!
BUT HE'S STILL NOT LETTING GO OF THAT UNDERWEAR!
WHAT EVIL!
AN' DEN, EVIL QUEEN-
GO!
VSSSH
HEY YOU!
SHE TOOK OFF WITH THE MONEY!
WHAT EVIL!
OH, MY SIS-TER...

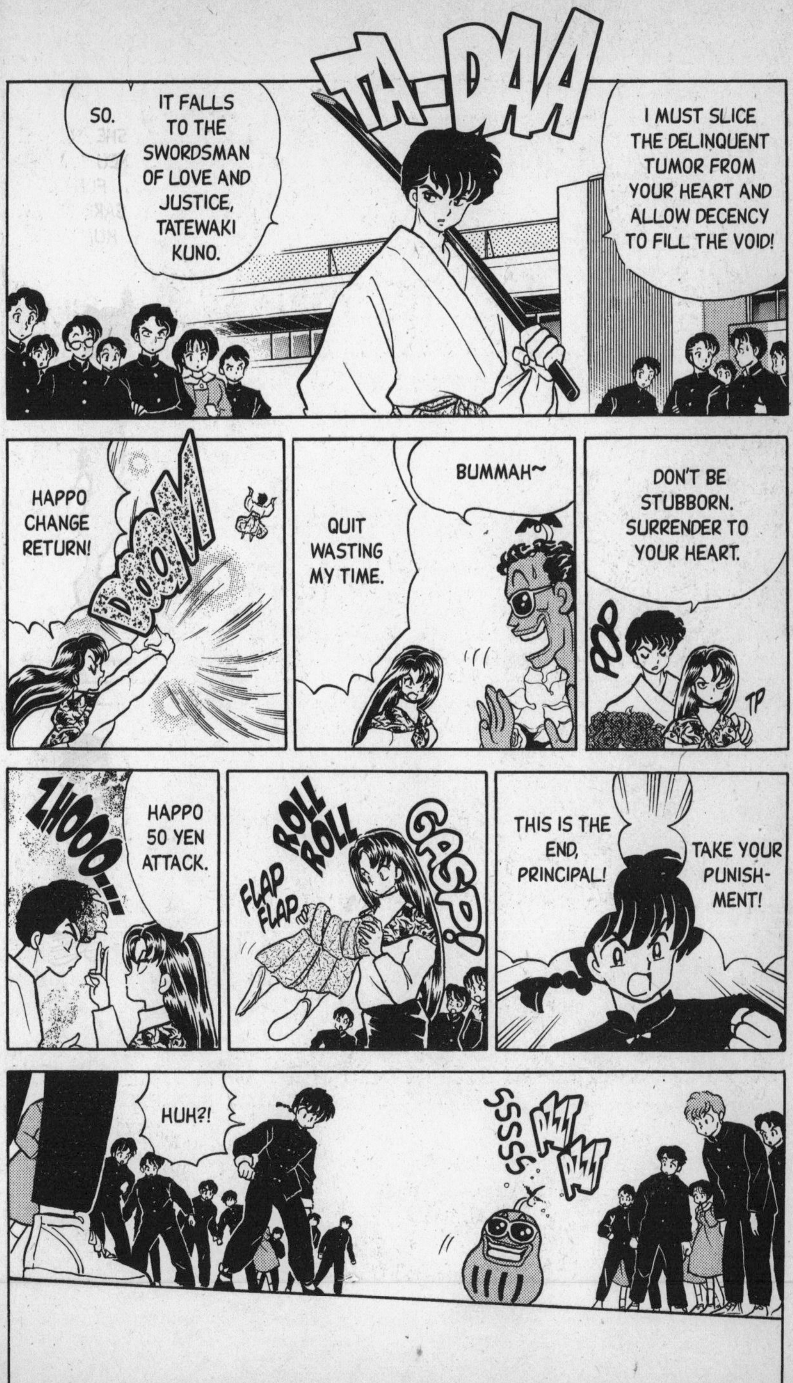
TA-DAA
SO.
IT FALLS TO THE SWORDSMAN OF LOVE AND JUSTICE, TATEWAKI KUNO.
I MUST SLICE THE DELINQUENT TUMOR FROM YOUR HEART AND ALLOW DECENCY TO FILL THE VOID!
HAPPO CHANGE RETURN!
BOOM
QUIT WASTING MY TIME.
BUMMAH~
POP
DON'T BE STUBBORN. SURRENDER TO YOUR HEART.
TP
ZHOOO...!!
HAPPO 50 YEN ATTACK.
ROLL ROLL
FLAP FLAP
GASP!
THIS IS THE END, PRINCIPAL!
TAKE YOUR PUNISH-MENT!
HUH?!
SSSS
PZZT PZZT

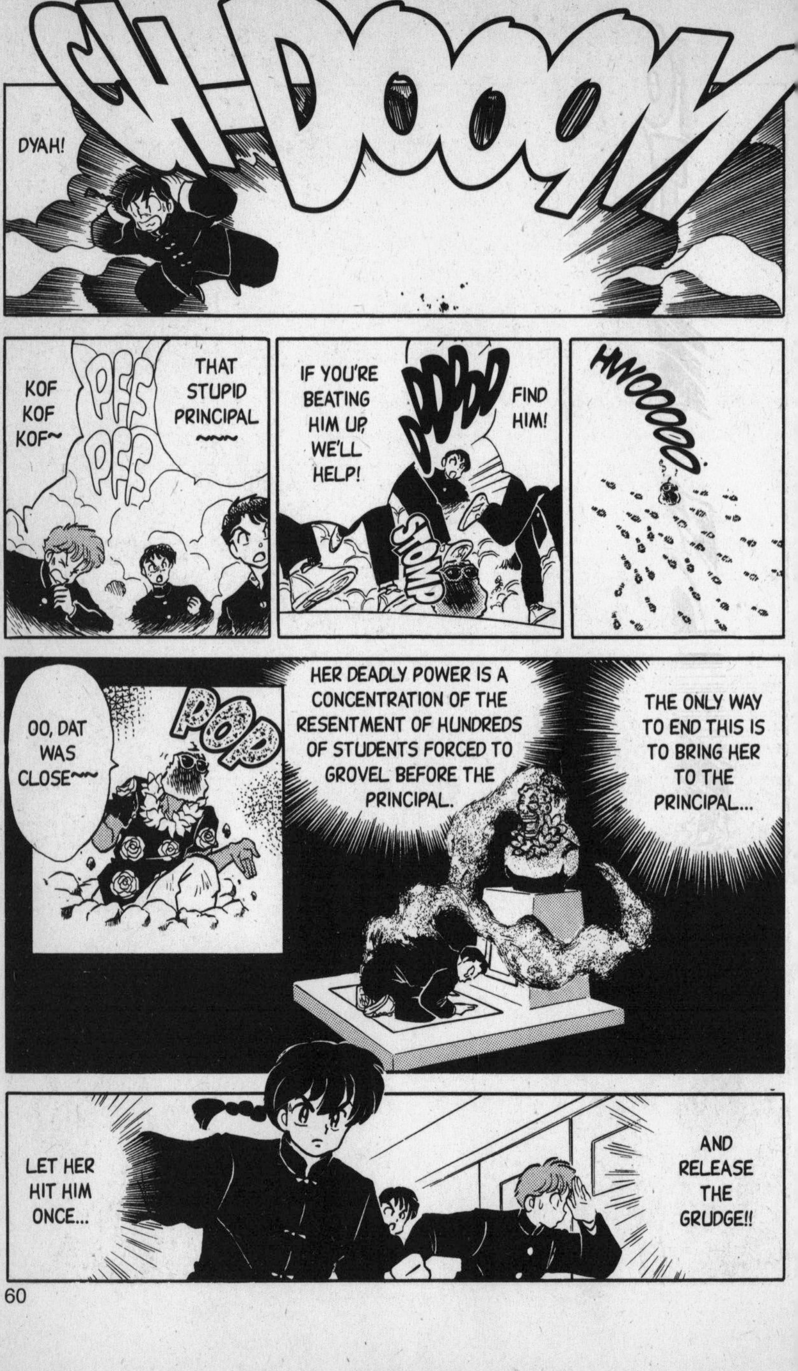
CH-DOOOM!
DYAH!
KOF KOF KOF~
PFF PFF PFF
THAT STUPID PRINCIPAL ~~~
IF YOU'RE BEATING HIM UP, WE'LL HELP!
DDDDD
FIND HIM!
STOMP
HWOOOOOO
OO, DAT WAS CLOSE~~
POP
HER DEADLY POWER IS A CONCENTRATION OF THE RESENTMENT OF HUNDREDS OF STUDENTS FORCED TO GROVEL BEFORE THE PRINCIPAL.
THE ONLY WAY TO END THIS IS TO BRING HER TO THE PRINCIPAL...
LET HER HIT HIM ONCE...
AND RELEASE THE GRUDGE!!

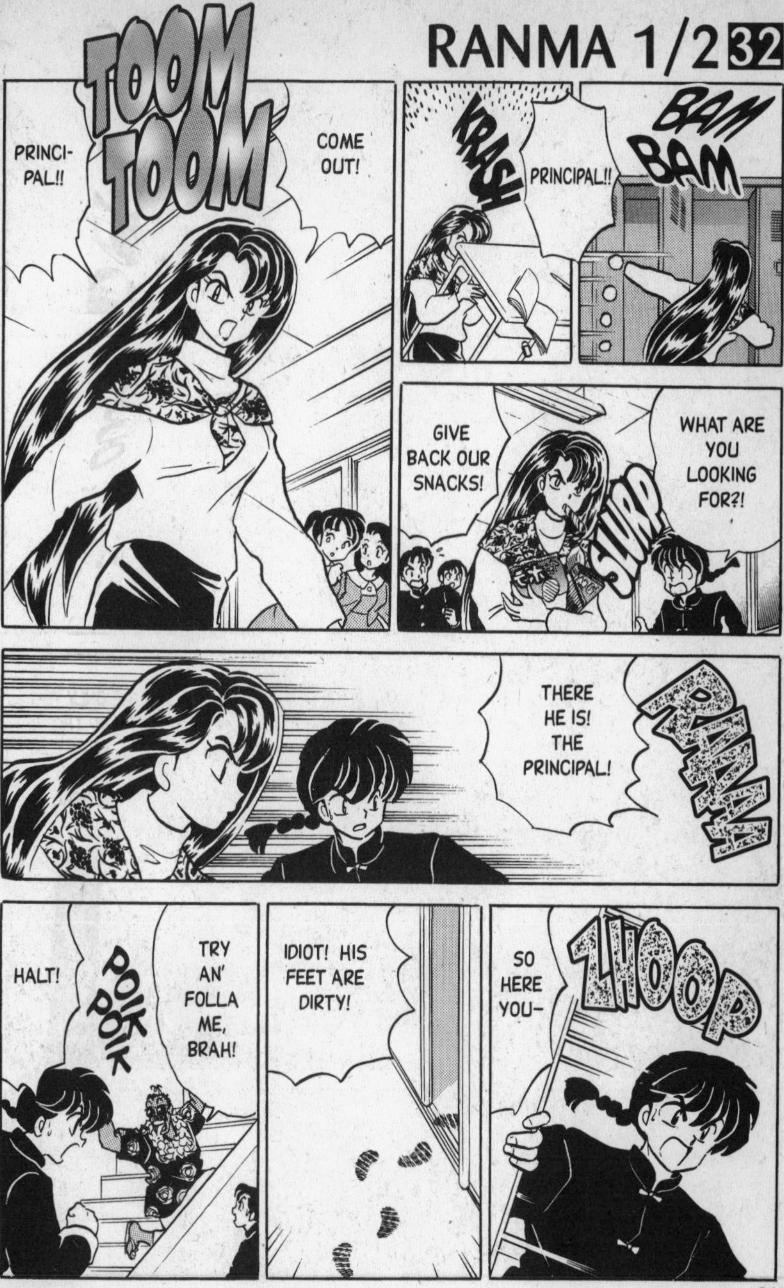
PRINCI-PAL!!
TOOM TOOM
COME OUT!
KRASH
PRINCIPAL!!
BAM BAM
GIVE BACK OUR SNACKS!
SLURP
WHAT ARE YOU LOOKING FOR?!
THERE HE IS! THE PRINCIPAL!
RANMA
HALT!
POIK POIK
TRY AN' FOLLA ME, BRAH!
IDIOT! HIS FEET ARE DIRTY!
SO HERE YOU-
ZHOOP

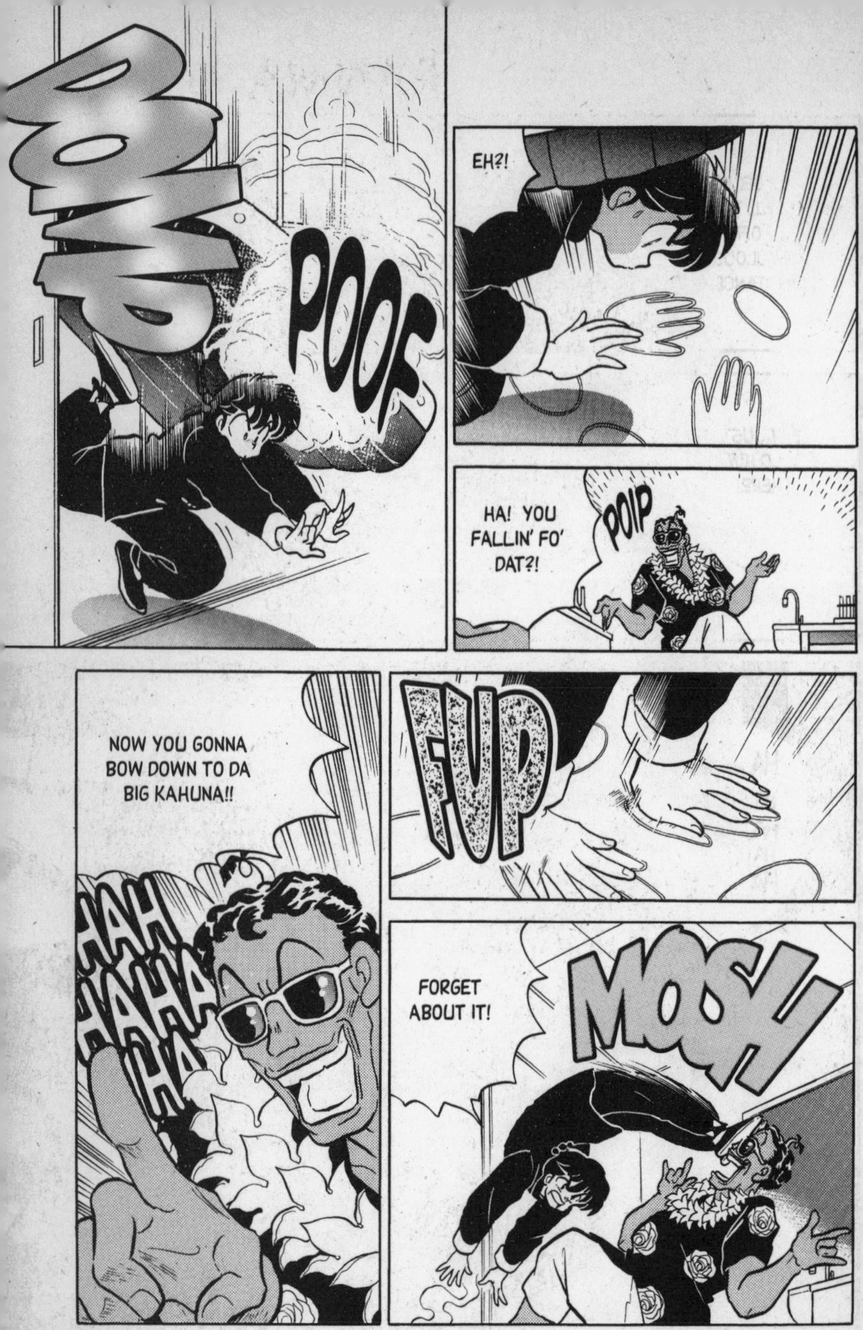
POOF
EH?!
HA! YOU FALLIN' FO' DAT?!
POIP
NOW YOU GONNA BOW DOWN TO DA BIG KAHUNA!!
HAH HAHA HAHA HA
FUP
FORGET ABOUT IT!
MOSH

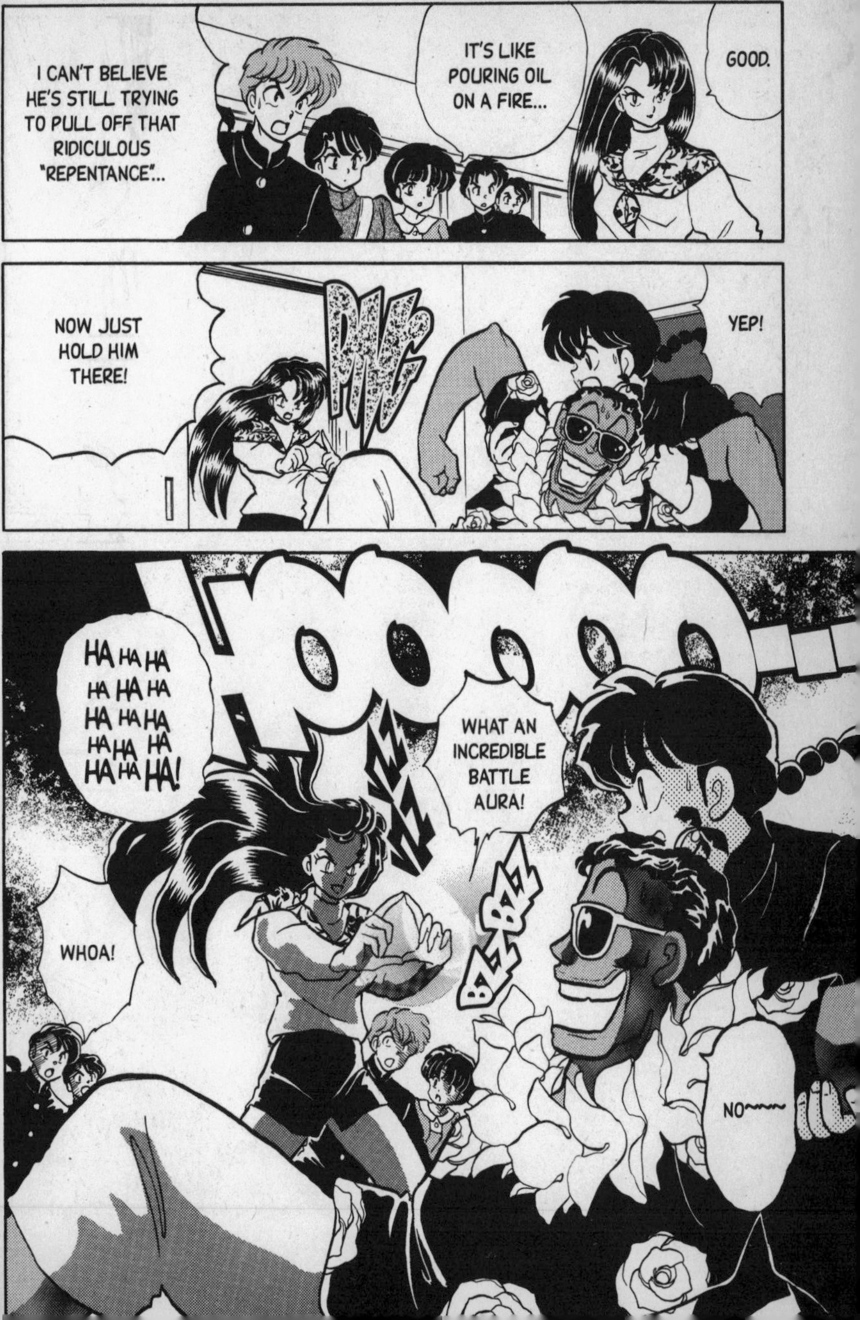
I CAN'T BELIEVE HE'S STILL TRYING TO PULL OFF THAT RIDICULOUS "REPENTANCE"...
IT'S LIKE POURING OIL ON A FIRE...
GOOD.
NOW JUST HOLD HIM THERE!
YEP!
HA HA HA HA HA HA HA HA HA HA HA HA HA HA HA!
WHAT AN INCREDIBLE BATTLE AURA!
WHOA!
NO~~~~

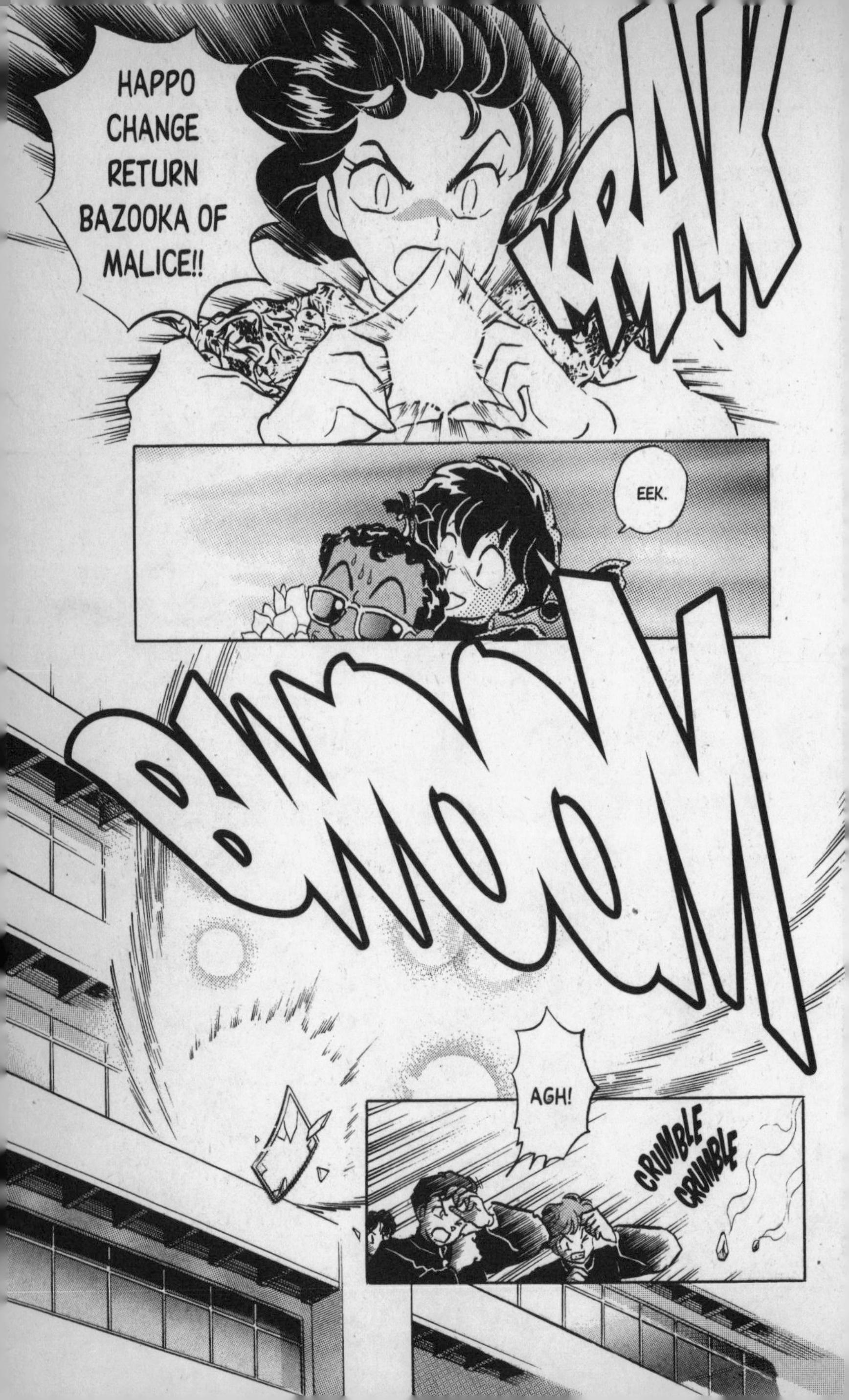
HAPPO CHANGE RETURN BAZOOKA OF MALICE!!
KRAK
EEK.
BWOOM
AGH!
CRUMBLE CRUMBLE

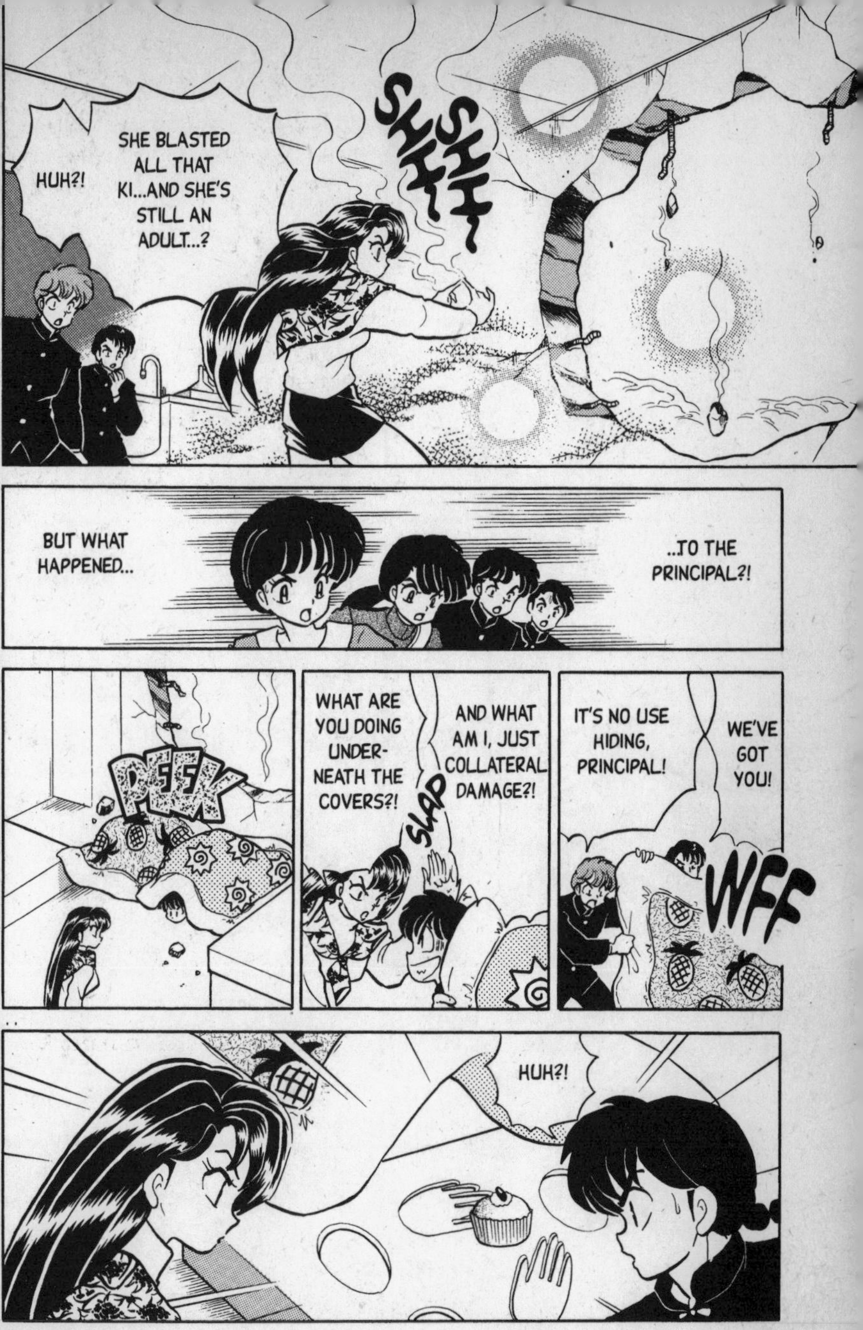
HUH?!
SHE BLASTED ALL THAT KI...AND SHE'S STILL AN ADULT...?
SHHH~
BUT WHAT HAPPENED...
...TO THE PRINCIPAL?!
PFSSK
WHAT ARE YOU DOING UNDER-NEATH THE COVERS?!
SLAP
AND WHAT AM I, JUST COLLATERAL DAMAGE?!
IT'S NO USE HIDING, PRINCIPAL!
WE'VE GOT YOU!
WFF
HUH?!

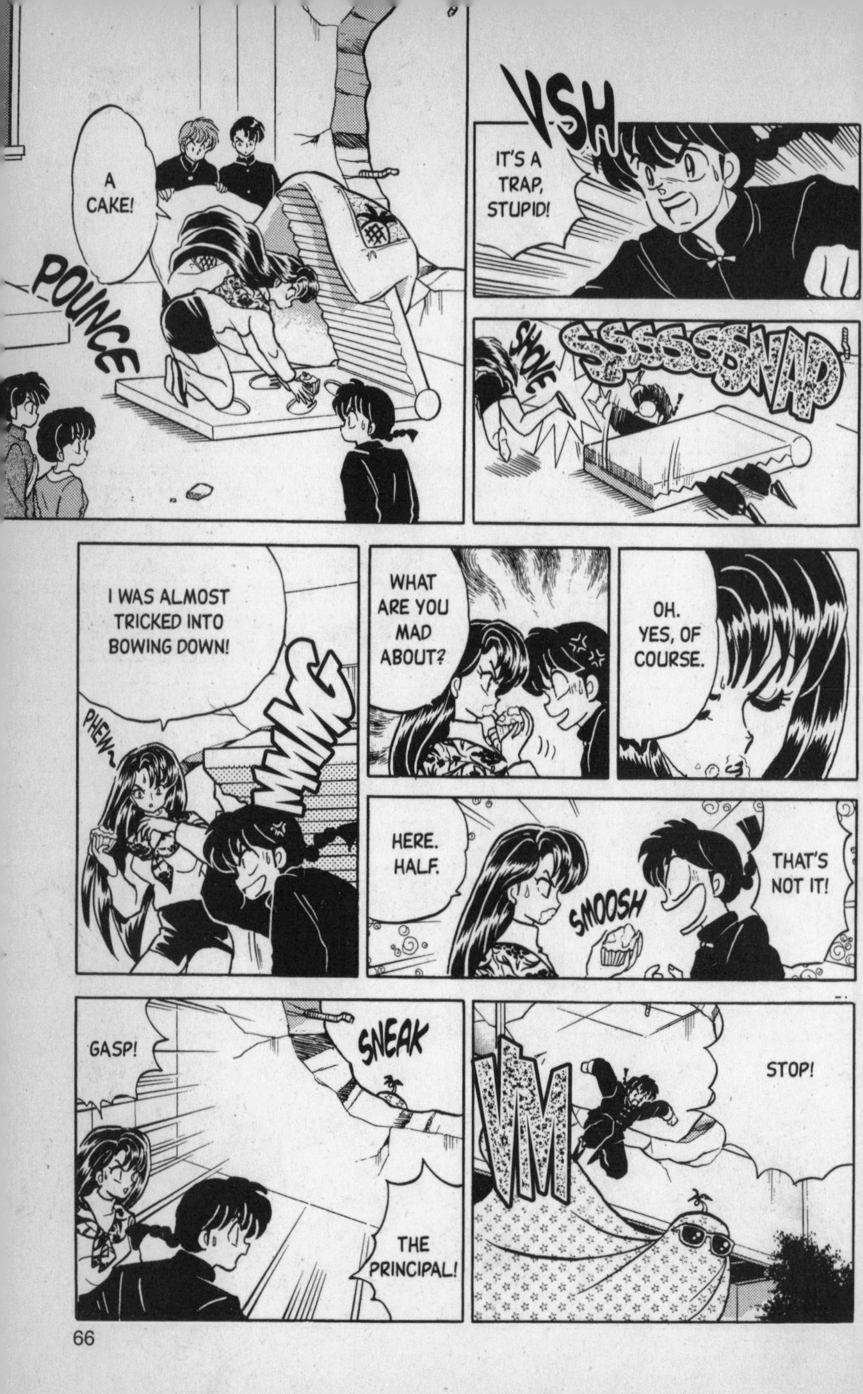
A CAKE!
POUNCE
VSH
IT'S A TRAP, STUPID!
SHOVE
SSSSSSNAP
I WAS ALMOST TRICKED INTO BOWING DOWN!
PHEW~
MMMG
WHAT ARE YOU MAD ABOUT?
OH. YES, OF COURSE.
HERE. HALF.
SMOOSH
THAT'S NOT IT!
GASP!
SNEAK
THE PRINCIPAL!
VM
STOP!

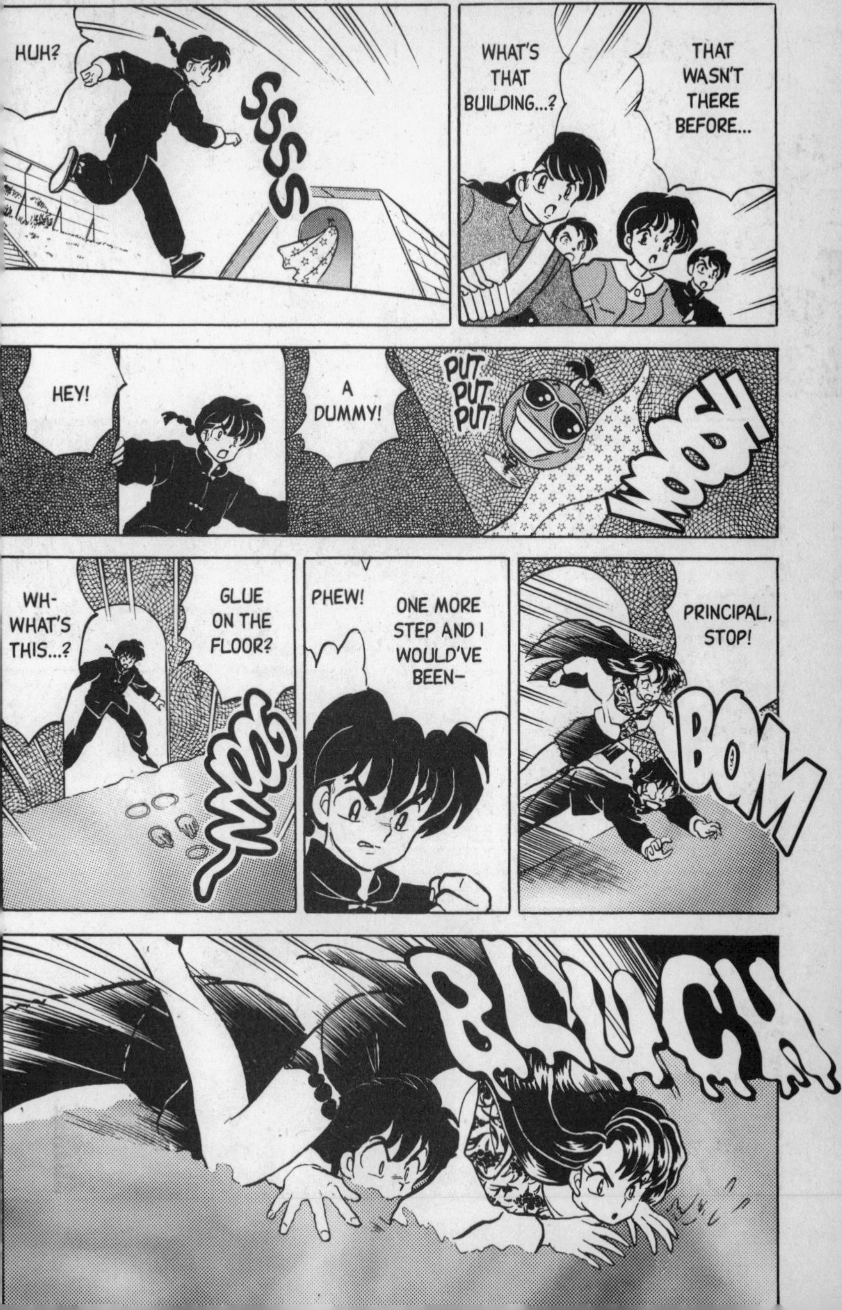
HUH?
SSSS
WHAT'S THAT BUILDING...?
THAT WASN'T THERE BEFORE...
HEY!
A DUMMY!
PUT PUT PUT
WOOSH
WH- WHAT'S THIS...?
GLUE ON THE FLOOR?
WOOO
PHEW!
ONE MORE STEP AND I WOULD'VE BEEN-
PRINCIPAL, STOP!
BOM
BLUUCH

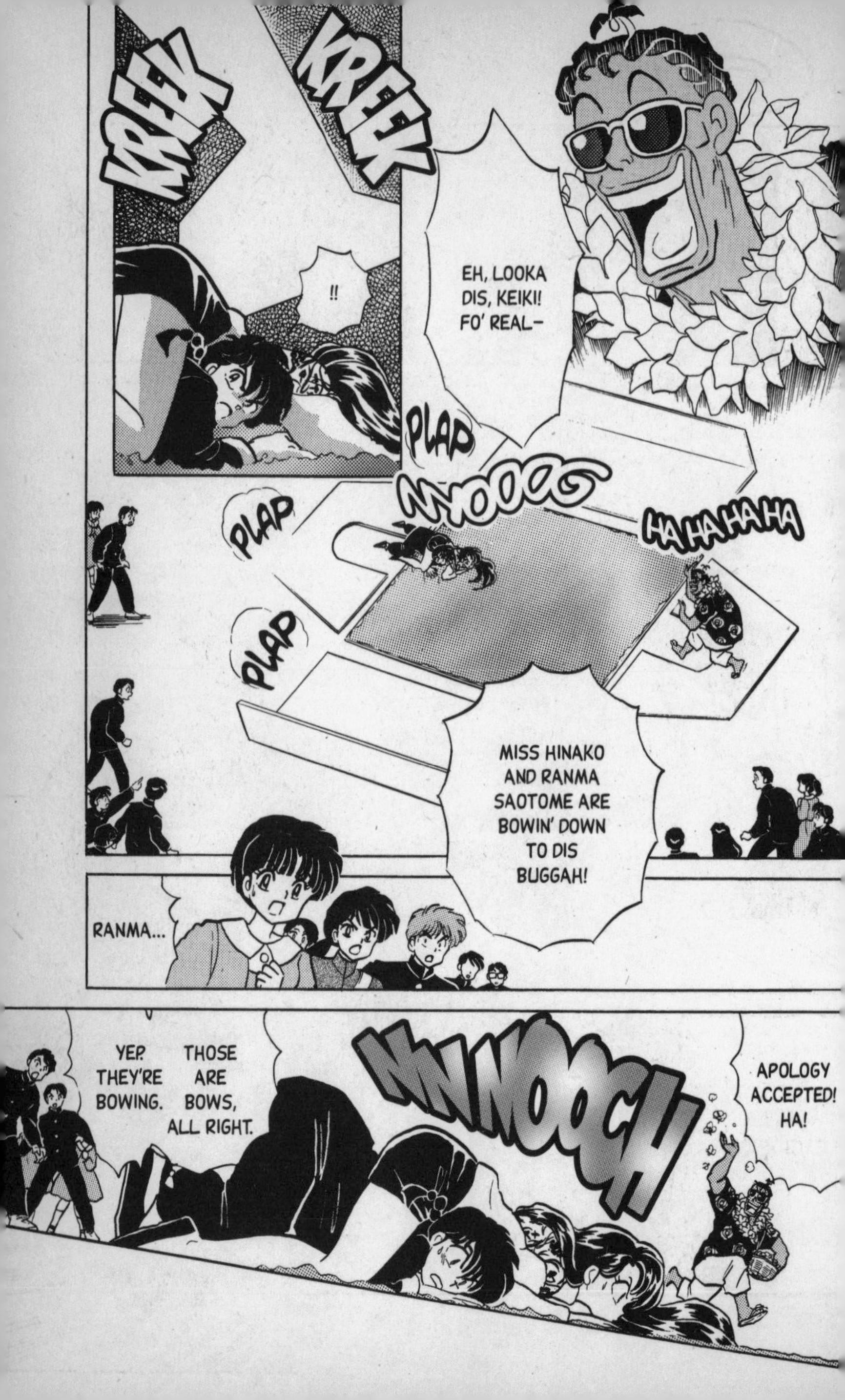
KREEK
KREEK
!!
EH, LOOKA DIS, KEIKI! FO' REAL—
PLAP
NYOOOG
PLAP
PLAP
HA HA HA HA
MISS HINAKO AND RANMA SAOTOME ARE BOWIN' DOWN TO DIS BUGGAH!
RANMA...
YEP. THEY'RE BOWING.
THOSE ARE BOWS, ALL RIGHT.
MMMOOCH
APOLOGY ACCEPTED! HA!

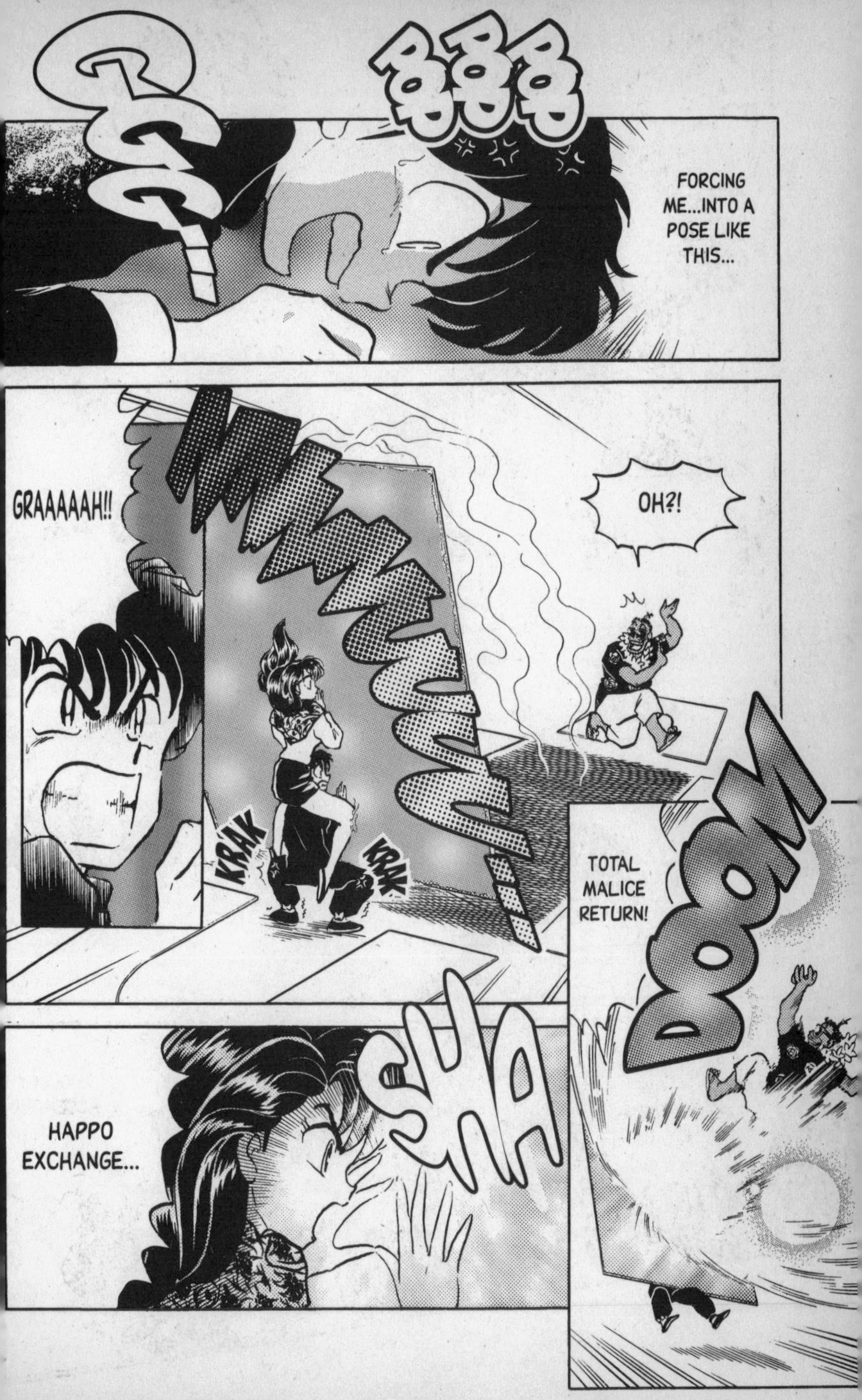
GGG
BBBB
FORCING ME...INTO A POSE LIKE THIS...
GRAAAAAH!!
OH?!
KRAK
KRAK
TOTAL MALICE RETURN!
DOOM
HAPPO EXCHANGE...
SHA

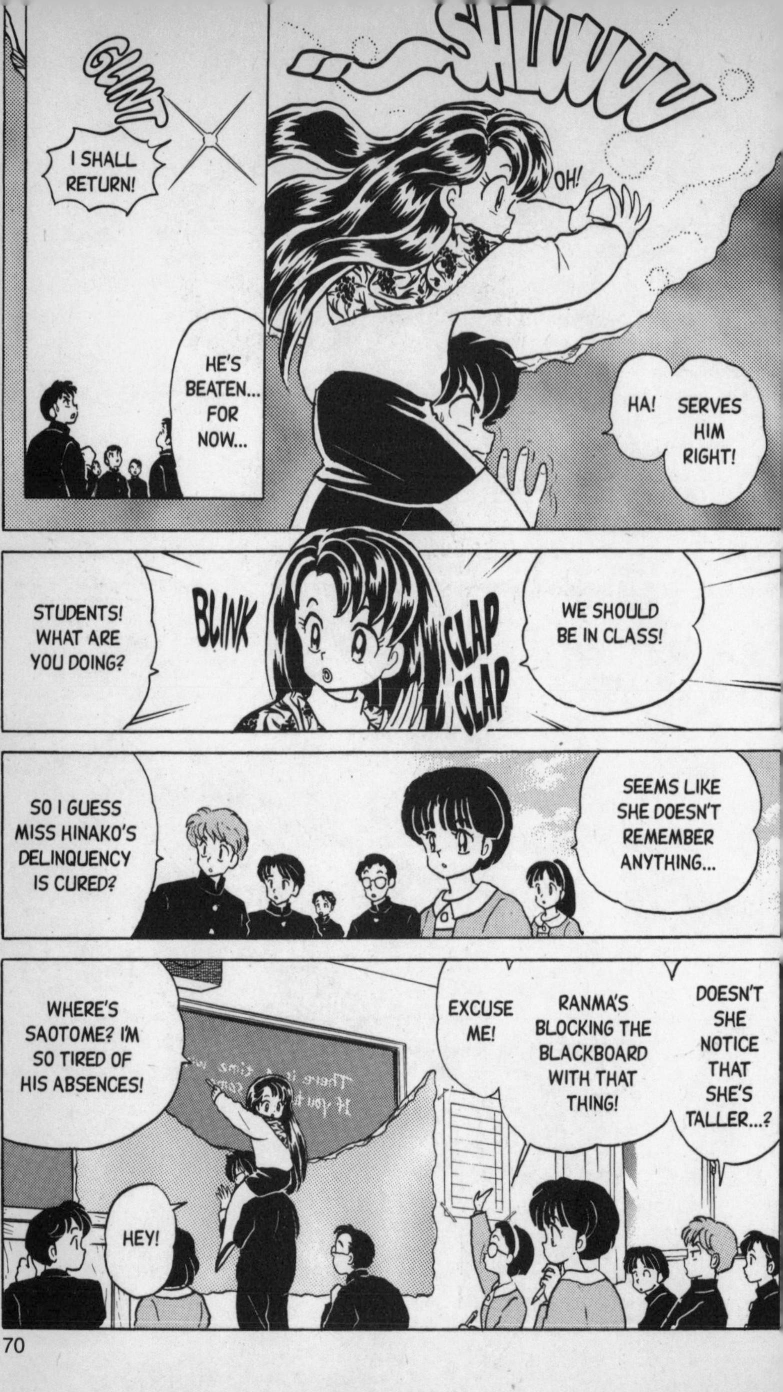
GLINT
I SHALL RETURN!
SHUUUUU
OH!
HE'S BEATEN... FOR NOW...
HA! SERVES HIM RIGHT!
STUDENTS! WHAT ARE YOU DOING?
BLINK
CLAP CLAP
WE SHOULD BE IN CLASS!
SO I GUESS MISS HINAKO'S DELINQUENCY IS CURED?
SEEMS LIKE SHE DOESN'T REMEMBER ANYTHING...
WHERE'S SAOTOME? I'M SO TIRED OF HIS ABSENCES!
HEY!
EXCUSE ME!
RANMA'S BLOCKING THE BLACKBOARD WITH THAT THING!
DOESN'T SHE NOTICE THAT SHE'S TALLER...?

PART 5

BUSTED!

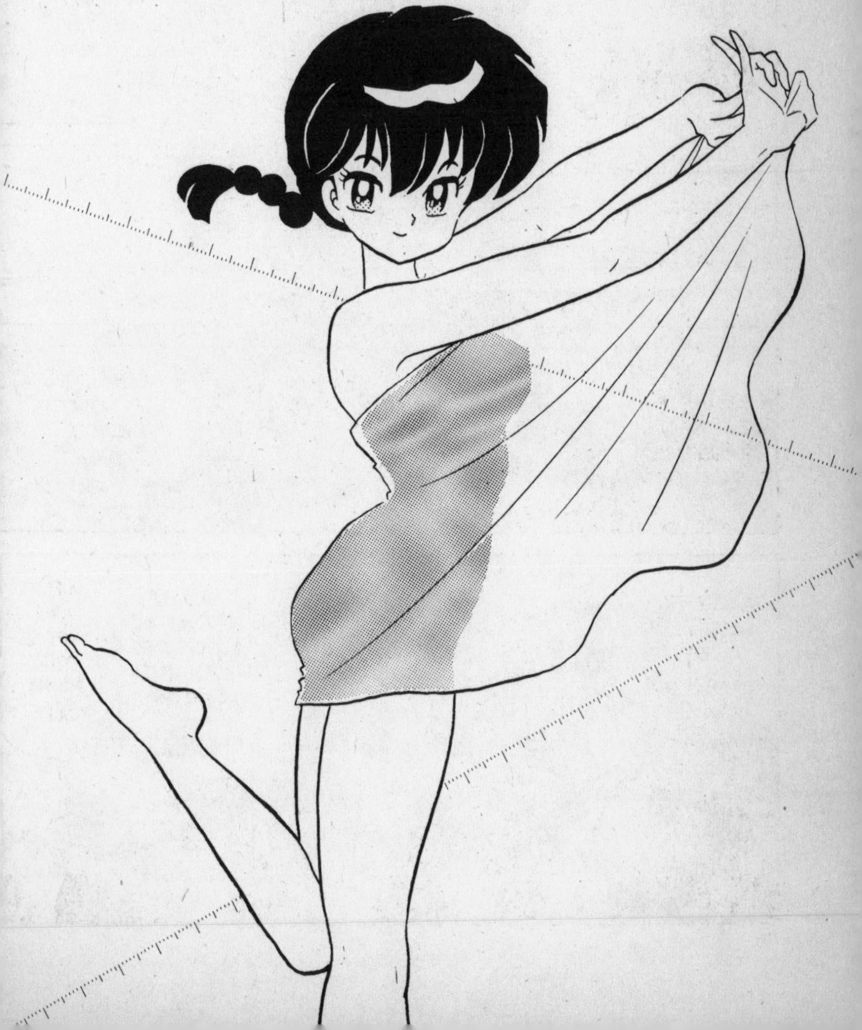

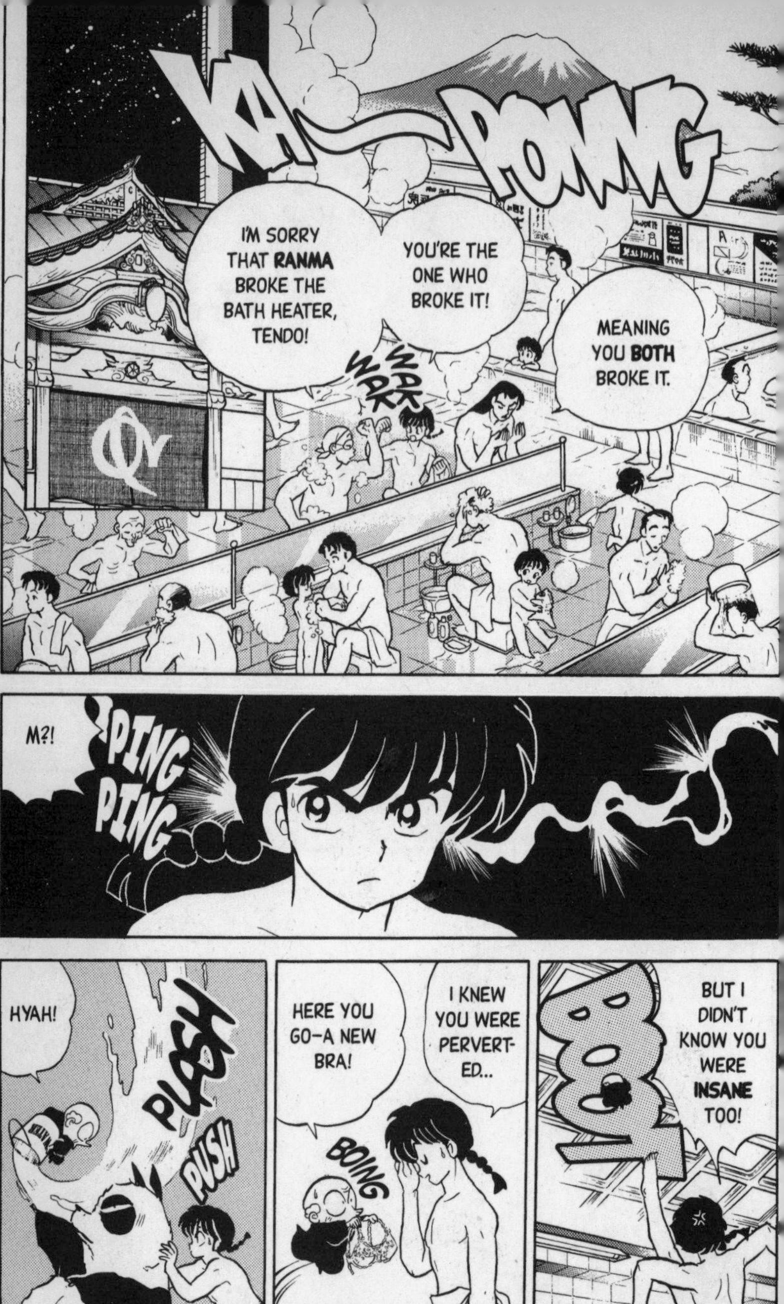
KA-POWNG
I'M SORRY THAT RANMA BROKE THE BATH HEATER, TENDO!
YOU'RE THE ONE WHO BROKE IT!
WAK WAK
MEANING YOU BOTH BROKE IT.
M?!
PING PING
HYAH!
PLOSH
PUSH
HERE YOU GO—A NEW BRA!
I KNEW YOU WERE PERVERT-ED...
BOING
BUT I DIDN'T KNOW YOU WERE INSANE TOO!

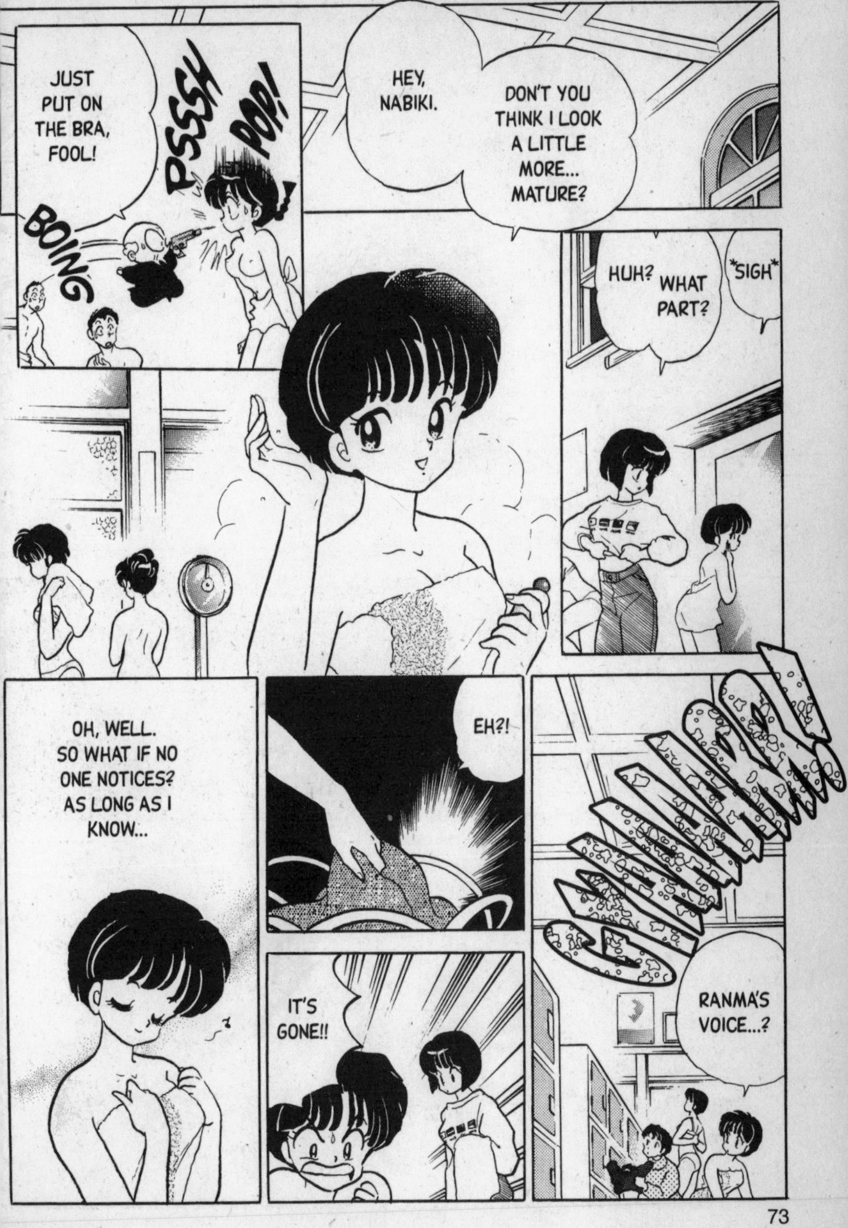
JUST PUT ON THE BRA, FOOL!
PSSSH
POP!
BOING
HEY, NABIKI.
DON'T YOU THINK I LOOK A LITTLE MORE... MATURE?
HUH?
WHAT PART?
SIGH
OH, WELL. SO WHAT IF NO ONE NOTICES? AS LONG AS I KNOW...
EH?!
IT'S GONE!!
RANMA'S VOICE...?

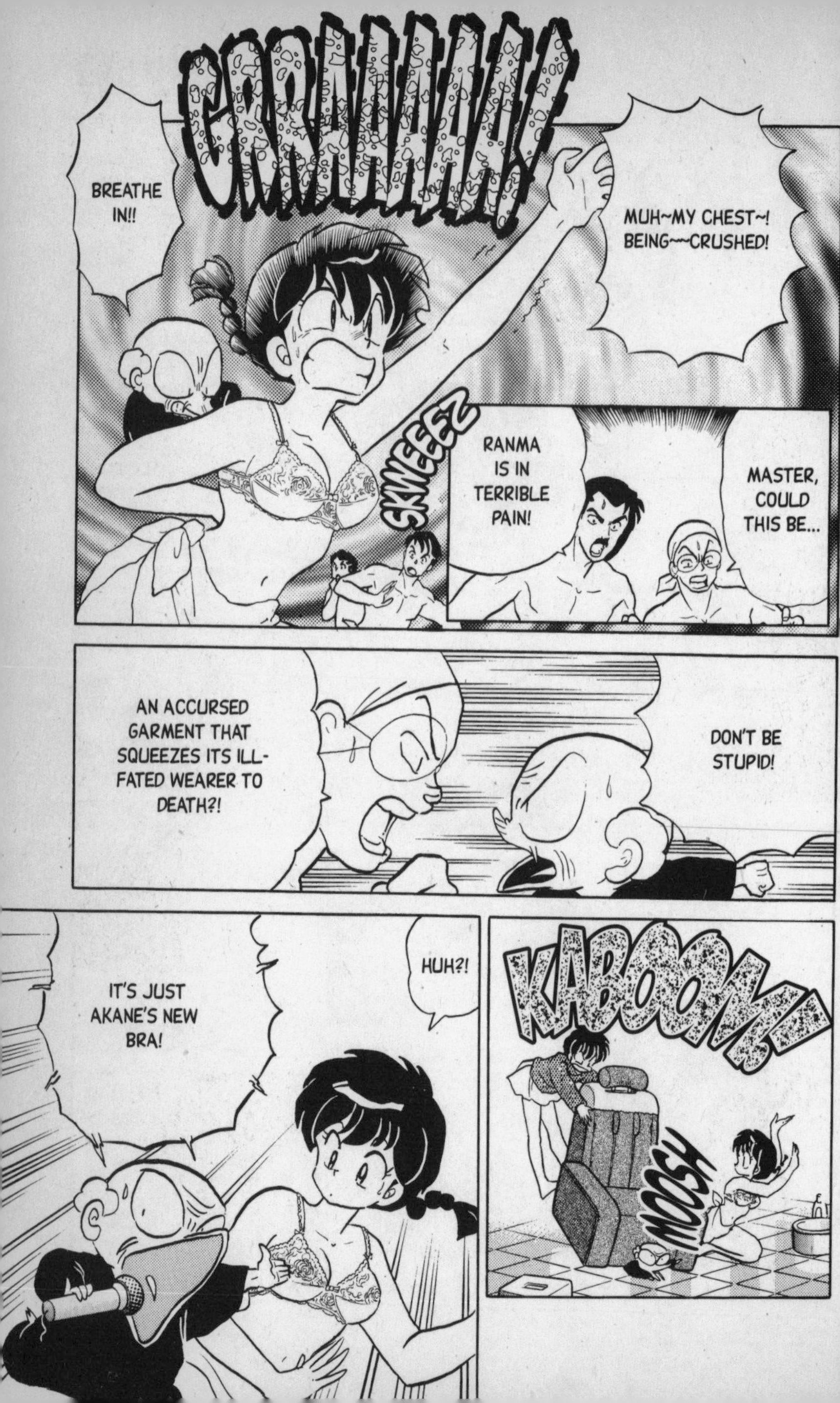
GRAAAAH!
BREATHE IN!!
MUH~MY CHEST~! BEING~~CRUSHED!
SKWEEEZ
RANMA IS IN TERRIBLE PAIN!
MASTER, COULD THIS BE...
AN ACCURSED GARMENT THAT SQUEEZES ITS ILL-FATED WEARER TO DEATH?!
DON'T BE STUPID!
IT'S JUST AKANE'S NEW BRA!
HUH?!
KABOOM!
MOOSH

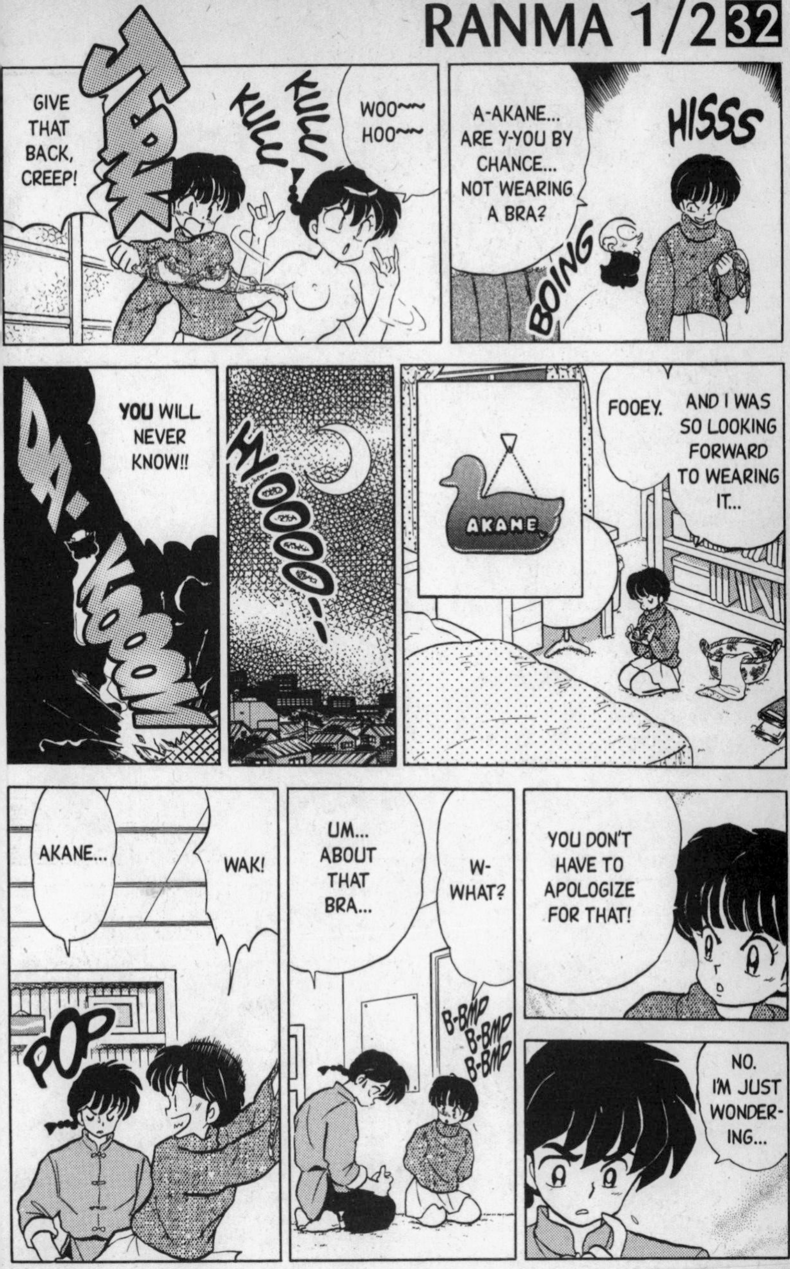
GIVE THAT BACK, CREEP!
KULU KULU
WOO~~ HOO~~
A-AKANE... ARE Y-YOU BY CHANCE... NOT WEARING A BRA?
HISSS
BOING
YOU WILL NEVER KNOW!!
AKANE
FOOEY.
AND I WAS SO LOOKING FORWARD TO WEARING IT...
AKANE...
WAK!
POP
UM... ABOUT THAT BRA...
W- WHAT?
B-BMP B-BMP B-BMP
YOU DON'T HAVE TO APOLOGIZE FOR THAT!
NO. I'M JUST WONDER- ING...

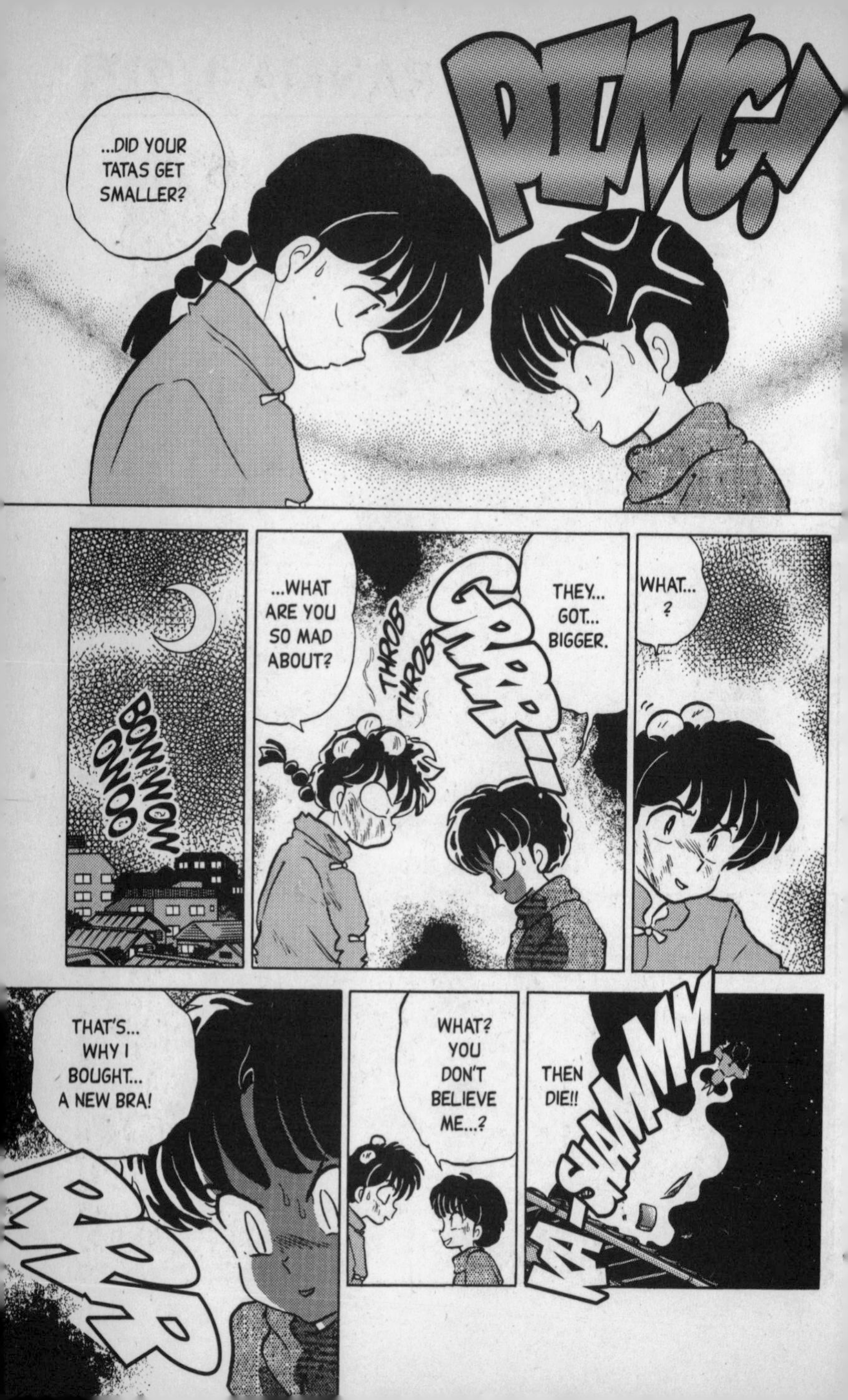
...DID YOUR TATAS GET SMALLER?
PIING!
BOWWOW OWOO
...WHAT ARE YOU SO MAD ABOUT?
THROB THROB
GRRR...
THEY... GOT... BIGGER.
WHAT...?
THAT'S... WHY I BOUGHT... A NEW BRA!
RRRR
WHAT? YOU DON'T BELIEVE ME...?
THEN DIE!!
KA-SHAMMM

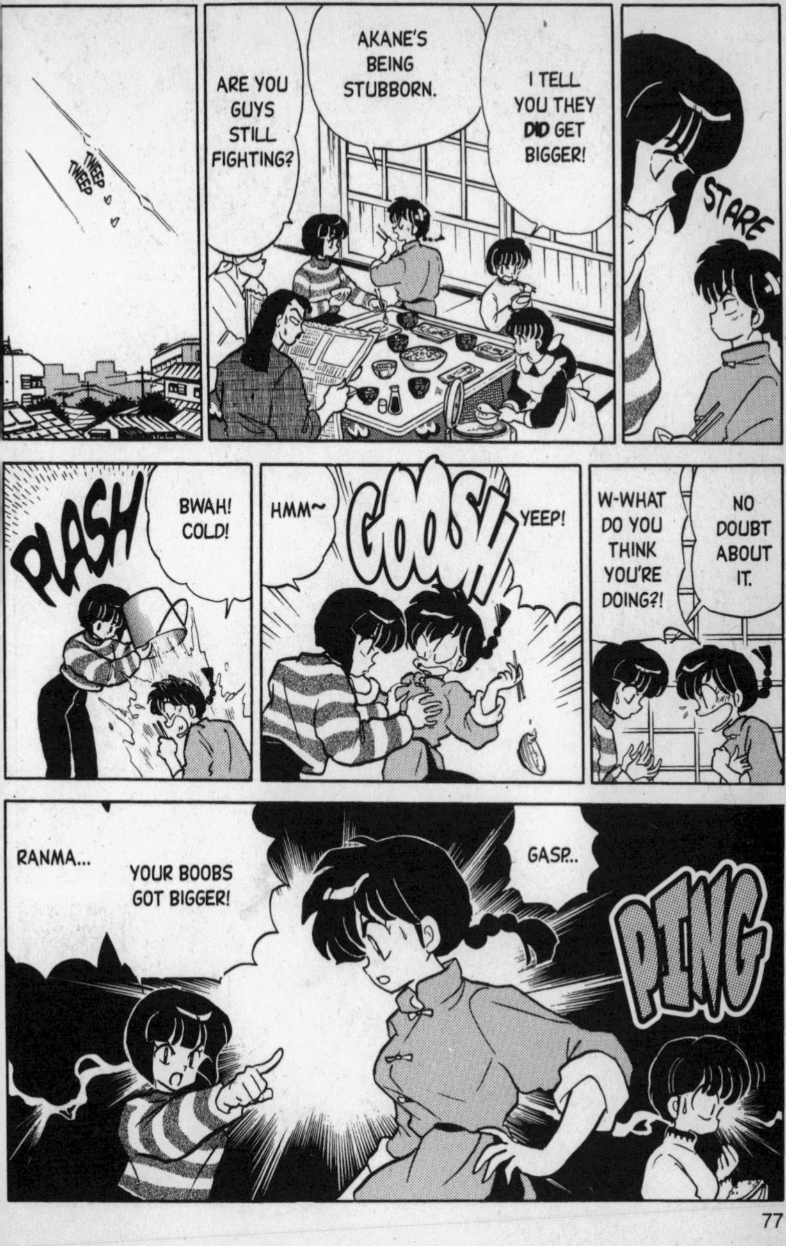
TWEEP
TWEEP
ARE YOU GUYS STILL FIGHTING?
AKANE'S BEING STUBBORN.
I TELL YOU THEY **DID** GET BIGGER!
STARE
PLASH
BWAH! COLD!
HMM~
GOOSH
YEEP!
W-WHAT DO YOU THINK YOU'RE DOING?!
NO DOUBT ABOUT IT.
RANMA...
YOUR BOOBS GOT BIGGER!
GASP...
PING

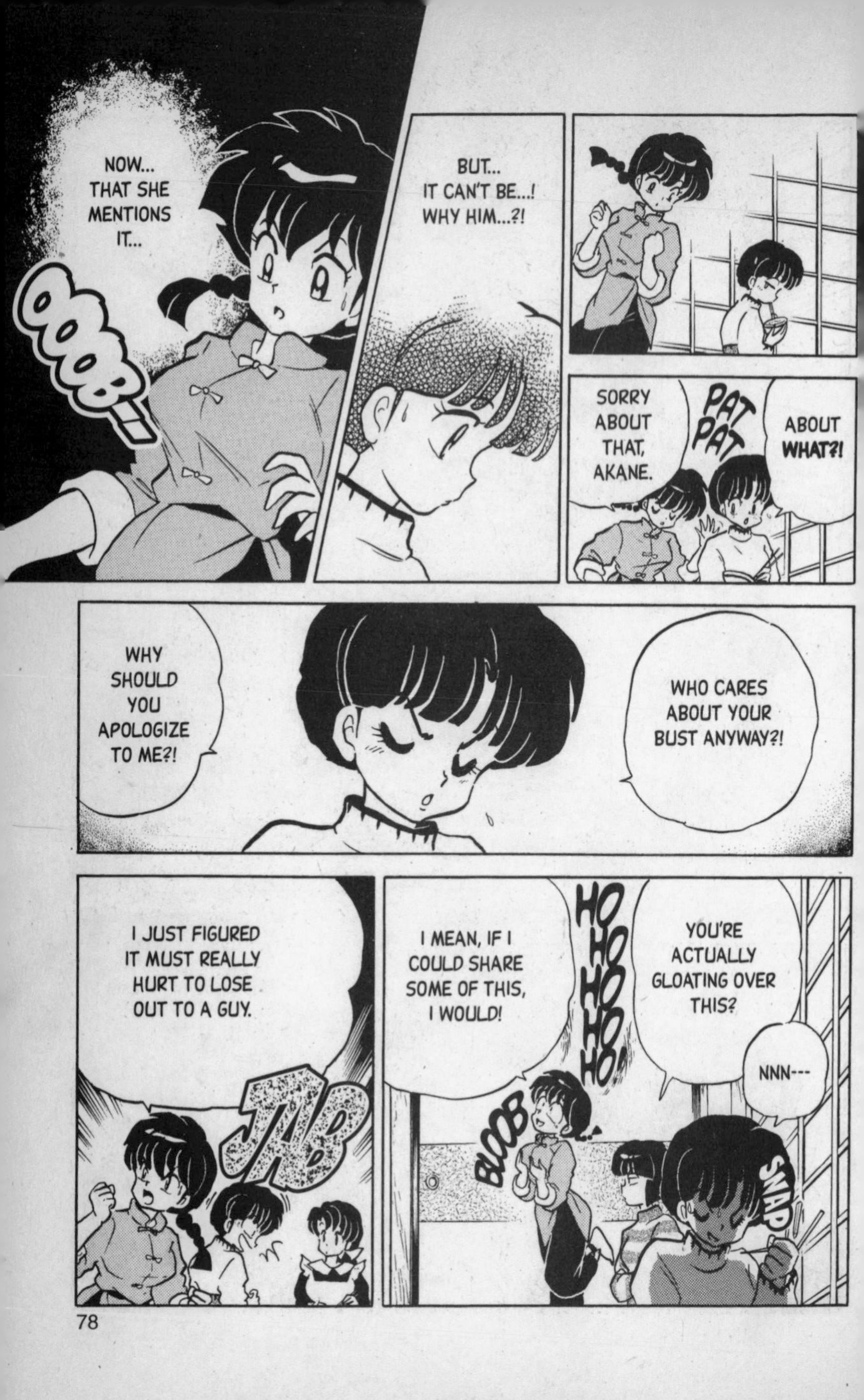
NOW... THAT SHE MENTIONS IT...
OOOB
BUT... IT CAN'T BE...! WHY HIM...?!
SORRY ABOUT THAT, AKANE.
PAT PAT
ABOUT WHAT?!
WHY SHOULD YOU APOLOGIZE TO ME?!
WHO CARES ABOUT YOUR BUST ANYWAY?!
I JUST FIGURED IT MUST REALLY HURT TO LOSE OUT TO A GUY.
JAB
I MEAN, IF I COULD SHARE SOME OF THIS, I WOULD!
HO HO HO HO HO HO
BLOOB
YOU'RE ACTUALLY GLOATING OVER THIS?
NNN---
SNAP

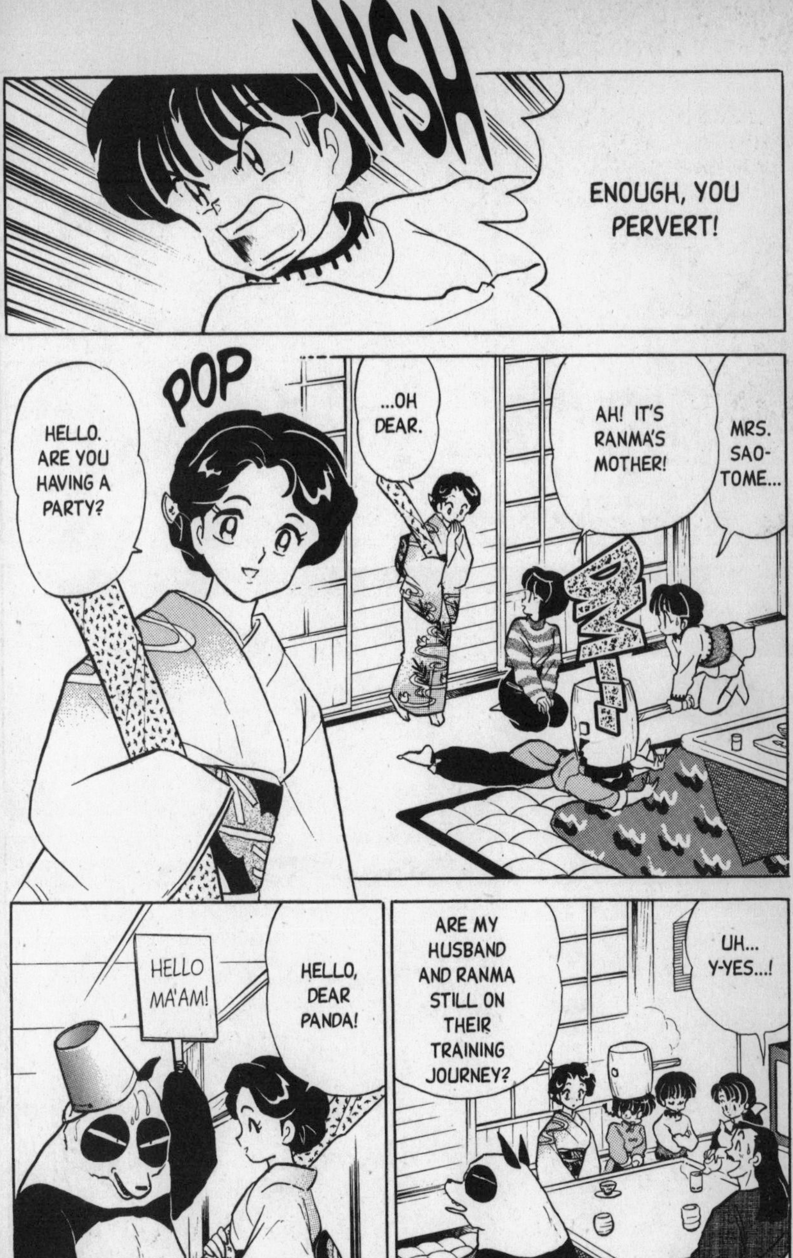
WSH
ENOUGH, YOU PERVERT!
POP
HELLO. ARE YOU HAVING A PARTY?
...OH DEAR.
AH! IT'S RANMA'S MOTHER!
MRS. SAO-TOME...
HELLO MA'AM!
HELLO, DEAR PANDA!
ARE MY HUSBAND AND RANMA STILL ON THEIR TRAINING JOURNEY?
UH... Y-YES...!

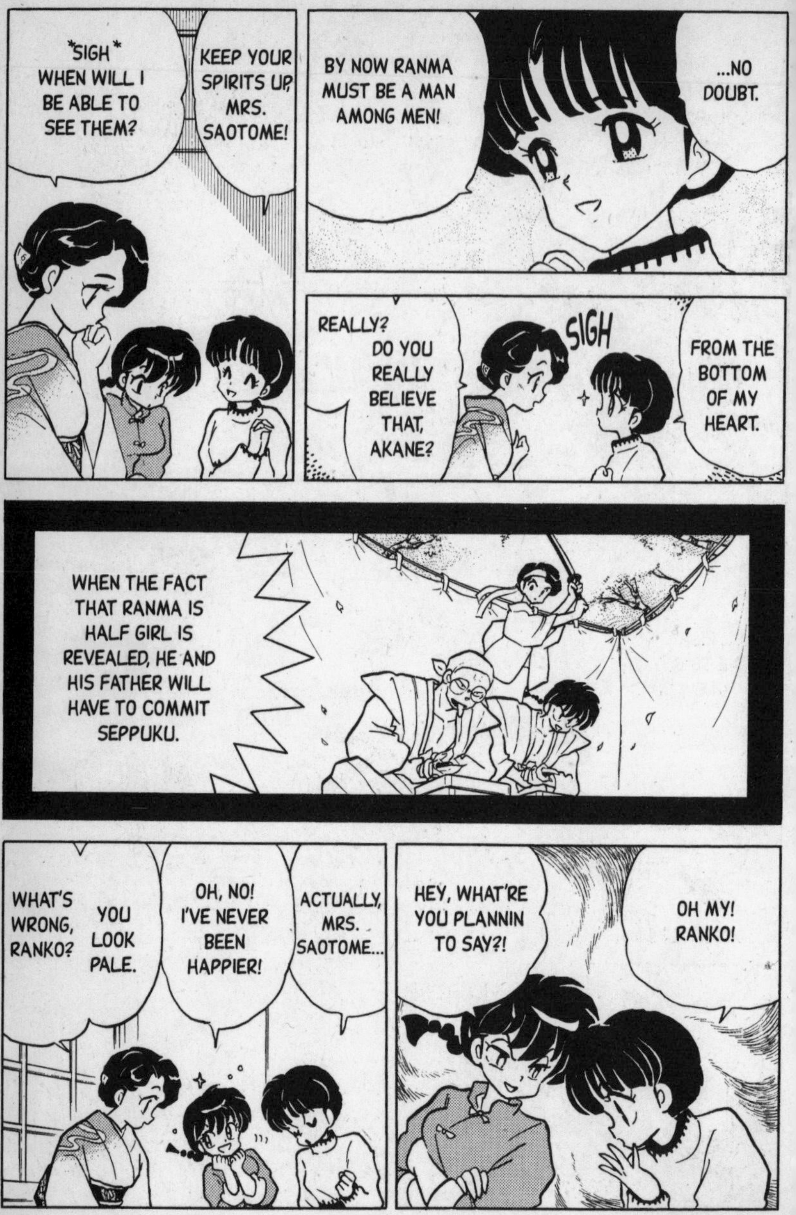
SIGH WHEN WILL I BE ABLE TO SEE THEM?
KEEP YOUR SPIRITS UP, MRS. SAOTOME!
BY NOW RANMA MUST BE A MAN AMONG MEN!
...NO DOUBT.
REALLY? DO YOU REALLY BELIEVE THAT, AKANE?
SIGH
FROM THE BOTTOM OF MY HEART.
WHEN THE FACT THAT RANMA IS HALF GIRL IS REVEALED, HE AND HIS FATHER WILL HAVE TO COMMIT SEPPUKU.
WHAT'S WRONG, RANKO?
YOU LOOK PALE.
OH, NO! I'VE NEVER BEEN HAPPIER!
ACTUALLY, MRS. SAOTOME...
HEY, WHAT'RE YOU PLANNIN TO SAY?!
OH MY! RANKO!

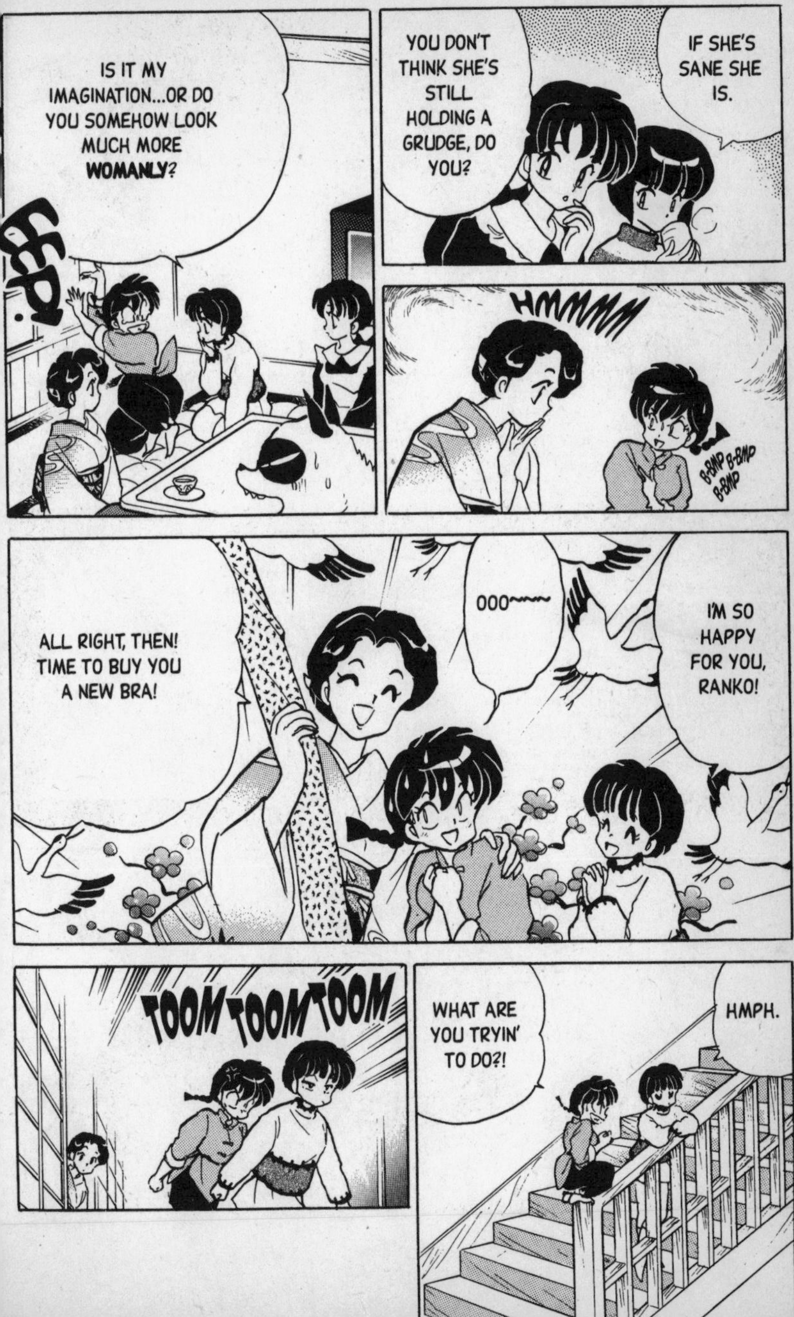
IS IT MY IMAGINATION...OR DO YOU SOMEHOW LOOK MUCH MORE **WOMANLY**?
EEP!
YOU DON'T THINK SHE'S STILL HOLDING A GRUDGE, DO YOU?
IF SHE'S SANE SHE IS.
HMMMM
B-BMP B-BMP B-BMP
ALL RIGHT, THEN! TIME TO BUY YOU A NEW BRA!
OOO~~~
I'M SO HAPPY FOR YOU, RANKO!
TOOM TOOM TOOM
WHAT ARE YOU TRYIN' TO DO?!
HMPH.

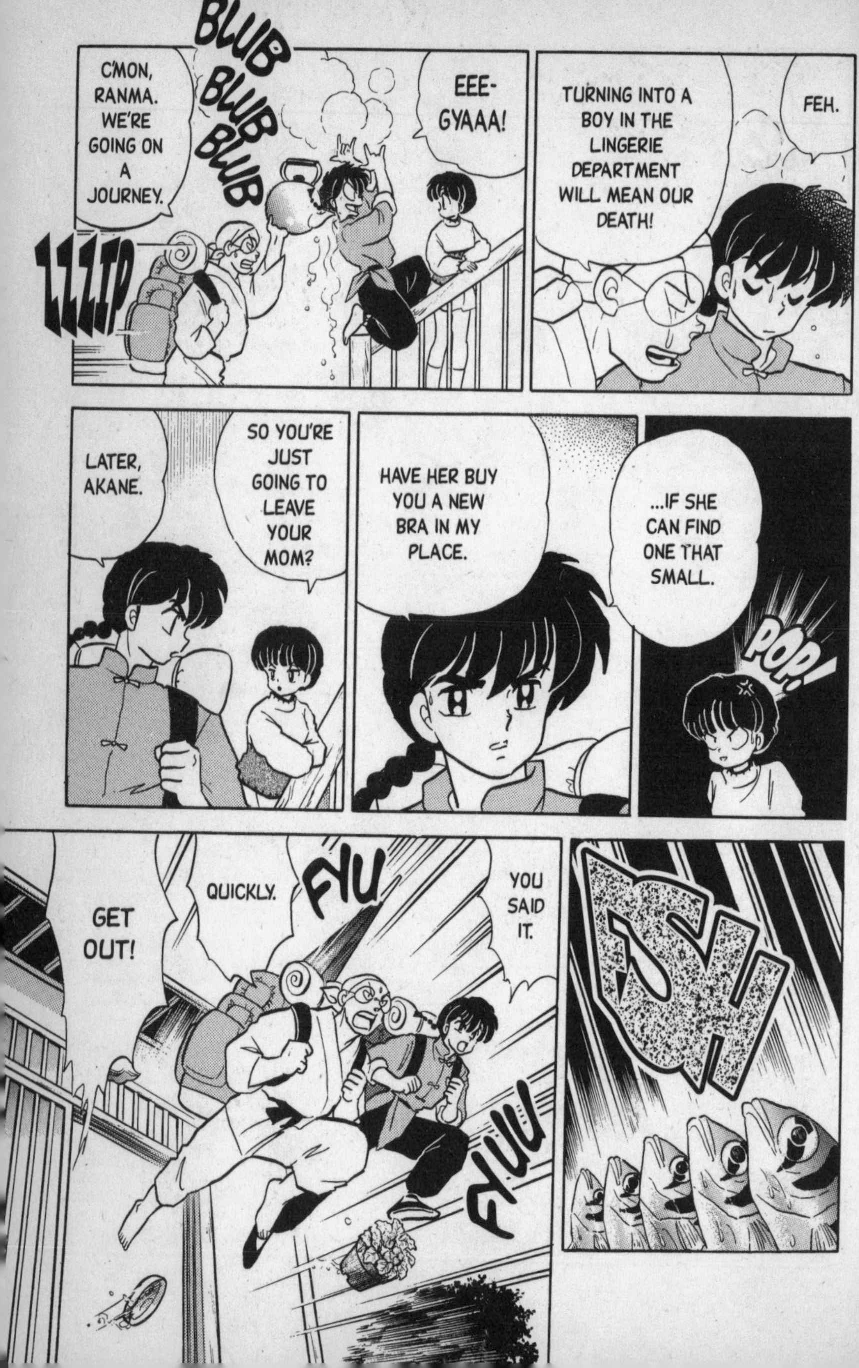
BLUB BLUB BLUB
C'MON, RANMA. WE'RE GOING ON A JOURNEY.
ZZZIP
EEE-GYAAA!
TURNING INTO A BOY IN THE LINGERIE DEPARTMENT WILL MEAN OUR DEATH!
FEH.
LATER, AKANE.
SO YOU'RE JUST GOING TO LEAVE YOUR MOM?
HAVE HER BUY YOU A NEW BRA IN MY PLACE.
...IF SHE CAN FIND ONE THAT SMALL.
POP!
GET OUT!
QUICKLY.
FYU
YOU SAID IT.
FYUU
FSH

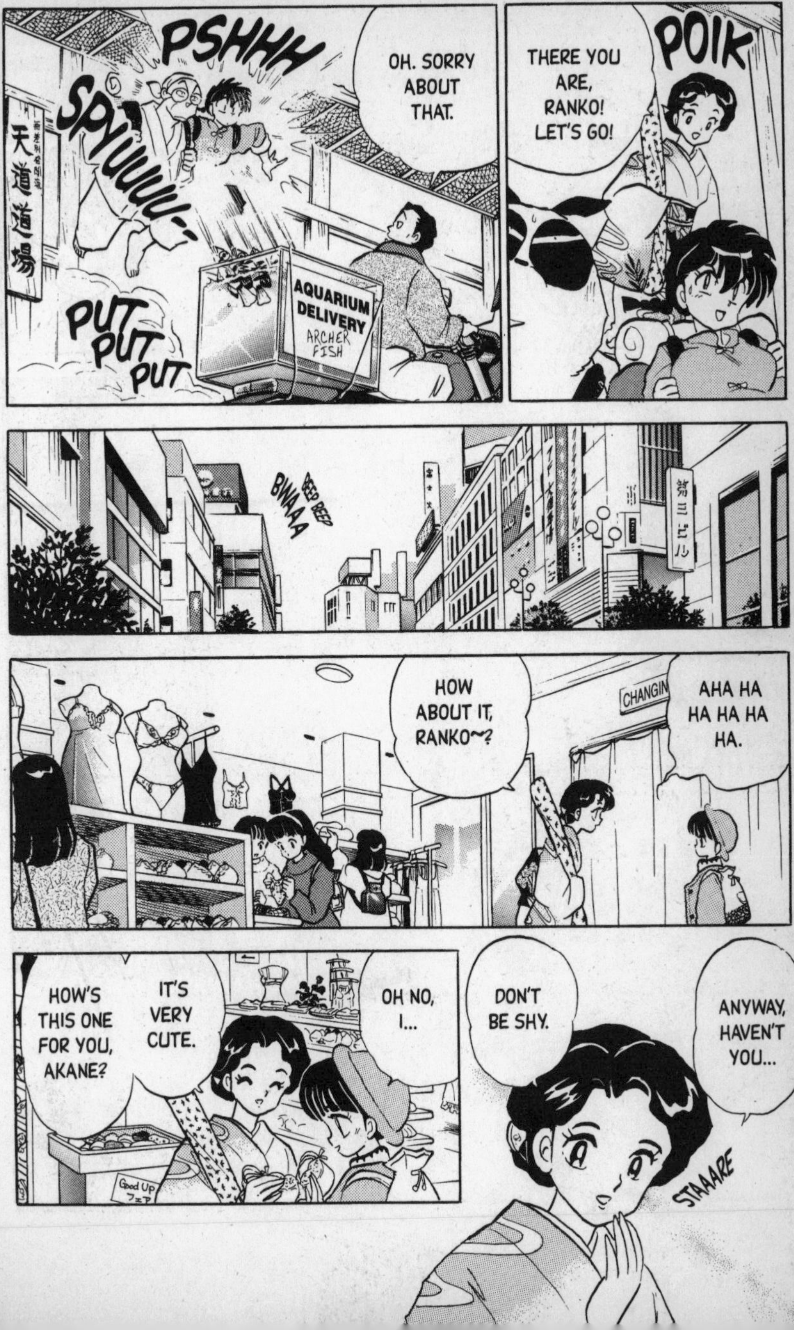
PSHHH
SPYUUUUU
天道道場
PUT PUT PUT
AQUARIUM DELIVERY
ARCHER FISH
OH. SORRY ABOUT THAT.
POIK
THERE YOU ARE, RANKO! LET'S GO!
BWAAA
BEEP BEEP
HOW ABOUT IT, RANKO~?
CHANGIN
AHA HA HA HA HA HA.
HOW'S THIS ONE FOR YOU, AKANE?
IT'S VERY CUTE.
OH NO, I...
Good UP フェア
DON'T BE SHY.
ANYWAY, HAVEN'T YOU...
STAARE

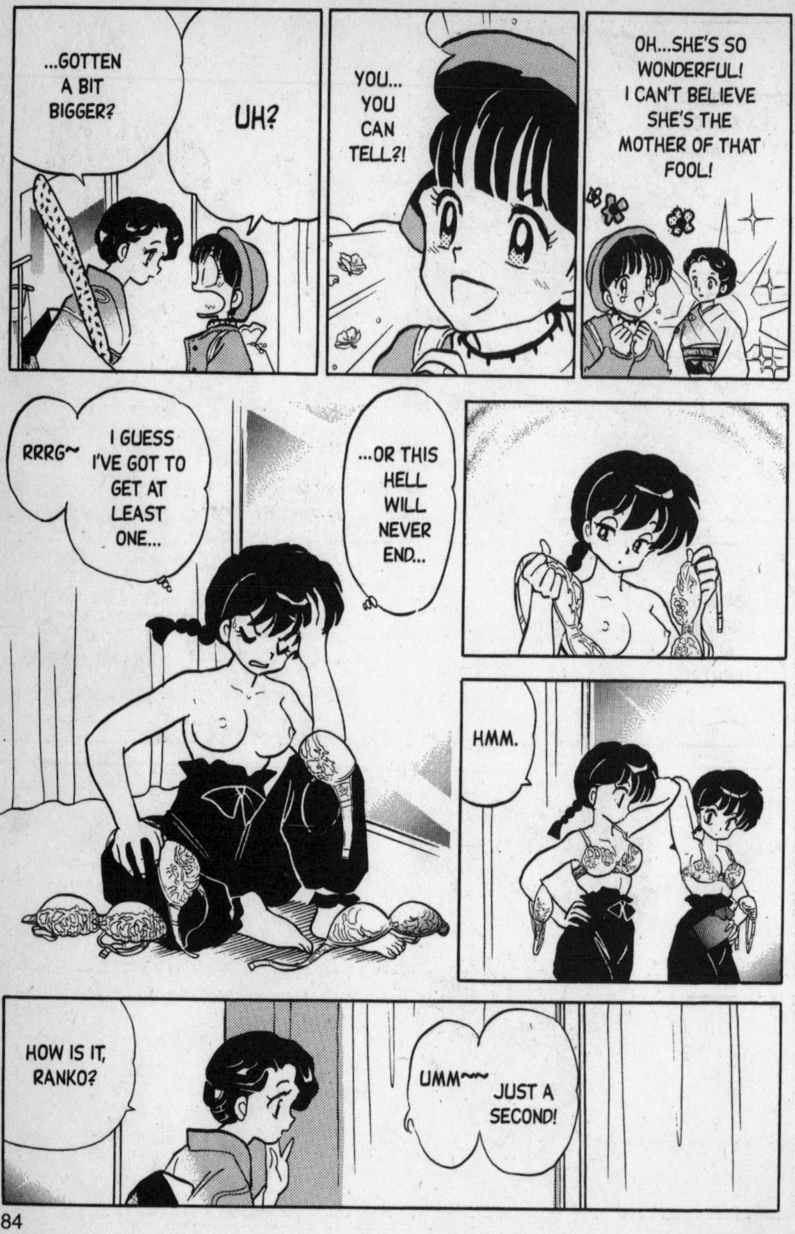
...GOTTEN A BIT BIGGER?
UH?
YOU... YOU CAN TELL?!
OH...SHE'S SO WONDERFUL! I CAN'T BELIEVE SHE'S THE MOTHER OF THAT FOOL!
RRRG~
I GUESS I'VE GOT TO GET AT LEAST ONE...
...OR THIS HELL WILL NEVER END...
HMM.
HOW IS IT, RANKO?
UMM~~
JUST A SECOND!

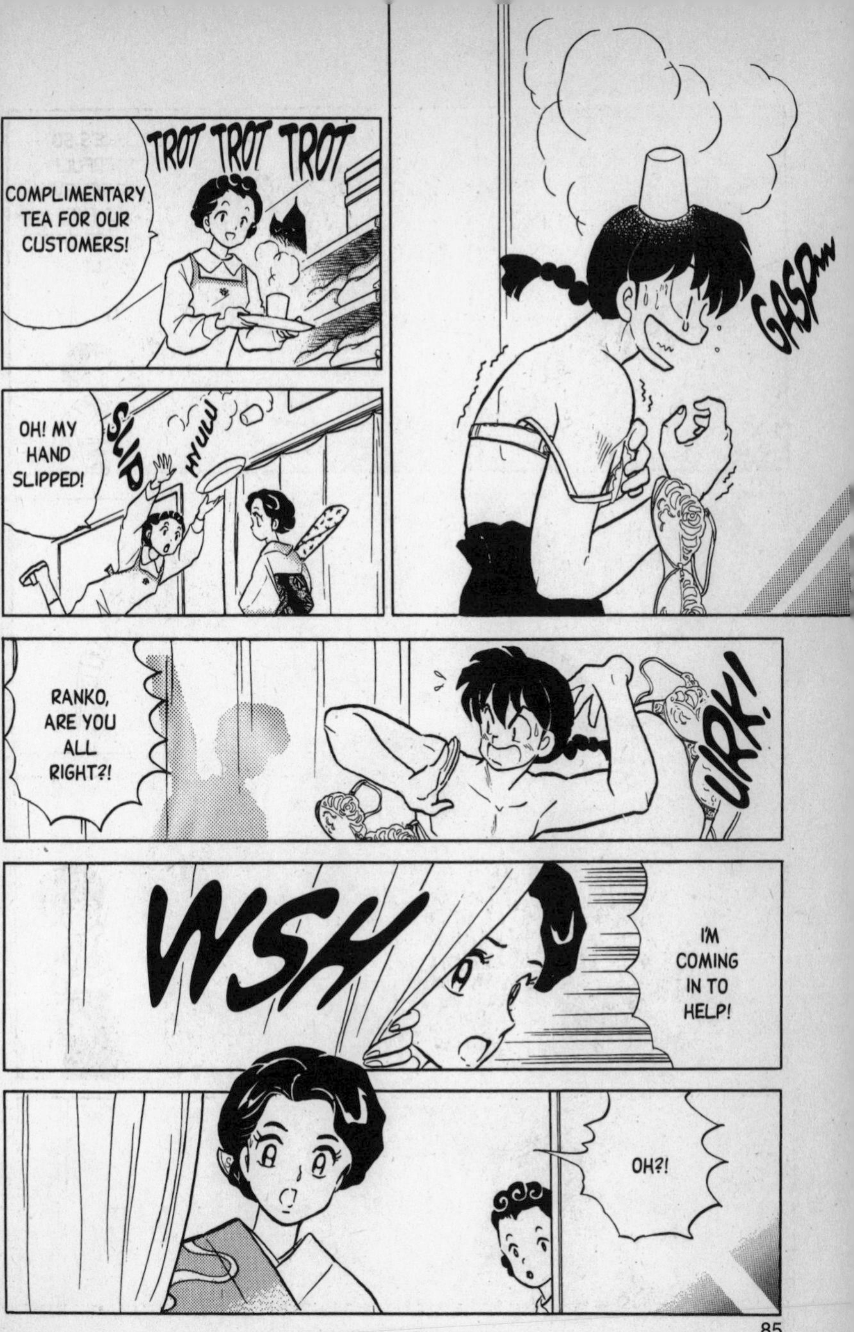
TROT TROT TROT
COMPLIMENTARY TEA FOR OUR CUSTOMERS!
SLIP
HYULU
OH! MY HAND SLIPPED!
GASP
RANKO, ARE YOU ALL RIGHT?!
URK!
WSH
I'M COMING IN TO HELP!
OH?!

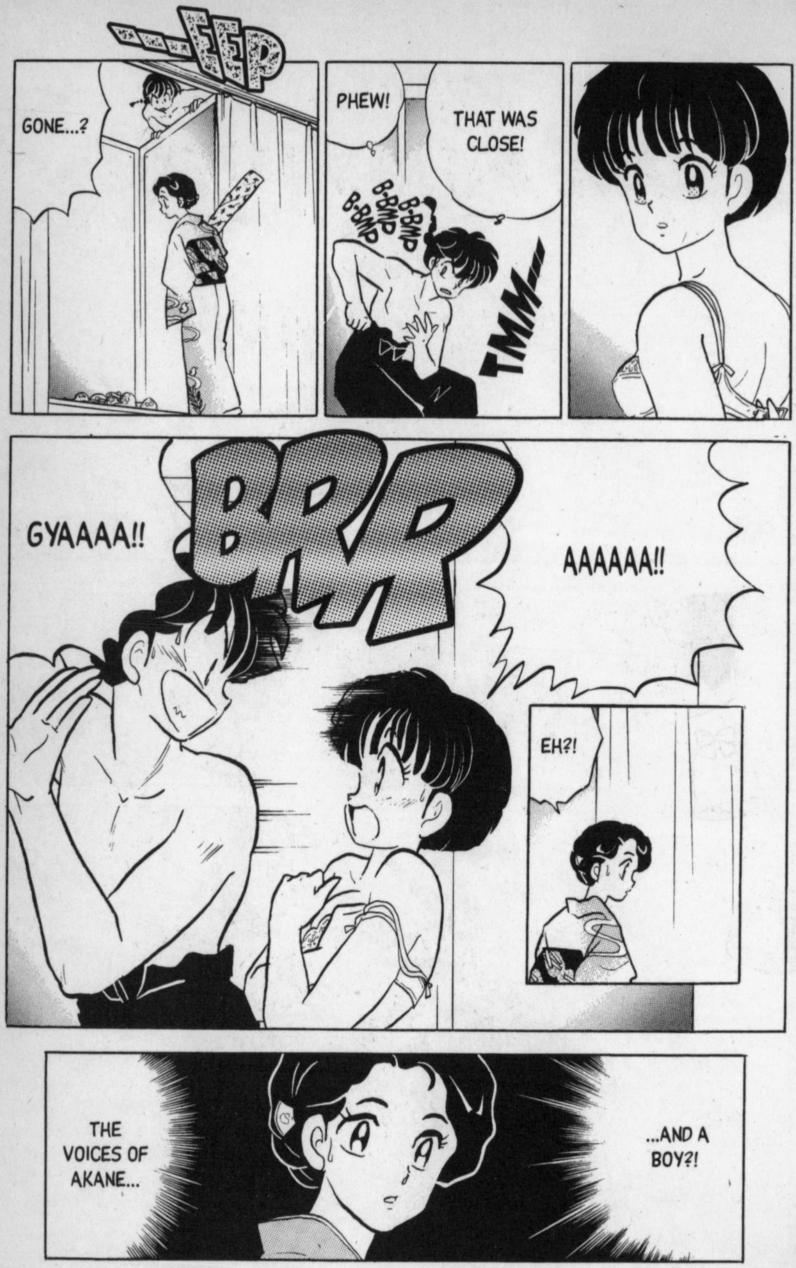
--EEP
GONE...?
PHEW!
THAT WAS CLOSE!
B-BMP B-BMP B-BMP
TMM...
GYAAAA!!
BRR
AAAAAA!!
EH?!
THE VOICES OF AKANE...
...AND A BOY?!

PART 6

THE PUNISHMENT OF PERV-BOY!

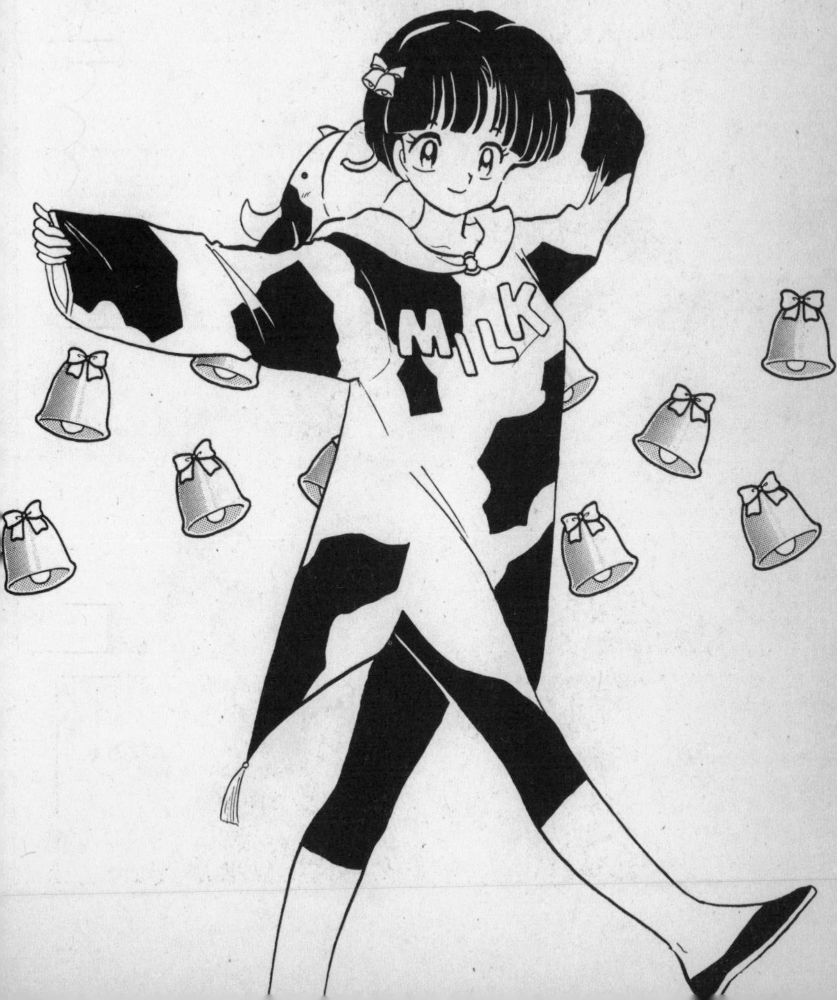
MILK

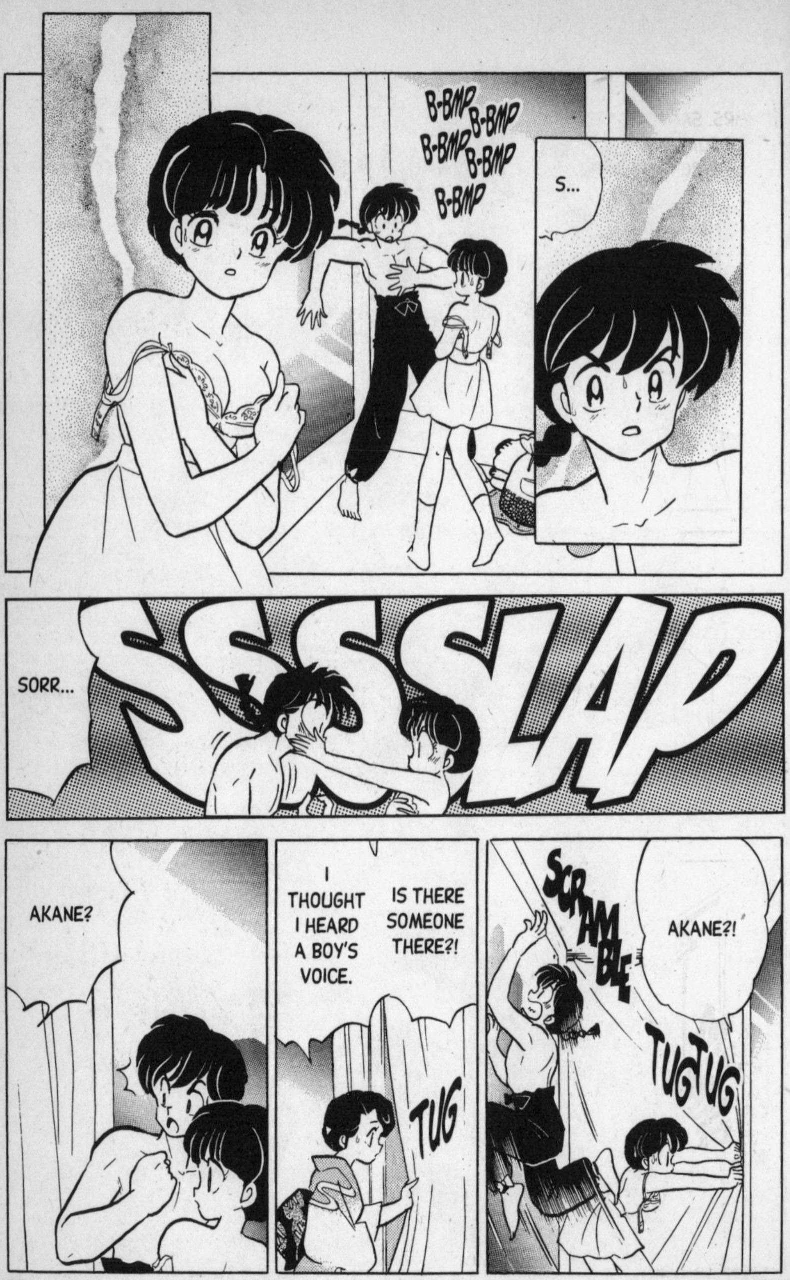
B-BMP B-BMP
B-BMP B-BMP
B-BMP
S...
SORR...
SSSLAP
AKANE?
I THOUGHT I HEARD A BOY'S VOICE.
IS THERE SOMEONE THERE?!
TUG
SCRAMBLE
AKANE?!
TUG TUG

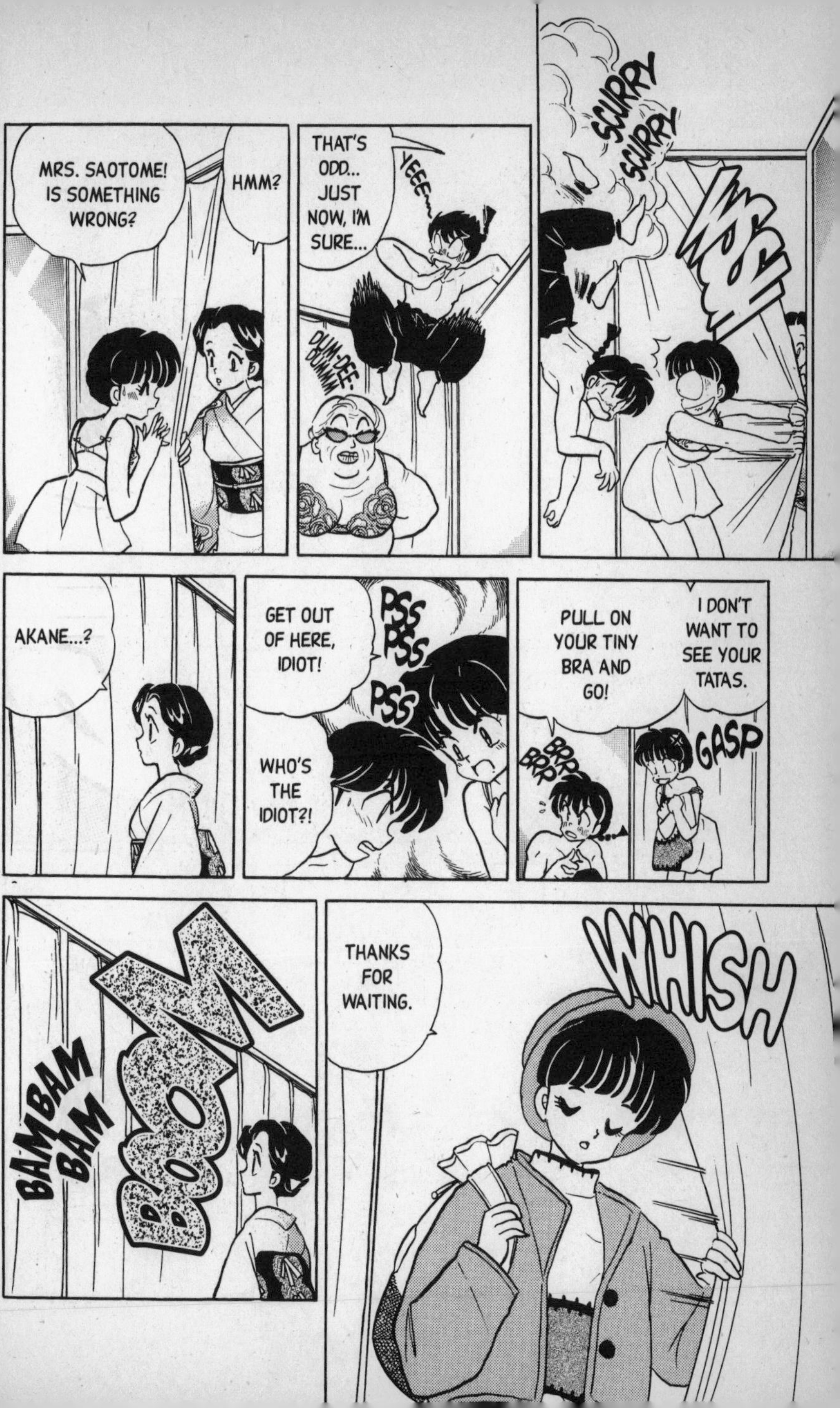
MRS. SAOTOME! IS SOMETHING WRONG?
HMM?
THAT'S ODD... JUST NOW, I'M SURE...
YEEE...
DUM-DEE-DUMMM
SCURRY SCURRY
WOSH
AKANE...?
GET OUT OF HERE, IDIOT!
PSS PSS PSS
WHO'S THE IDIOT?!
PULL ON YOUR TINY BRA AND GO!
I DON'T WANT TO SEE YOUR TATAS.
BRR BRR
GASP
BAMBAM BAM
BOOM
THANKS FOR WAITING.
WHISH

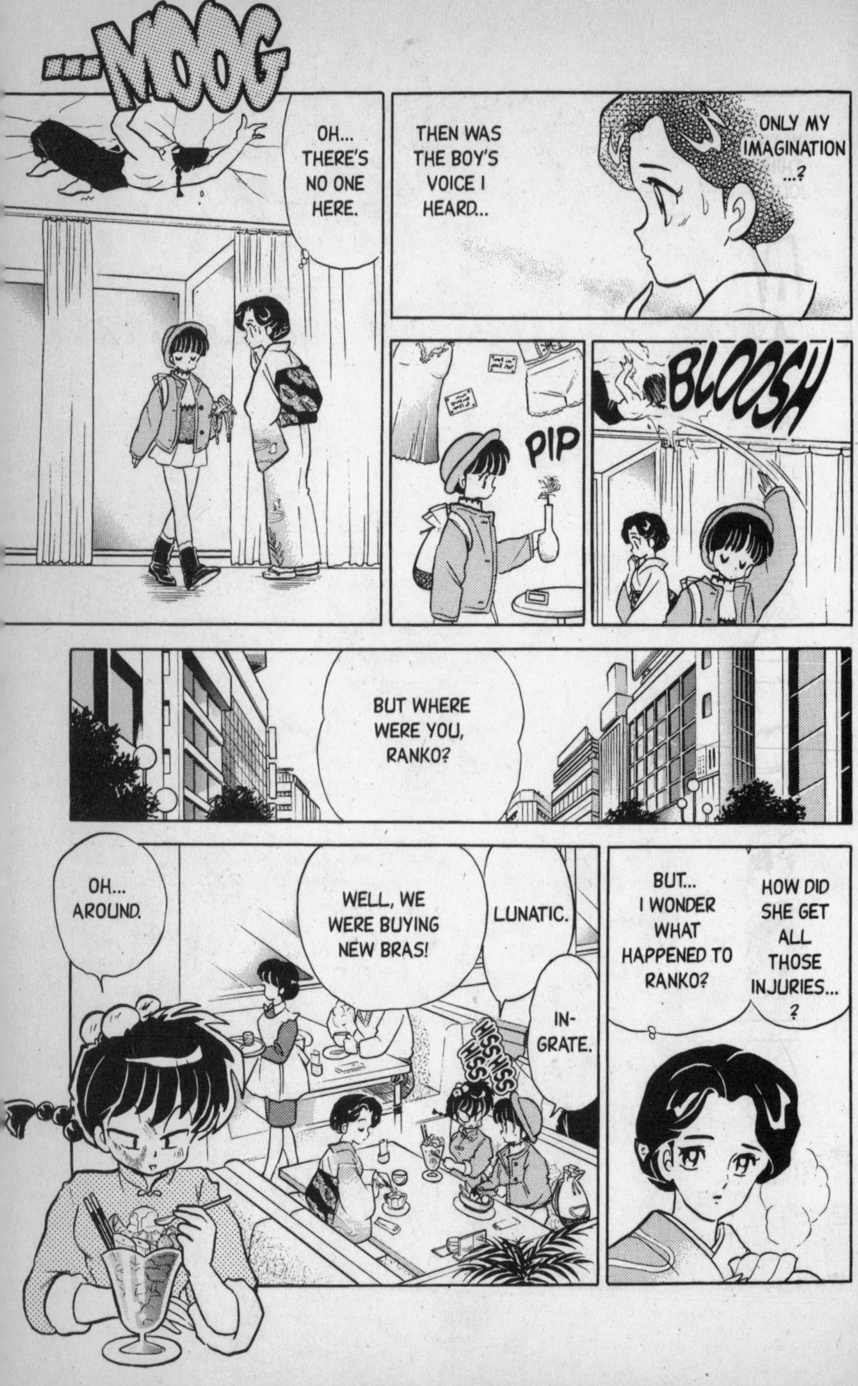
...MOOG
OH... THERE'S NO ONE HERE.
THEN WAS THE BOY'S VOICE I HEARD...
ONLY MY IMAGINATION ...?
PIP
BLOOSH
BUT WHERE WERE YOU, RANKO?
OH... AROUND.
WELL, WE WERE BUYING NEW BRAS!
LUNATIC.
IN-GRATE.
HISS HISS
BUT... I WONDER WHAT HAPPENED TO RANKO?
HOW DID SHE GET ALL THOSE INJURIES... ?

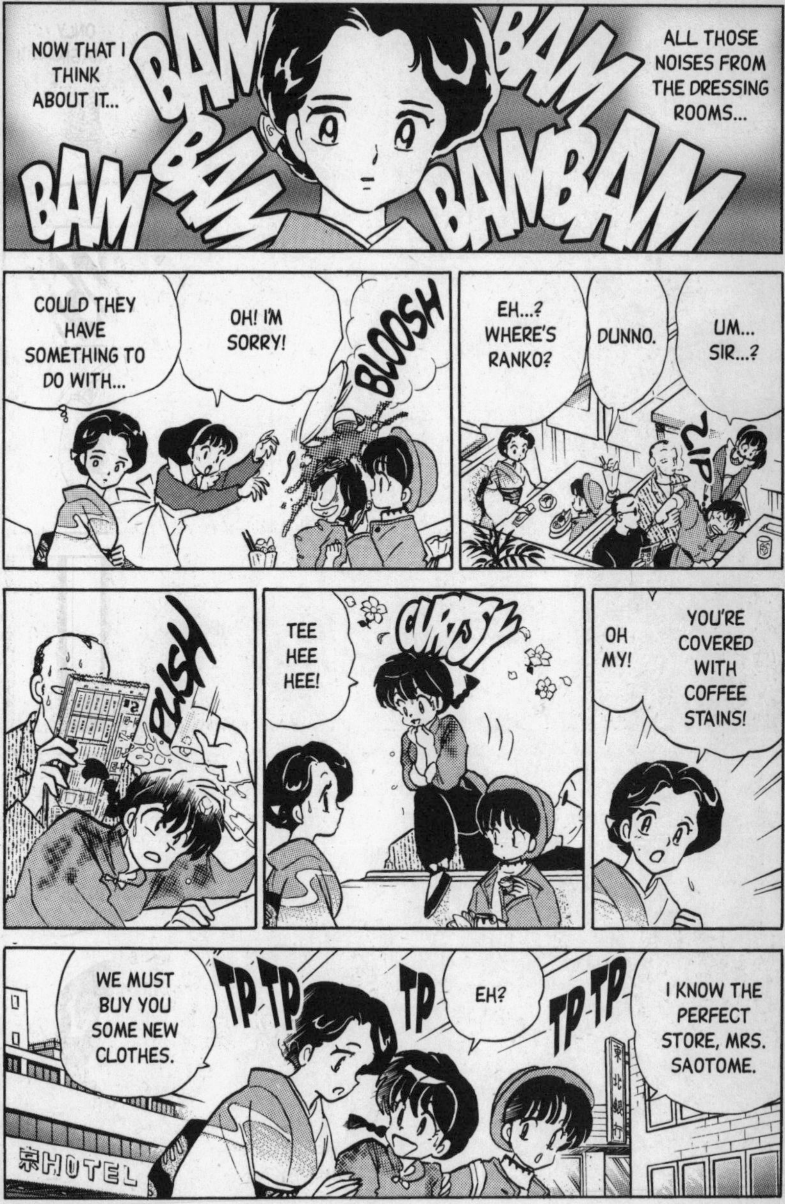
NOW THAT I THINK ABOUT IT...
BAM
BAM
BAM
BAM
BAMBAM
ALL THOSE NOISES FROM THE DRESSING ROOMS...
COULD THEY HAVE SOMETHING TO DO WITH...
OH! I'M SORRY!
BLOOSH
EH...? WHERE'S RANKO?
DUNNO.
UM... SIR...?
ZIP
PUSH
TEE HEE HEE!
CURTSY
OH MY!
YOU'RE COVERED WITH COFFEE STAINS!
WE MUST BUY YOU SOME NEW CLOTHES.
TP TP
TP
EH?
TP-TP
I KNOW THE PERFECT STORE, MRS. SAOTOME.

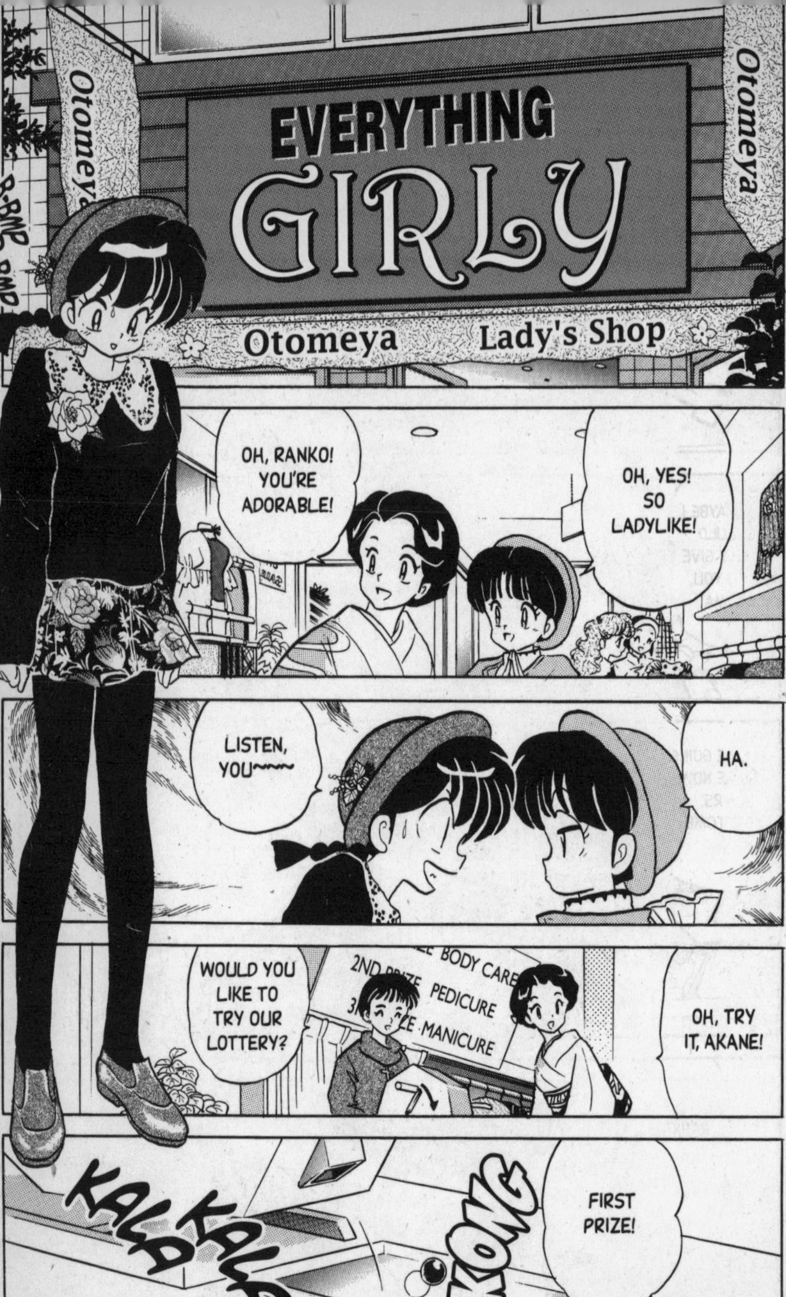
Otomeya
Otomeya
EVERYTHING
GIRLY
Otomeya Lady's Shop
B-BMP B-BMP B-BMP
OH, RANKO! YOU'RE ADORABLE!
OH, YES! SO LADYLIKE!
LISTEN, YOU~~~
HA.
WOULD YOU LIKE TO TRY OUR LOTTERY?
BODY CARE
2ND PRIZE PEDICURE
MANICURE
OH, TRY IT, AKANE!
KALA KALA
KONG
FIRST PRIZE!

CONGRATULATIONS!

YOU'VE WON A "BODY CARE" GIFT CARD!

BO... 1ST PRI... ...ND PRIZE ...URE 3RD P... ...URE

WHY, AKANE! LOOK AT YOU!

HEH-HEH... I GUESS I AM PRETTY LUCKY...

69.2 KG → 48.2 KG
THIS COULD BE YOU!

BUT MAYBE I SHOULD REALLY GIVE IT TO YOU, RANMA.

OH, NO, AKANE. KEEP IT FOR YOURSELF.

SEE? THEY HAVE A "BOSOM CARE" COURSE!

MAYBE YOU CAN MAKE YOUR TATAS BIGGER.

I'LL BE GOING HOME NOW, MRS. SAOTOME.

HM...?

WOOSH

G'BYE.

AKANE?

Lady's S...

RANKO... DID YOU HAVE A FIGHT WITH AKANE?

HUH...?

OH, NO, NO~~~

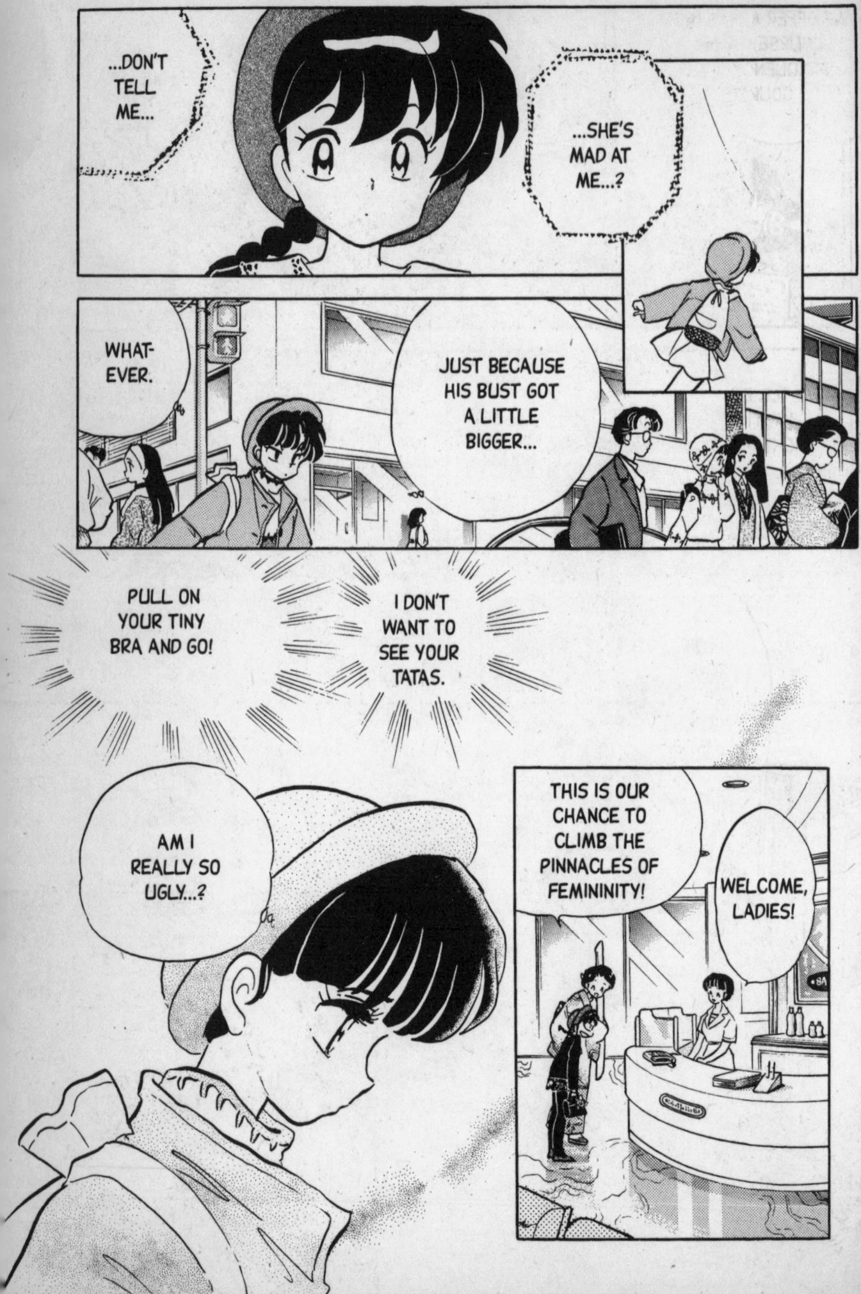

...DON'T TELL ME...
...SHE'S MAD AT ME...?
WHATEVER.
JUST BECAUSE HIS BUST GOT A LITTLE BIGGER...
PULL ON YOUR TINY BRA AND GO!
I DON'T WANT TO SEE YOUR TATAS.
AM I REALLY SO UGLY...?
THIS IS OUR CHANCE TO CLIMB THE PINNACLES OF FEMININITY!
WELCOME, LADIES!

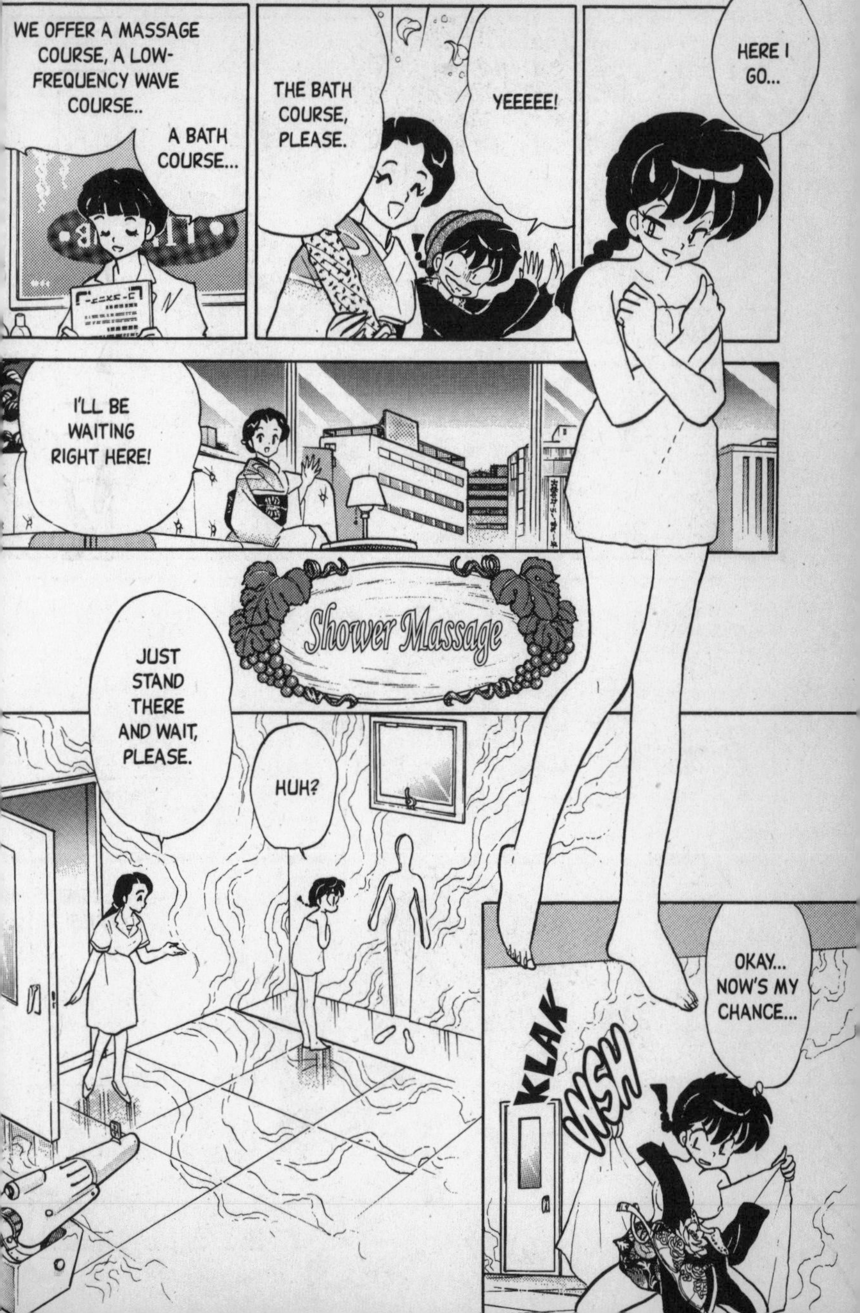
WE OFFER A MASSAGE COURSE, A LOW-FREQUENCY WAVE COURSE..
A BATH COURSE...
THE BATH COURSE, PLEASE.
YEEEEE!
HERE I GO...
I'LL BE WAITING RIGHT HERE!
Shower Massage
JUST STAND THERE AND WAIT, PLEASE.
HUH?
OKAY... NOW'S MY CHANCE...
KLAK
WSH

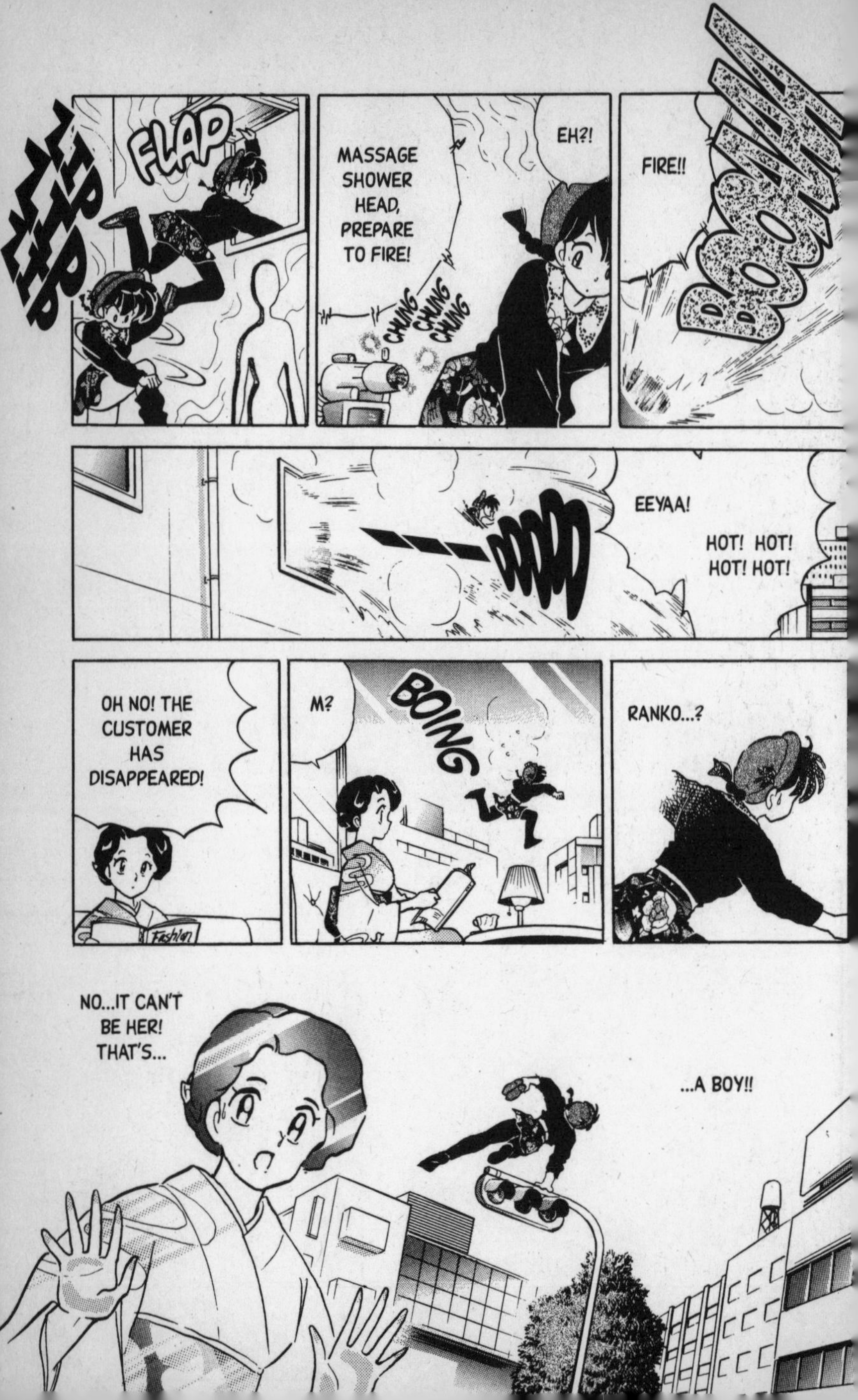

RIP RIP
FLAP
MASSAGE SHOWER HEAD, PREPARE TO FIRE!
CHUNG CHUNG CHUNG
EH?!
FIRE!!
EEYAA!
HOT! HOT! HOT! HOT!
OH NO! THE CUSTOMER HAS DISAPPEARED!
Fashion
M?
BOING
RANKO...?
NO...IT CAN'T BE HER! THAT'S...
...A BOY!!

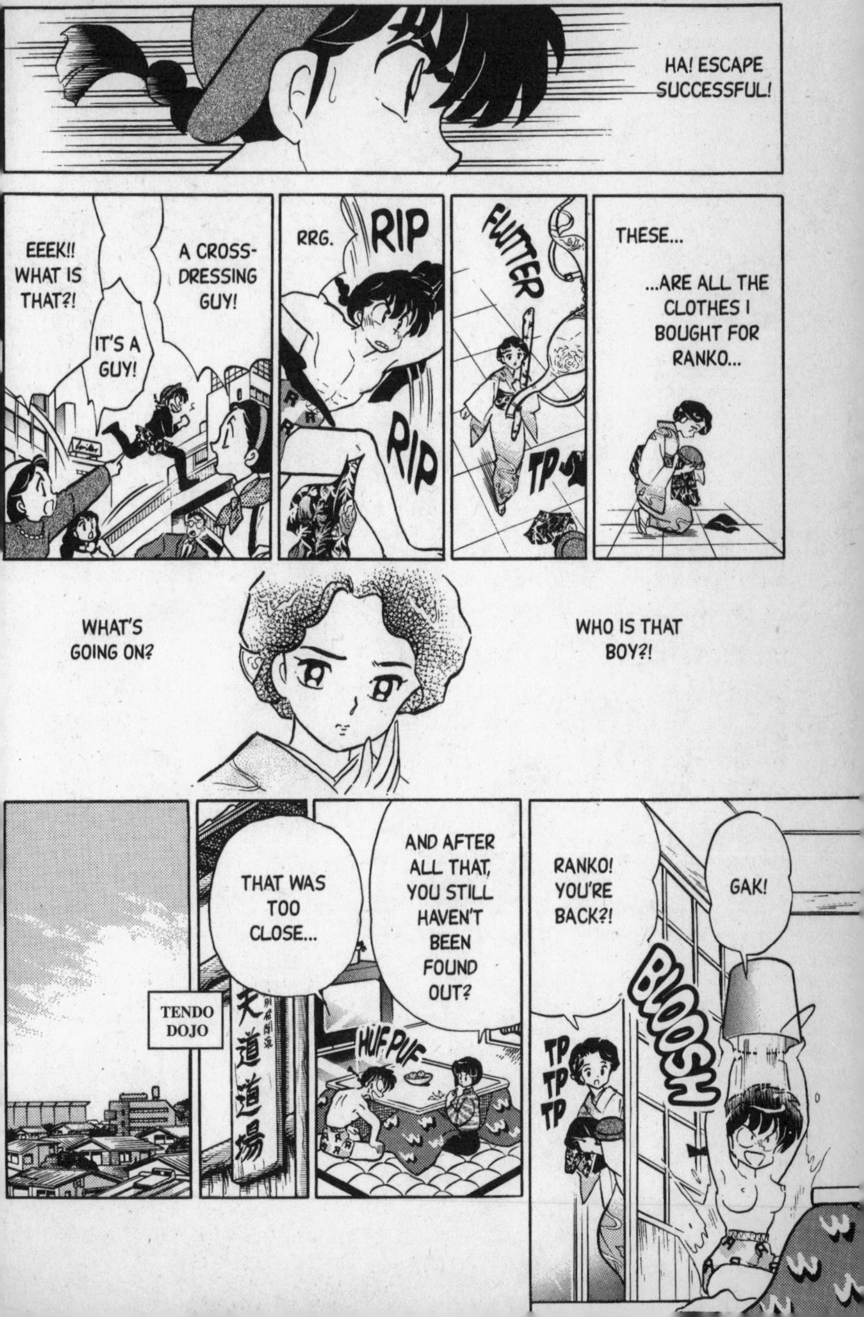
HA! ESCAPE SUCCESSFUL!
EEEK!! WHAT IS THAT?!
IT'S A GUY!
A CROSS-DRESSING GUY!
RRG.
RIP
RIP
FLUTTER
TP
THESE...
...ARE ALL THE CLOTHES I BOUGHT FOR RANKO...
WHAT'S GOING ON?
WHO IS THAT BOY?!
TENDO DOJO
天道道場
THAT WAS TOO CLOSE...
AND AFTER ALL THAT, YOU STILL HAVEN'T BEEN FOUND OUT?
HUF PUF
RANKO! YOU'RE BACK?!
TP TP TP
GAK!
BLOOSH

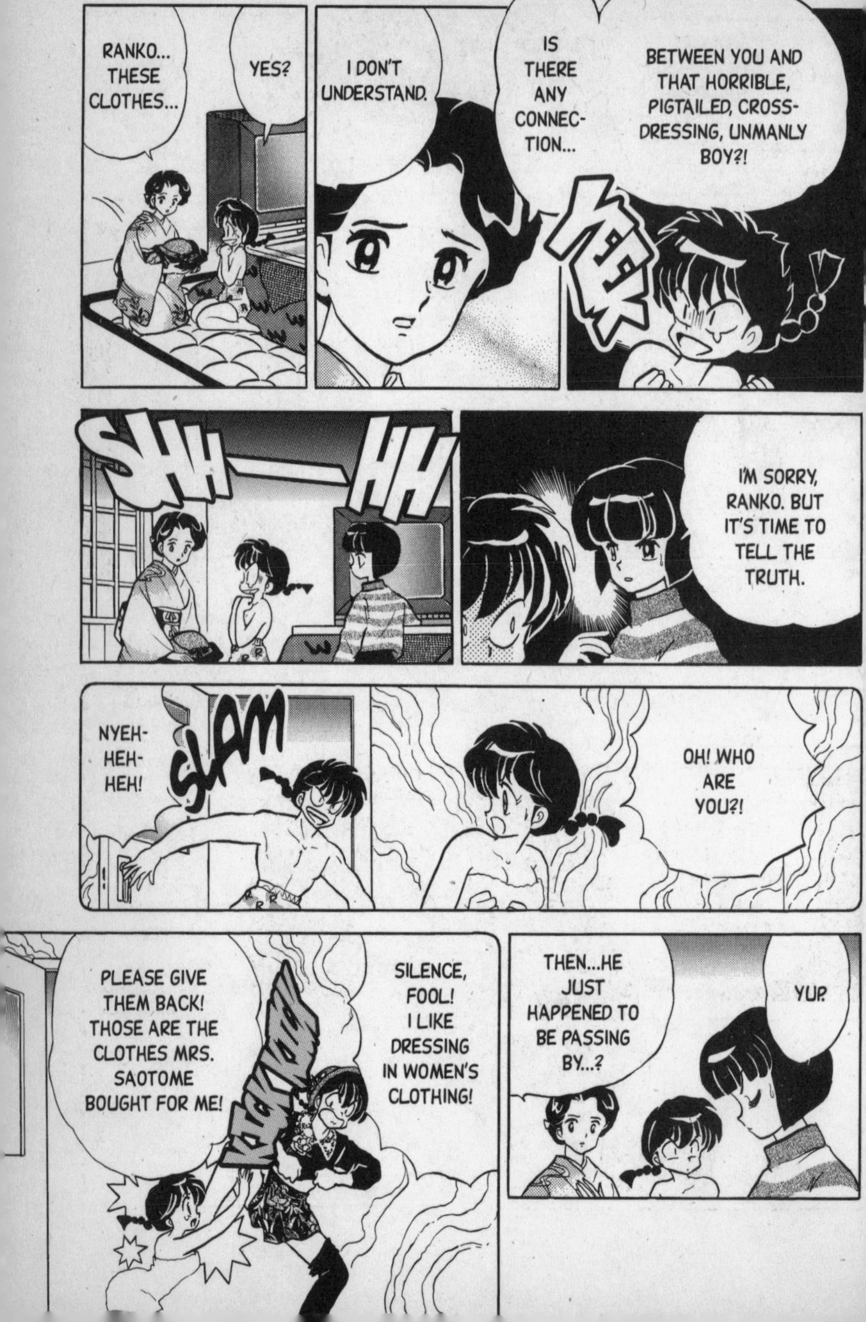

RANKO... THESE CLOTHES...
YES?
I DON'T UNDERSTAND.
IS THERE ANY CONNECTION...
BETWEEN YOU AND THAT HORRIBLE, PIGTAILED, CROSS-DRESSING, UNMANLY BOY?!
YIPE
SHH
HH
I'M SORRY, RANKO. BUT IT'S TIME TO TELL THE TRUTH.
NYEH-HEH-HEH!
SLAM
OH! WHO ARE YOU?!
PLEASE GIVE THEM BACK! THOSE ARE THE CLOTHES MRS. SAOTOME BOUGHT FOR ME!
SILENCE, FOOL! I LIKE DRESSING IN WOMEN'S CLOTHING!
THEN...HE JUST HAPPENED TO BE PASSING BY...?
YUP.

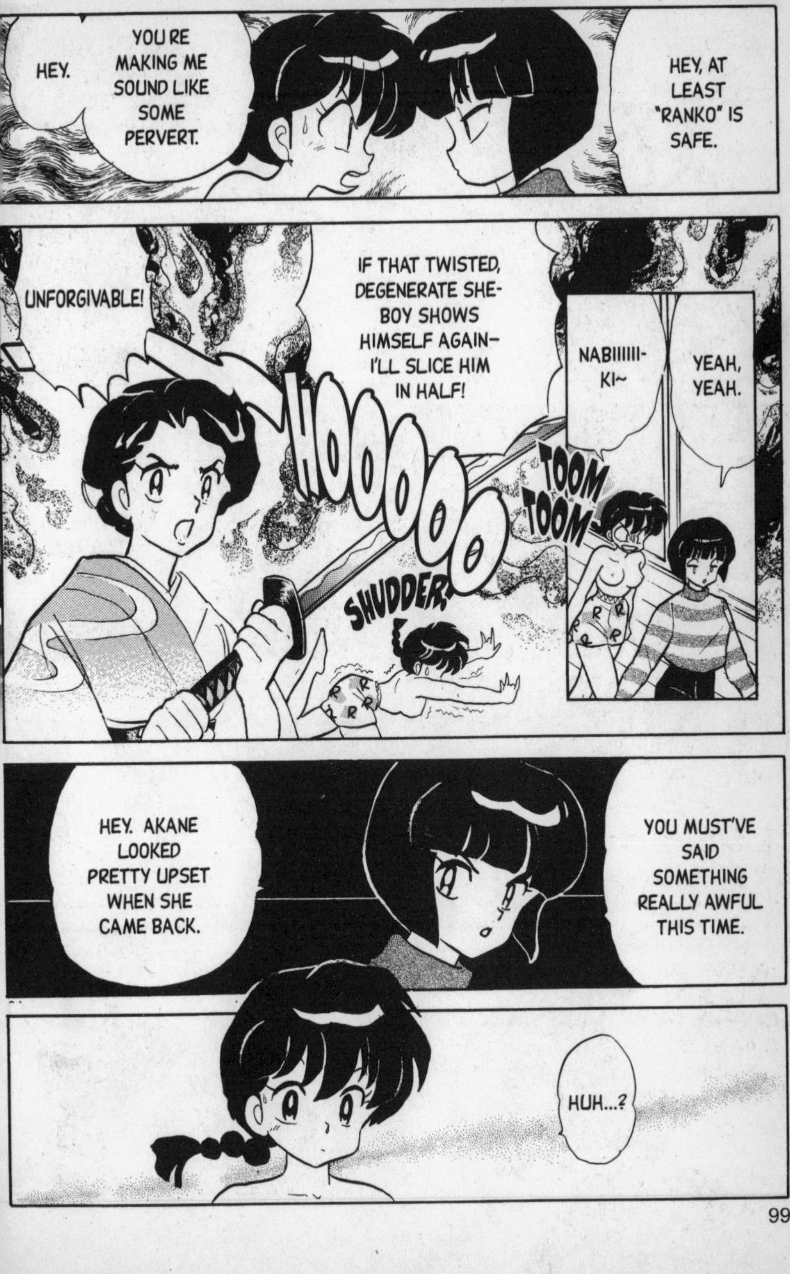
HEY.
YOU RE MAKING ME SOUND LIKE SOME PERVERT.
HEY, AT LEAST "RANKO" IS SAFE.
UNFORGIVABLE!
IF THAT TWISTED, DEGENERATE SHE-BOY SHOWS HIMSELF AGAIN—I'LL SLICE HIM IN HALF!
HOOOOOO
SHUDDER
NABIIIIII-KI~
YEAH, YEAH.
TOOM TOOM
HEY. AKANE LOOKED PRETTY UPSET WHEN SHE CAME BACK.
YOU MUST'VE SAID SOMETHING REALLY AWFUL THIS TIME.
HUH...?

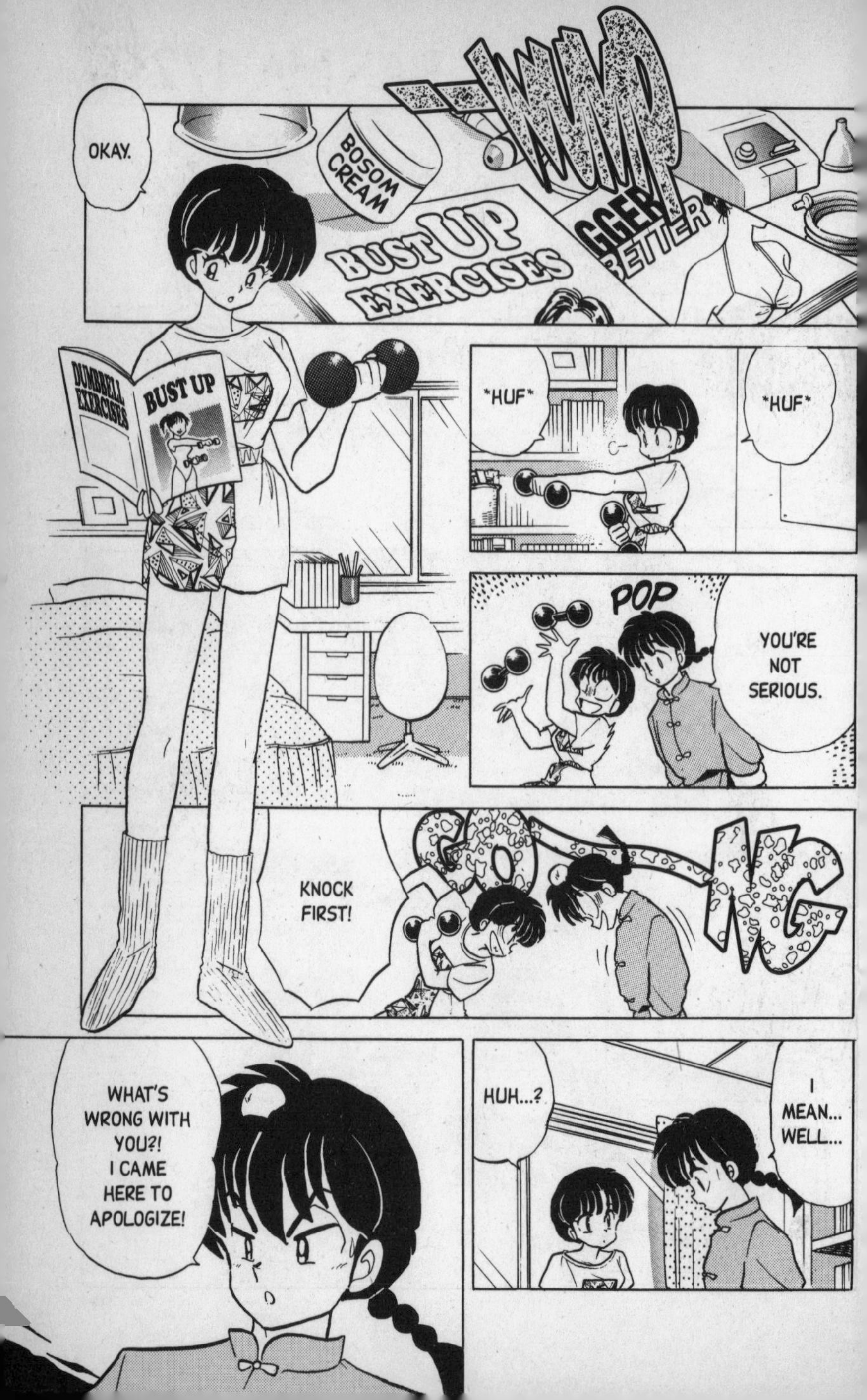
OKAY.
BOSOM CREAM
BUST UP EXERCISES
WUMP
GGER BETTER
DUMBBELL EXERCISES
BUST UP
HUF
HUF
POP
YOU'RE NOT SERIOUS.
KNOCK FIRST!
GONG
WHAT'S WRONG WITH YOU?! I CAME HERE TO APOLOGIZE!
HUH...?
I MEAN... WELL...

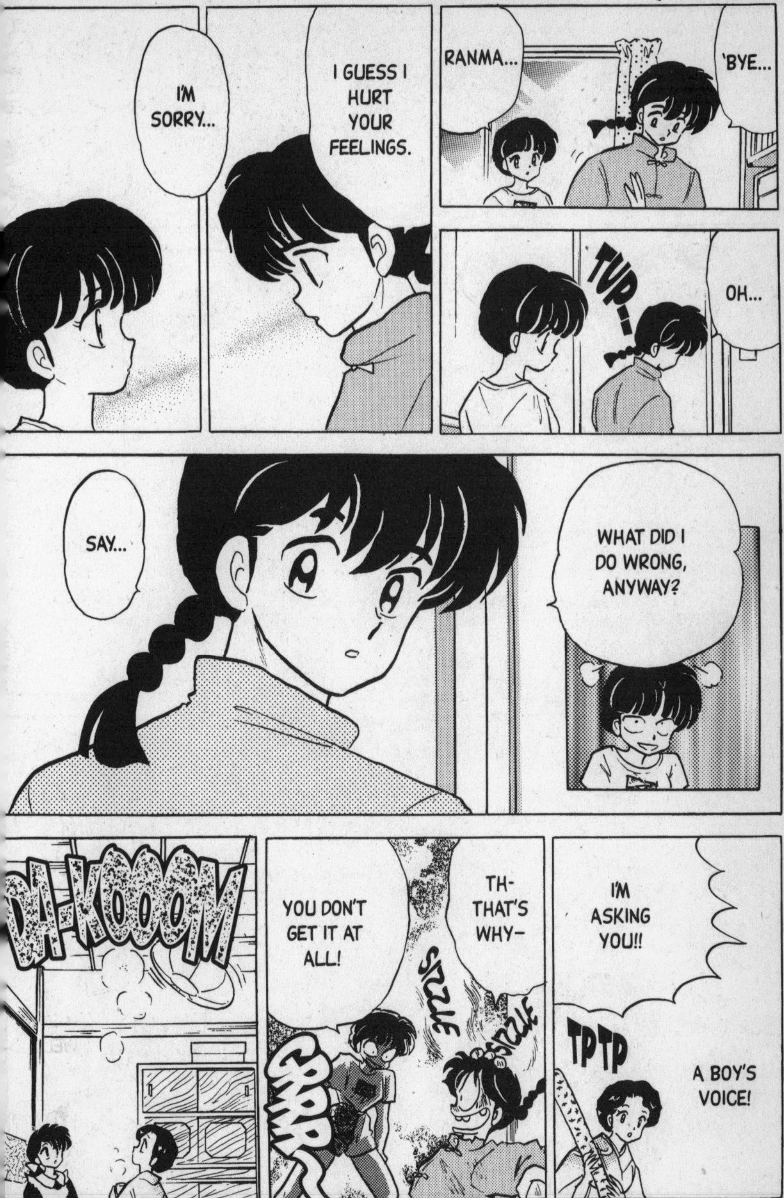
I'M SORRY...
I GUESS I HURT YOUR FEELINGS.
RANMA...
'BYE...
TUP--
OH...
SAY...
WHAT DID I DO WRONG, ANYWAY?
DA-KOOOM
YOU DON'T GET IT AT ALL!
TH- THAT'S WHY-
SIZZLE
SIZZLE
GRRR
I'M ASKING YOU!!
TPTP
A BOY'S VOICE!

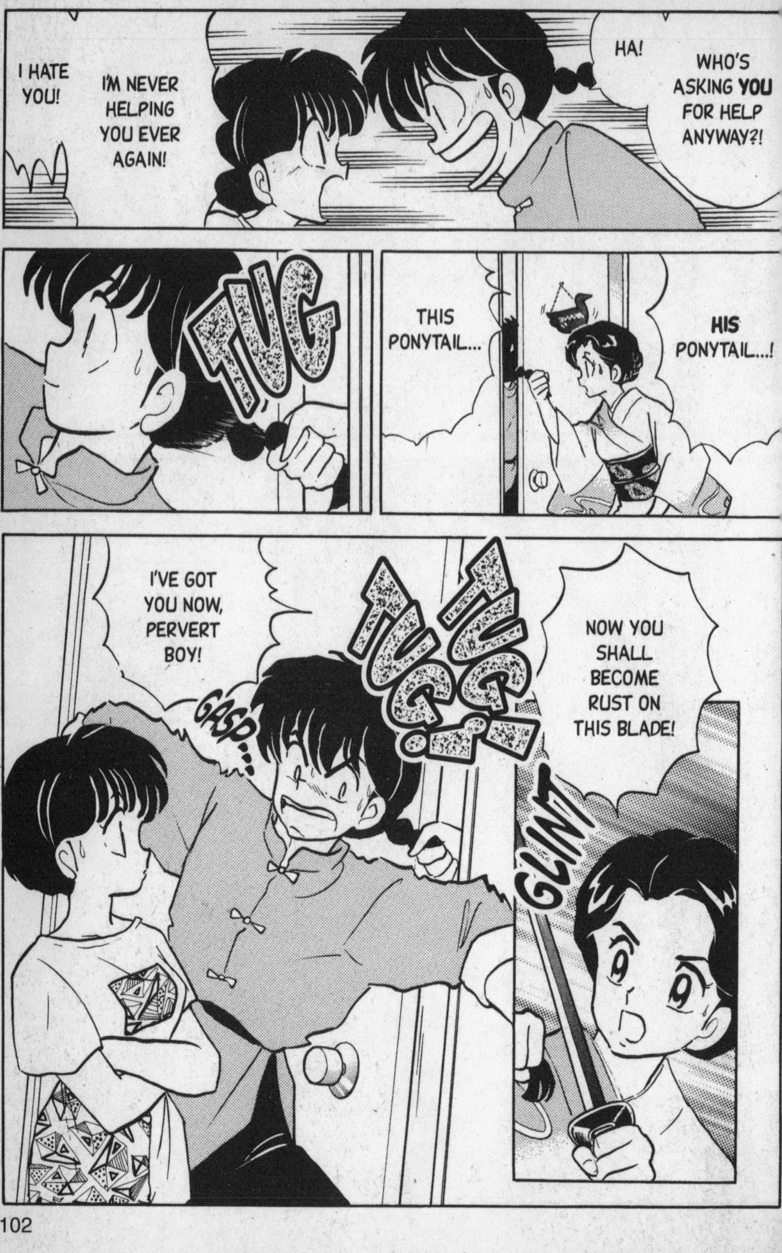
I HATE YOU!
I'M NEVER HELPING YOU EVER AGAIN!
HA!
WHO'S ASKING **YOU** FOR HELP ANYWAY?!
TUG
THIS PONYTAIL...
HIS PONYTAIL...!
I'VE GOT YOU NOW, PERVERT BOY!
GASP...
TUG TUG!
NOW YOU SHALL BECOME RUST ON THIS BLADE!
GLINT

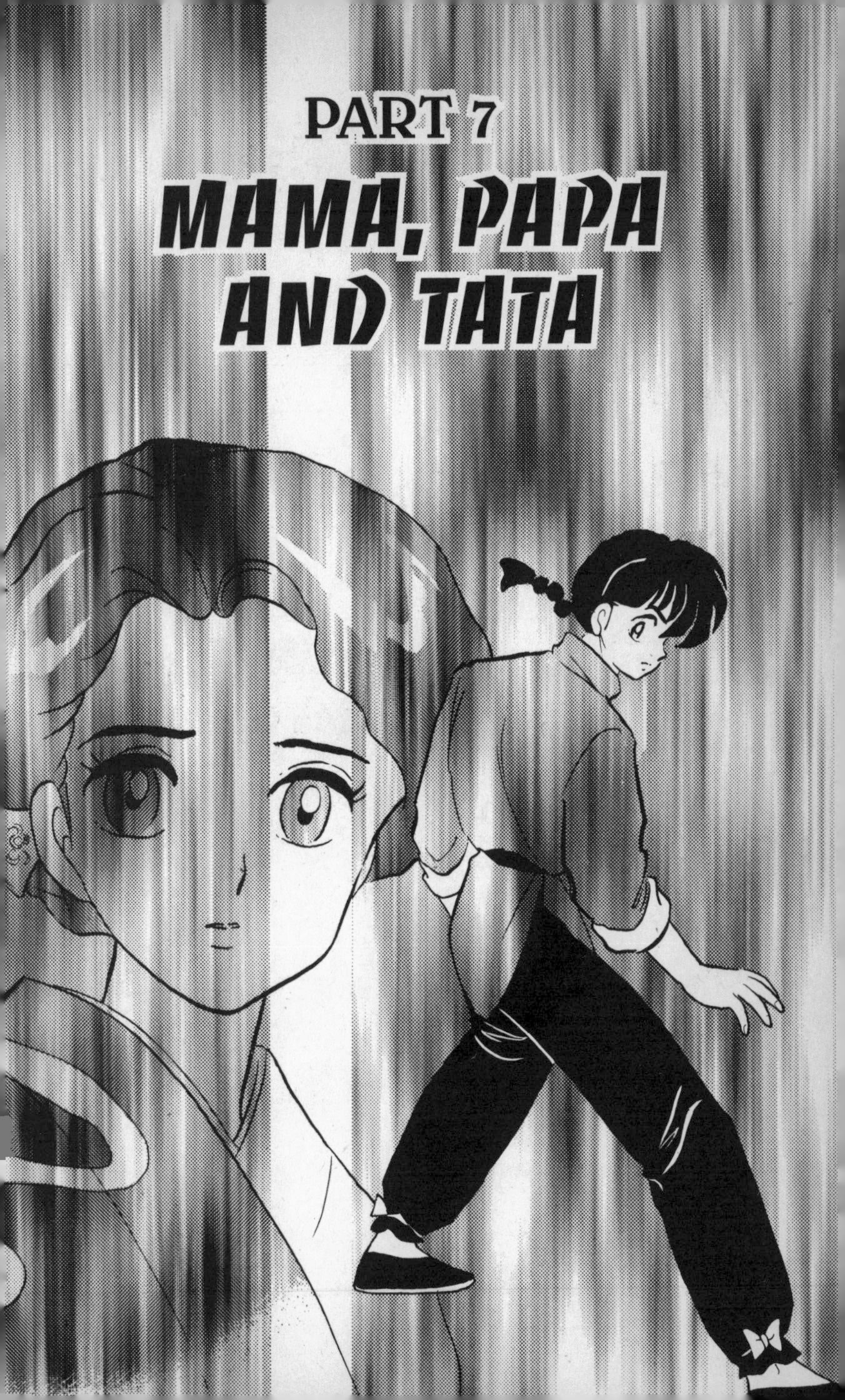
PART 7
MAMA, PAPA AND TATA

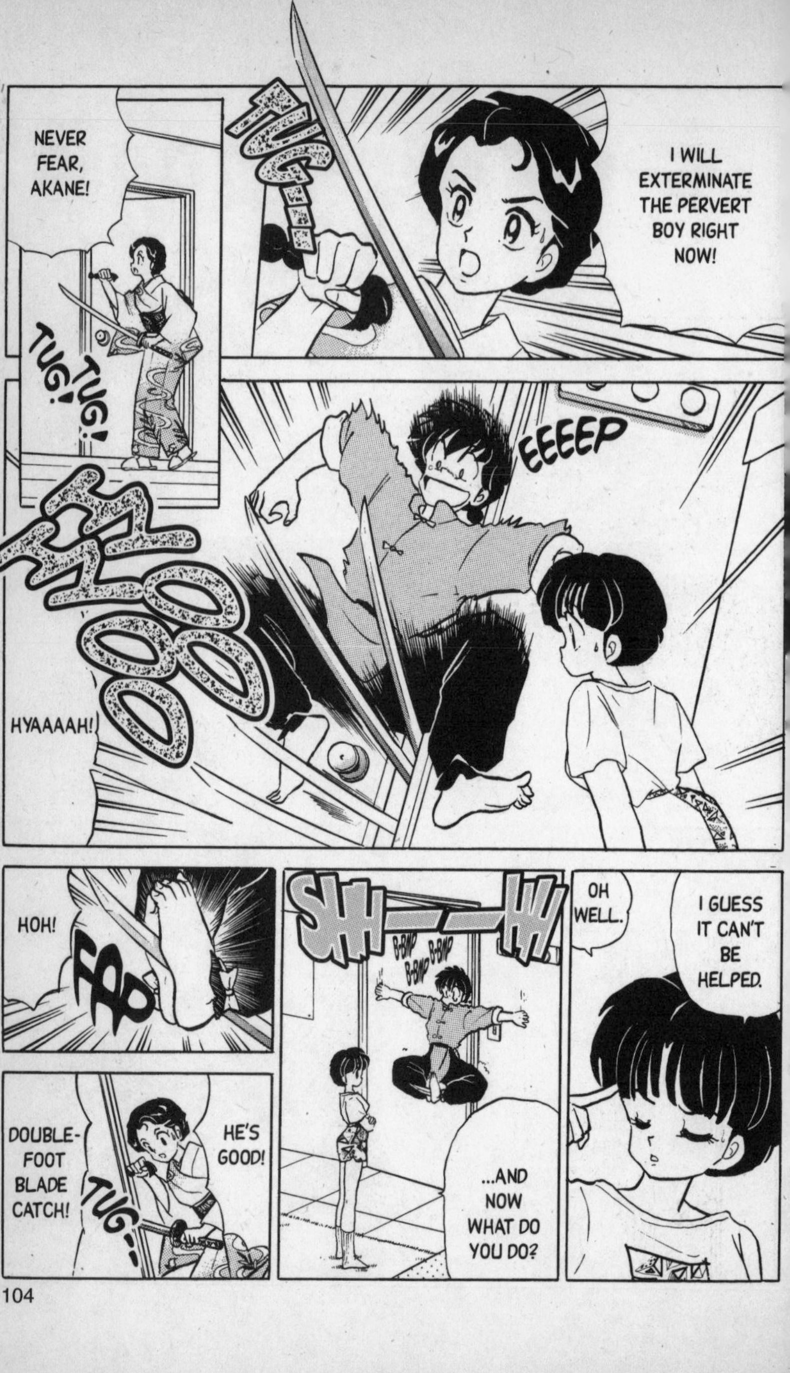
NEVER FEAR, AKANE!
TUG! TUG!
TUG...!
I WILL EXTERMINATE THE PERVERT BOY RIGHT NOW!
HYAAAAH!
EEEEP
HOH!
FAP
DOUBLE-FOOT BLADE CATCH!
HE'S GOOD!
TUG...
SHH—H
B-BMP B-BMP B-BMP
...AND NOW WHAT DO YOU DO?
OH WELL.
I GUESS IT CAN'T BE HELPED.

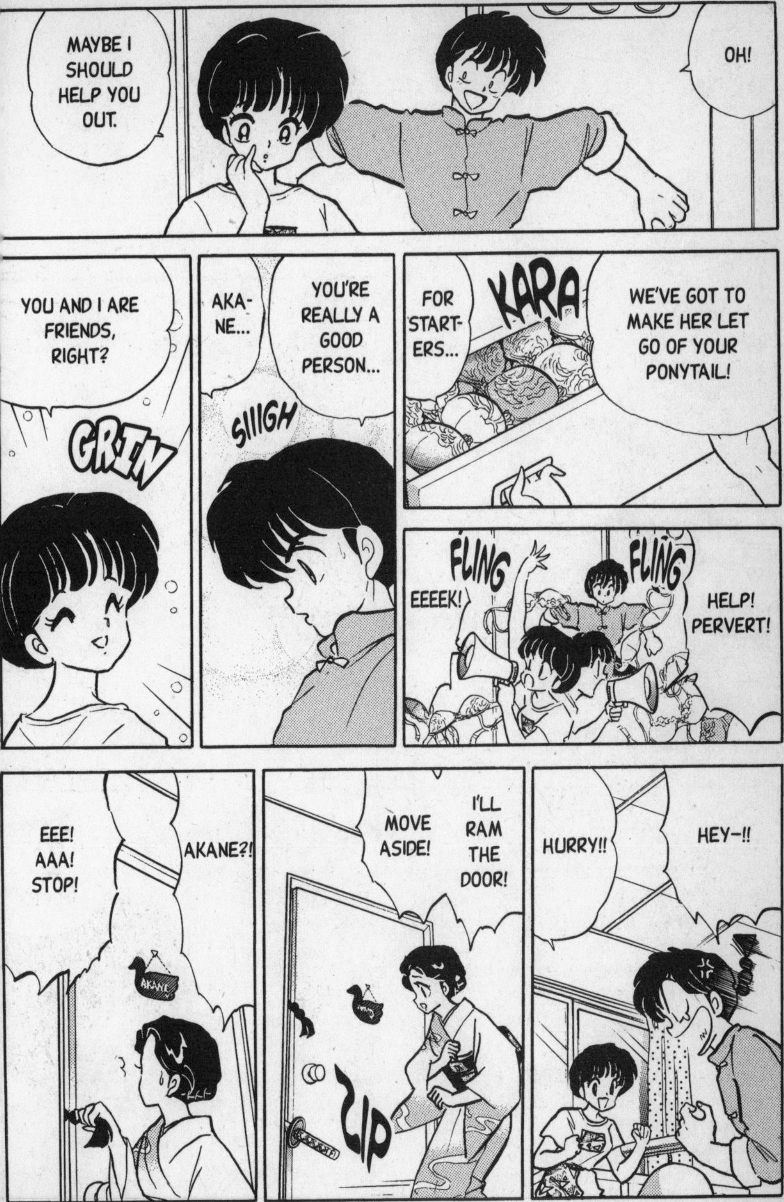
MAYBE I SHOULD HELP YOU OUT.
OH!
YOU AND I ARE FRIENDS, RIGHT?
GRIN
AKANE...
YOU'RE REALLY A GOOD PERSON...
SIIIGH
FOR STARTERS...
KARA
WE'VE GOT TO MAKE HER LET GO OF YOUR PONYTAIL!
FLING
EEEEK!
FLING
HELP! PERVERT!
EEE! AAA! STOP!
AKANE?!
MOVE ASIDE!
I'LL RAM THE DOOR!
ZIP
HURRY!!
HEY-!!

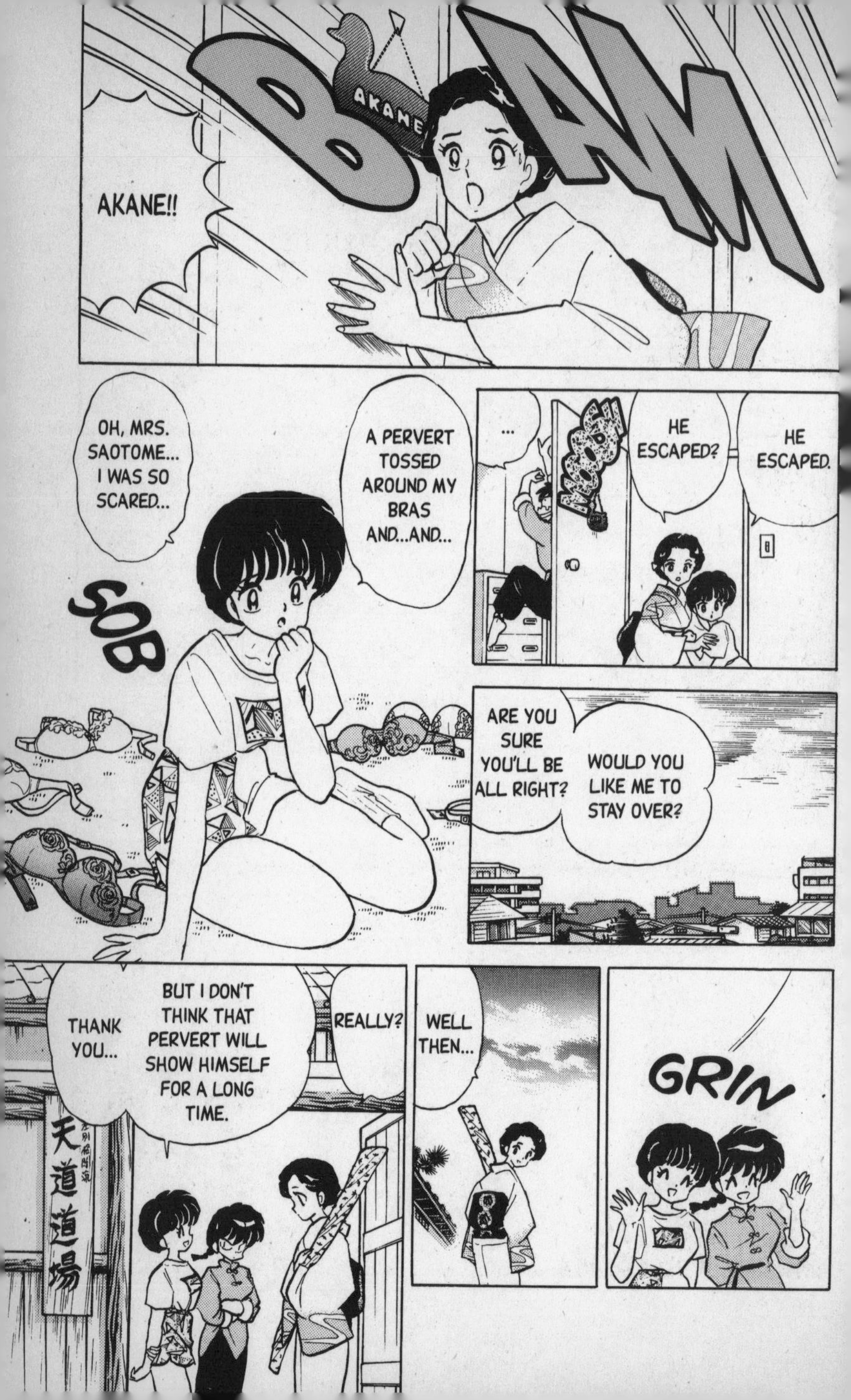
BAM
AKANE
AKANE!!
OH, MRS. SAOTOME... I WAS SO SCARED...
A PERVERT TOSSED AROUND MY BRAS AND...AND...
SOB
...
HE ESCAPED?
HE ESCAPED.
ARE YOU SURE YOU'LL BE ALL RIGHT?
WOULD YOU LIKE ME TO STAY OVER?
THANK YOU...
BUT I DON'T THINK THAT PERVERT WILL SHOW HIMSELF FOR A LONG TIME.
REALLY?
天道道場
WELL THEN...
GRIN

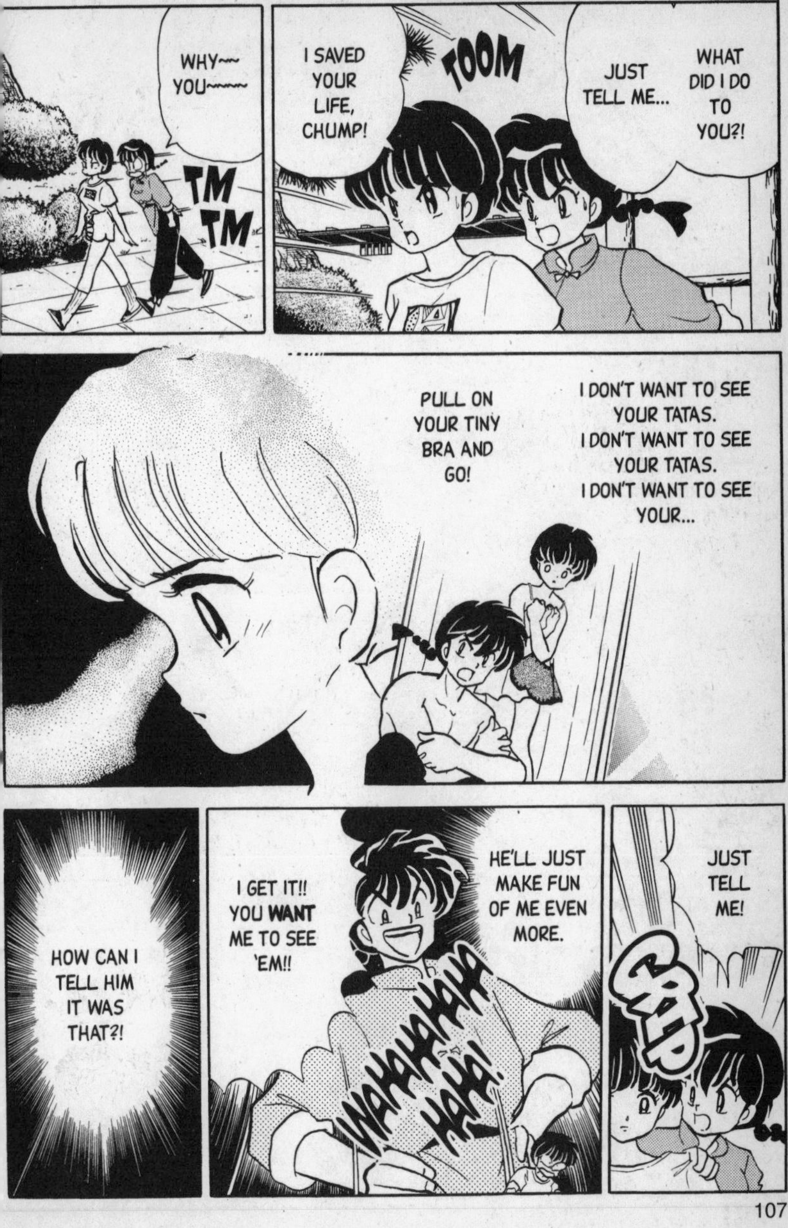
WHY~~ YOU~~~~
TM TM
I SAVED YOUR LIFE, CHUMP!
TOOM
JUST TELL ME...
WHAT DID I DO TO YOU?!
PULL ON YOUR TINY BRA AND GO!
I DON'T WANT TO SEE YOUR TATAS. I DON'T WANT TO SEE YOUR TATAS. I DON'T WANT TO SEE YOUR...
HOW CAN I TELL HIM IT WAS THAT?!
I GET IT!! YOU WANT ME TO SEE 'EM!!
WAHAHAHAHA HAHA!
HE'LL JUST MAKE FUN OF ME EVEN MORE.
JUST TELL ME!
GRIP

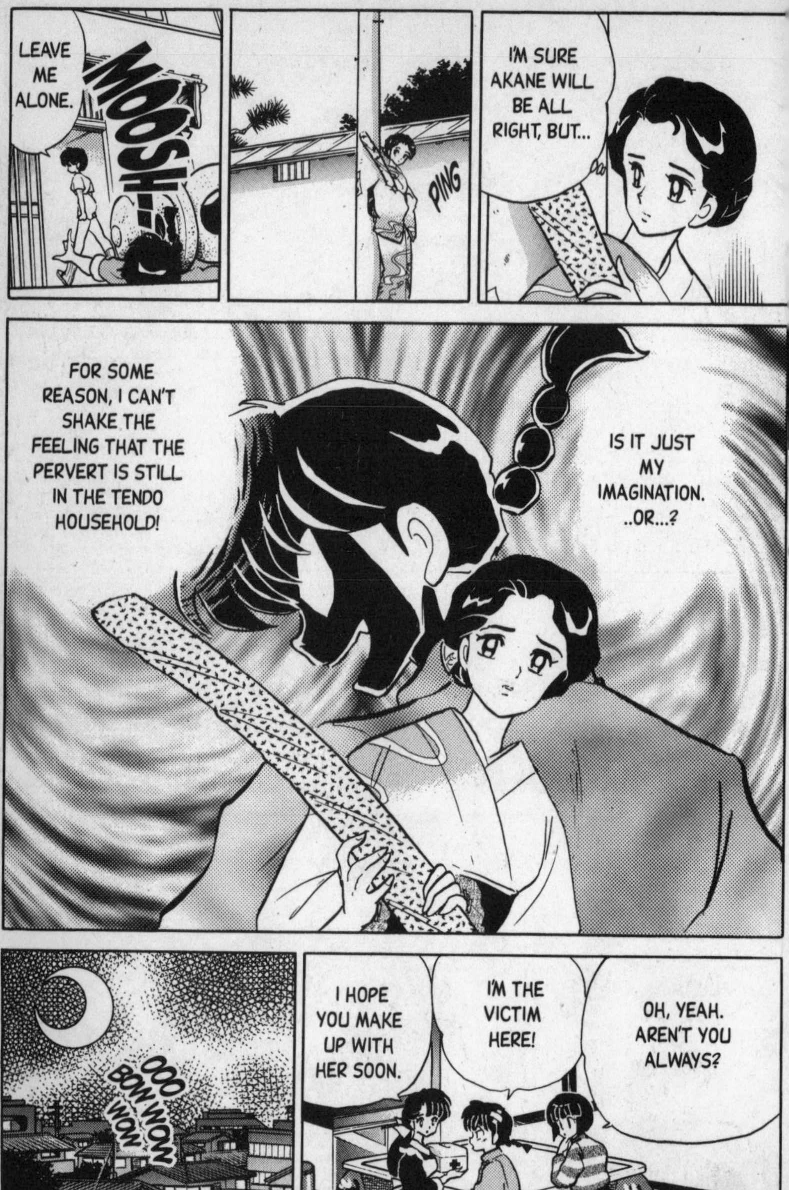
LEAVE ME ALONE.
MOOSH
PING
I'M SURE AKANE WILL BE ALL RIGHT, BUT...
FOR SOME REASON, I CAN'T SHAKE THE FEELING THAT THE PERVERT IS STILL IN THE TENDO HOUSEHOLD!
IS IT JUST MY IMAGINATION. ..OR...?
OOO BOW WOW WOW
I HOPE YOU MAKE UP WITH HER SOON.
I'M THE VICTIM HERE!
OH, YEAH. AREN'T YOU ALWAYS?

ALL I DID WAS MAKE FUN OF AKANE'S UNDERSIZED BREASTS!

WHAT'S WRONG WITH THAT?

HIC!

KRASSSSH!!

...

THAT'S YOUR FATHER.

NO, NO!

I DON'T WANT TO SEE MY PAPA THIS WAY....

SOB SOB

I DON'T WANT TO SEE MY PAPA...

I DON'T WANT TO SEE YOUR TATAS.

RAN-MA...

YOU ACTUALLY **SAID** THAT?!

HOW SHOULD I KNOW THAT WOULD HURT HER FEELINGS?

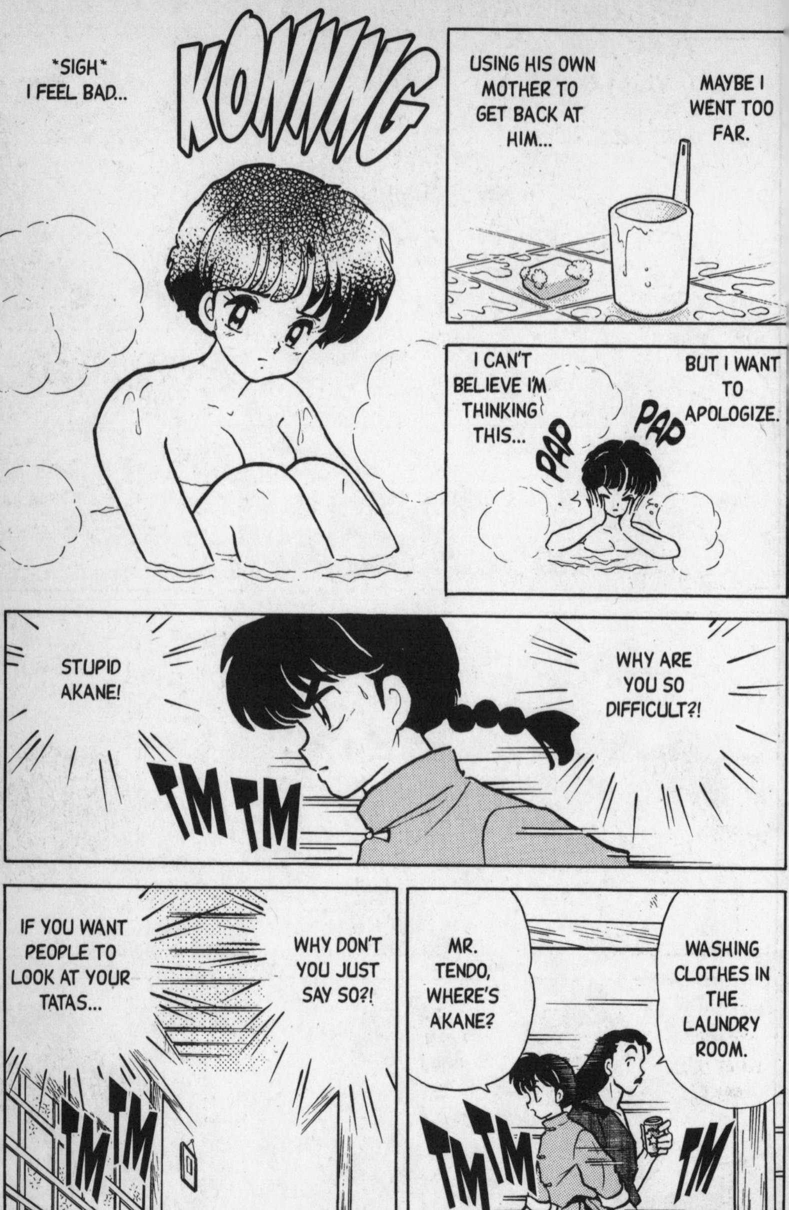
SIGH
I FEEL BAD...
KONNNG
USING HIS OWN MOTHER TO GET BACK AT HIM...
MAYBE I WENT TOO FAR.
I CAN'T BELIEVE I'M THINKING THIS...
PAP
PAP
BUT I WANT TO APOLOGIZE.
STUPID AKANE!
TM TM
WHY ARE YOU SO DIFFICULT?!
IF YOU WANT PEOPLE TO LOOK AT YOUR TATAS...
WHY DON'T YOU JUST SAY SO?!
TM TM
MR. TENDO, WHERE'S AKANE?
WASHING CLOTHES IN THE LAUNDRY ROOM.
TM TM
TM

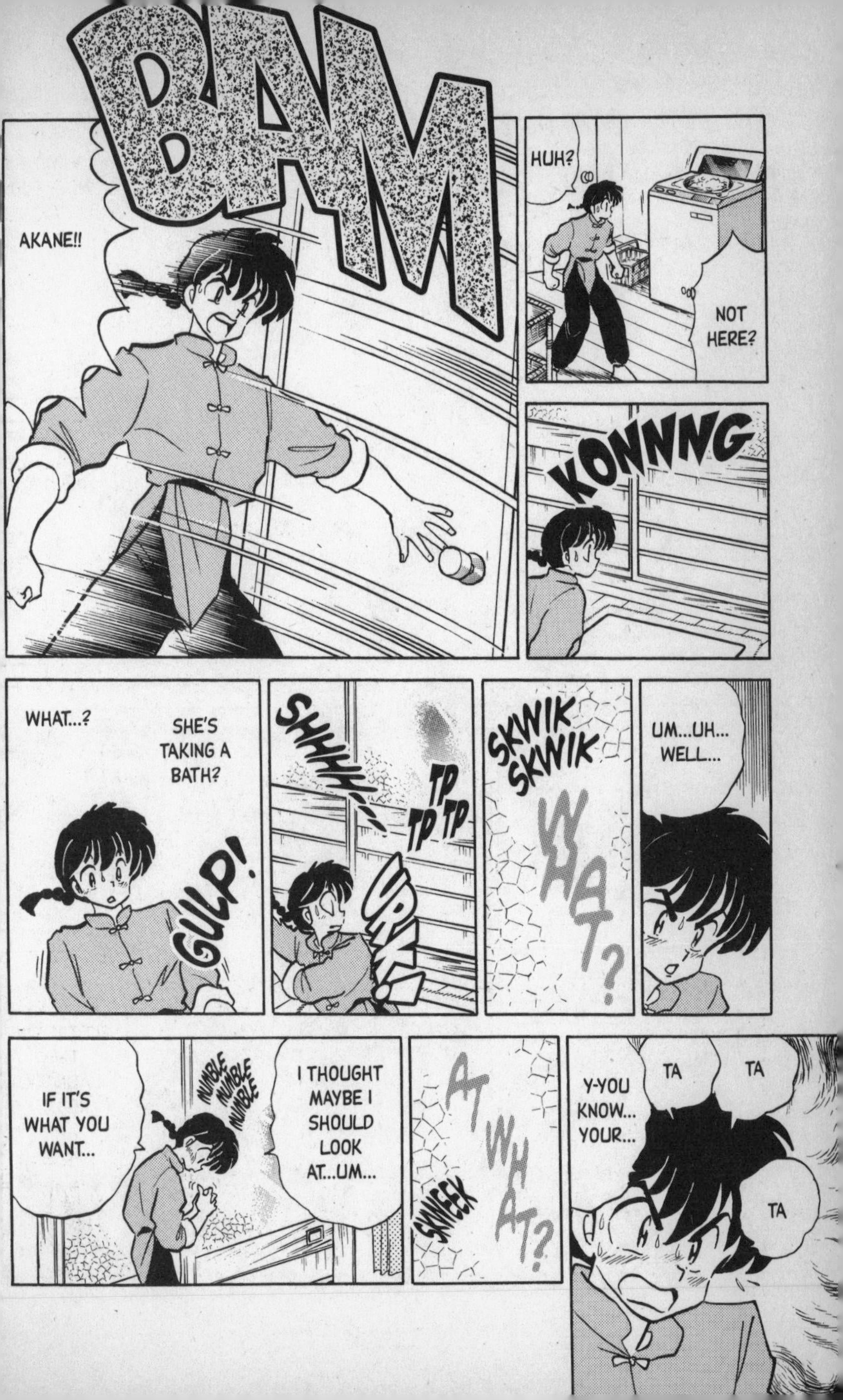
BAM
AKANE!!
HUH?
NOT HERE?
KONNNG
WHAT...?
SHE'S TAKING A BATH?
GULP!
SHHHH---
TP TP TP TP
URK!
SKWIK SKWIK
WHAT?
UM...UH... WELL...
IF IT'S WHAT YOU WANT...
MUMBLE MUMBLE MUMBLE
I THOUGHT MAYBE I SHOULD LOOK AT...UM...
AT WHAT?
SKWEEK
Y-YOU KNOW... YOUR...
TA
TA
TA

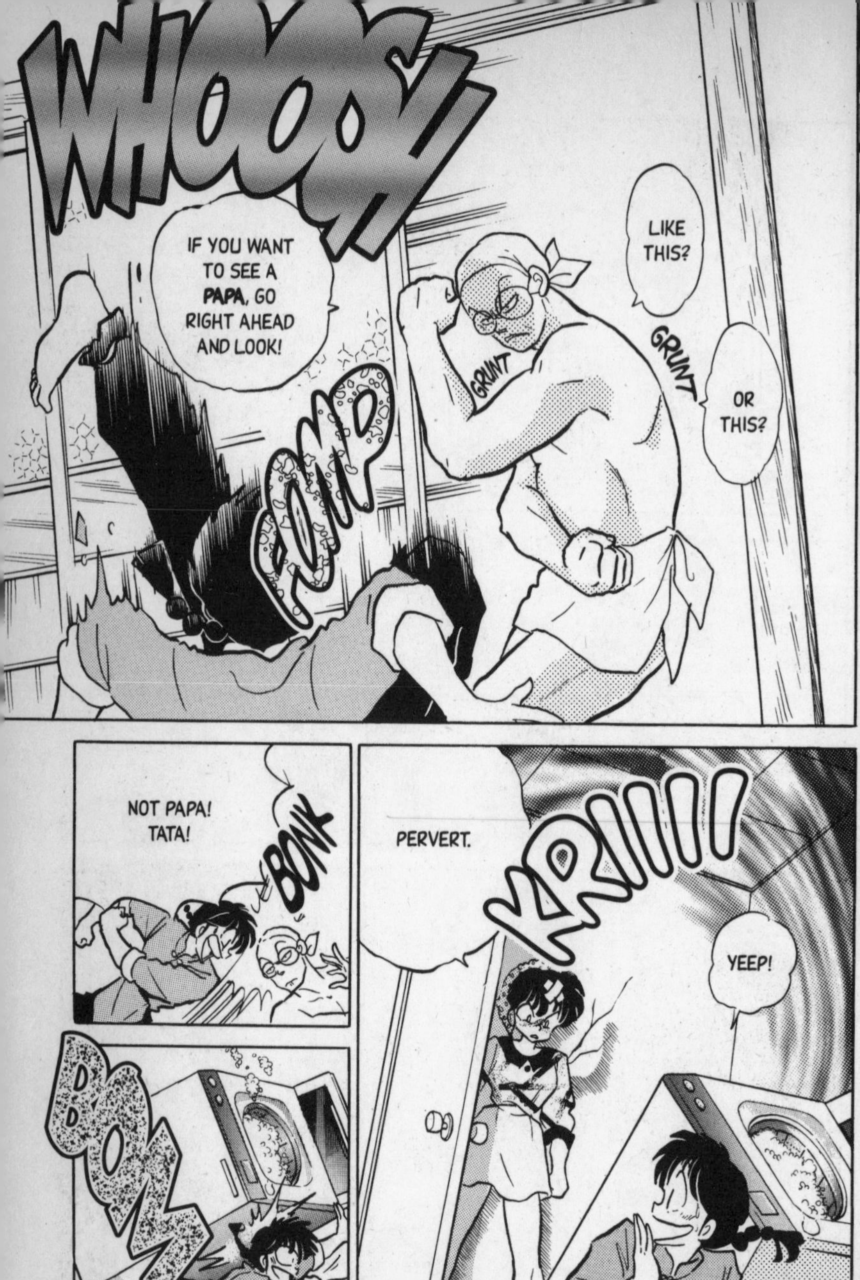
WHOOOSH!
IF YOU WANT TO SEE A **PAPA**, GO RIGHT AHEAD AND LOOK!
FOMP
GRUNT
LIKE THIS?
GRUNT
OR THIS?
NOT PAPA! TATA!
BONK
PERVERT.
KRIIIII
YEEP!

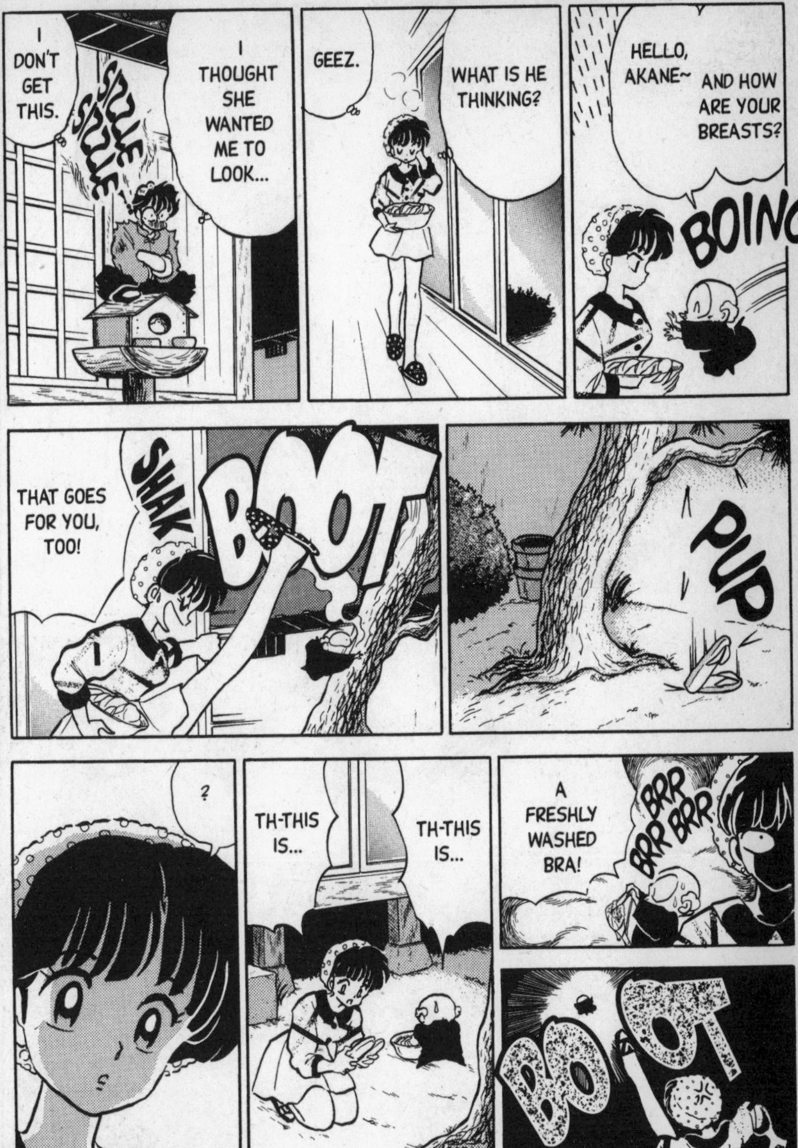
I DON'T GET THIS.
SIZZLE SIZZLE
I THOUGHT SHE WANTED ME TO LOOK...
GEEZ.
WHAT IS HE THINKING?
HELLO, AKANE~
AND HOW ARE YOUR BREASTS?
BOING
THAT GOES FOR YOU, TOO!
SHAK
BOOT
PUP
?
TH-THIS IS...
TH-THIS IS...
A FRESHLY WASHED BRA!
BRR BRR BRR BRR
BOOT

THESE ARE
MRS.
SAOTOME'S
SLIPPERS...!

BUT
WHY...?

PITTER PITTER PATTER
TONK

A TAKE-
OUT
BOWL?!

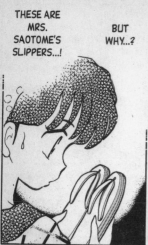

NO ONE'S
GOTTEN
TAKE-
OUT.

AND IT'S
EVEN
WASHED!

BUT THAT
MUST
MEAN...

AKANE.

PSSH

EH?

I GOT A NEW
POLAROID.

COOL.

BEEE

GAH!
THAT'S...

MRS.
SAOTOME'S
SWORD BAG!!

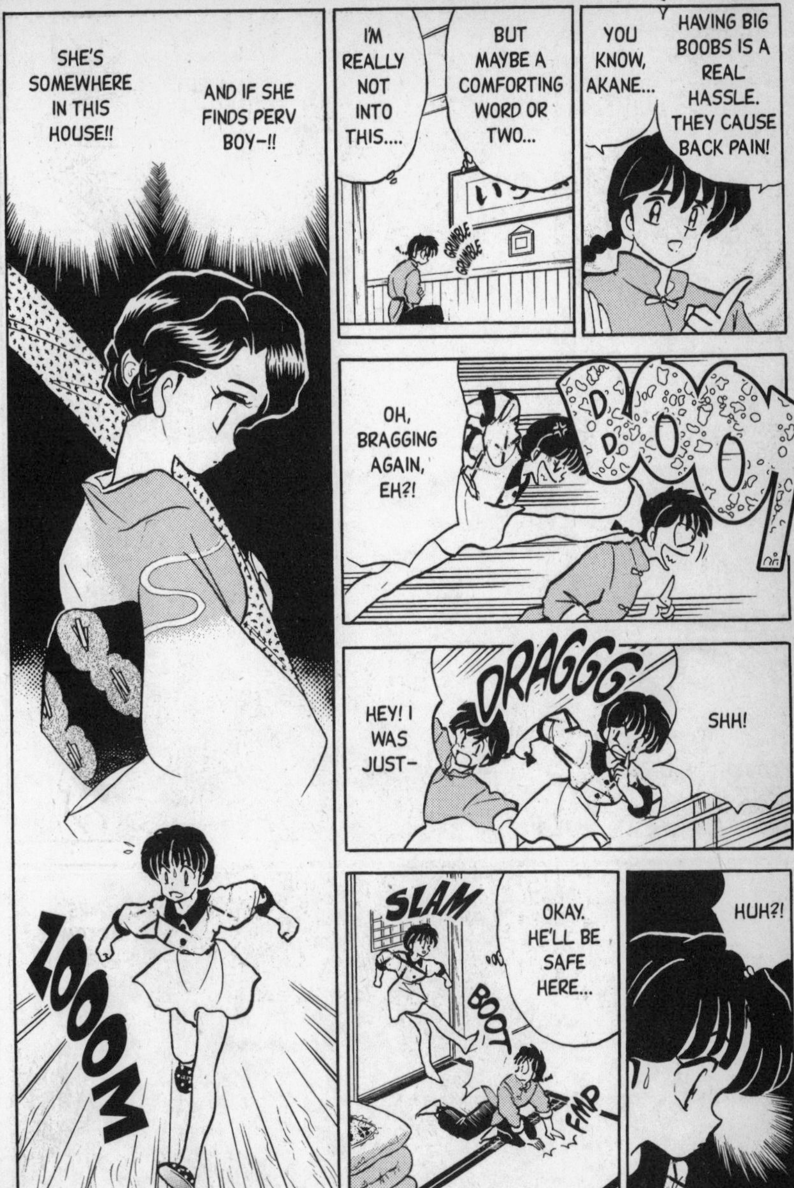
SHE'S SOMEWHERE IN THIS HOUSE!!
AND IF SHE FINDS PERV BOY-!!
ZOOOOM
I'M REALLY NOT INTO THIS....
BUT MAYBE A COMFORTING WORD OR TWO...
GRUMBLE GRUMBLE
YOU KNOW, AKANE...
HAVING BIG BOOBS IS A REAL HASSLE. THEY CAUSE BACK PAIN!
OH, BRAGGING AGAIN, EH?!
BOOT
DRAGGG
HEY! I WAS JUST-
SHH!
SLAM
OKAY. HE'LL BE SAFE HERE...
BOOT
FMP
HUH?!

GAH!

KIMONO HEM...?!

SHE'S IN THE CLOSET!

?

POOF

H-HEY...

MMF

...

B-BMP B-BMP B-BMP

SHE'S NOT MOVING.

SHE HASN'T NOTICED YET!

PHEW!

EVEN A GREAT WARRIOR...

CAN FALL ASLEEP.

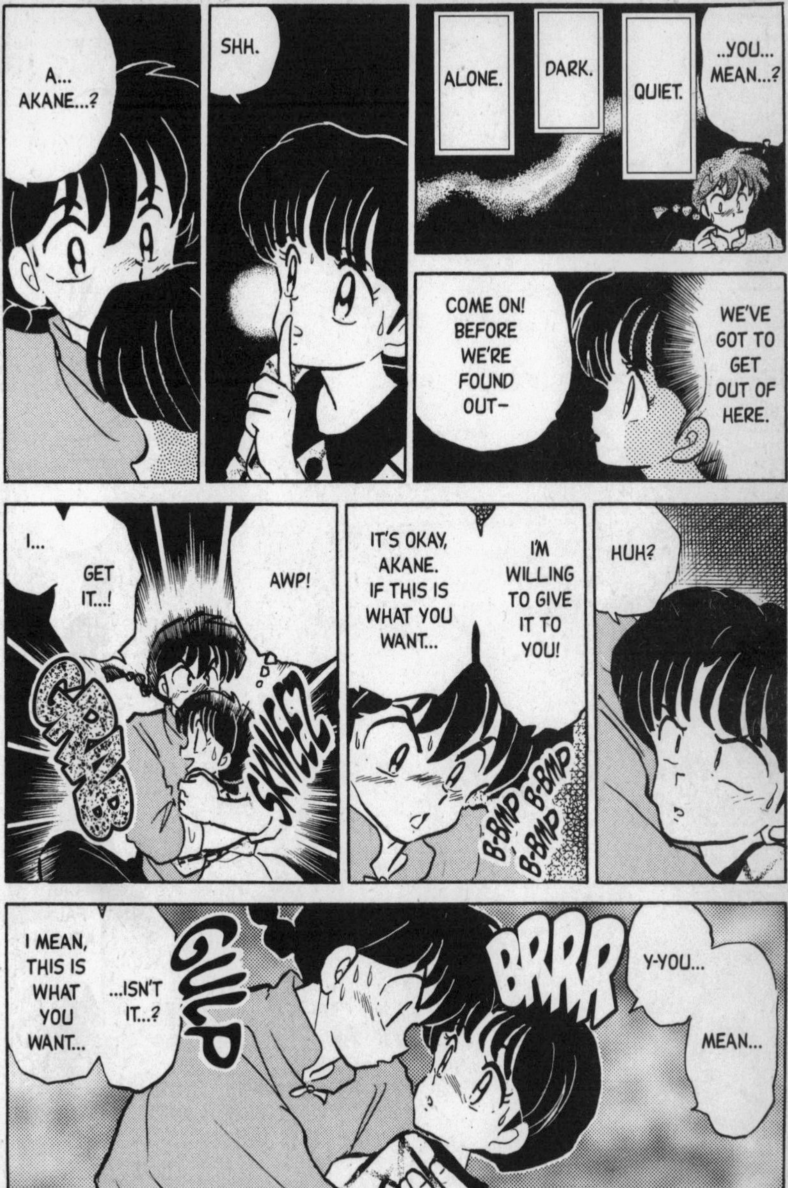
A... AKANE...?
SHH.
ALONE.
DARK.
QUIET.
..YOU... MEAN...?
COME ON! BEFORE WE'RE FOUND OUT–
WE'VE GOT TO GET OUT OF HERE.
I...
GET IT...!
AWP!
GRAB
SKWEEZ
IT'S OKAY, AKANE. IF THIS IS WHAT YOU WANT...
I'M WILLING TO GIVE IT TO YOU!
B-BMP B-BMP B-BMP B-BMP
HUH?
I MEAN, THIS IS WHAT YOU WANT...
...ISN'T IT...?
GULP
BRRR
Y-YOU...
MEAN...

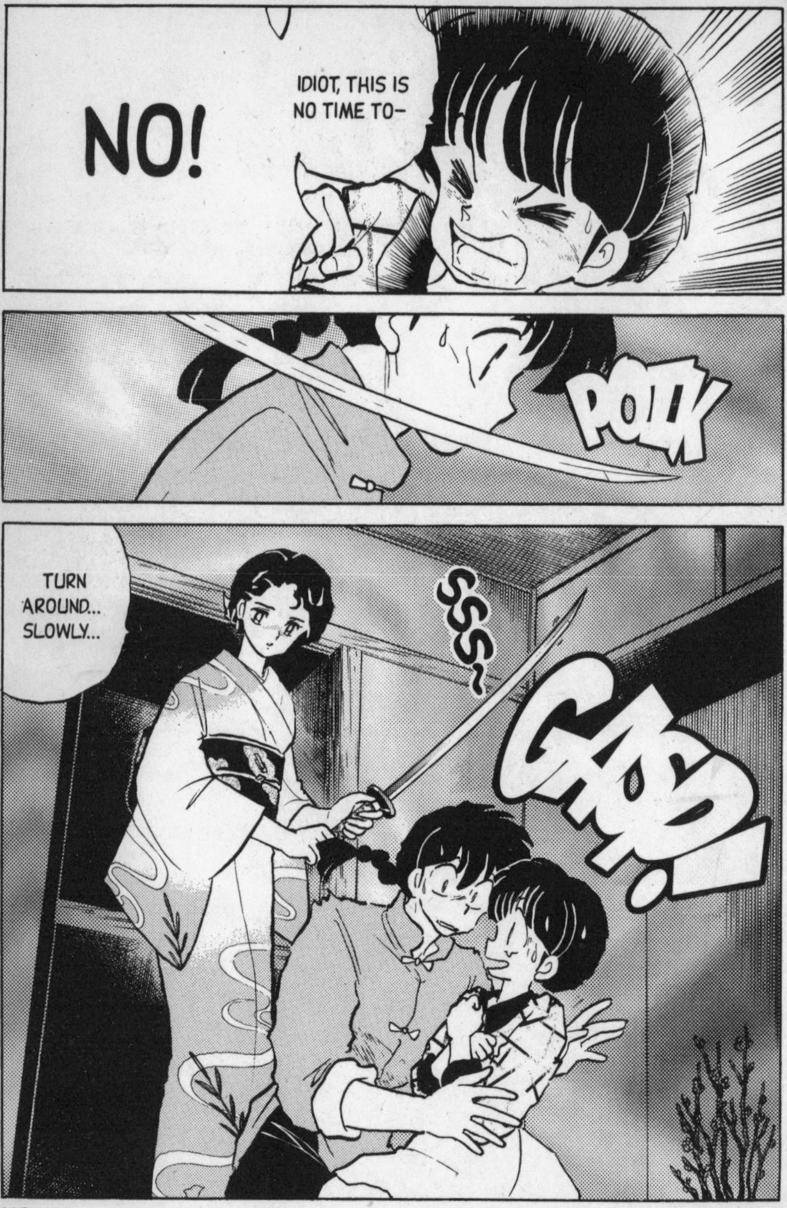
NO!
IDIOT, THIS IS NO TIME TO—
POKK
TURN AROUND... SLOWLY...
SSS~
GASP!

PART 8
LOOKING HIS BEST

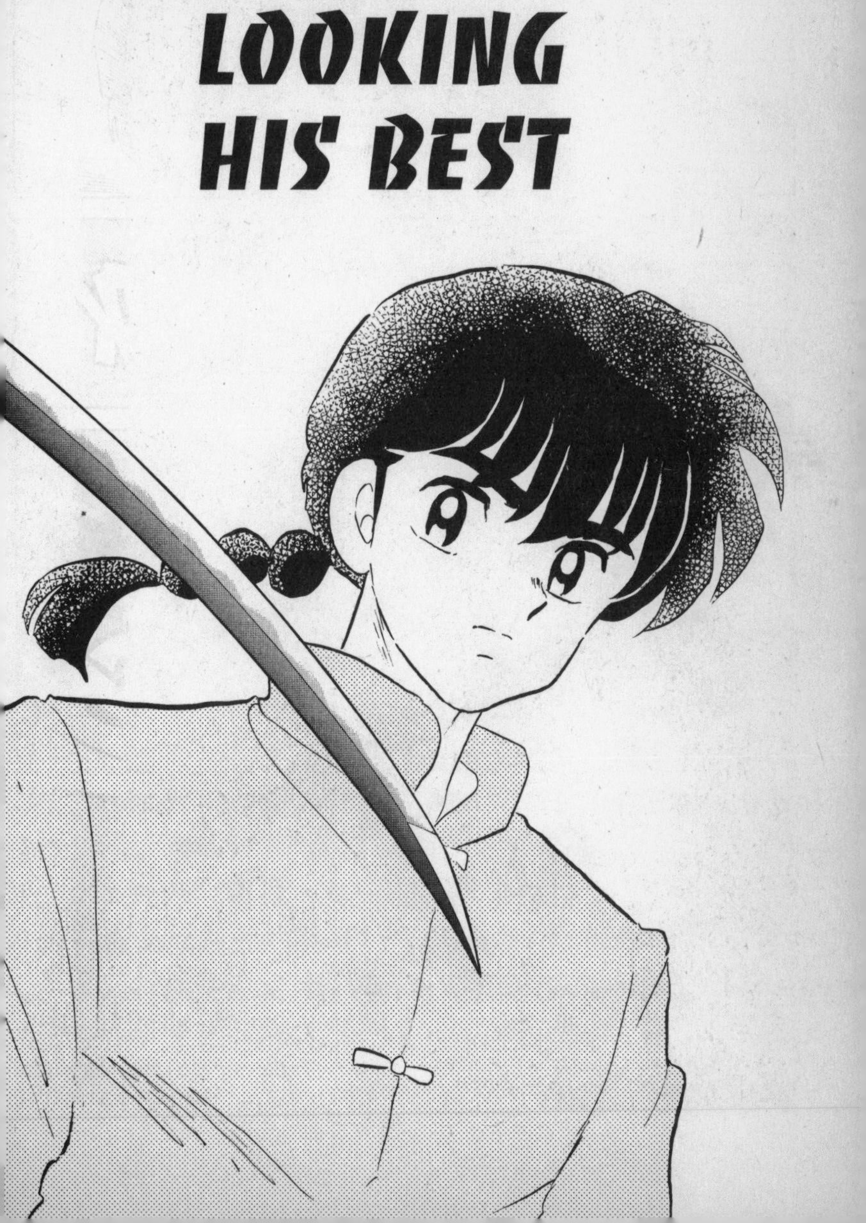

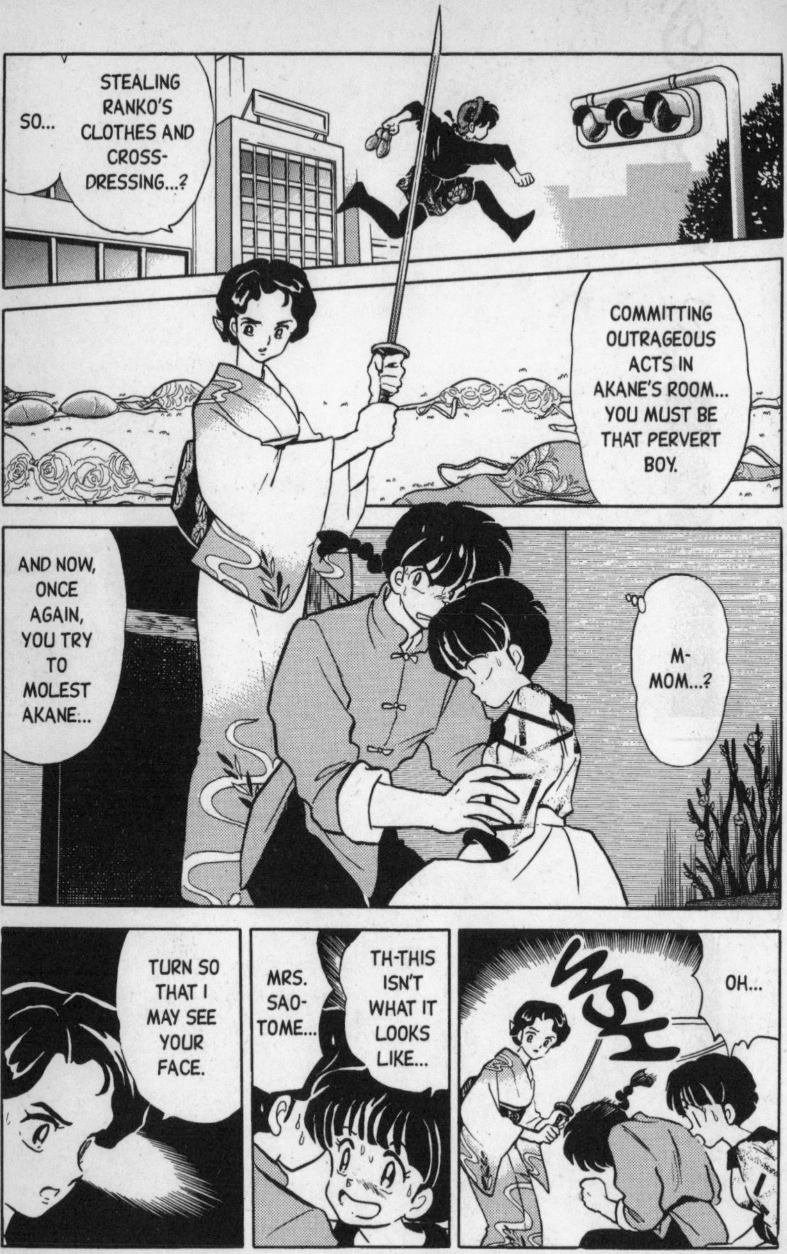
SO...
STEALING RANKO'S CLOTHES AND CROSS-DRESSING...?
COMMITTING OUTRAGEOUS ACTS IN AKANE'S ROOM... YOU MUST BE THAT PERVERT BOY.
AND NOW, ONCE AGAIN, YOU TRY TO MOLEST AKANE...
M-MOM...?
TURN SO THAT I MAY SEE YOUR FACE.
MRS. SAO-TOME...
TH-THIS ISN'T WHAT IT LOOKS LIKE...
WSH
OH...

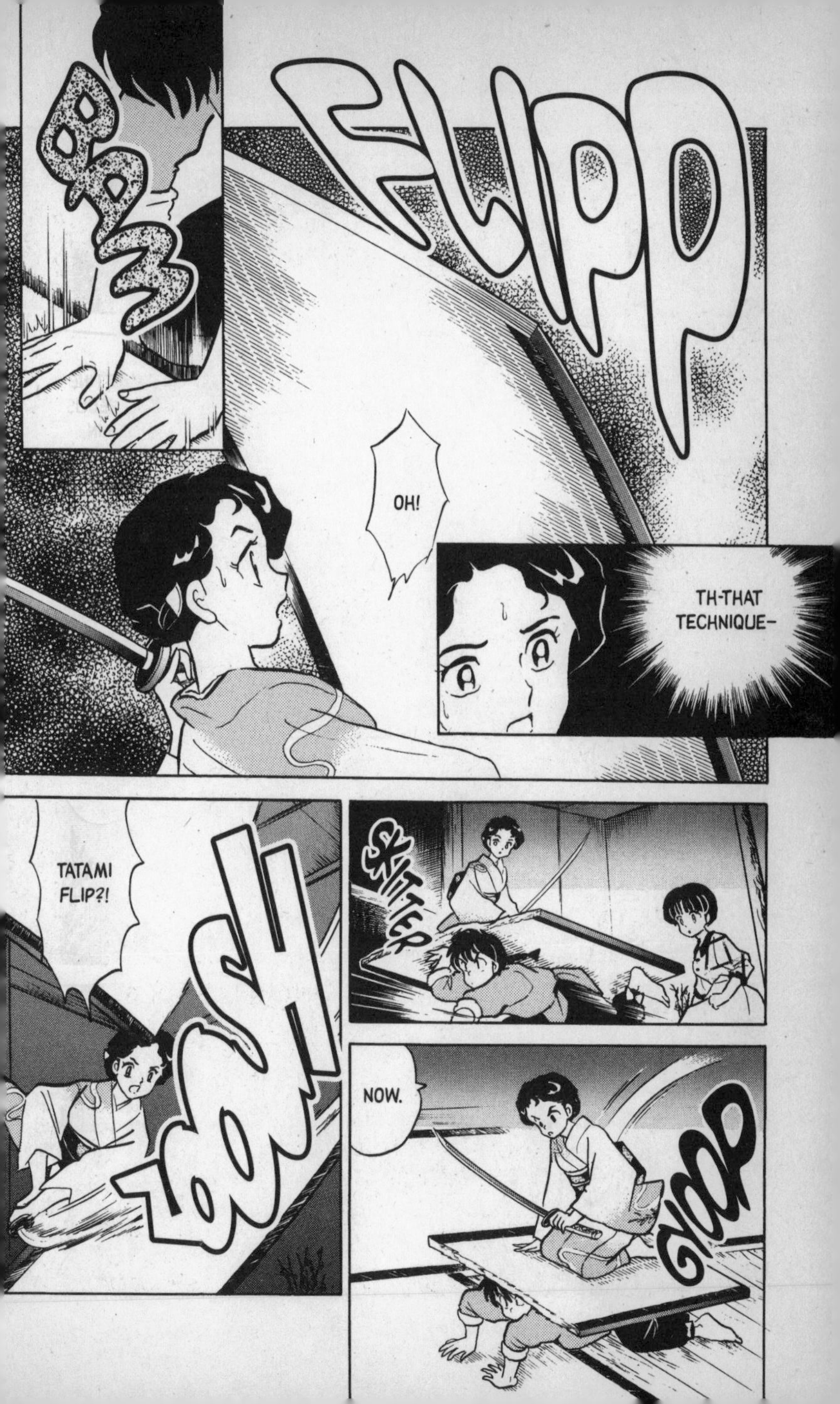
BAMM
FLIPP
OH!
TH-THAT TECHNIQUE–
TATAMI FLIP?!
FOOSH
SKITTER
NOW.
GWOOP

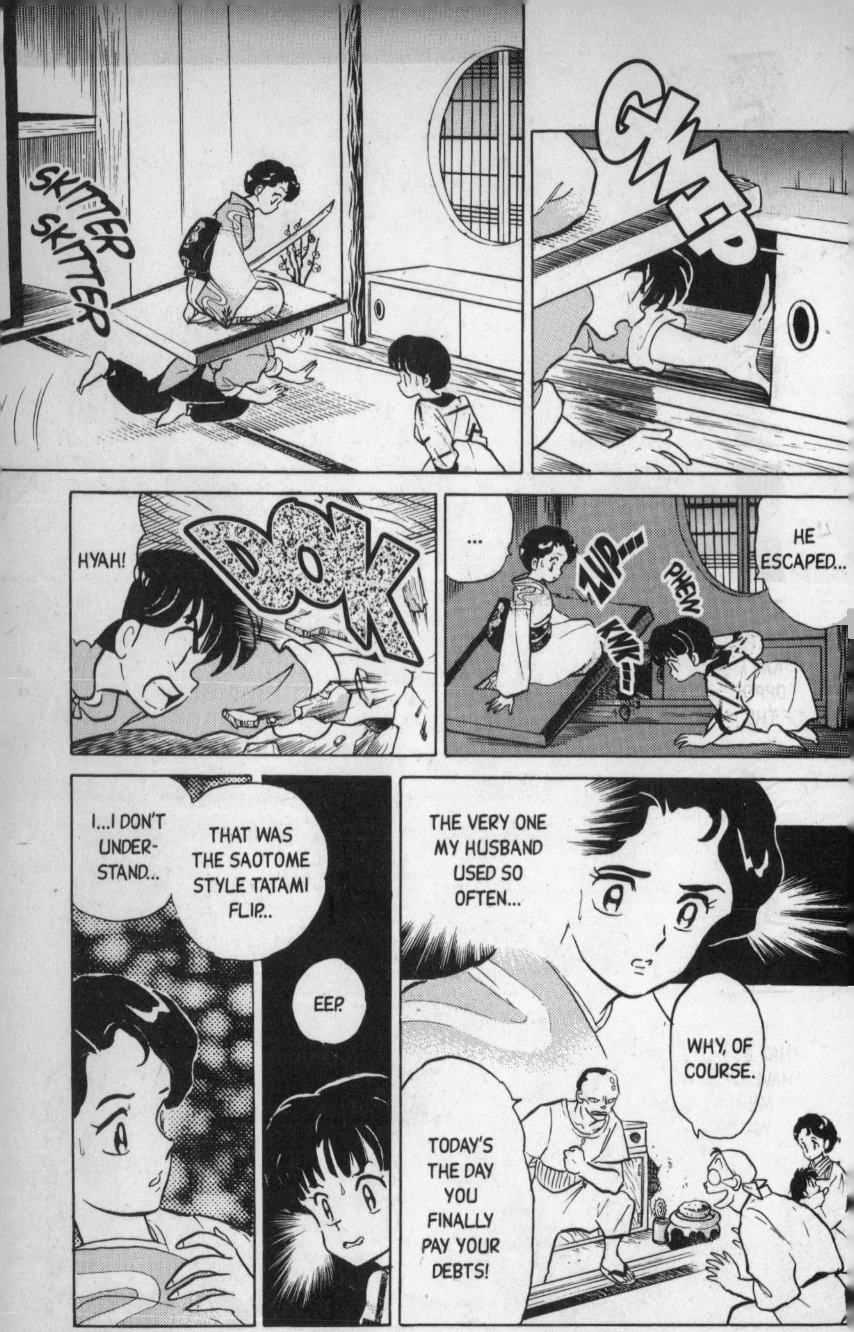
SKITTER SKITTER
GWAEP
HYAH!
DOK
...
ZUP...
PHEW
KNK...
HE ESCAPED...
I...I DON'T UNDER-STAND...
THAT WAS THE SAOTOME STYLE TATAMI FLIP..
EEP.
THE VERY ONE MY HUSBAND USED SO OFTEN...
WHY, OF COURSE.
TODAY'S THE DAY YOU FINALLY PAY YOUR DEBTS!

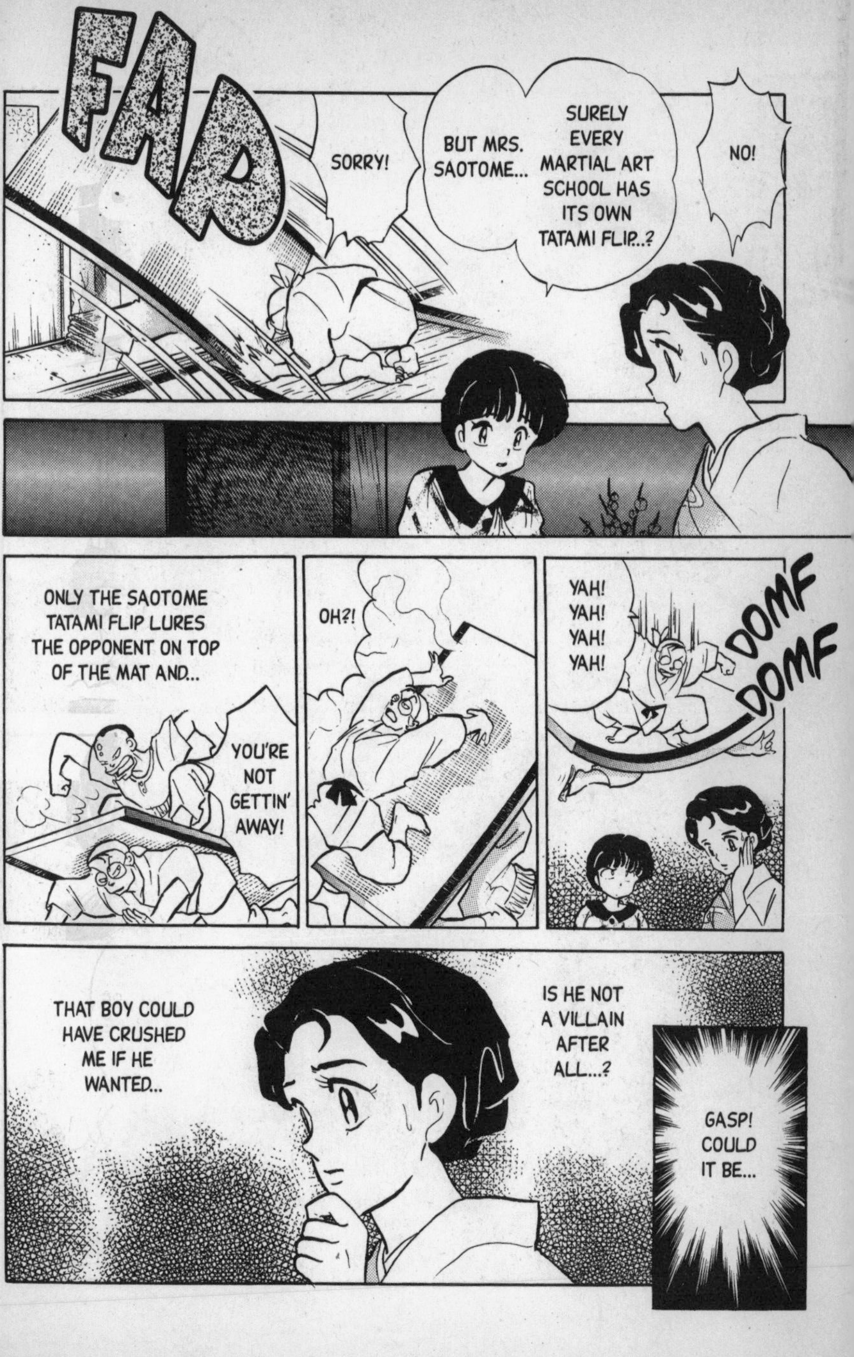
FAP
SORRY!
BUT MRS. SAOTOME...
SURELY EVERY MARTIAL ART SCHOOL HAS ITS OWN TATAMI FLIP...?
NO!
ONLY THE SAOTOME TATAMI FLIP LURES THE OPPONENT ON TOP OF THE MAT AND...
YOU'RE NOT GETTIN' AWAY!
OH?!
YAH! YAH! YAH! YAH!
DOMF DOMF
THAT BOY COULD HAVE CRUSHED ME IF HE WANTED...
IS HE NOT A VILLAIN AFTER ALL...?
GASP! COULD IT BE...

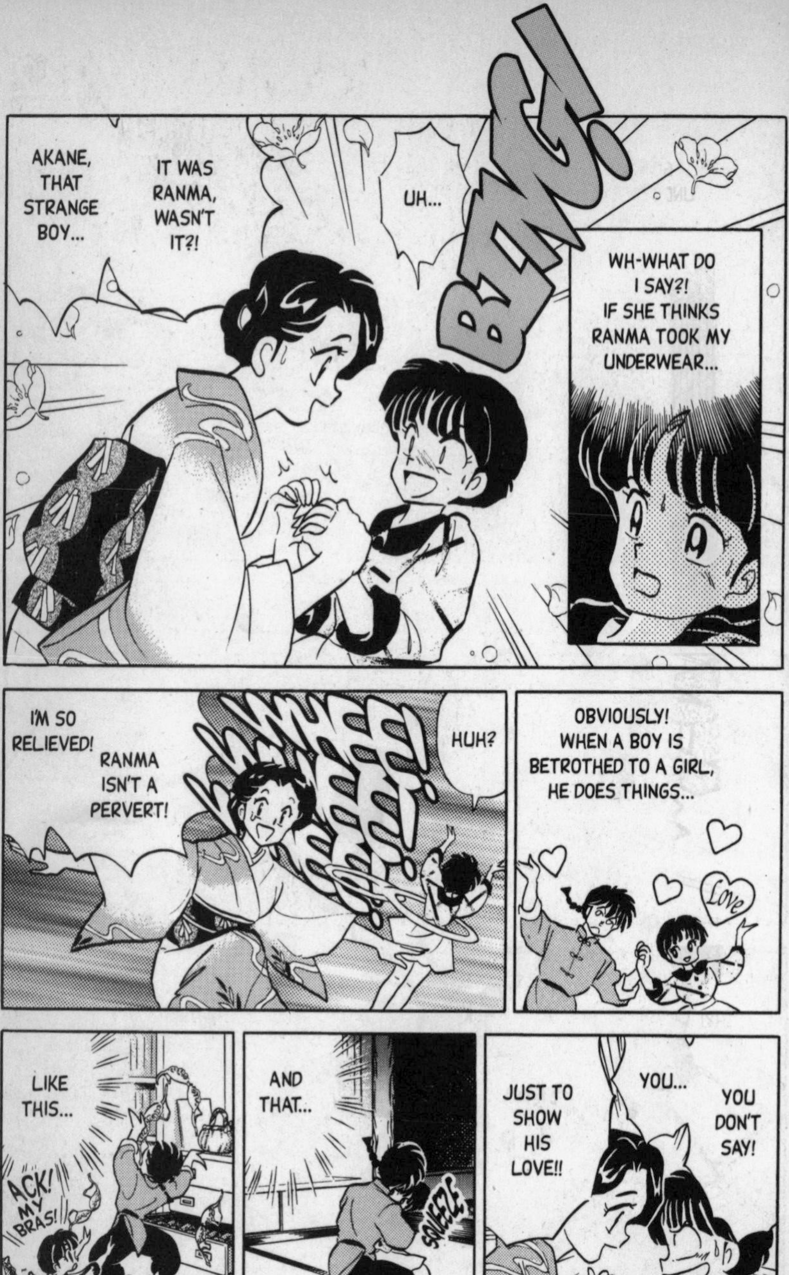
AKANE, THAT STRANGE BOY...
IT WAS RANMA, WASN'T IT?!
UH...
BLING!
WH-WHAT DO I SAY?! IF SHE THINKS RANMA TOOK MY UNDERWEAR...
I'M SO RELIEVED!
RANMA ISN'T A PERVERT!
HUH?
OBVIOUSLY! WHEN A BOY IS BETROTHED TO A GIRL, HE DOES THINGS...
Love
LIKE THIS...
ACK! MY BRAS!
AND THAT...
SQUEEZE
JUST TO SHOW HIS LOVE!!
YOU...
YOU DON'T SAY!

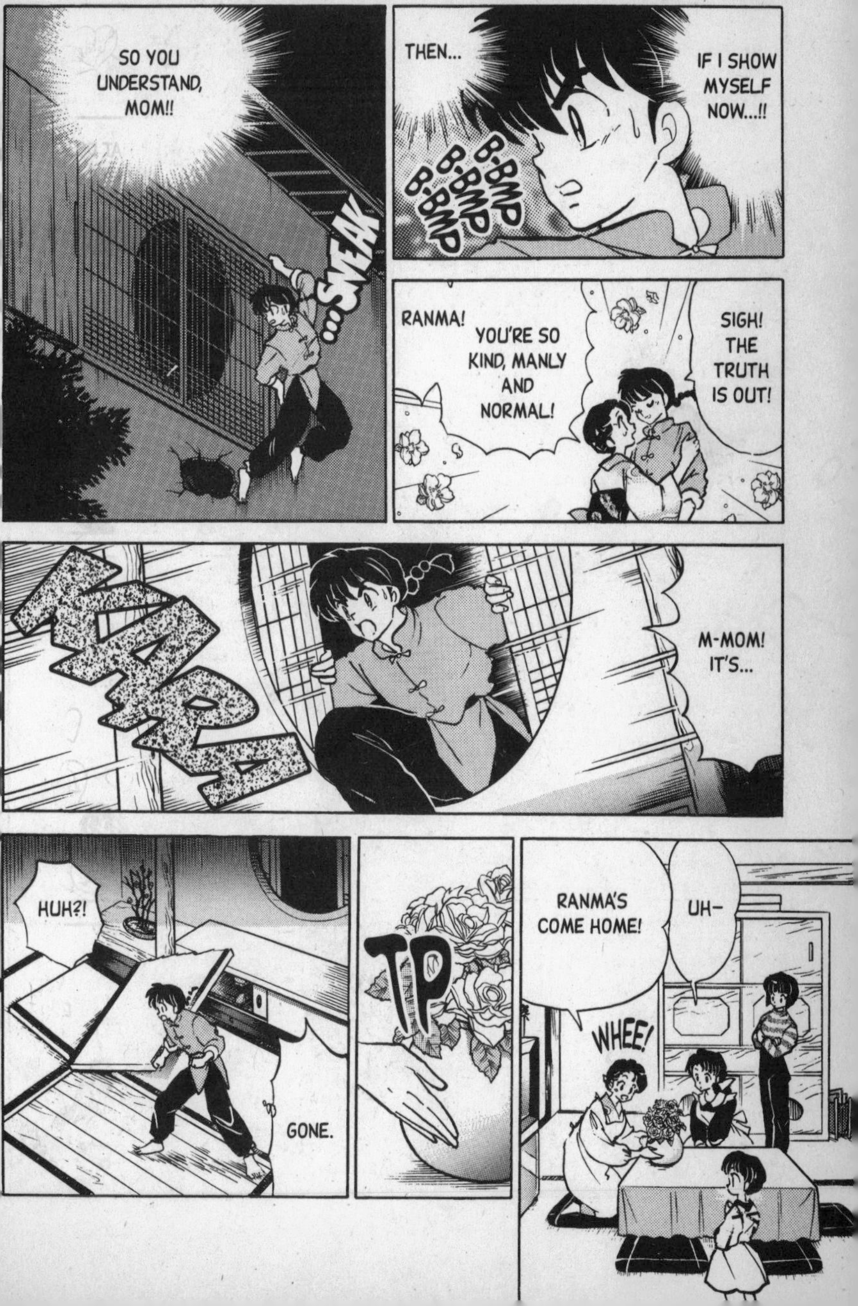
SO YOU UNDERSTAND, MOM!!
...SNEAK
THEN...
IF I SHOW MYSELF NOW...!!
B-BMP B-BMP B-BMP
RANMA!
YOU'RE SO KIND, MANLY AND NORMAL!
SIGH! THE TRUTH IS OUT!
M-MOM! IT'S...
HUH?!
GONE.
TP
RANMA'S COME HOME!
UH-
WHEE!

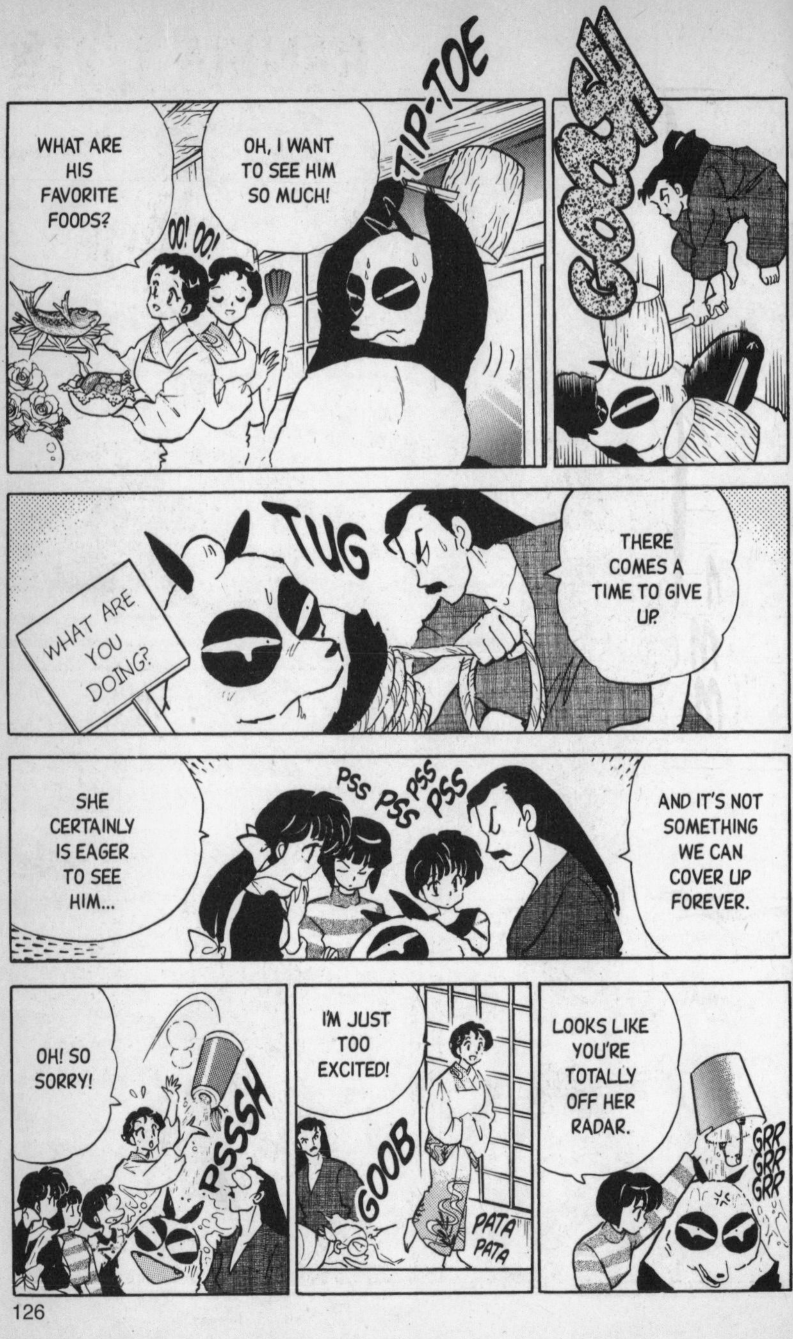
WHAT ARE HIS FAVORITE FOODS?
OO! OO!
OH, I WANT TO SEE HIM SO MUCH!
TIP-TOE
GOOSH
WHAT ARE YOU DOING?
TUG
THERE COMES A TIME TO GIVE UP.
SHE CERTAINLY IS EAGER TO SEE HIM...
PSS PSS PSS PSS
AND IT'S NOT SOMETHING WE CAN COVER UP FOREVER.
OH! SO SORRY!
PSSSH
I'M JUST TOO EXCITED!
GOOB
PATA PATA
LOOKS LIKE YOU'RE TOTALLY OFF HER RADAR.
GRR GRR GRR

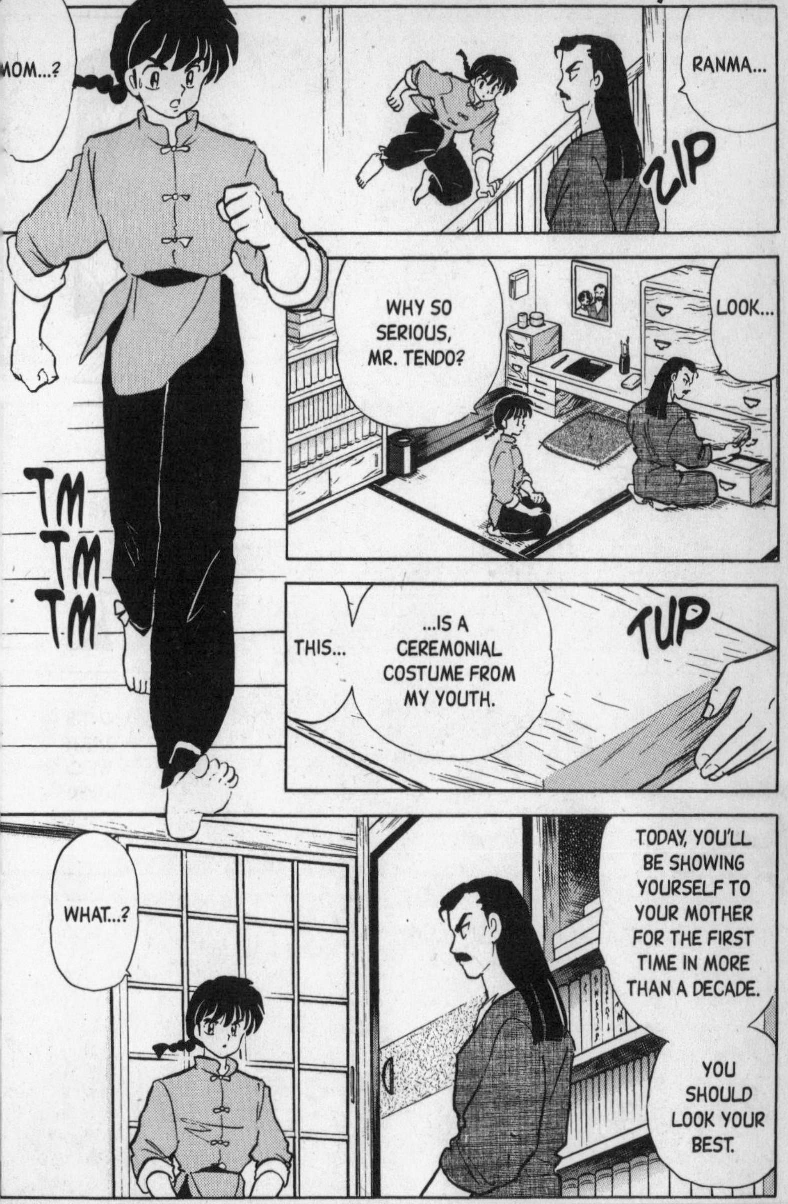
MOM...?
TM
TM
TM
RANMA...
ZIP
WHY SO SERIOUS, MR. TENDO?
LOOK...
THIS...
...IS A CEREMONIAL COSTUME FROM MY YOUTH.
TUP
WHAT...?
TODAY, YOU'LL BE SHOWING YOURSELF TO YOUR MOTHER FOR THE FIRST TIME IN MORE THAN A DECADE.
YOU SHOULD LOOK YOUR BEST.

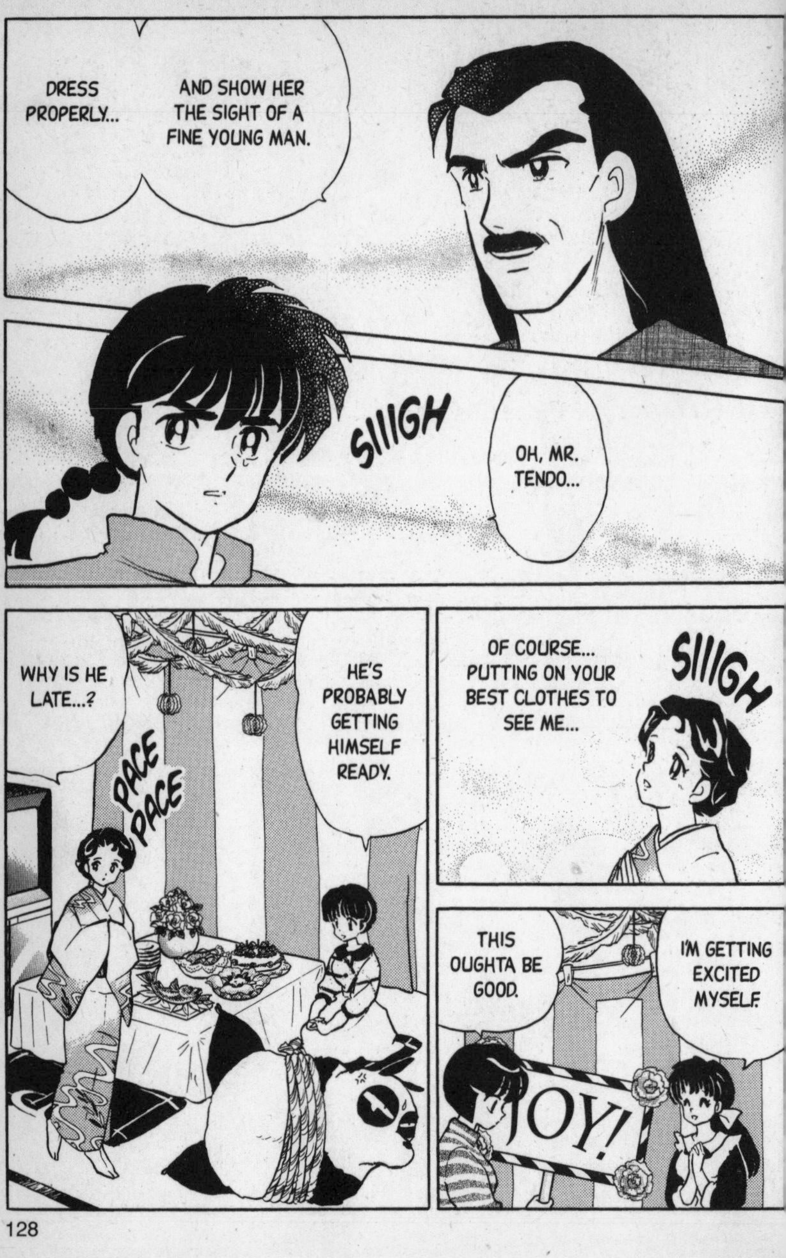
DRESS PROPERLY...
AND SHOW HER THE SIGHT OF A FINE YOUNG MAN.
SIIIGH
OH, MR. TENDO...
WHY IS HE LATE...?
PACE PACE
HE'S PROBABLY GETTING HIMSELF READY.
OF COURSE... PUTTING ON YOUR BEST CLOTHES TO SEE ME...
SIIIGH
THIS OUGHTA BE GOOD.
I'M GETTING EXCITED MYSELF.
JOY!

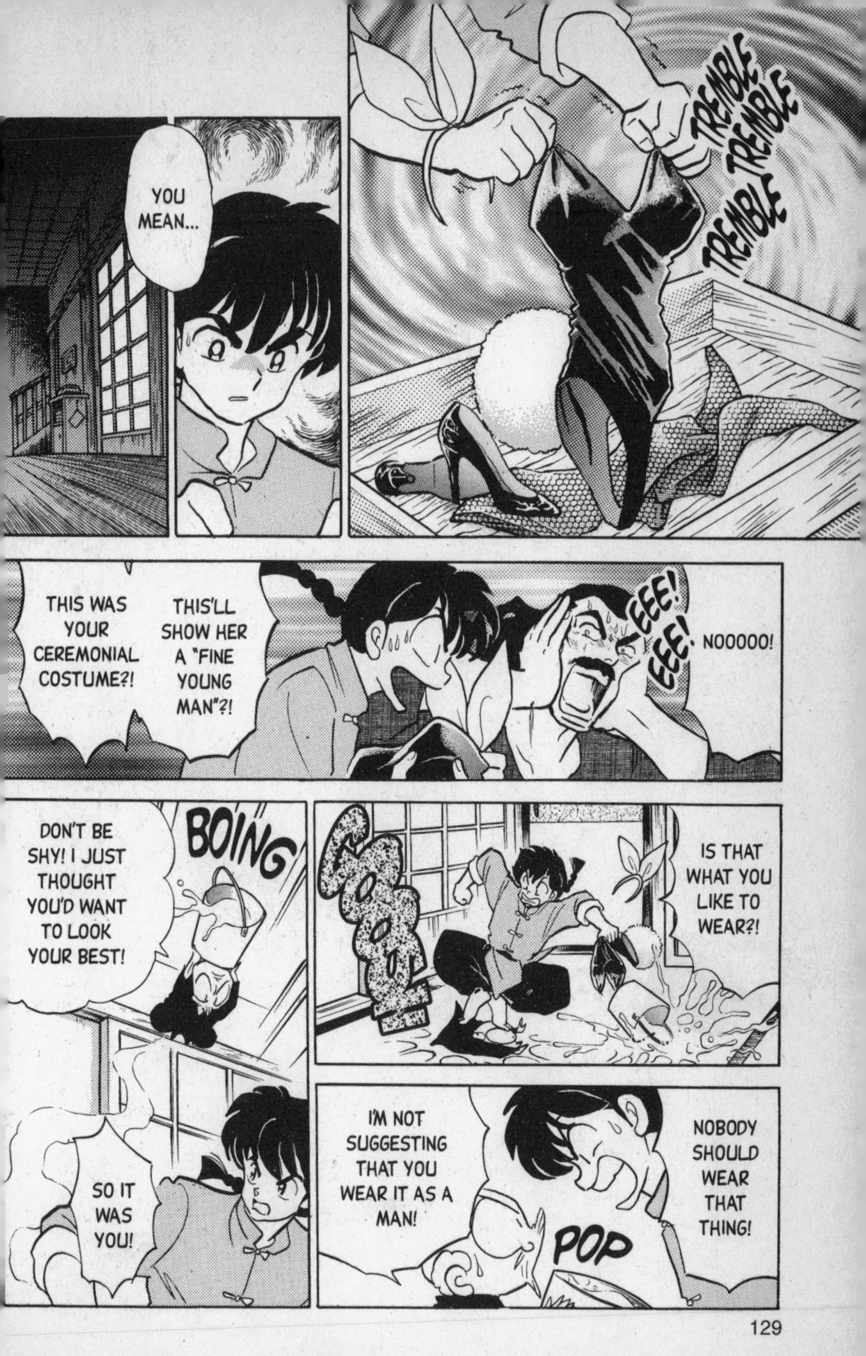
YOU MEAN...
TREMBLE TREMBLE TREMBLE
THIS WAS YOUR CEREMONIAL COSTUME?!
THIS'LL SHOW HER A "FINE YOUNG MAN"?!
EEE! EEE!
NOOOOO!
DON'T BE SHY! I JUST THOUGHT YOU'D WANT TO LOOK YOUR BEST!
BOING
GOOOO
IS THAT WHAT YOU LIKE TO WEAR?!
SO IT WAS YOU!
I'M NOT SUGGESTING THAT YOU WEAR IT AS A MAN!
NOBODY SHOULD WEAR THAT THING!
POP

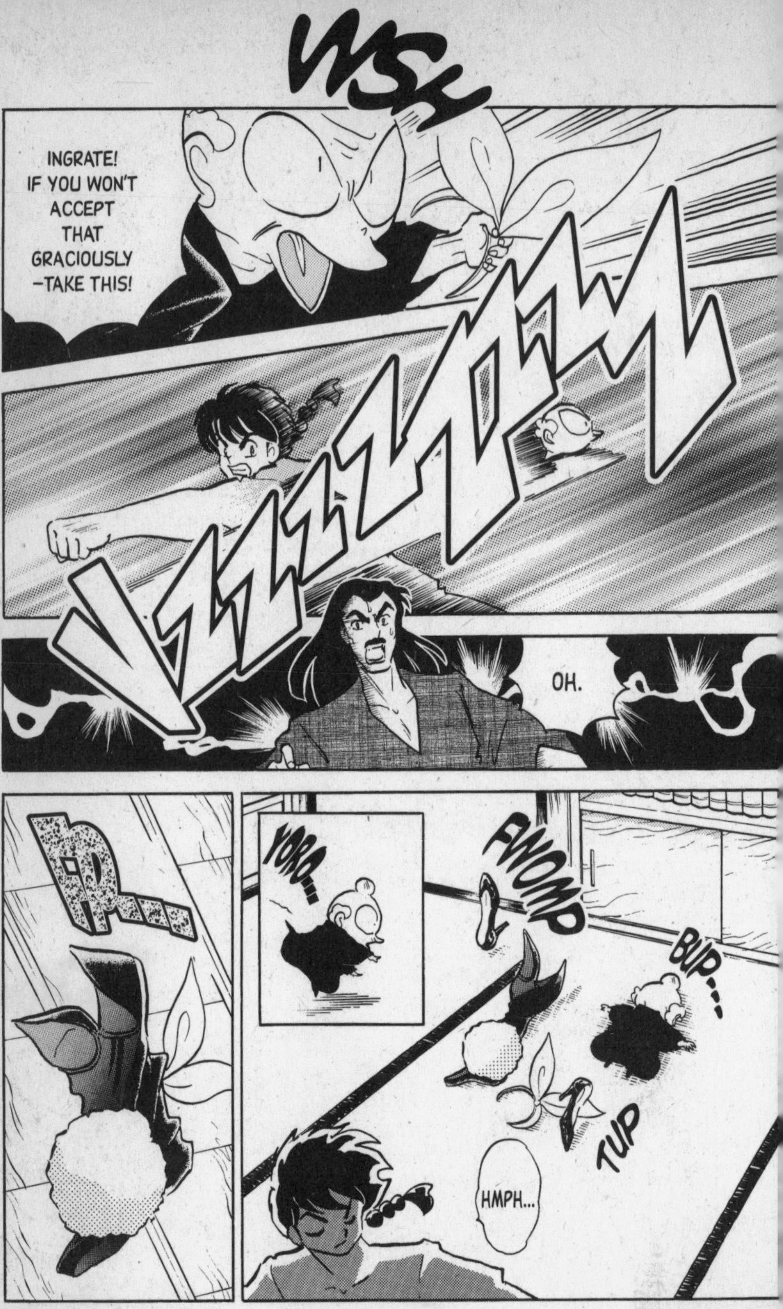
WSH
INGRATE! IF YOU WON'T ACCEPT THAT GRACIOUSLY —TAKE THIS!
OH.
YORO...
FWOMP
BUP...
TUP
HMPH...

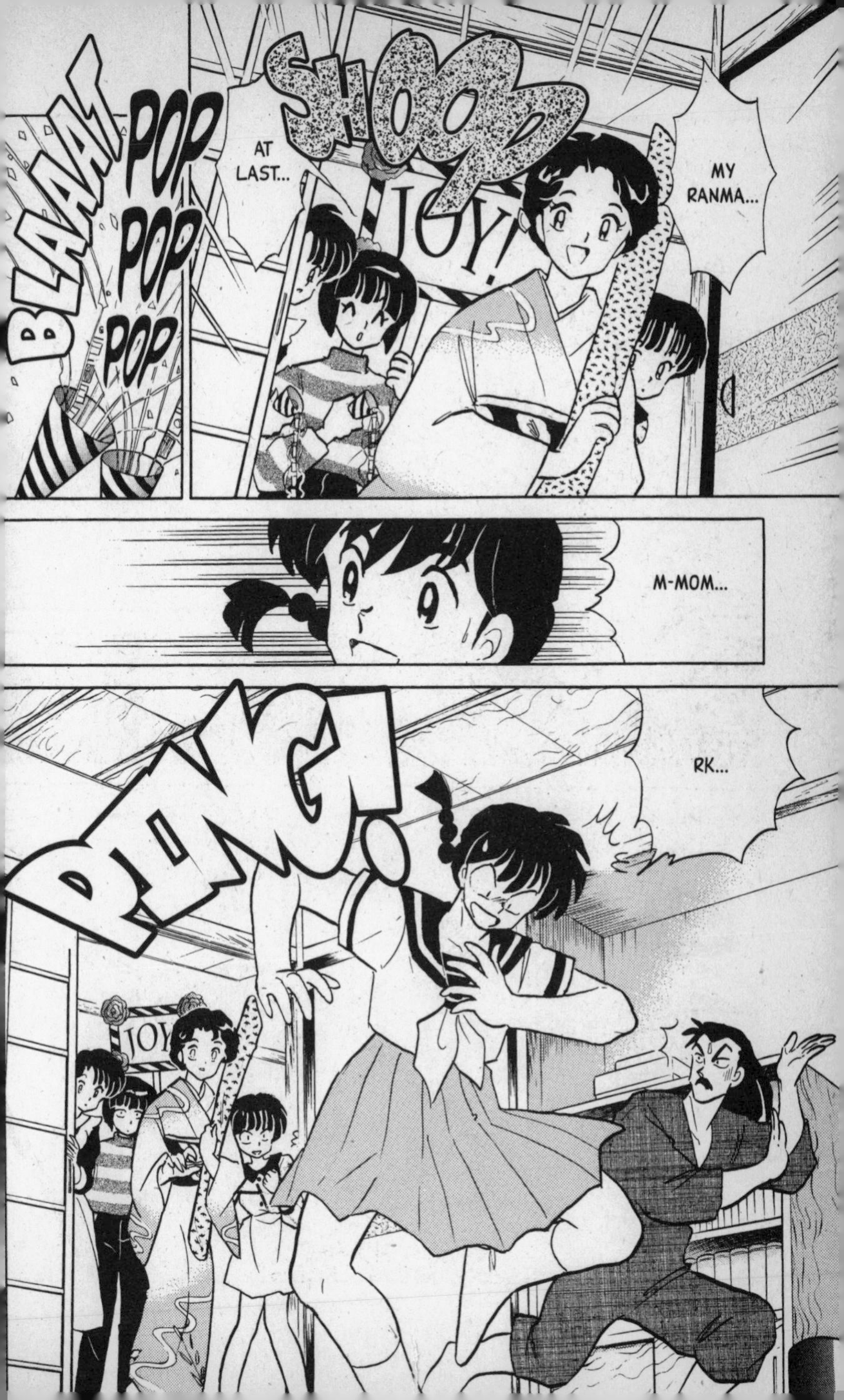
BLAAAT
POP
POP
POP
POP
AT LAST...
SHOOP
JOY!
MY RANMA...
M-MOM...
RK...
BOING!
JOY

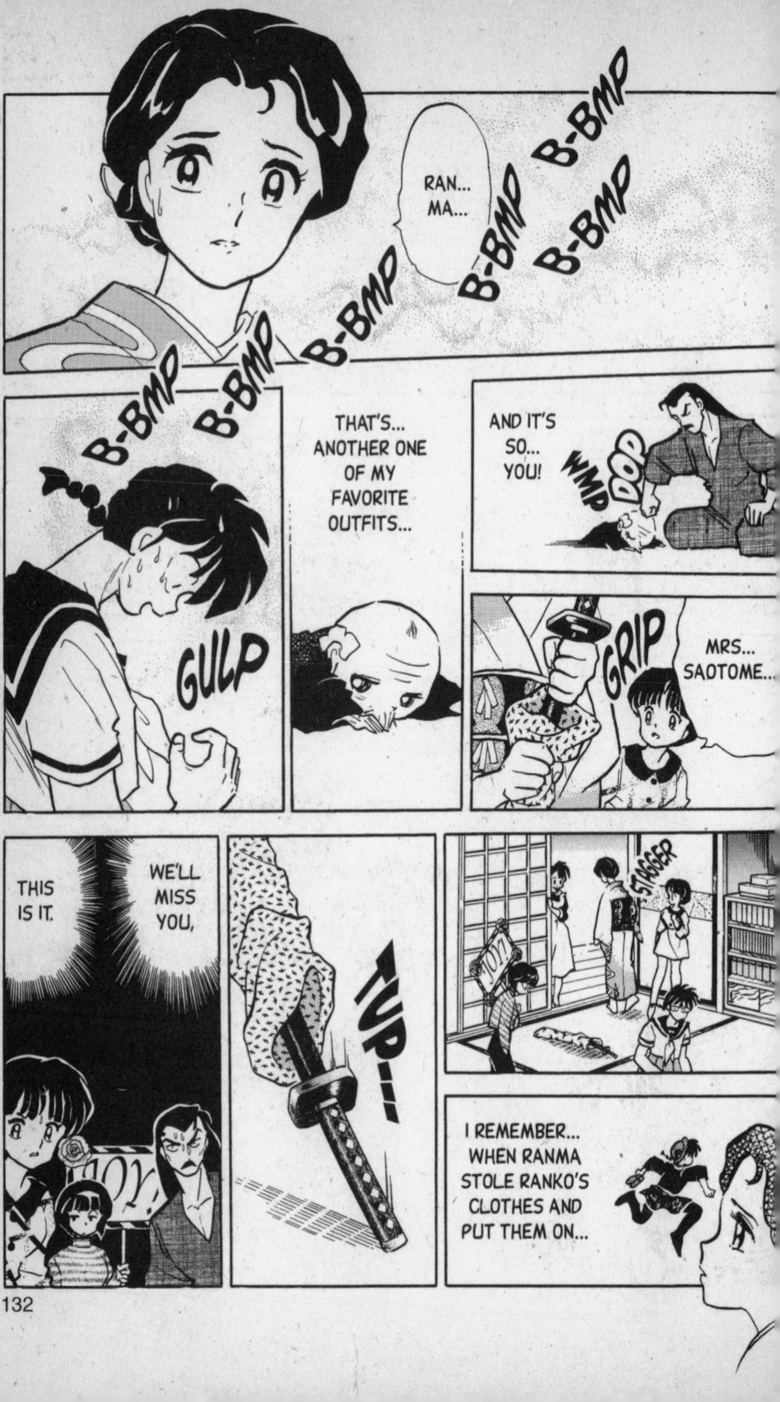

RAN... MA...
B-BMP B-BMP B-BMP B-BMP B-BMP
B-BMP B-BMP
GULP
THAT'S... ANOTHER ONE OF MY FAVORITE OUTFITS...
AND IT'S SO... YOU!
WMP
DOP
GRIP
MRS... SAOTOME...
THIS IS IT.
WE'LL MISS YOU,
TUP...
STAGGER
I REMEMBER... WHEN RANMA STOLE RANKO'S CLOTHES AND PUT THEM ON...

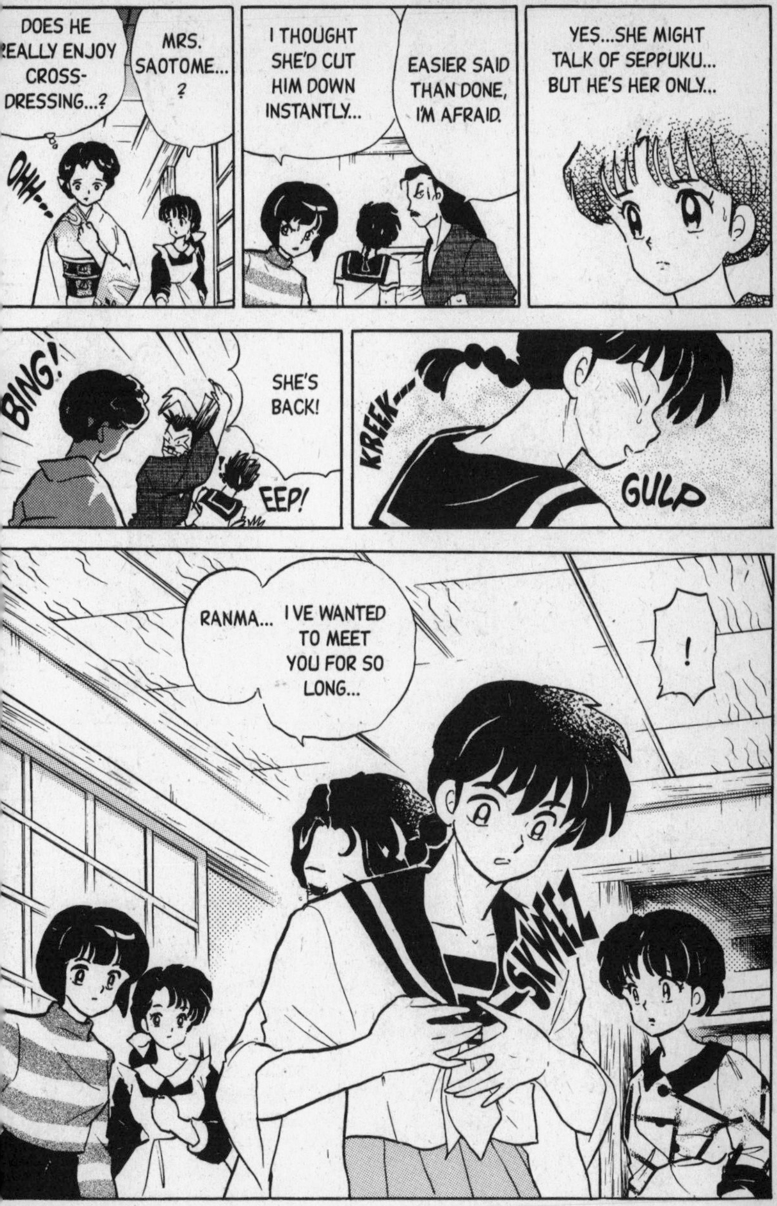
DOES HE REALLY ENJOY CROSS-DRESSING...?
MRS. SAOTOME...?
OHH...
I THOUGHT SHE'D CUT HIM DOWN INSTANTLY...
EASIER SAID THAN DONE, I'M AFRAID.
YES...SHE MIGHT TALK OF SEPPUKU... BUT HE'S HER ONLY...
BING!
SHE'S BACK!
EEP!
KREEK...
GULP
RANMA...
I'VE WANTED TO MEET YOU FOR SO LONG...
!
SKWEEZ

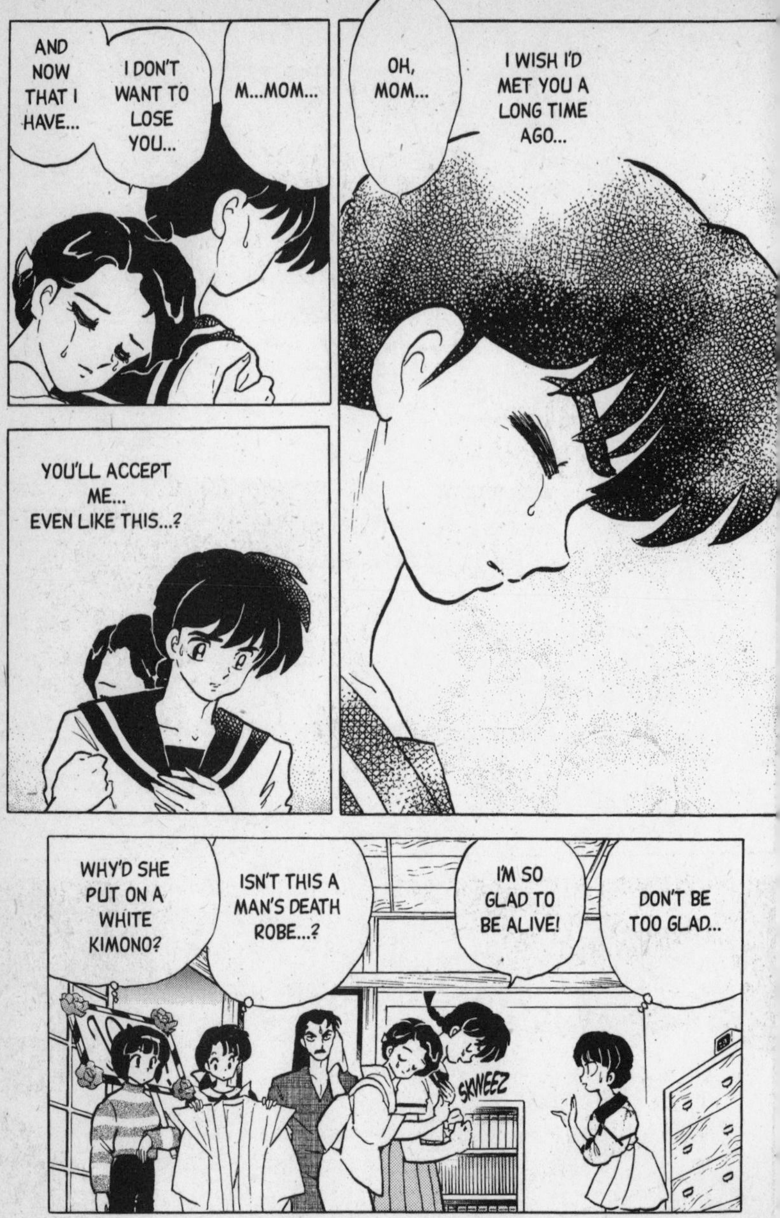
AND NOW THAT I HAVE...
I DON'T WANT TO LOSE YOU...
M...MOM...
YOU'LL ACCEPT ME... EVEN LIKE THIS...?
OH, MOM...
I WISH I'D MET YOU A LONG TIME AGO...
WHY'D SHE PUT ON A WHITE KIMONO?
ISN'T THIS A MAN'S DEATH ROBE...?
I'M SO GLAD TO BE ALIVE!
DON'T BE TOO GLAD...
SKWEEZ

PART 9

SEE ME FOR WHAT I AM

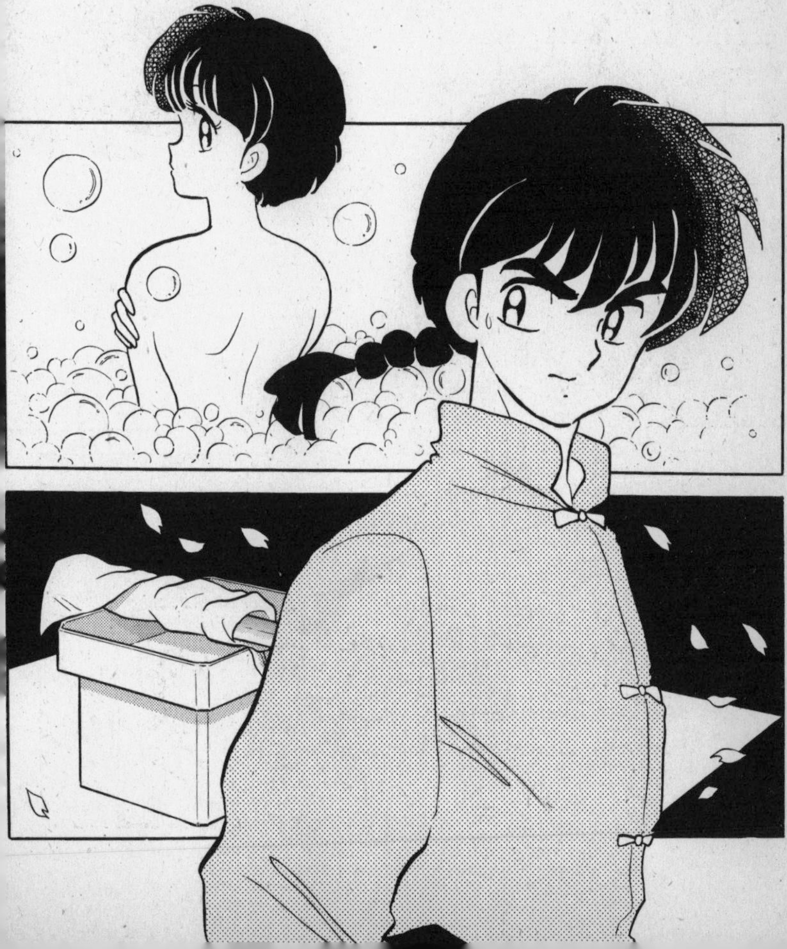

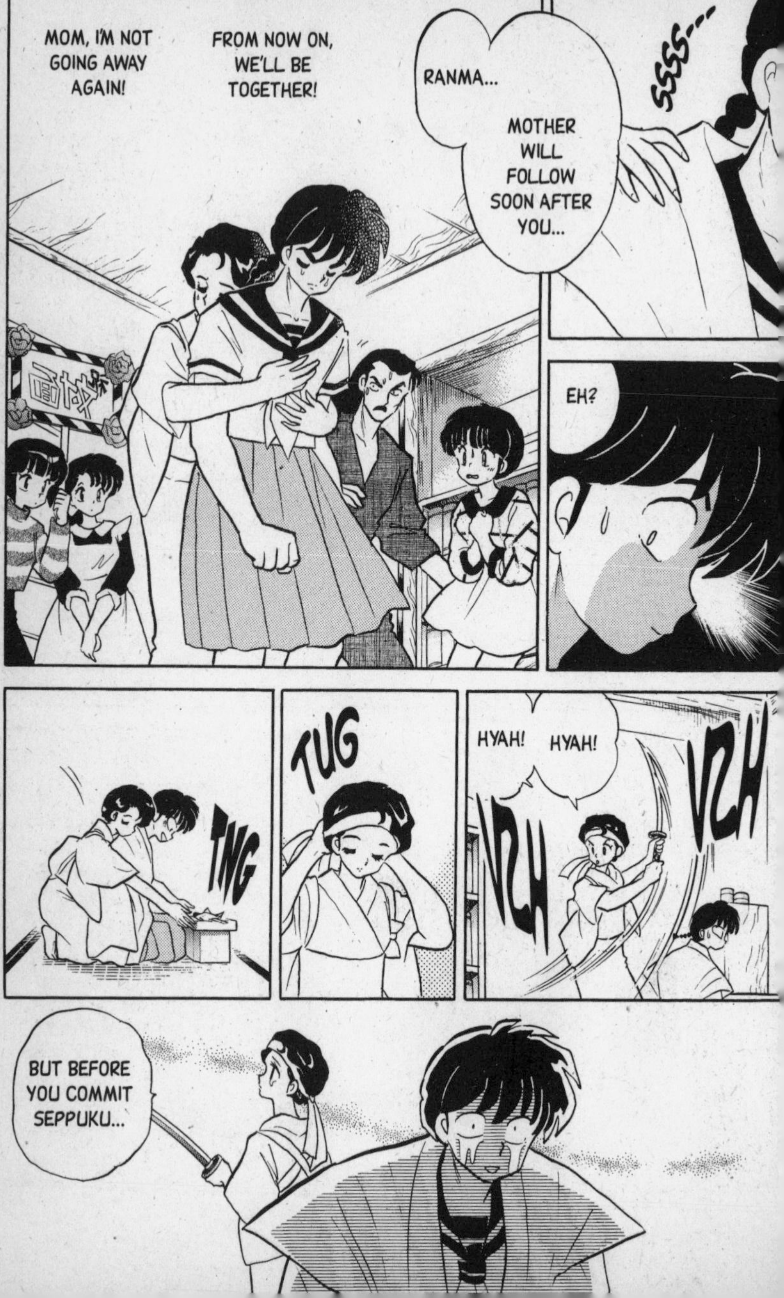
MOM, I'M NOT GOING AWAY AGAIN!
FROM NOW ON, WE'LL BE TOGETHER!
RANMA...
MOTHER WILL FOLLOW SOON AFTER YOU...
SSSS---
EH?
TNG
TUG
HYAH!
HYAH!
VZH
VZH
BUT BEFORE YOU COMMIT SEPPUKU...

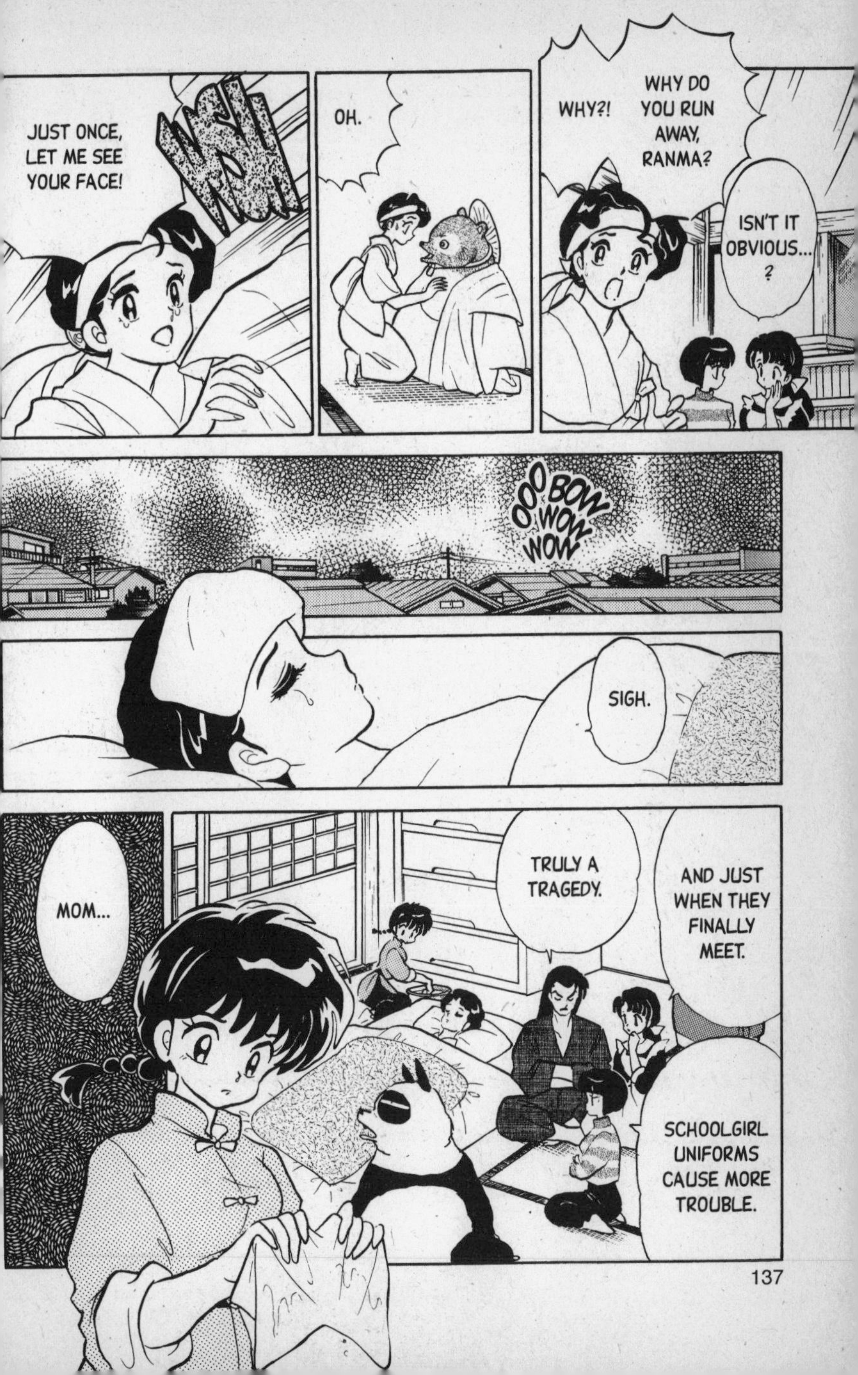
JUST ONCE, LET ME SEE YOUR FACE!
WSH
OH.
WHY?!
WHY DO YOU RUN AWAY, RANMA?
ISN'T IT OBVIOUS...?
OOO BOW WOW WOW
SIGH.
MOM...
TRULY A TRAGEDY.
AND JUST WHEN THEY FINALLY MEET.
SCHOOLGIRL UNIFORMS CAUSE MORE TROUBLE.

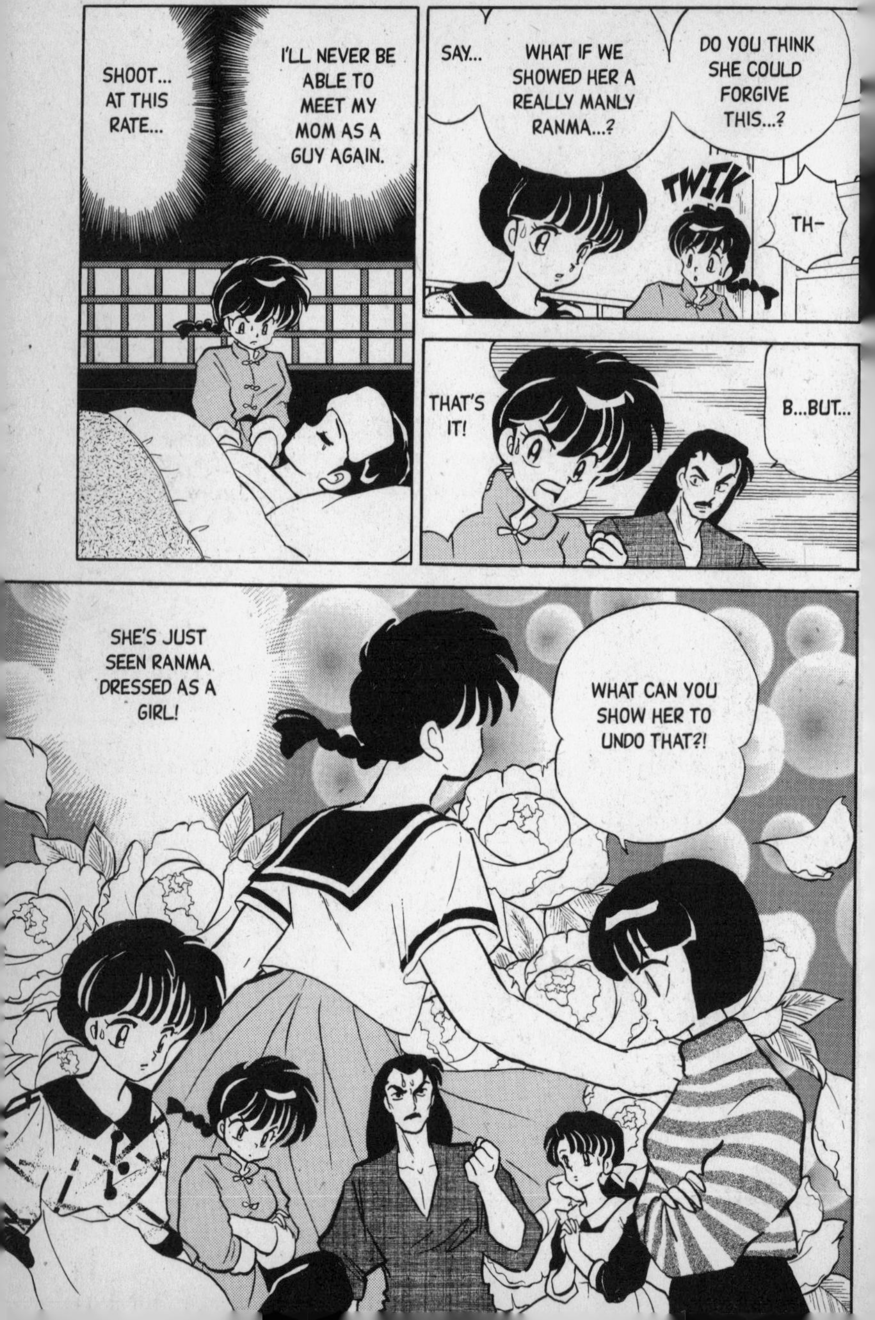
SHOOT... AT THIS RATE...
I'LL NEVER BE ABLE TO MEET MY MOM AS A GUY AGAIN.
SAY...
WHAT IF WE SHOWED HER A REALLY MANLY RANMA...?
DO YOU THINK SHE COULD FORGIVE THIS...?
TWIK
TH-
THAT'S IT!
B...BUT...
SHE'S JUST SEEN RANMA DRESSED AS A GIRL!
WHAT CAN YOU SHOW HER TO UNDO THAT?!

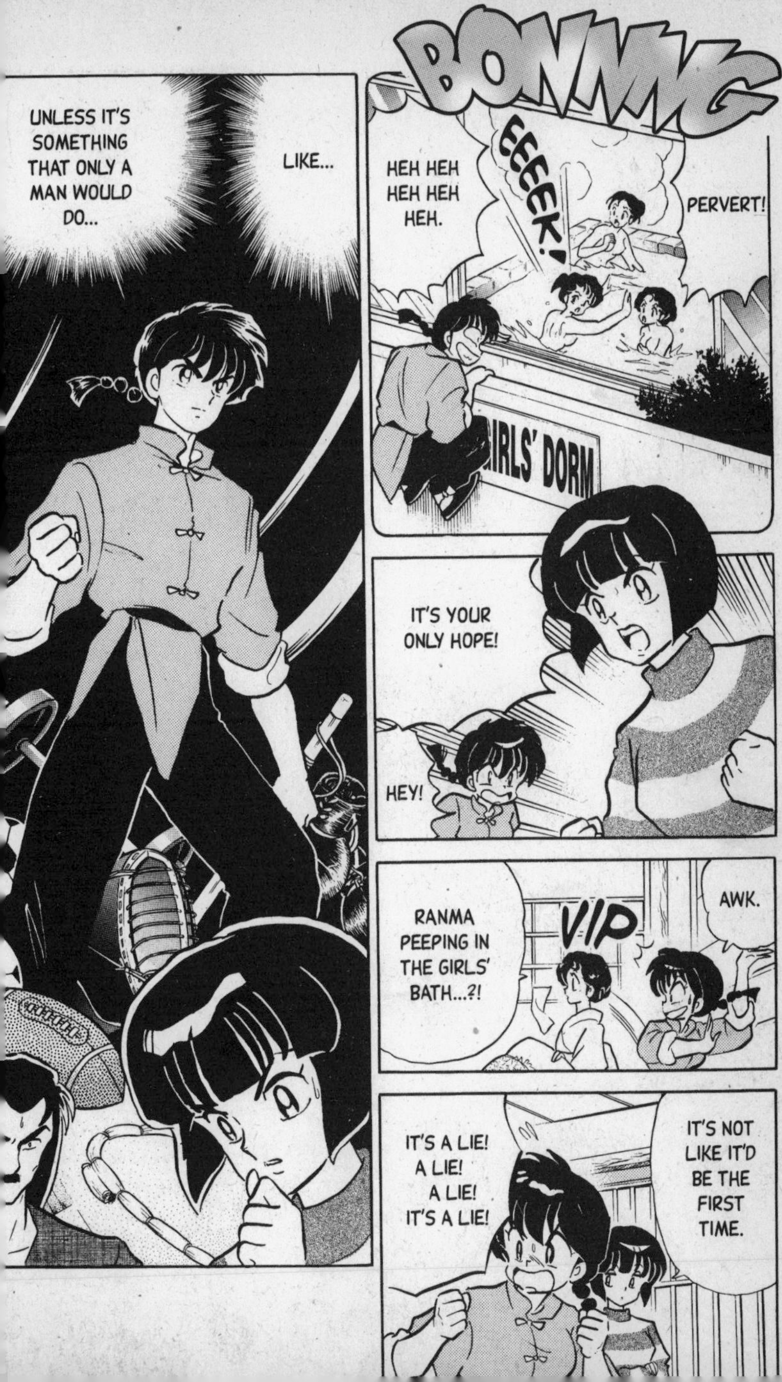
UNLESS IT'S SOMETHING THAT ONLY A MAN WOULD DO...
LIKE...
BONNNG
HEH HEH HEH HEH HEH.
EEEEK!
PERVERT!
GIRLS' DORM
IT'S YOUR ONLY HOPE!
HEY!
RANMA PEEPING IN THE GIRLS' BATH...?!
VIP
AWK.
IT'S A LIE! A LIE! A LIE! IT'S A LIE!
IT'S NOT LIKE IT'D BE THE FIRST TIME.

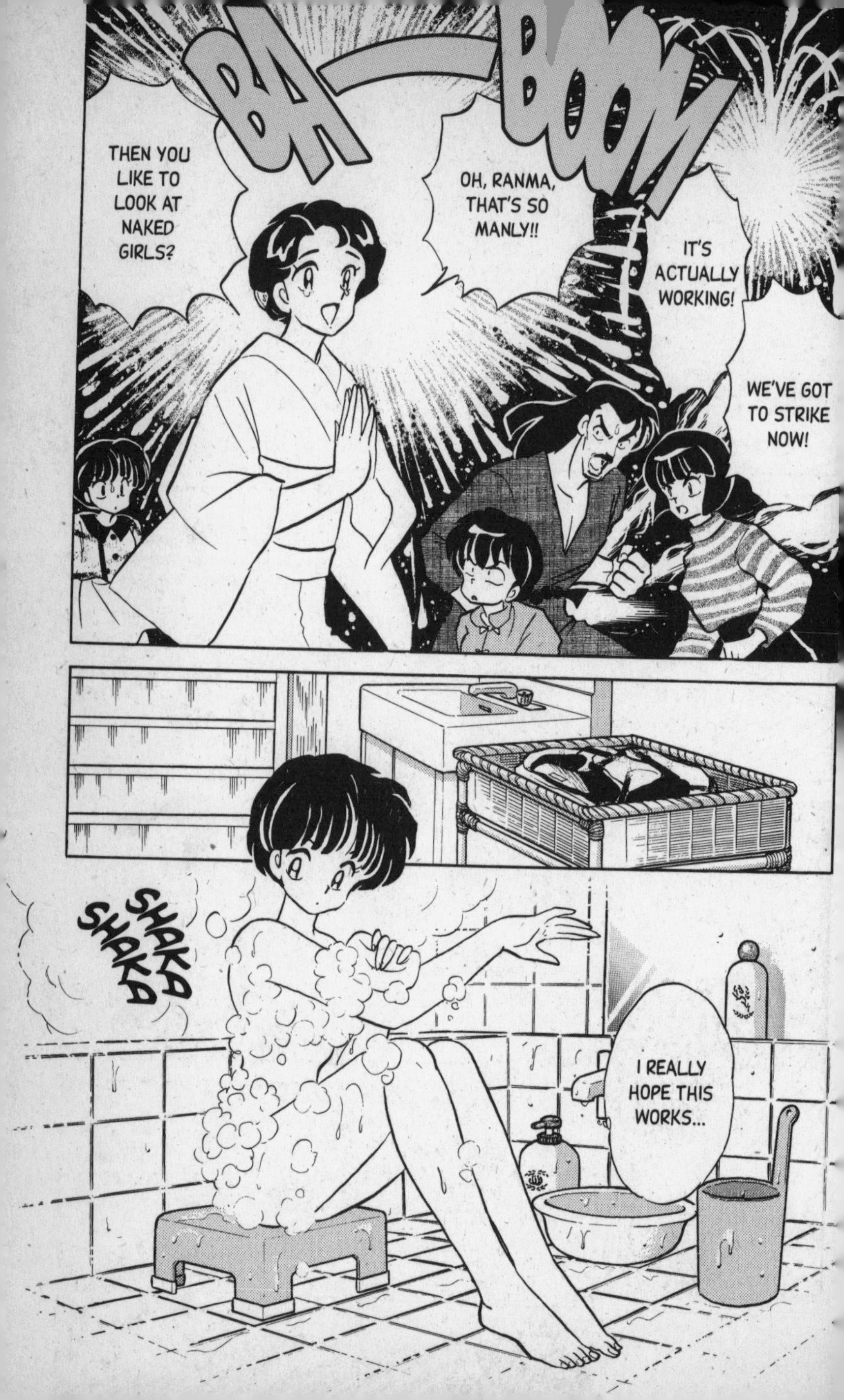
BA—BOOM
THEN YOU LIKE TO LOOK AT NAKED GIRLS?
OH, RANMA, THAT'S SO MANLY!!
IT'S ACTUALLY WORKING!
WE'VE GOT TO STRIKE NOW!
SHAKA SHAKA
I REALLY HOPE THIS WORKS...

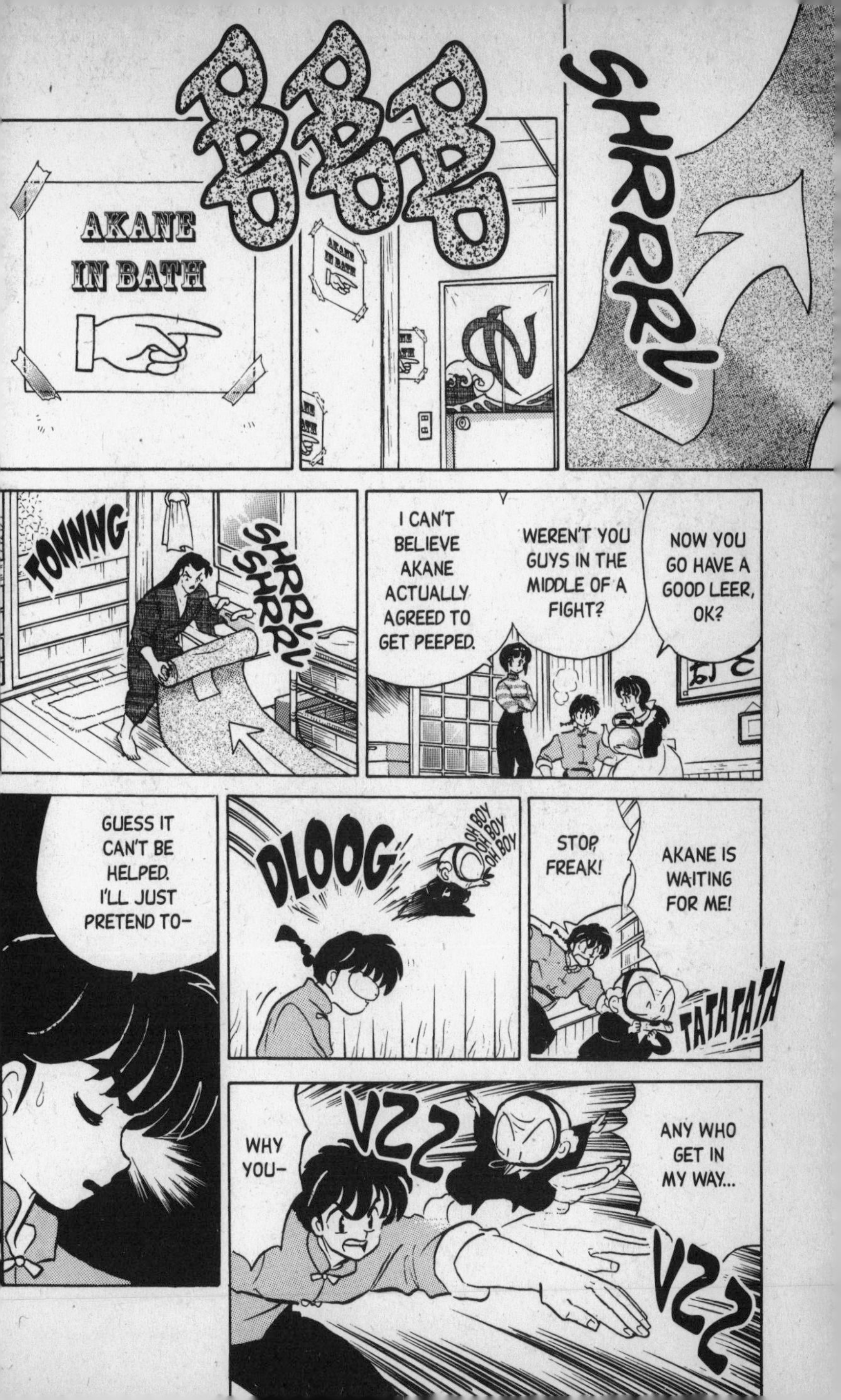
AKANE IN BATH
BBB
AKANE IN BATH
SHRRRU
TONNNG
SHRRU SHRRU
I CAN'T BELIEVE AKANE ACTUALLY AGREED TO GET PEEPED.
WEREN'T YOU GUYS IN THE MIDDLE OF A FIGHT?
NOW YOU GO HAVE A GOOD LEER, OK?
GUESS IT CAN'T BE HELPED. I'LL JUST PRETEND TO–
DLOOG
OH BOY OH BOY OH BOY
STOP, FREAK!
AKANE IS WAITING FOR ME!
TATATATA
WHY YOU–
VZZ
ANY WHO GET IN MY WAY...
VZZ

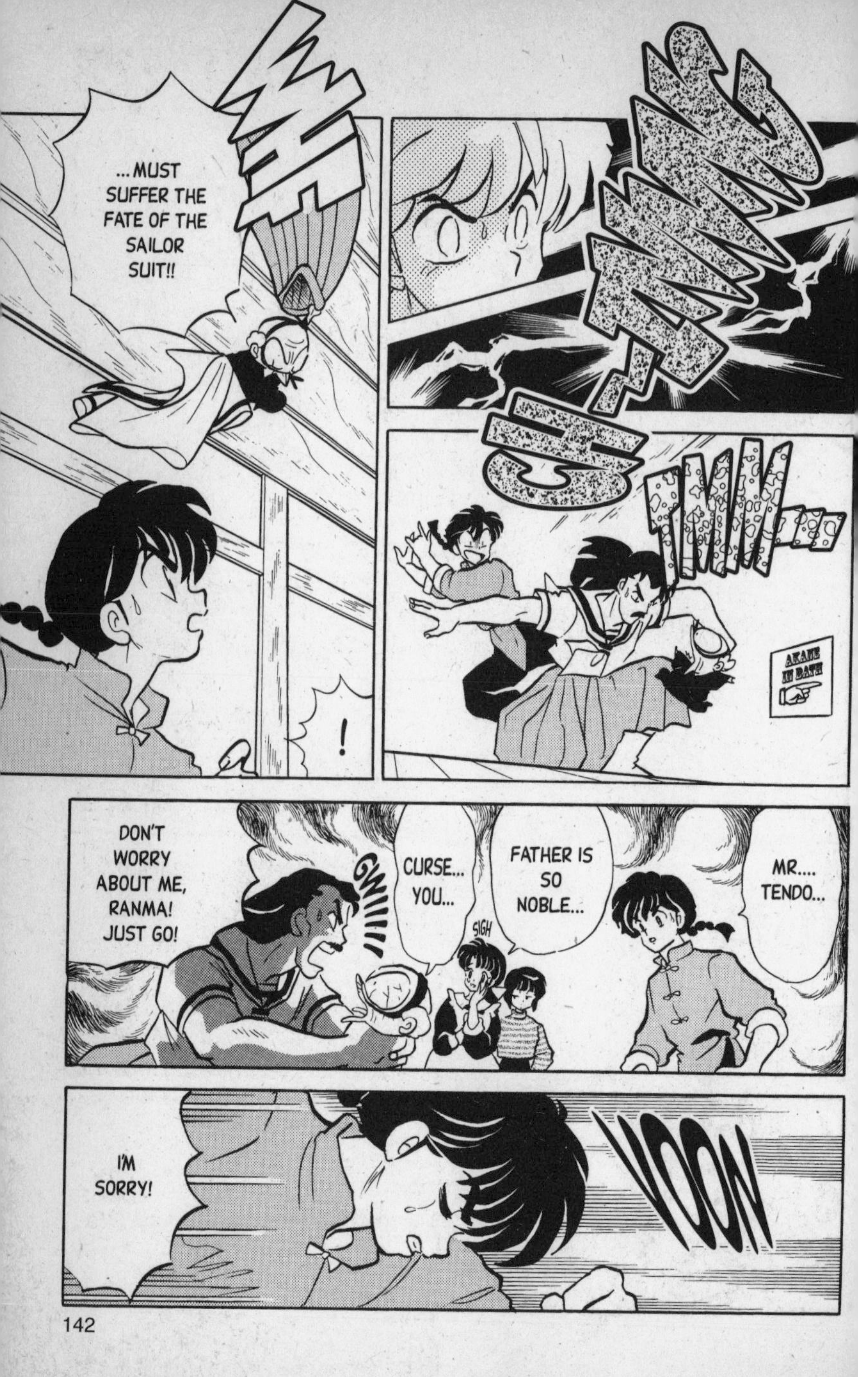

...MUST SUFFER THE FATE OF THE SAILOR SUIT!!
!
AKANE IN BATH
DON'T WORRY ABOUT ME, RANMA! JUST GO!
CURSE... YOU...
SIGH
FATHER IS SO NOBLE...
MR.... TENDO...
I'M SORRY!
VOOM

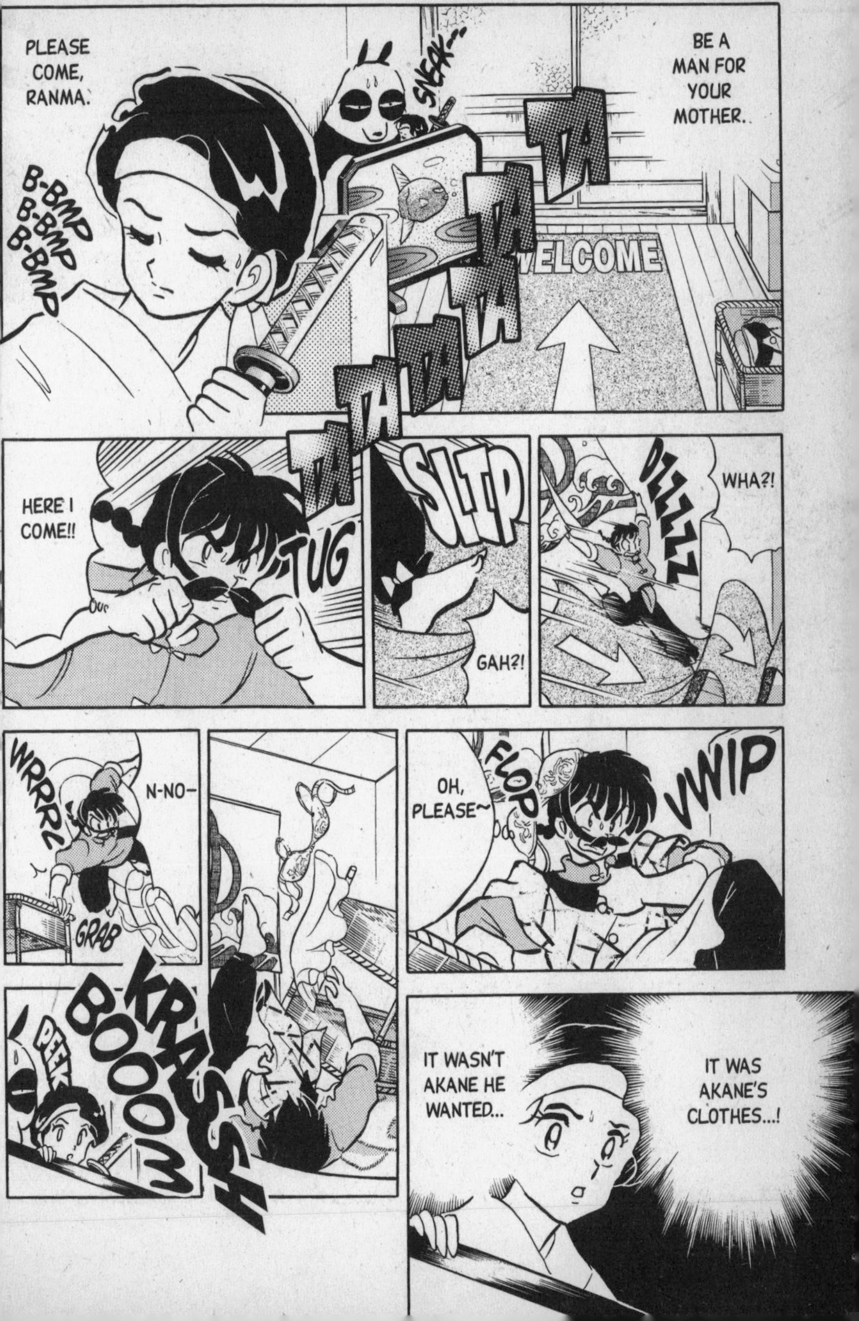
PLEASE COME, RANMA.
SNEAK--
BE A MAN FOR YOUR MOTHER..
B-BMP B-BMP B-BMP
TA TA TA TA TA TA TA
WELCOME
HERE I COME!!
TUG
SLTP
GAH?!
DZZZZZZ
WHA?!
WRRRRC
N-NO-
GRAB
OH, PLEASE~
FLOP
VWIP
PEEK
KRASH
BOOOM
IT WASN'T AKANE HE WANTED...
IT WAS AKANE'S CLOTHES...!

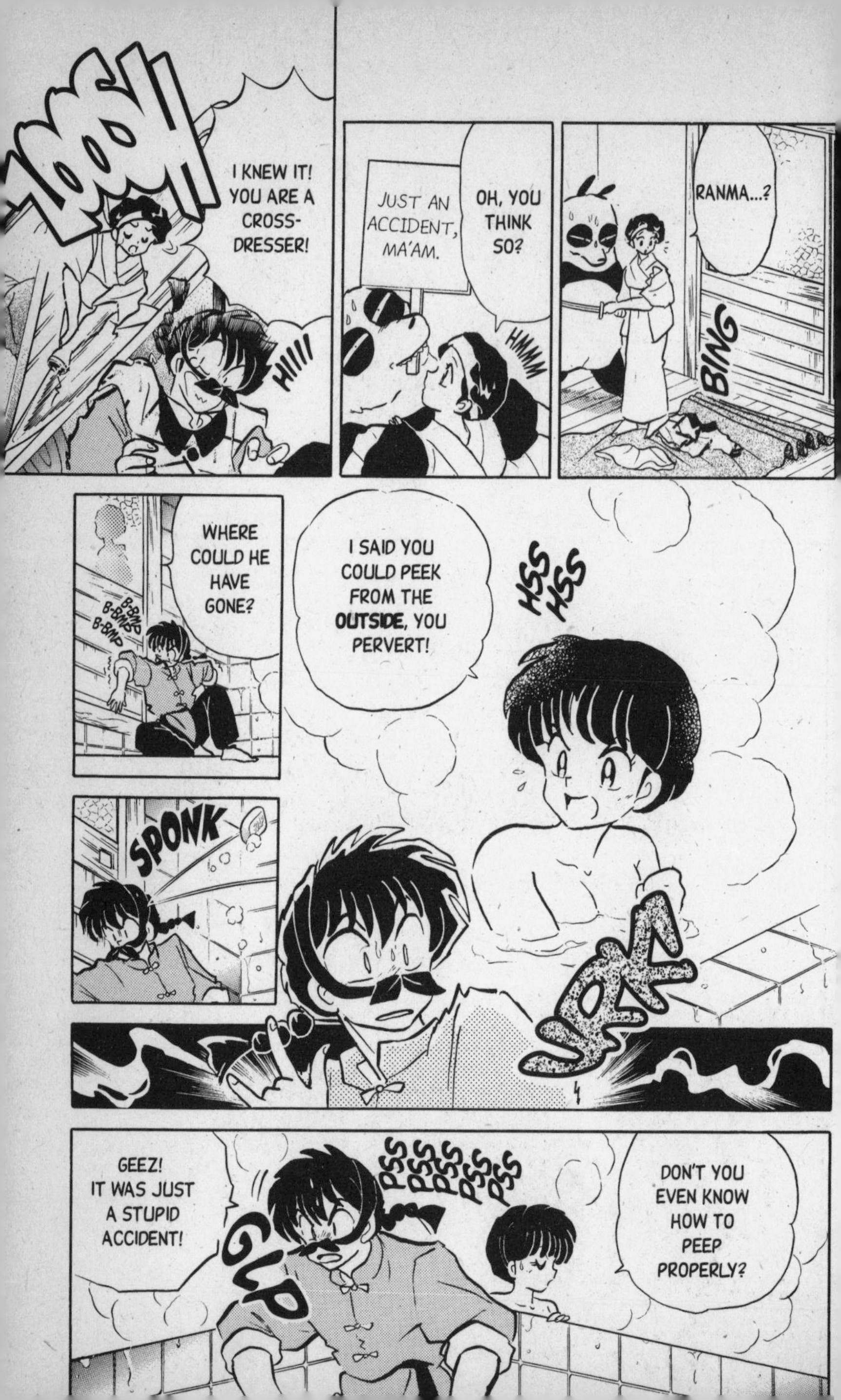
WHOOSH
I KNEW IT! YOU ARE A CROSS-DRESSER!
HI!!!
JUST AN ACCIDENT, MA'AM.
OH, YOU THINK SO?
HMMM
RANMA...?
BING
WHERE COULD HE HAVE GONE?
B-BMP B-BMP B-BMP
SPONK
I SAID YOU COULD PEEK FROM THE **OUTSIDE**, YOU PERVERT!
HSS HSS
GEEZ! IT WAS JUST A STUPID ACCIDENT!
GULP
PSS PSS PSS PSS PSS PSS
DON'T YOU EVEN KNOW HOW TO PEEP PROPERLY?

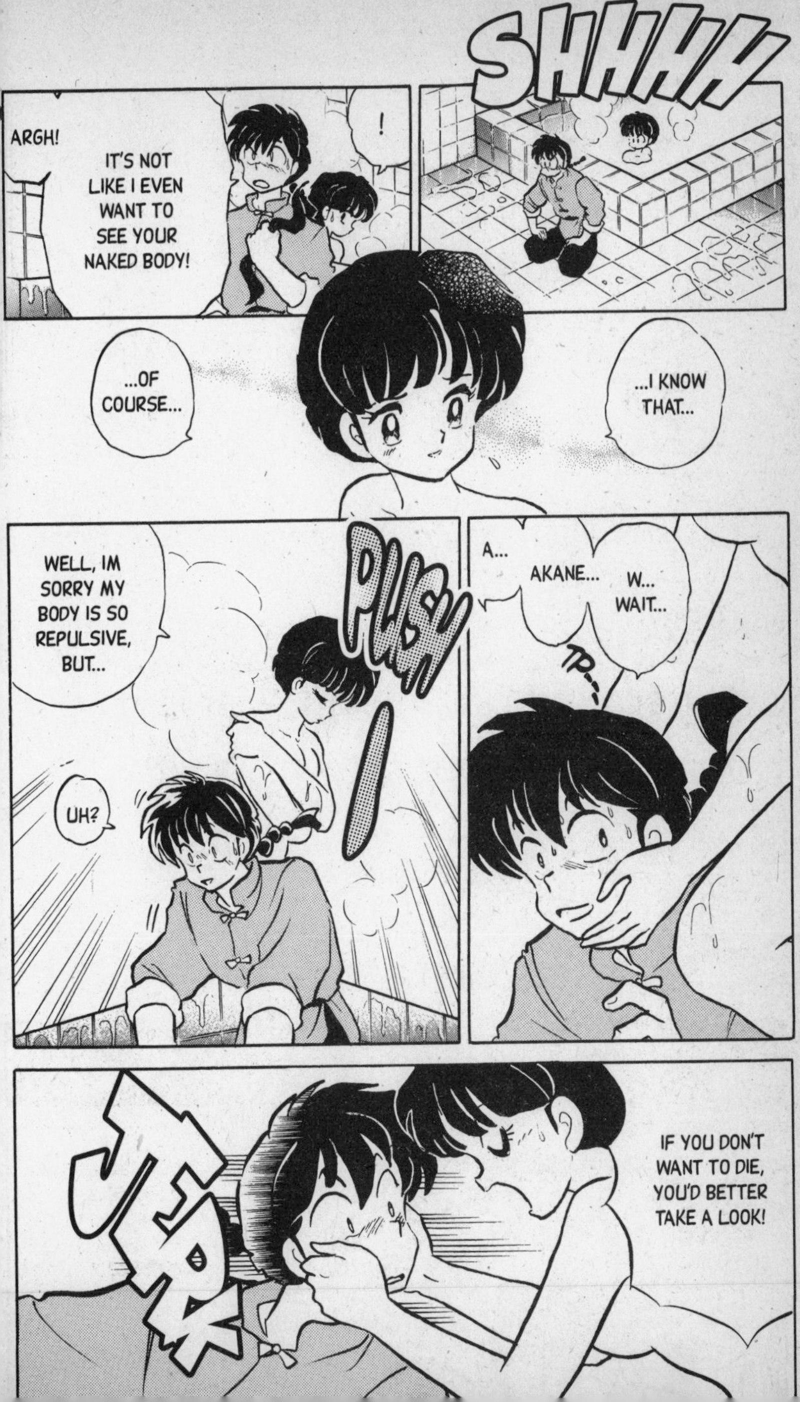
ARGH!
IT'S NOT LIKE I EVEN WANT TO SEE YOUR NAKED BODY!
!
SHHHH
...OF COURSE...
...I KNOW THAT...
WELL, IM SORRY MY BODY IS SO REPULSIVE, BUT...
PUSH
UH?
A...
AKANE...
W... WAIT...
TP...
JERK
IF YOU DON'T WANT TO DIE, YOU'D BETTER TAKE A LOOK!

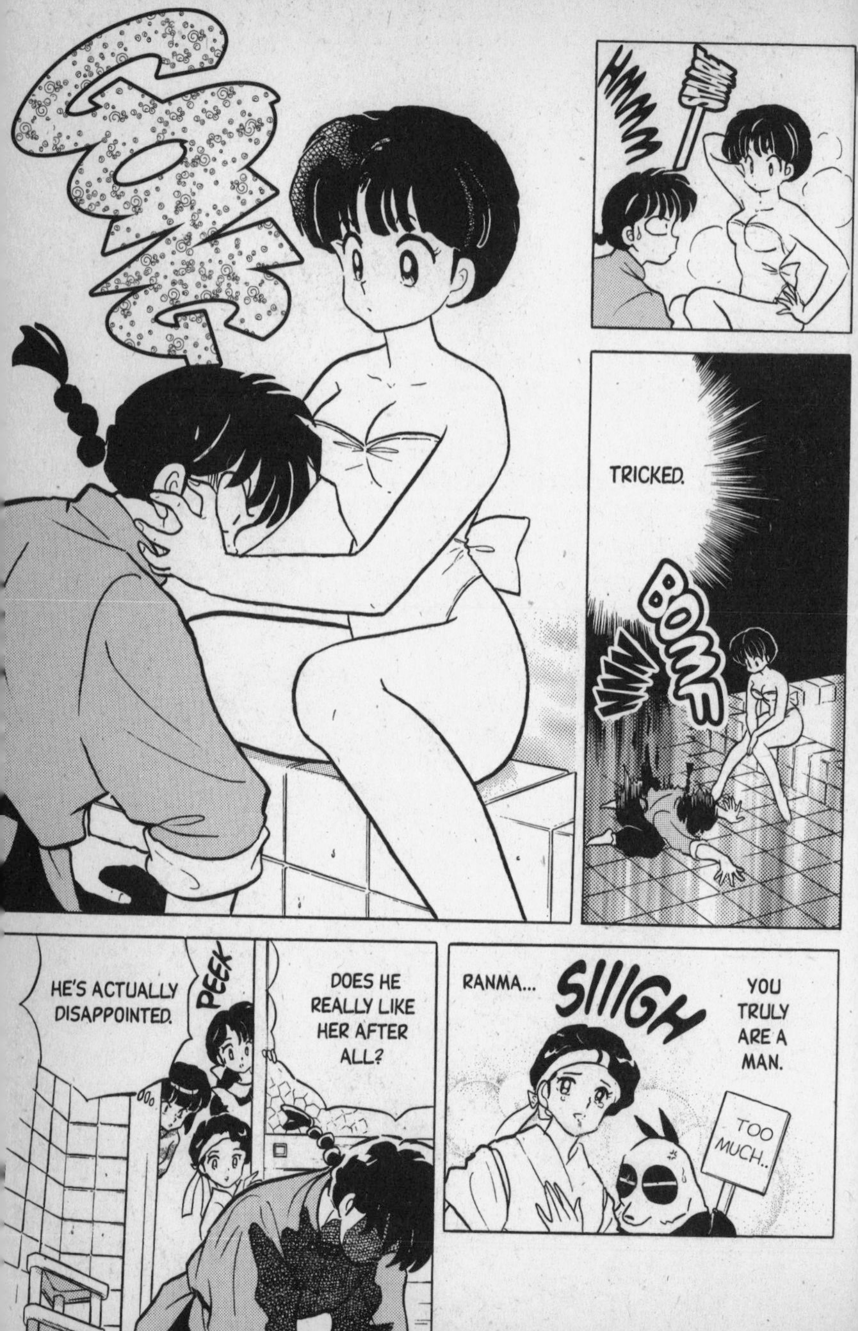
GONG
HMMM
TRICKED.
BOMF
WHAM
HE'S ACTUALLY DISAPPOINTED.
PEEK
DOES HE REALLY LIKE HER AFTER ALL?
RANMA...
SIIIGH
YOU TRULY ARE A MAN.
TOO MUCH..

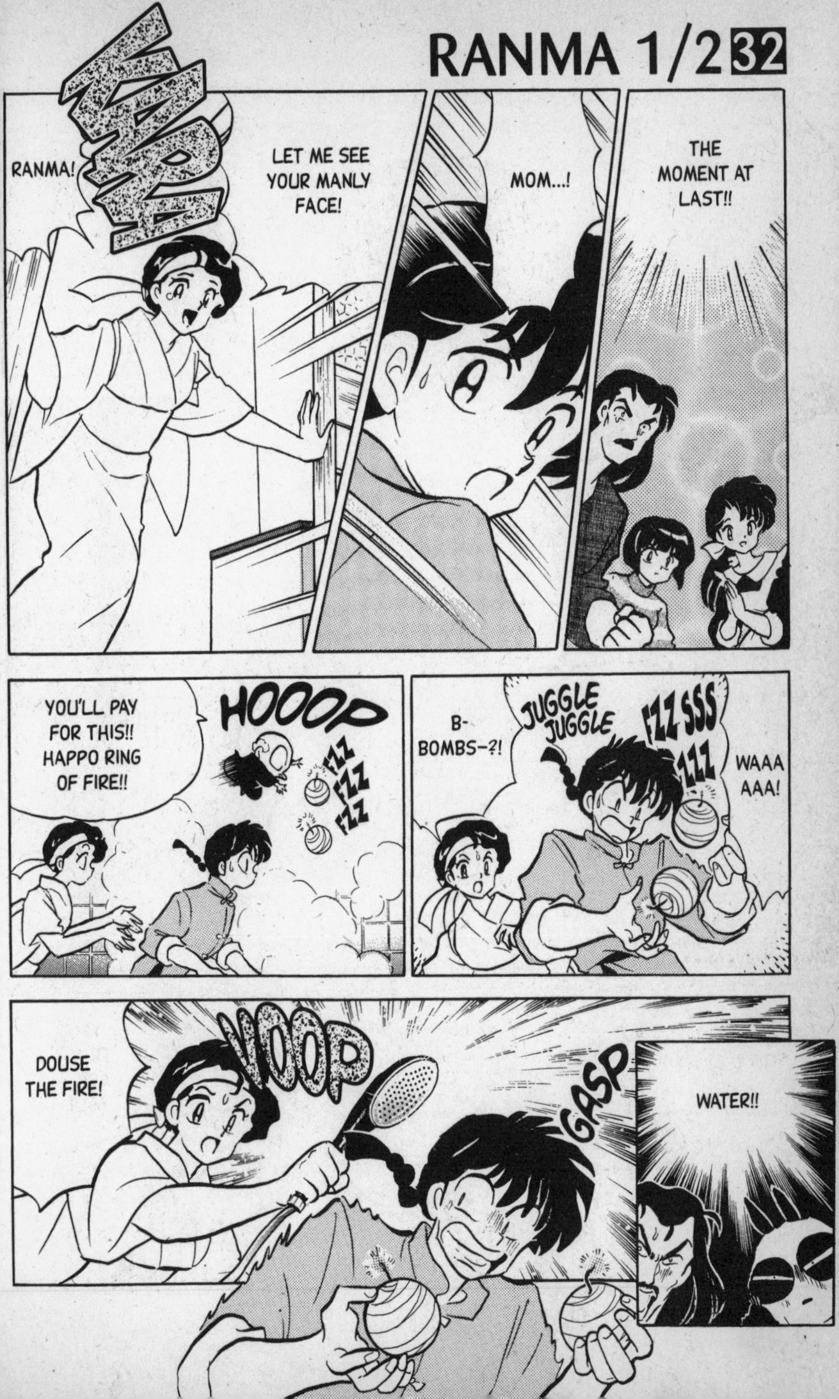
WAPA
RANMA!
LET ME SEE YOUR MANLY FACE!
MOM...!
THE MOMENT AT LAST!!
YOU'LL PAY FOR THIS!! HAPPO RING OF FIRE!!
HOOOP
FZZ FZZ FZZ
B- BOMBS-?!
JUGGLE JUGGLE
FZZ SSS ZZZ
WAAA AAA!
DOUSE THE FIRE!
VOOP
GASP
WATER!!

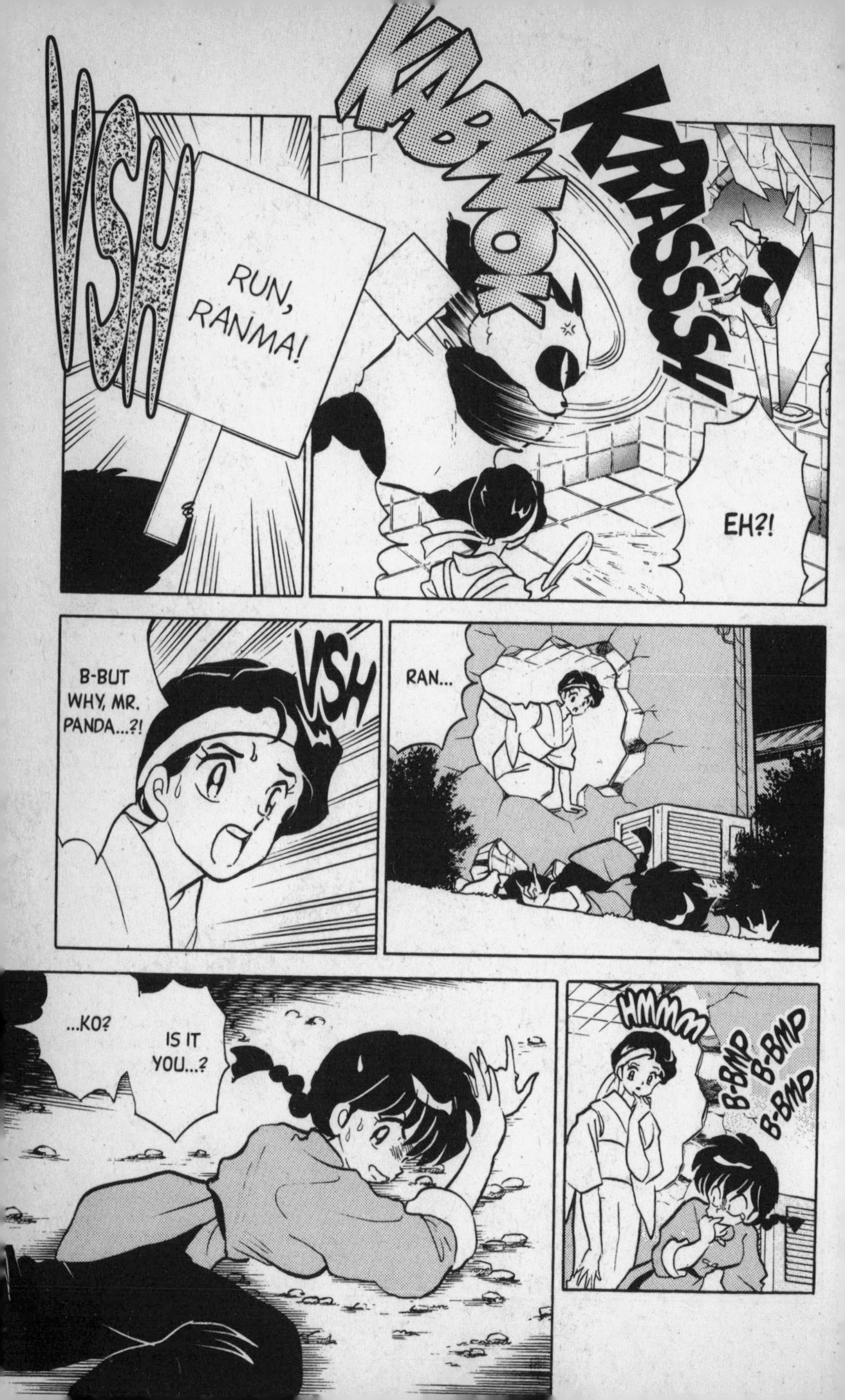
VSH
RUN, RANMA!
KABNOK
KRASSH!
EH?!
B-BUT WHY, MR. PANDA...?!
VSH
RAN...
...KO?
IS IT YOU...?
HMMM
B-BMP B-BMP B-BMP B-BMP

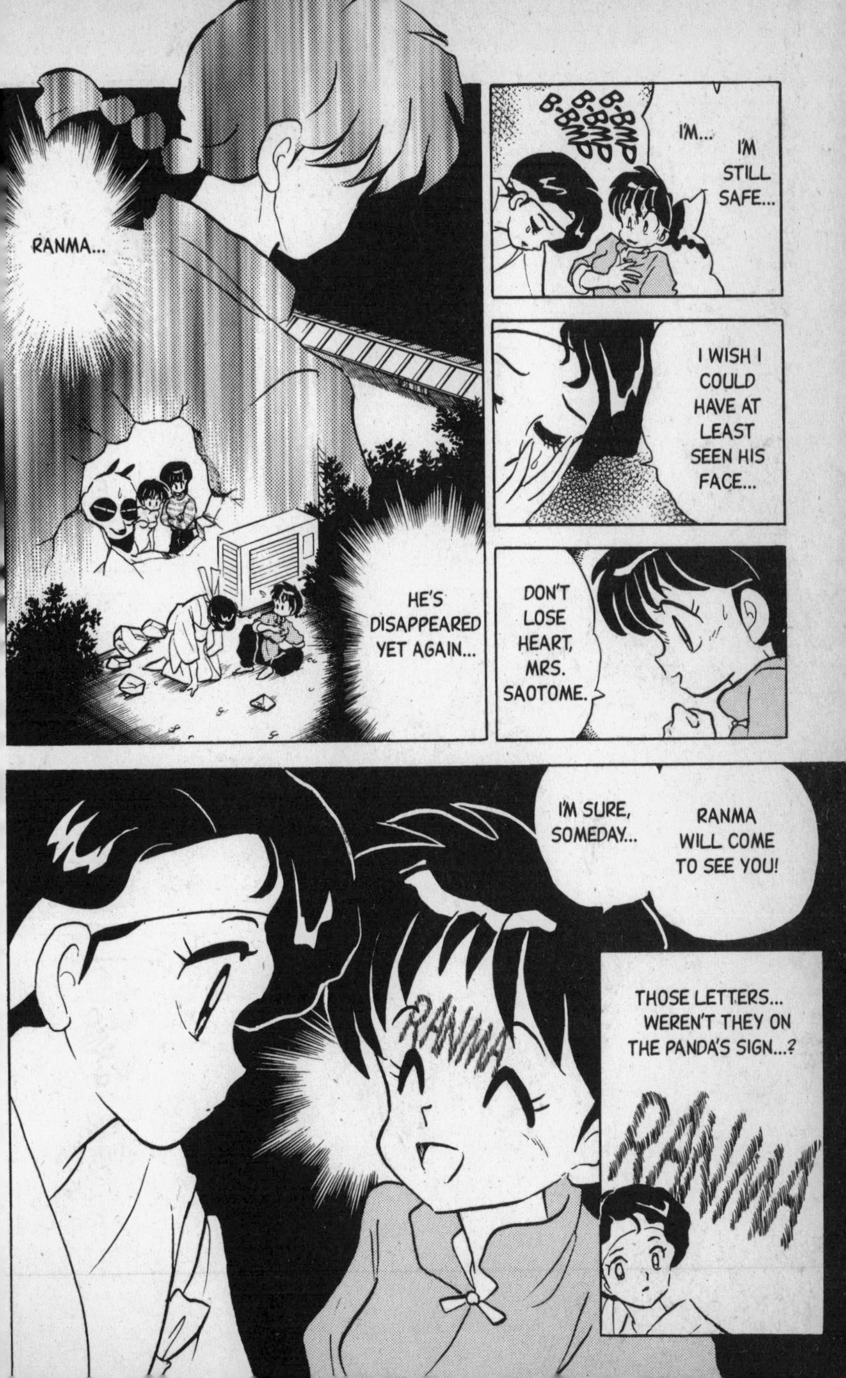
RANMA...
HE'S DISAPPEARED YET AGAIN...
B-BMP B-BMP B-BMP
I'M...
I'M STILL SAFE...
I WISH I COULD HAVE AT LEAST SEEN HIS FACE...
DON'T LOSE HEART, MRS. SAOTOME.
I'M SURE, SOMEDAY...
RANMA WILL COME TO SEE YOU!
THOSE LETTERS... WEREN'T THEY ON THE PANDA'S SIGN...?

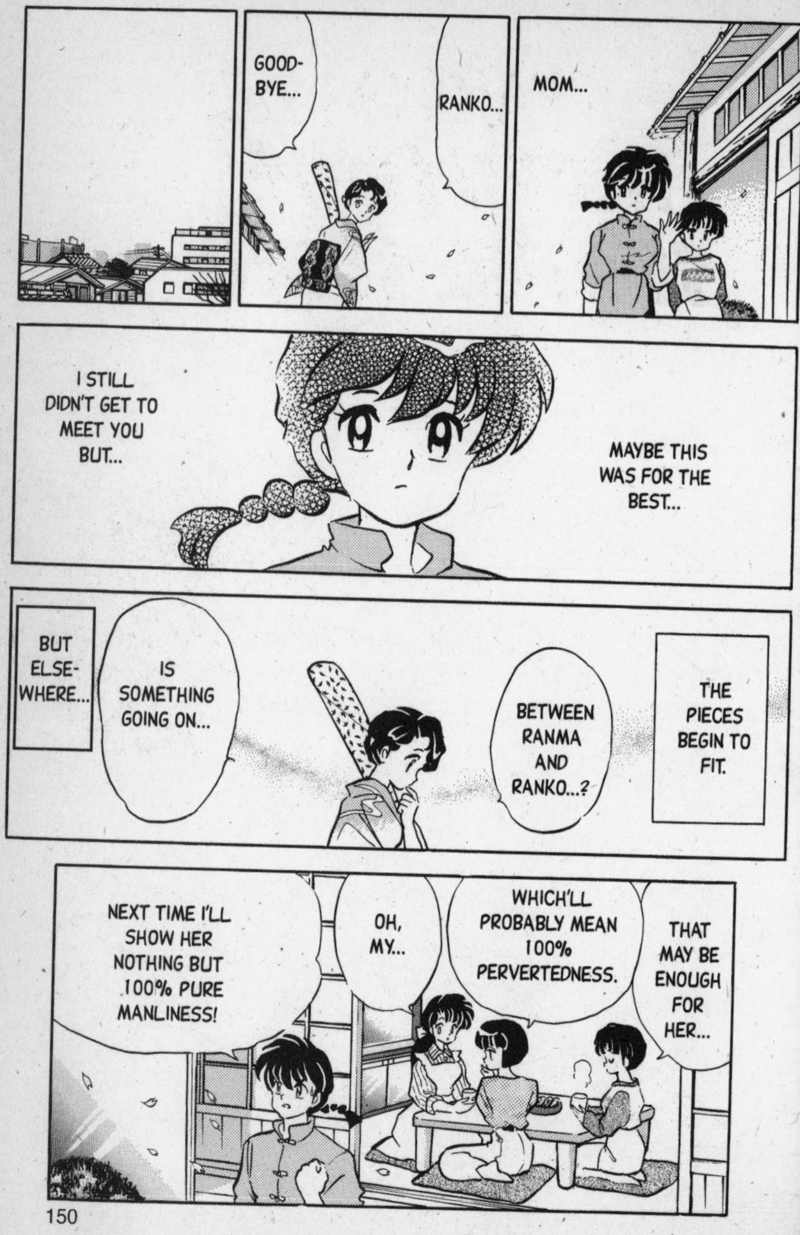

GOOD-BYE...
RANKO...
MOM...
I STILL DIDN'T GET TO MEET YOU BUT...
MAYBE THIS WAS FOR THE BEST...
BUT ELSE-WHERE...
IS SOMETHING GOING ON...
BETWEEN RANMA AND RANKO...?
THE PIECES BEGIN TO FIT.
NEXT TIME I'LL SHOW HER NOTHING BUT 100% PURE MANLINESS!
OH, MY...
WHICH'LL PROBABLY MEAN 100% PERVERTEDNESS.
THAT MAY BE ENOUGH FOR HER...

PART 10

INCENSE OF SPRING SLEEP

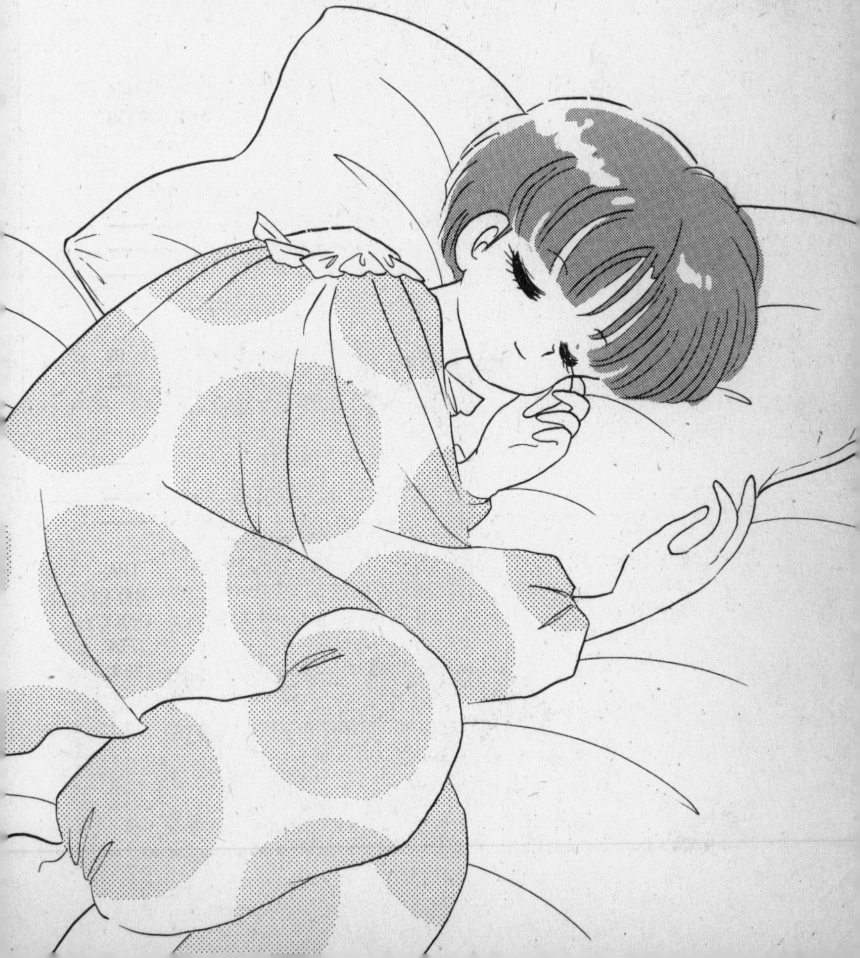

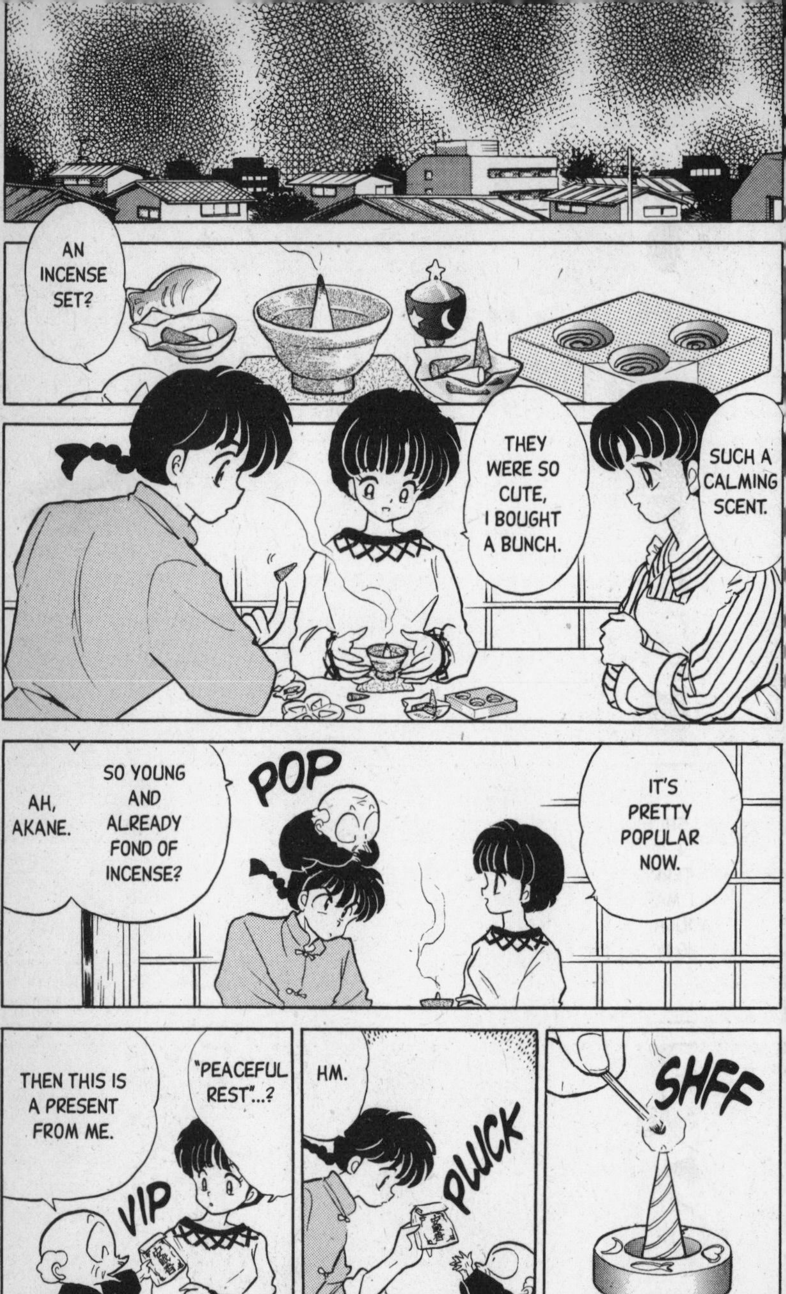
AN INCENSE SET?
THEY WERE SO CUTE, I BOUGHT A BUNCH.
SUCH A CALMING SCENT.
AH, AKANE.
SO YOUNG AND ALREADY FOND OF INCENSE?
POP
IT'S PRETTY POPULAR NOW.
THEN THIS IS A PRESENT FROM ME.
VIP
"PEACEFUL REST"...?
HM.
PLUCK
SHFF

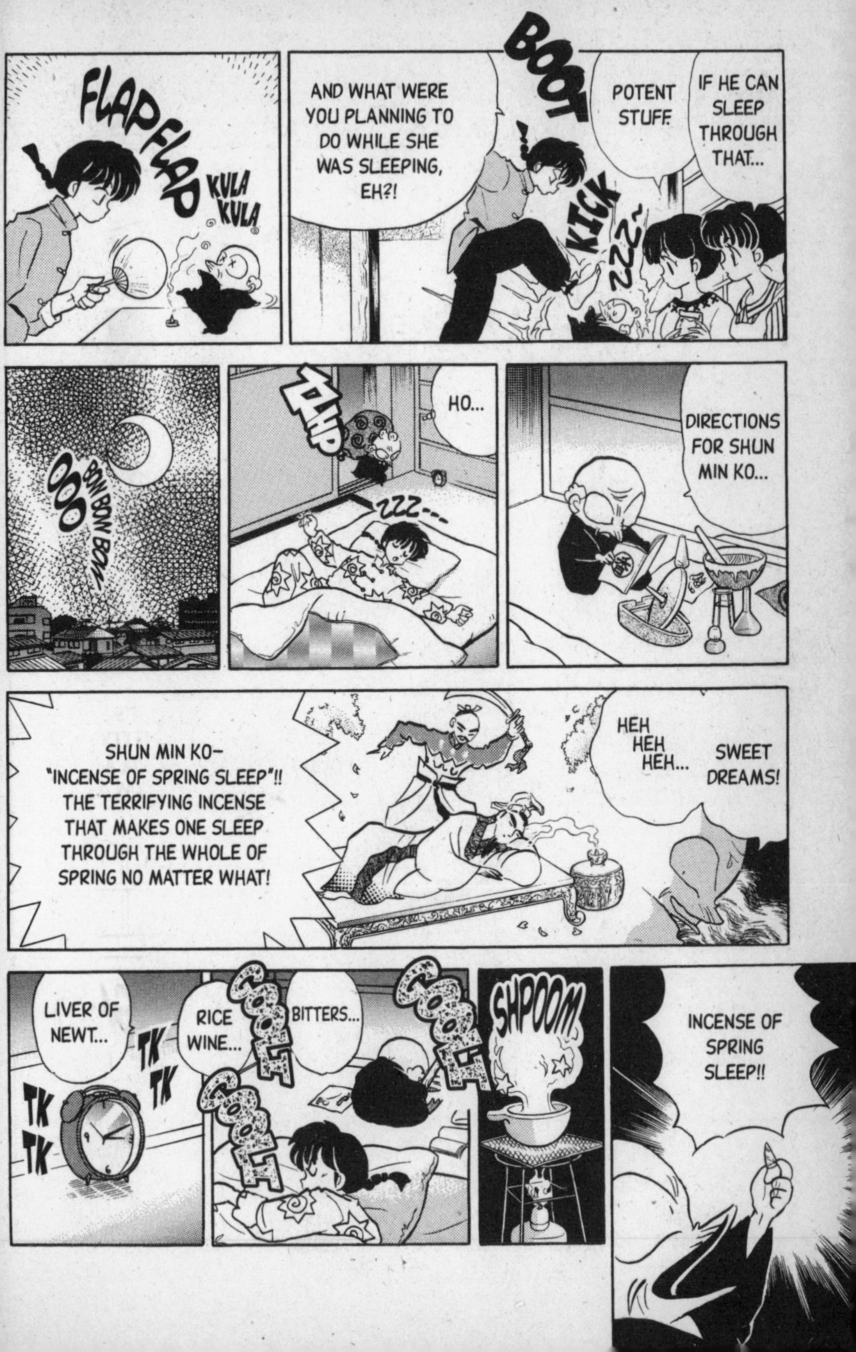
FLAP FLAP
KULA KULA
AND WHAT WERE YOU PLANNING TO DO WHILE SHE WAS SLEEPING, EH?!
BOOT
KICK
ZZZ~
POTENT STUFF.
IF HE CAN SLEEP THROUGH THAT...
BOW BOW BOW OOO
ZZZ---
HO...
DIRECTIONS FOR SHUN MIN KO...
SHUN MIN KO—"INCENSE OF SPRING SLEEP"!! THE TERRIFYING INCENSE THAT MAKES ONE SLEEP THROUGH THE WHOLE OF SPRING NO MATTER WHAT!
HEH HEH HEH...
SWEET DREAMS!
LIVER OF NEWT...
TK TK
TK TK
RICE WINE...
COOL
BITTERS...
COOL
SHPOOM
INCENSE OF SPRING SLEEP!!

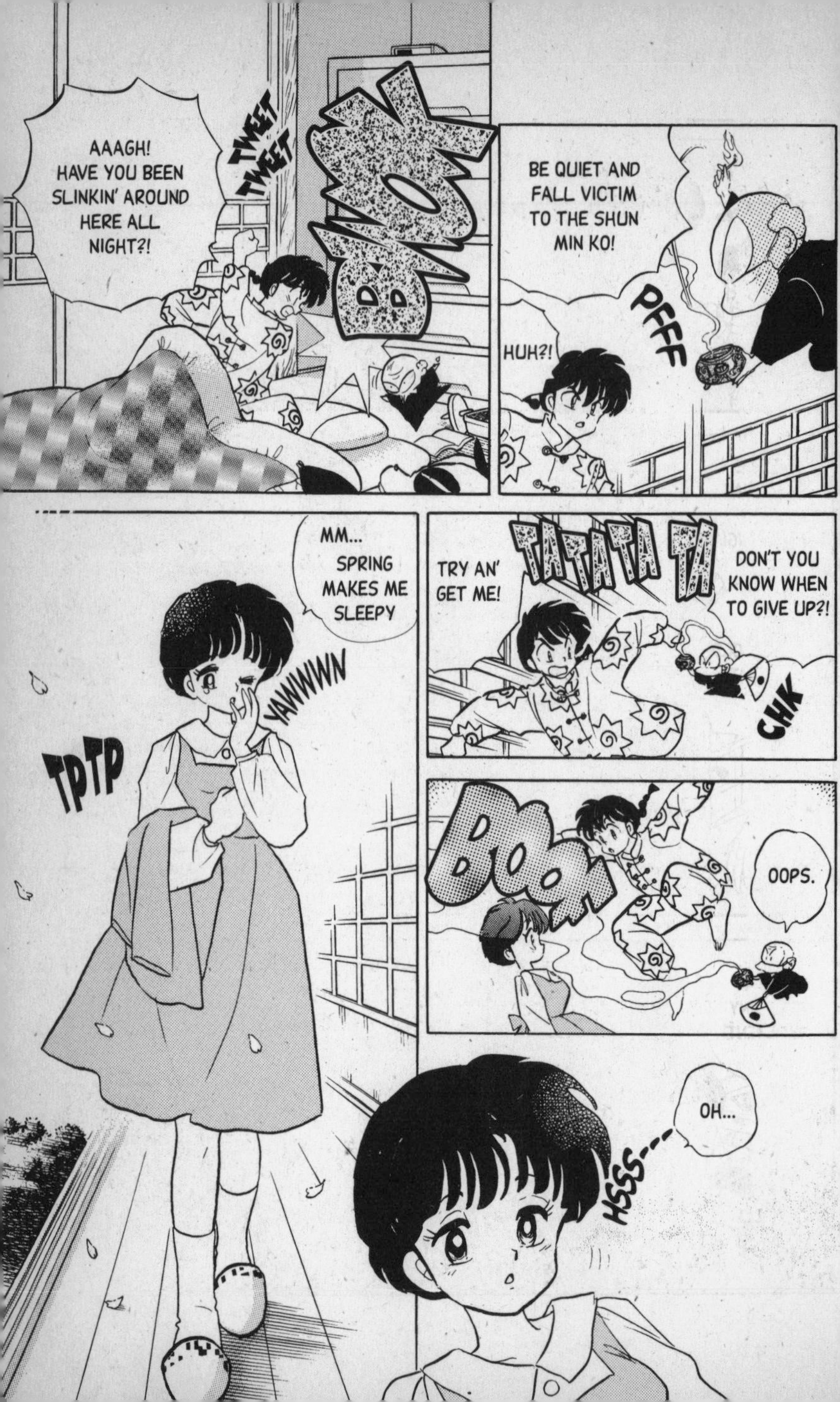
AAAGH! HAVE YOU BEEN SLINKIN' AROUND HERE ALL NIGHT?!
TWEET TWEET
BONK
BE QUIET AND FALL VICTIM TO THE SHUN MIN KO!
PFFF
HUH?!
MM... SPRING MAKES ME SLEEPY
YAWWWN
TPTP
TRY AN' GET ME!
TATATA TA
DON'T YOU KNOW WHEN TO GIVE UP?!
CHK
BOOM
OOPS.
HSSS...
OH...

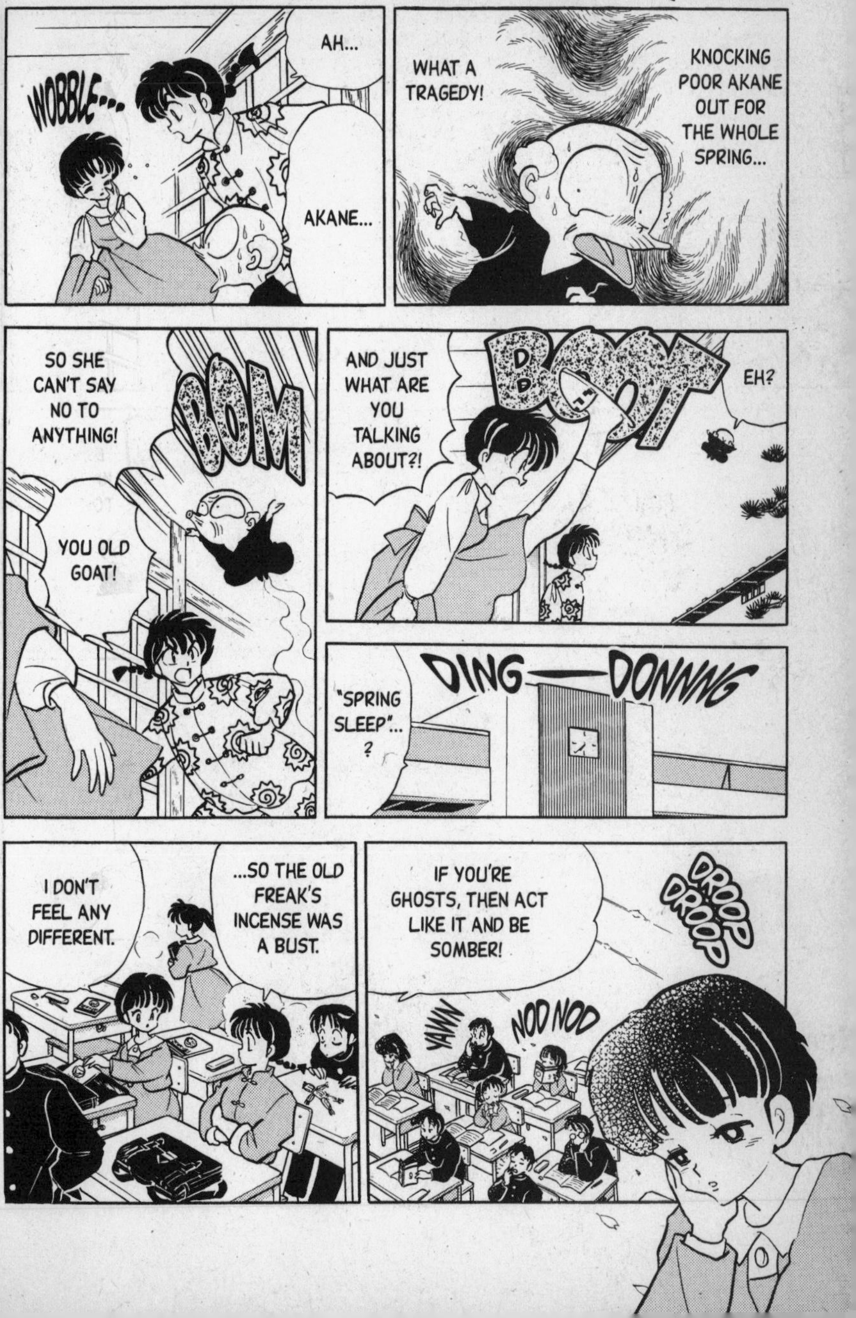
WOBBLE...
AH...
AKANE...
WHAT A TRAGEDY!
KNOCKING POOR AKANE OUT FOR THE WHOLE SPRING...
SO SHE CAN'T SAY NO TO ANYTHING!
BOM
YOU OLD GOAT!
AND JUST WHAT ARE YOU TALKING ABOUT?!
BOOT
EH?
"SPRING SLEEP"...?
DING—DONNNG
I DON'T FEEL ANY DIFFERENT.
...SO THE OLD FREAK'S INCENSE WAS A BUST.
IF YOU'RE GHOSTS, THEN ACT LIKE IT AND BE SOMBER!
YAWN
NOD NOD
DROOP DROOP

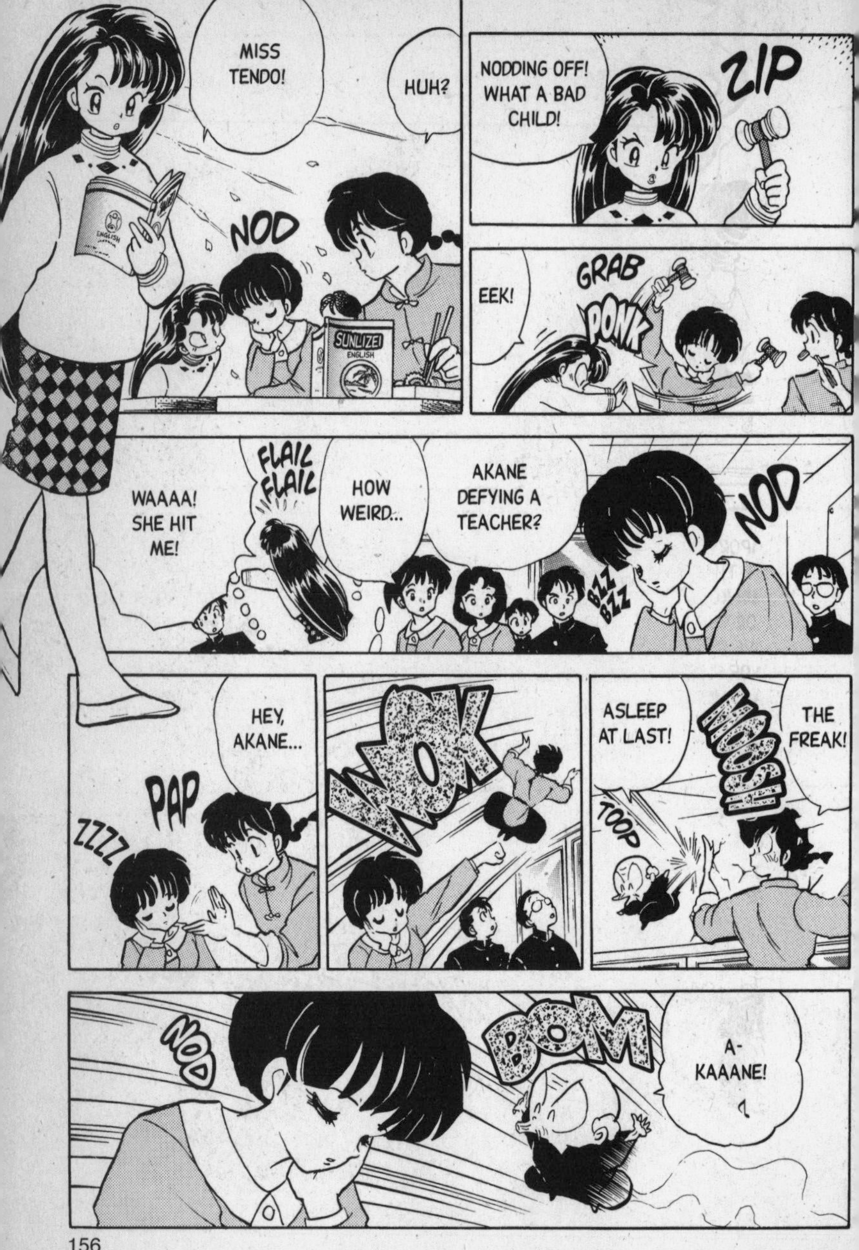
MISS TENDO!
HUH?
NOD
SUNLIZE!
ENGLISH
NODDING OFF! WHAT A BAD CHILD!
ZIP
EEK!
GRAB
PONK
WAAAA! SHE HIT ME!
FLAIL FLAIL
HOW WEIRD...
AKANE DEFYING A TEACHER?
NOD
BZZ BZZ
HEY, AKANE...
PAP
ZZZZ
WOK
ASLEEP AT LAST!
THE FREAK!
WOOSH
TOOP
NOD
BOM
A-KAAANE!

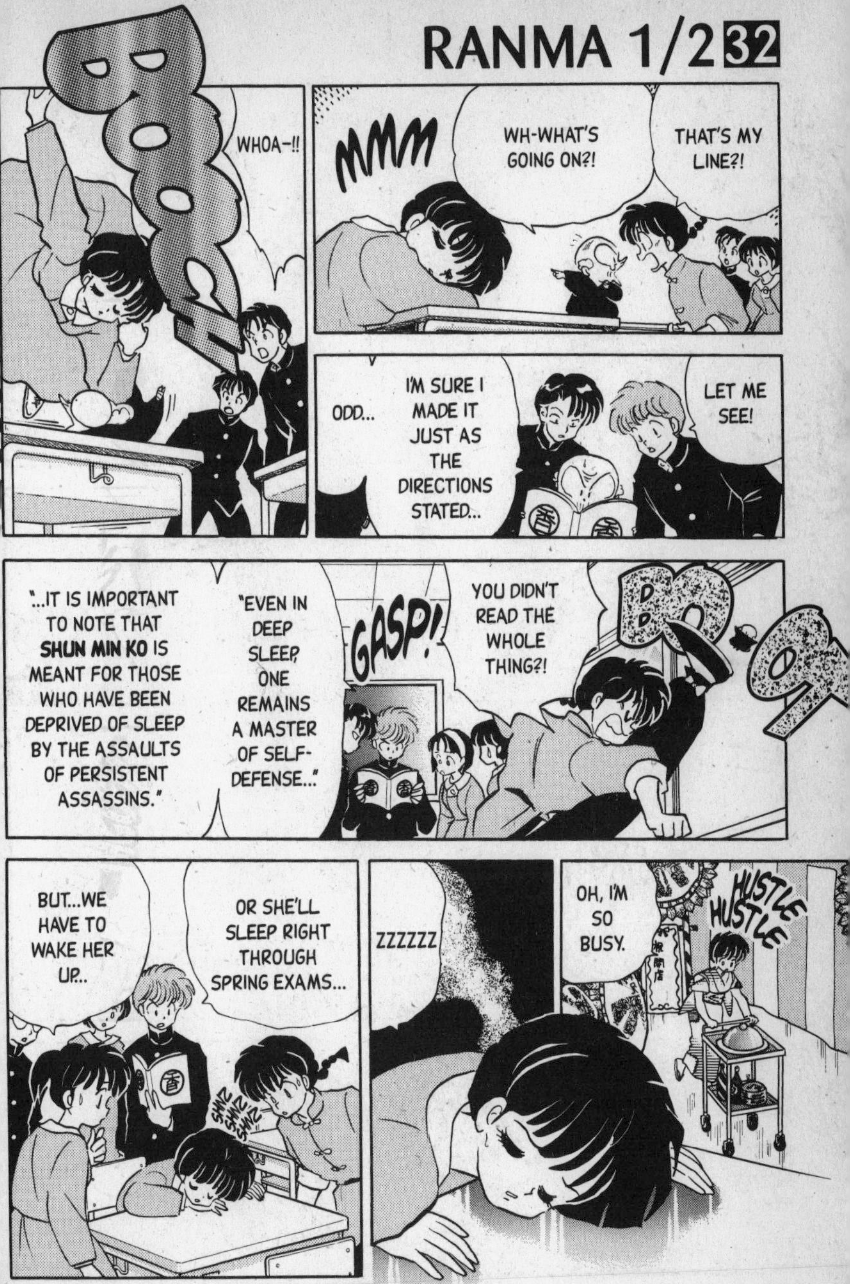
WHOA-!!
MMM
WH-WHAT'S GOING ON?!
THAT'S MY LINE?!
ODD...
I'M SURE I MADE IT JUST AS THE DIRECTIONS STATED...
LET ME SEE!
"...IT IS IMPORTANT TO NOTE THAT SHUN MIN KO IS MEANT FOR THOSE WHO HAVE BEEN DEPRIVED OF SLEEP BY THE ASSAULTS OF PERSISTENT ASSASSINS."
"EVEN IN DEEP SLEEP, ONE REMAINS A MASTER OF SELF-DEFENSE..."
GASP!
YOU DIDN'T READ THE WHOLE THING?!
BUT...WE HAVE TO WAKE HER UP..
OR SHE'LL SLEEP RIGHT THROUGH SPRING EXAMS...
ZZZZZZ
OH, I'M SO BUSY.
HUSTLE HUSTLE

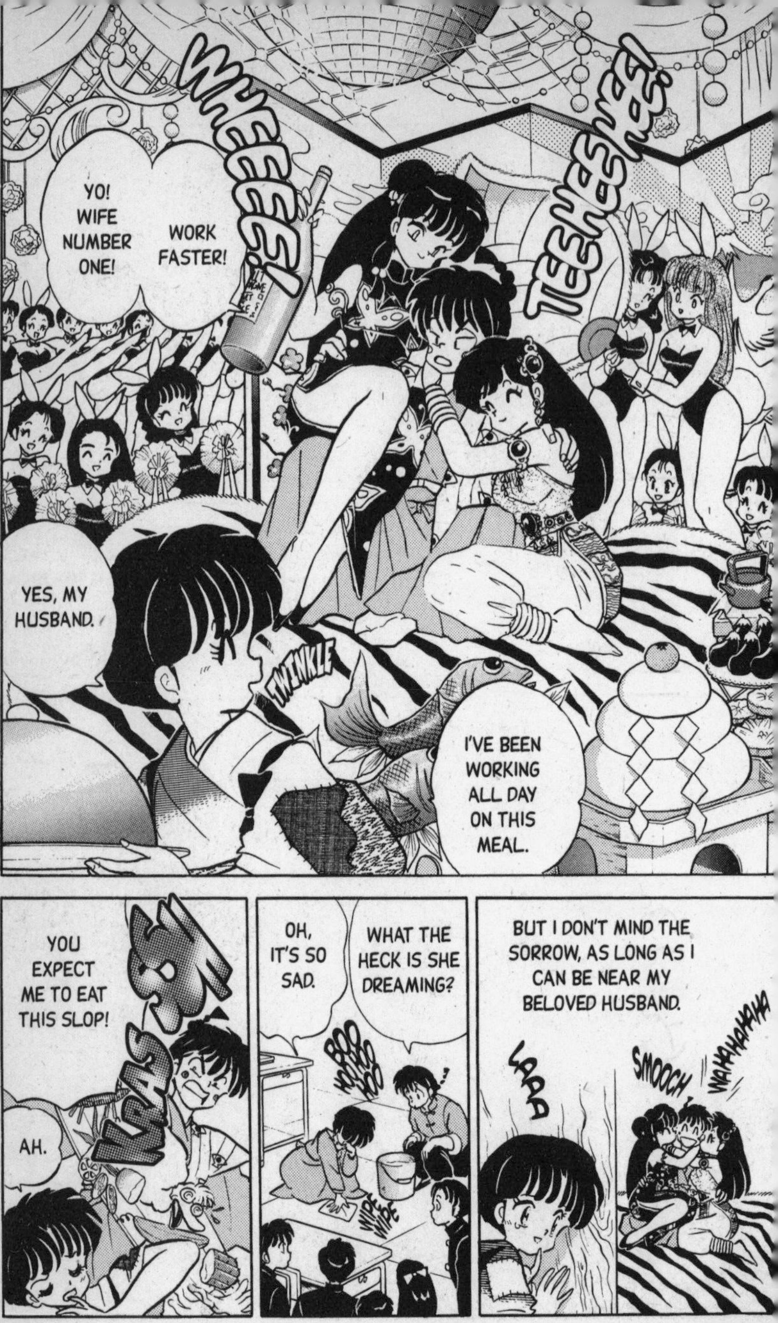
YO! WIFE NUMBER ONE!
WORK FASTER!
YES, MY HUSBAND.
TWINKLE
I'VE BEEN WORKING ALL DAY ON THIS MEAL.
YOU EXPECT ME TO EAT THIS SLOP!
AH.
OH, IT'S SO SAD.
WHAT THE HECK IS SHE DREAMING?
BOO HOO HOO HOO
WIPE WIPE
BUT I DON'T MIND THE SORROW, AS LONG AS I CAN BE NEAR MY BELOVED HUSBAND.
WAAA
SMOOCH
WAHAHAHAHA

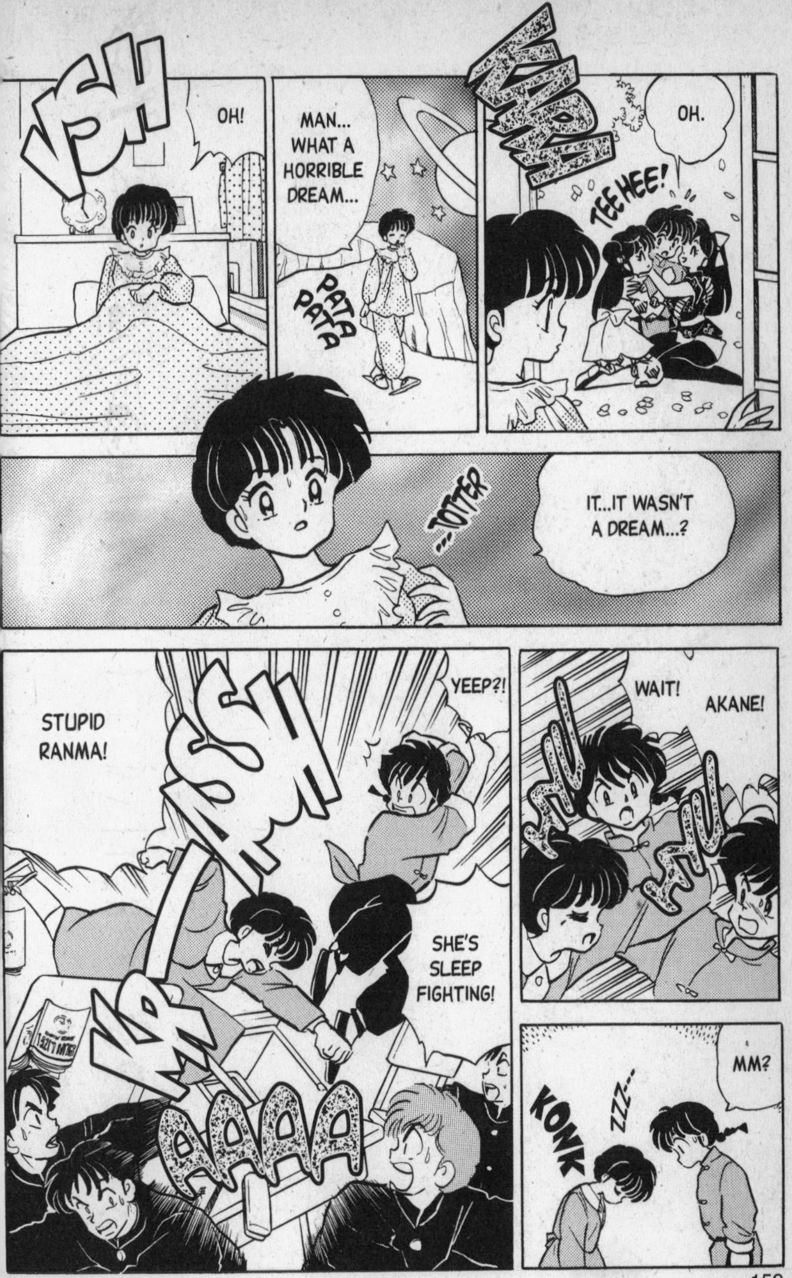
VSH
OH!
MAN... WHAT A HORRIBLE DREAM...
PATA PATA
OH.
TEE HEE!
...TOTTER
IT...IT WASN'T A DREAM...?
STUPID RANMA!
YEEP?!
SHE'S SLEEP FIGHTING!
WAIT!
AKANE!
KONK
ZZZ...
MM?

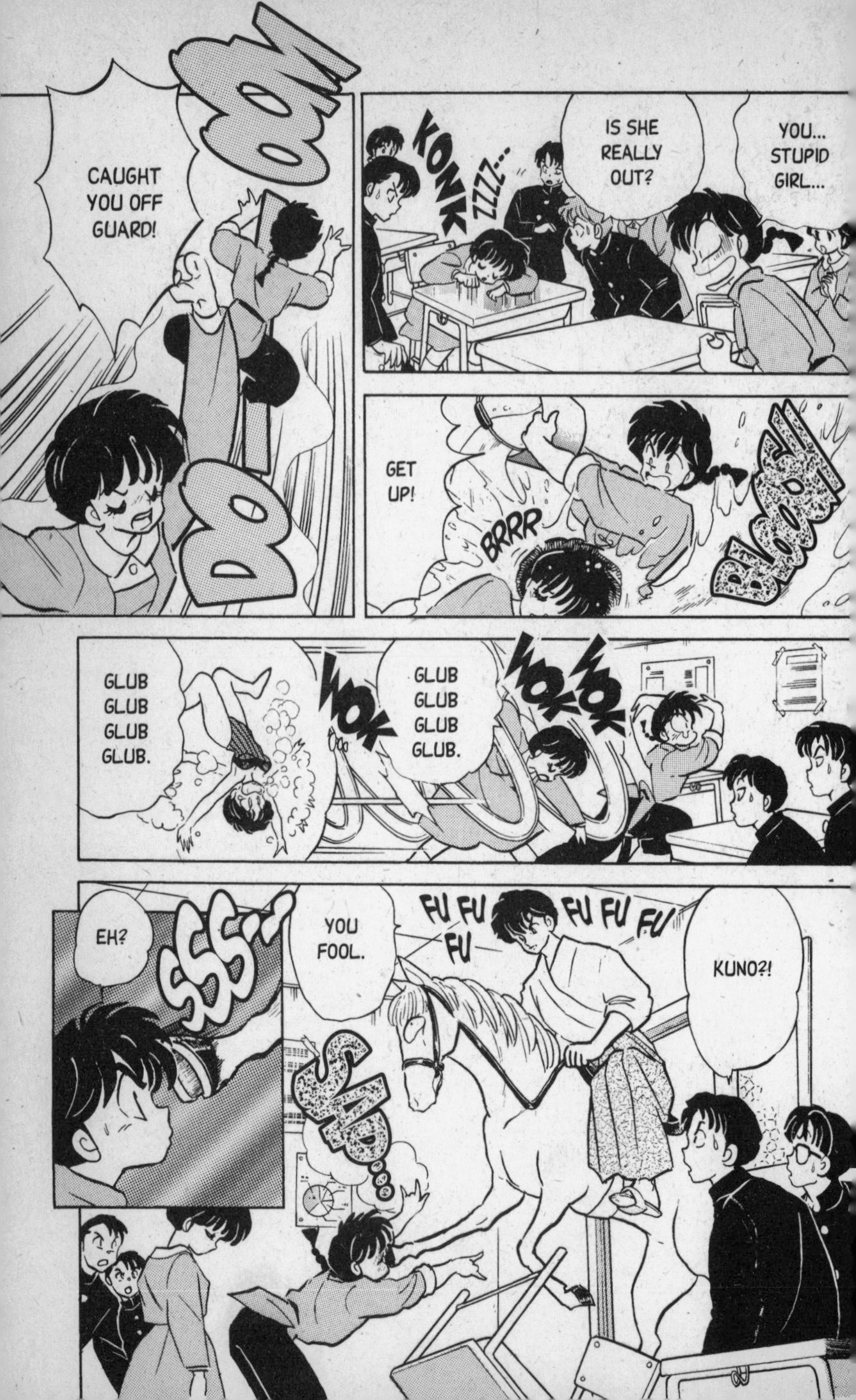
CAUGHT YOU OFF GUARD!
KONK
ZZZZ...
IS SHE REALLY OUT?
YOU... STUPID GIRL...
GET UP!
BRRR
GLUB GLUB GLUB GLUB.
WOK
GLUB GLUB GLUB GLUB.
WOK
WOK
EH?
SSS
YOU FOOL.
FU FU FU
FU FU FU
KUNO?!

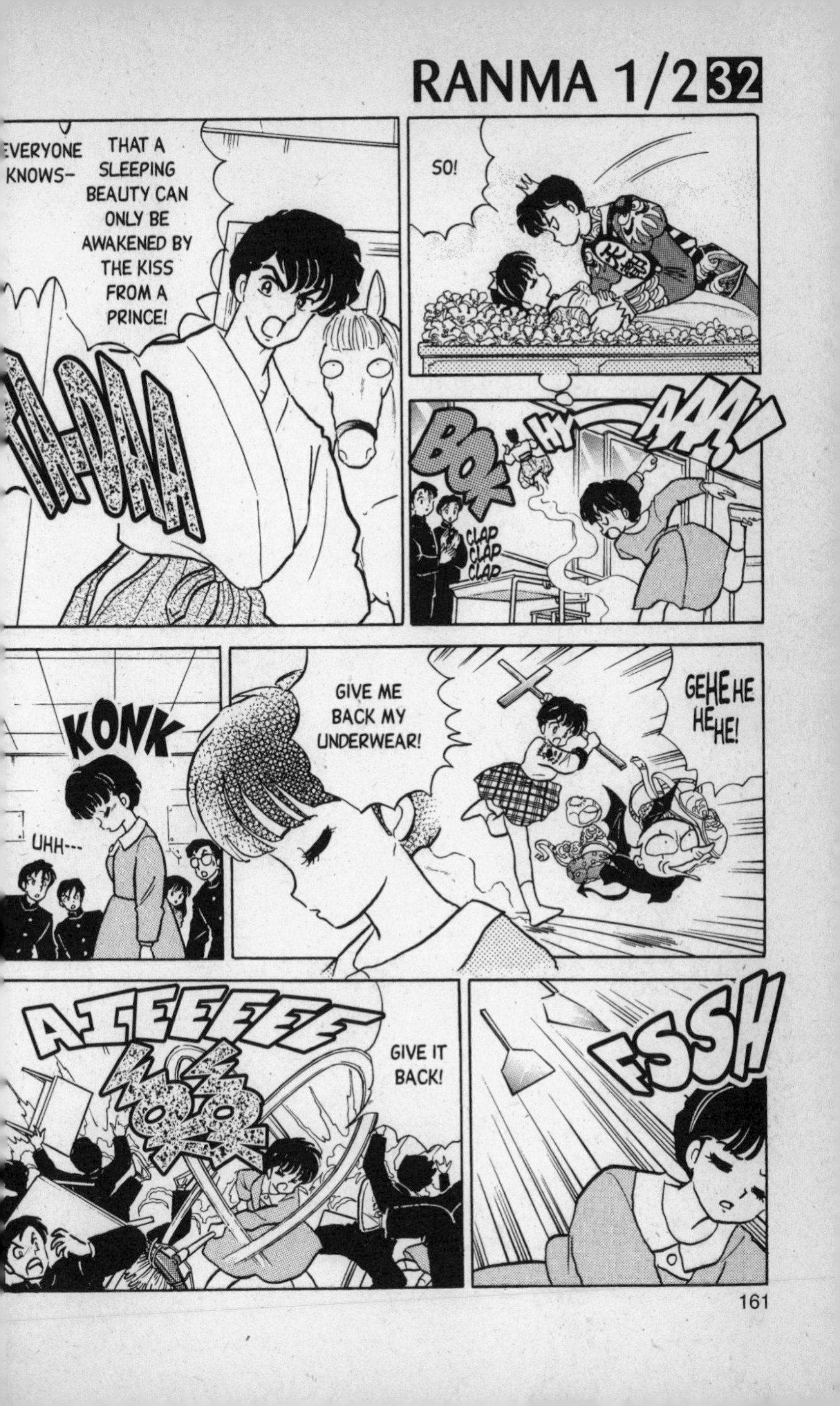
EVERYONE KNOWS—
THAT A SLEEPING BEAUTY CAN ONLY BE AWAKENED BY THE KISS FROM A PRINCE!
SO!
BOK
HY
AAA!
CLAP CLAP CLAP
KONK
UHH---
GIVE ME BACK MY UNDERWEAR!
GEHEHE HEHE!
A-IEEEEE
GIVE IT BACK!
ESSH

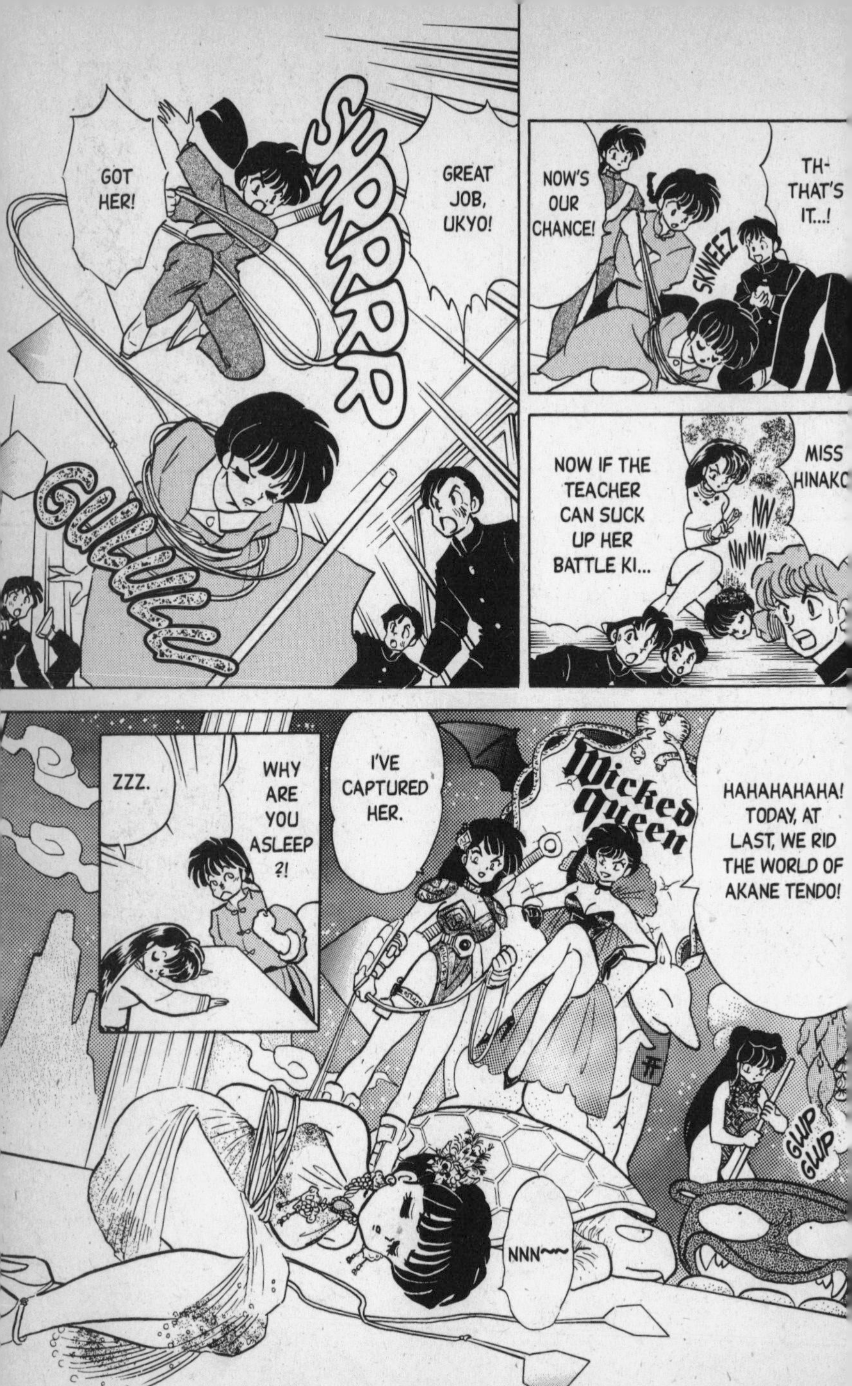
GOT HER!
SHRRR
GREAT JOB, UKYO!
GUUUU
NOW'S OUR CHANCE!
TH- THAT'S IT...!
SKWEEZ
NOW IF THE TEACHER CAN SUCK UP HER BATTLE KI...
MISS HINAK
ZZZ.
WHY ARE YOU ASLEEP ?!
I'VE CAPTURED HER.
Wicked Queen
HAHAHAHAHA! TODAY, AT LAST, WE RID THE WORLD OF AKANE TENDO!
GLUP GLUP
NNN~~

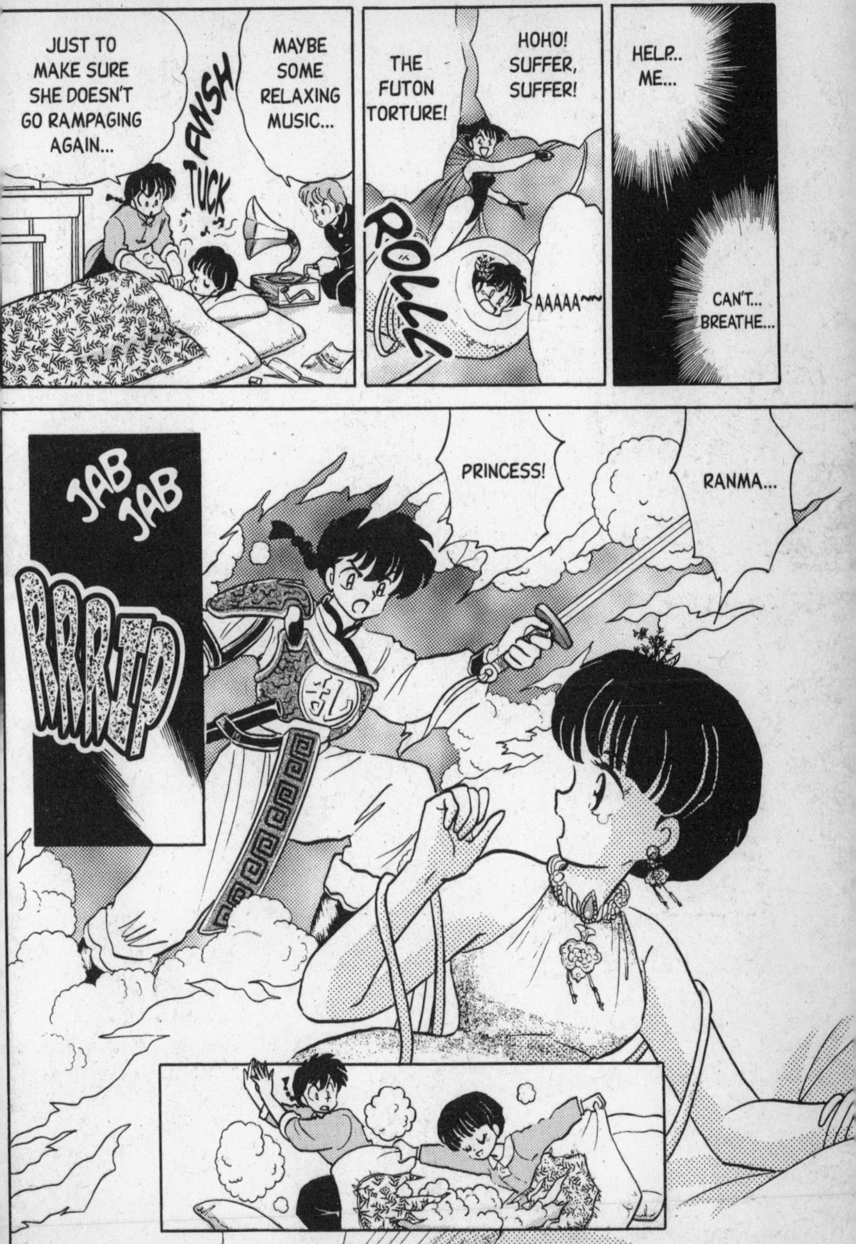
JUST TO MAKE SURE SHE DOESN'T GO RAMPAGING AGAIN...
FWSH
TUCK
MAYBE SOME RELAXING MUSIC...
THE FUTON TORTURE!
HOHO! SUFFER, SUFFER!
ROLL
AAAAA~~
HELP... ME...
CAN'T... BREATHE...
JAB JAB
RRRIP
PRINCESS!
RANMA...

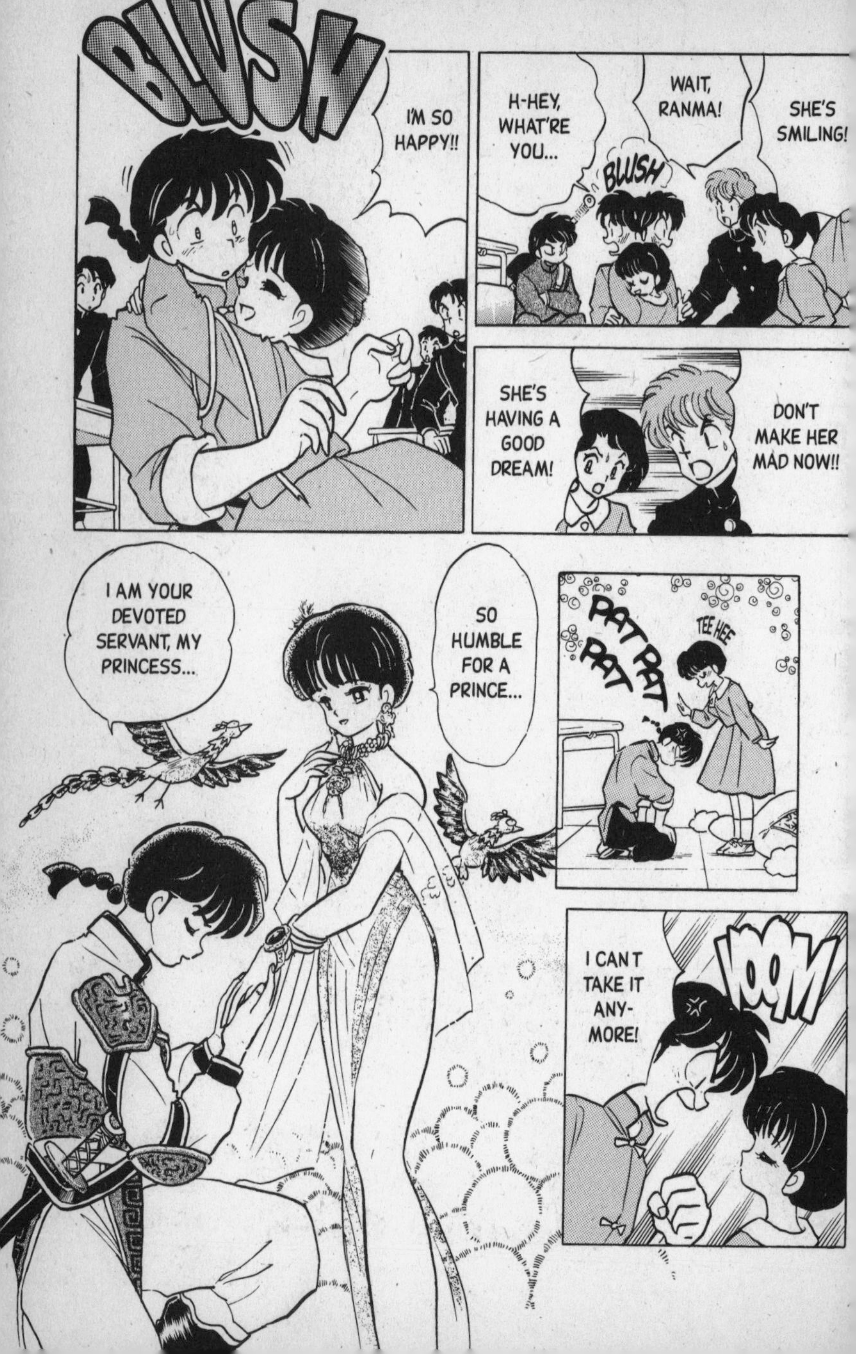
BLUSH
I'M SO HAPPY!!
H-HEY, WHAT'RE YOU...
BLUSH
WAIT, RANMA!
SHE'S SMILING!
SHE'S HAVING A GOOD DREAM!
DON'T MAKE HER MAD NOW!!
I AM YOUR DEVOTED SERVANT, MY PRINCESS...
SO HUMBLE FOR A PRINCE...
PAT PAT PAT
TEE HEE
I CANT TAKE IT ANY-MORE!
VOOM

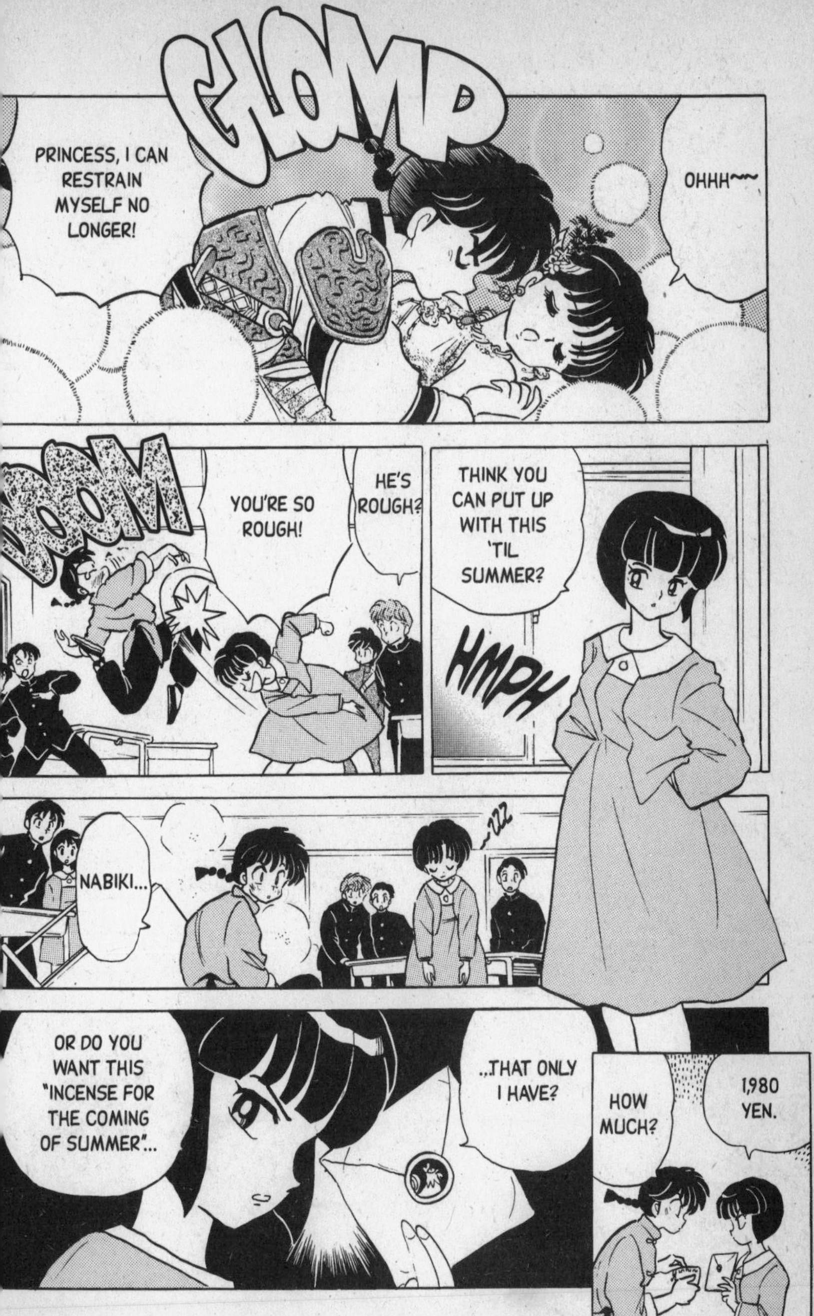
GLOMP
PRINCESS, I CAN RESTRAIN MYSELF NO LONGER!
OHHH~~
BOOM
YOU'RE SO ROUGH!
HE'S ROUGH?
THINK YOU CAN PUT UP WITH THIS 'TIL SUMMER?
HMPH
NABIKI...
~ZZZ
OR DO YOU WANT THIS "INCENSE FOR THE COMING OF SUMMER"...
..THAT ONLY I HAVE?
HOW MUCH?
1,980 YEN.

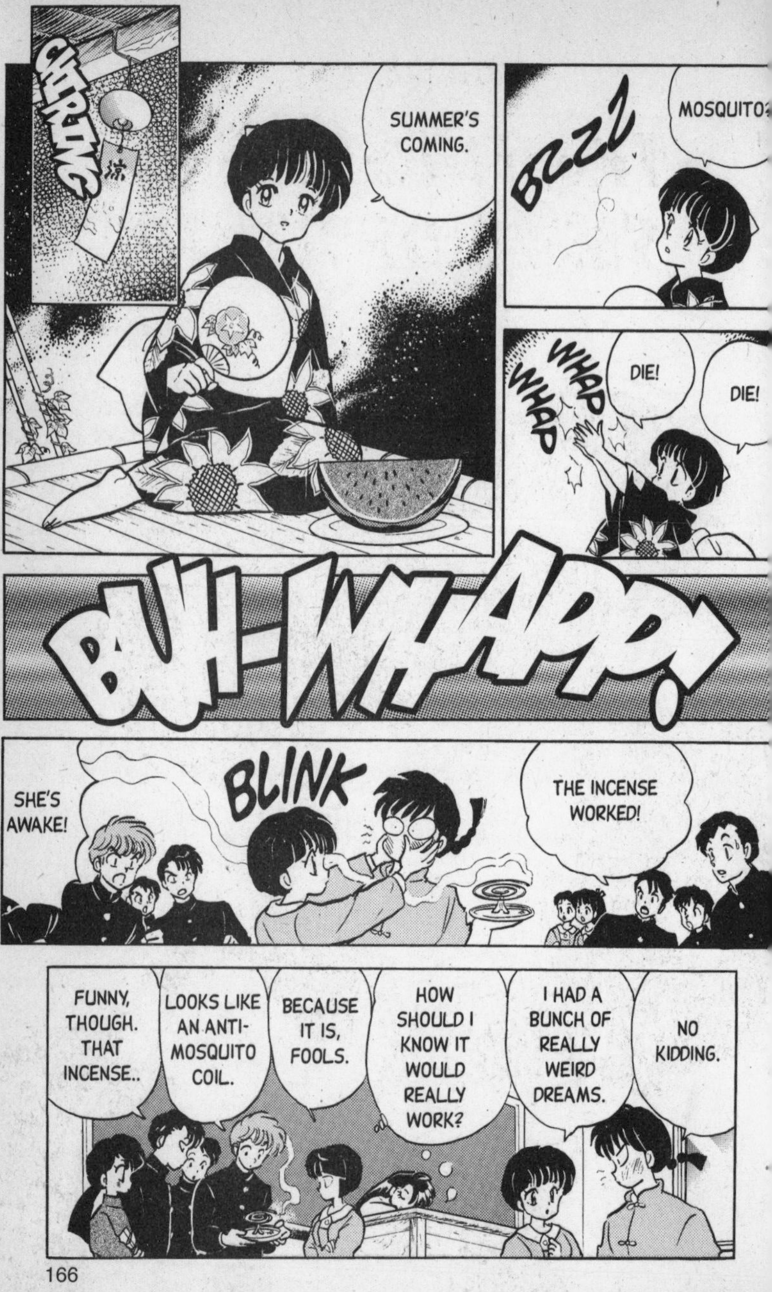
CHIRING
涼
SUMMER'S COMING.
BZZZ
MOSQUITO?
WHAP WHAP
DIE!
DIE!
BUH-WHAPP!
SHE'S AWAKE!
BLINK
THE INCENSE WORKED!
FUNNY, THOUGH. THAT INCENSE..
LOOKS LIKE AN ANTI-MOSQUITO COIL.
BECAUSE IT IS, FOOLS.
HOW SHOULD I KNOW IT WOULD REALLY WORK?
I HAD A BUNCH OF REALLY WEIRD DREAMS.
NO KIDDING.

PART 11

THE THREE-YEAR SMILE OF DEATH

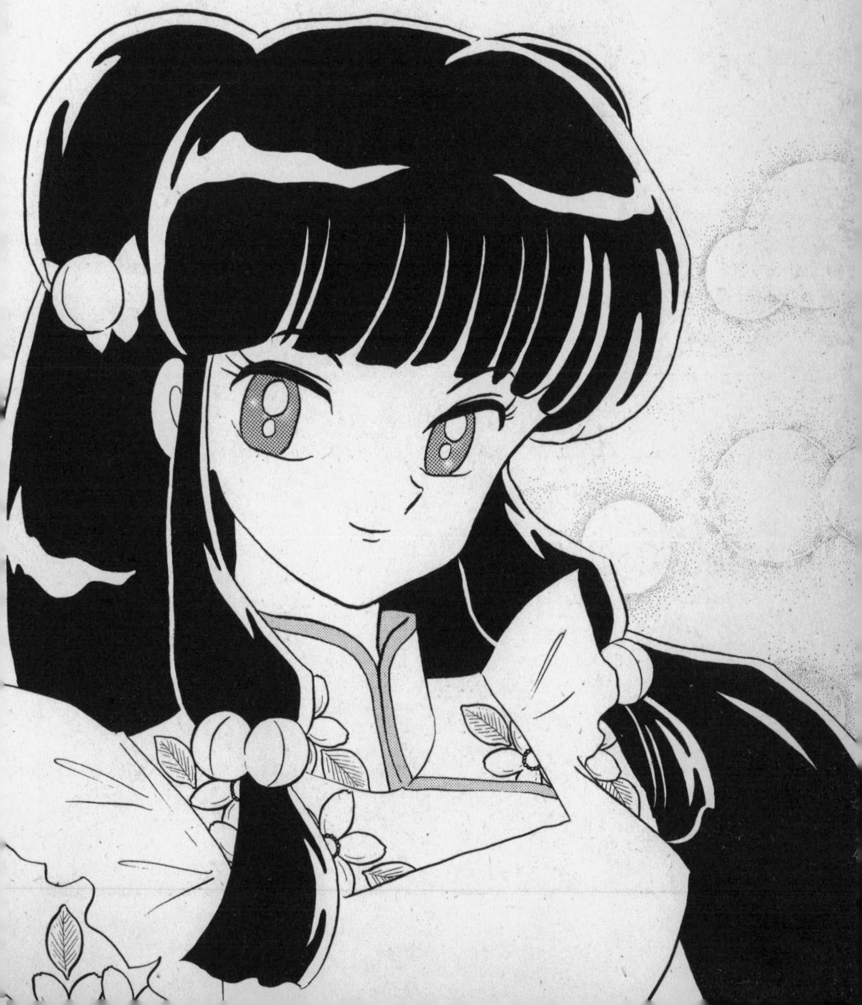

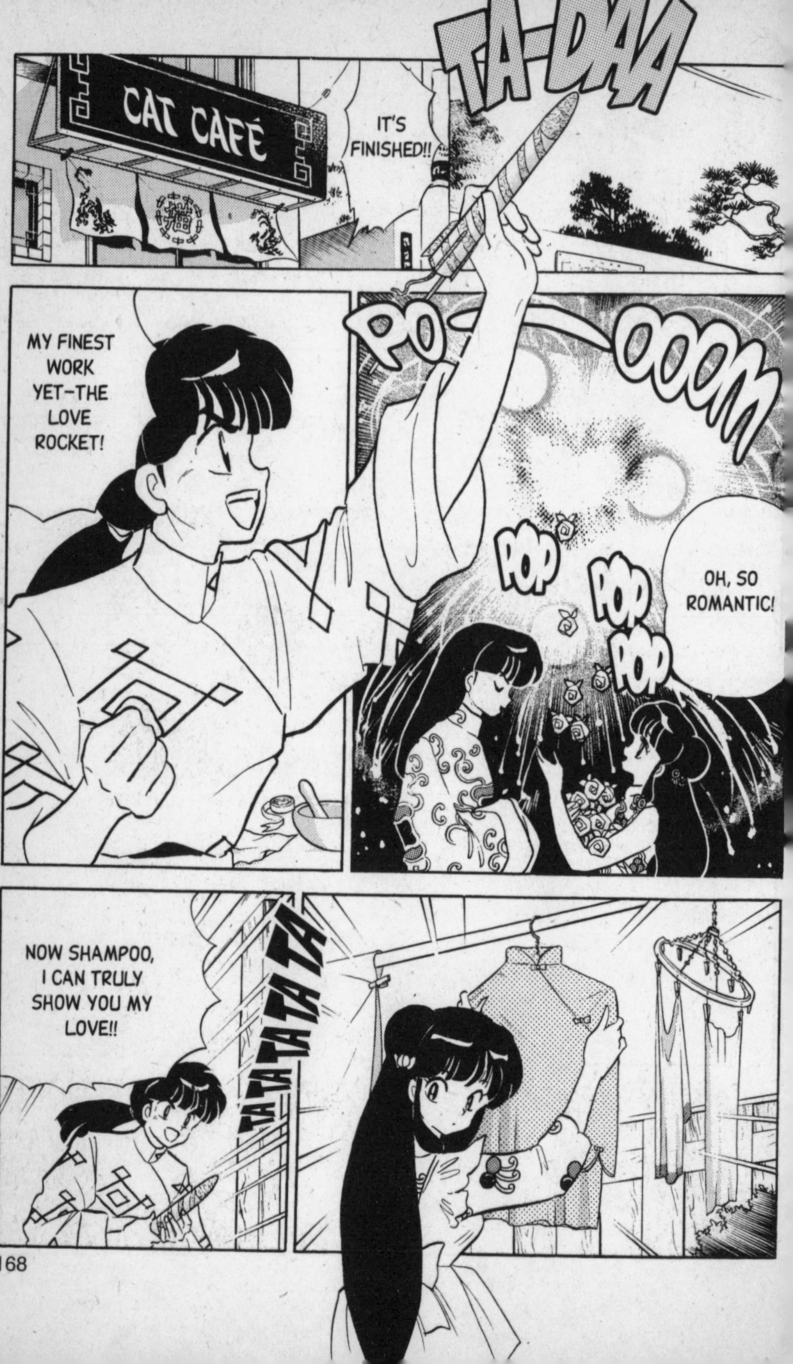
CAT CAFÉ
IT'S FINISHED!!
TA-DAA
MY FINEST WORK YET—THE LOVE ROCKET!
PO-OOOM
POP
POP
POP
OH, SO ROMANTIC!
NOW SHAMPOO, I CAN TRULY SHOW YOU MY LOVE!!
TA TA TA TA TA

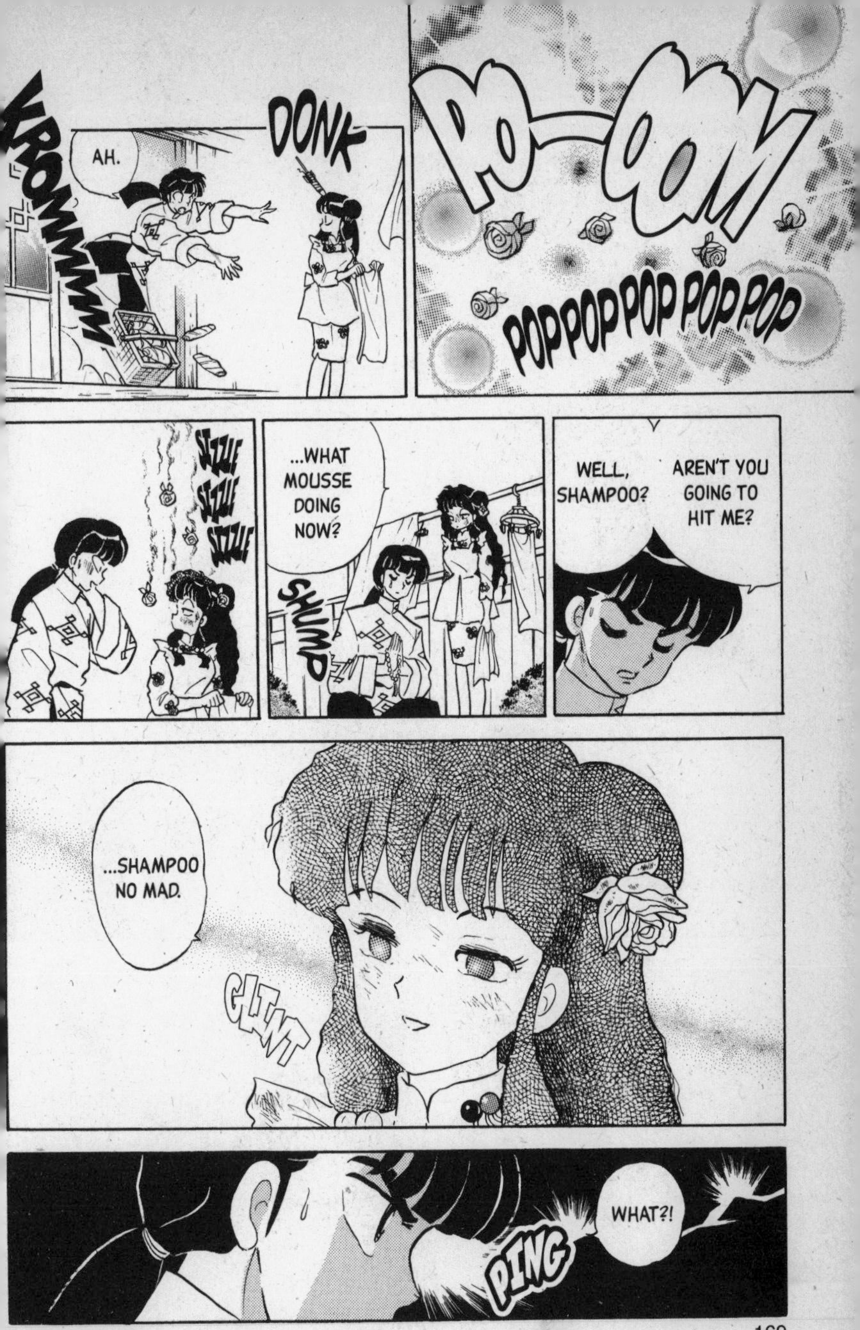
KROMMMMMM
AH.
DONK
PO—OOM
POPPOPPOPPOPPOP
SIZZLE SIZZLE SIZZLE
...WHAT MOUSSE DOING NOW?
SHUMP
WELL, SHAMPOO?
AREN'T YOU GOING TO HIT ME?
...SHAMPOO NO MAD.
GLINT
PING
WHAT?!

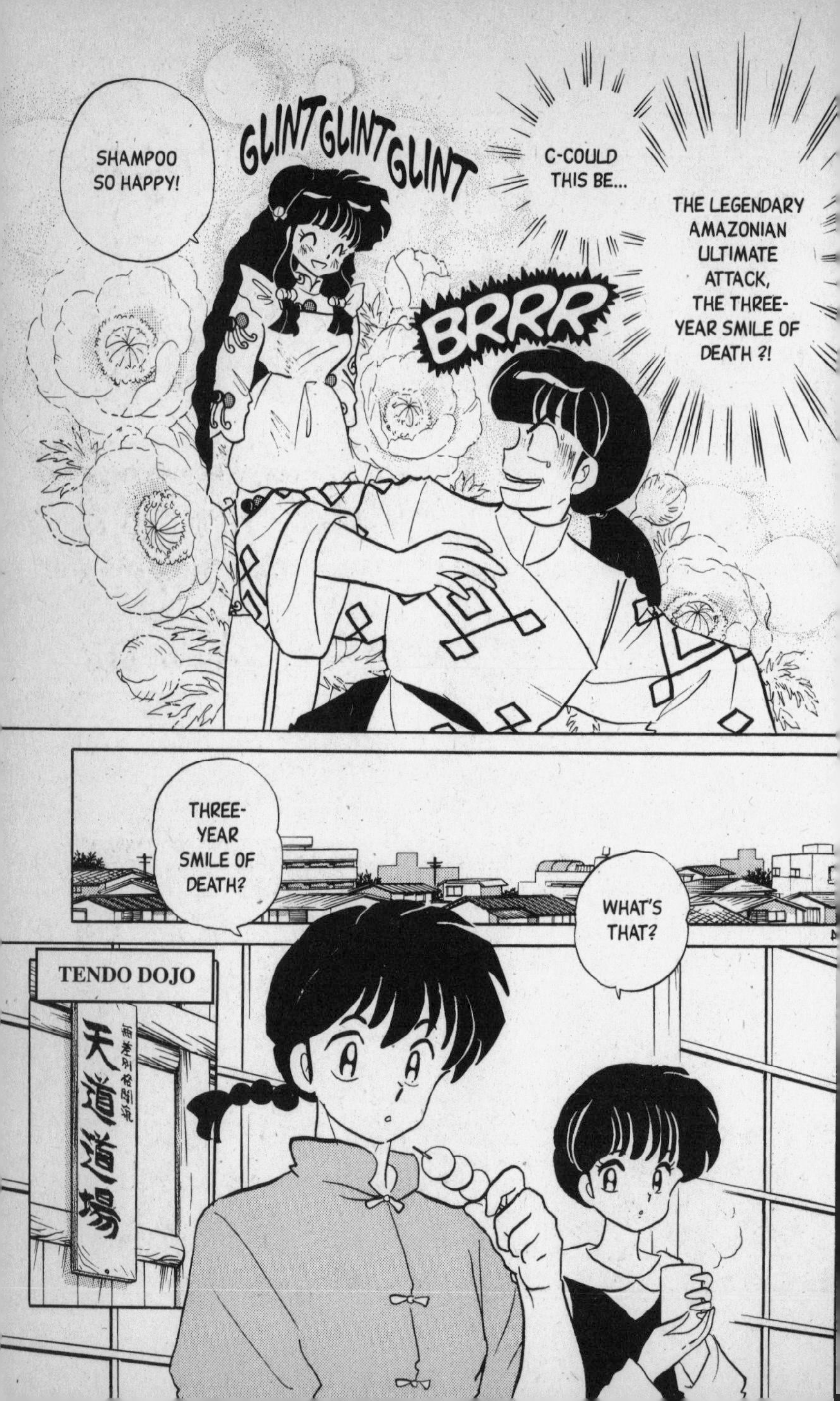
SHAMPOO SO HAPPY!
GLINT GLINT GLINT
BRRR
C-COULD THIS BE...
THE LEGENDARY AMAZONIAN ULTIMATE ATTACK, THE THREE-YEAR SMILE OF DEATH ?!
THREE-YEAR SMILE OF DEATH?
WHAT'S THAT?
TENDO DOJO
無差別格闘流
天道道場

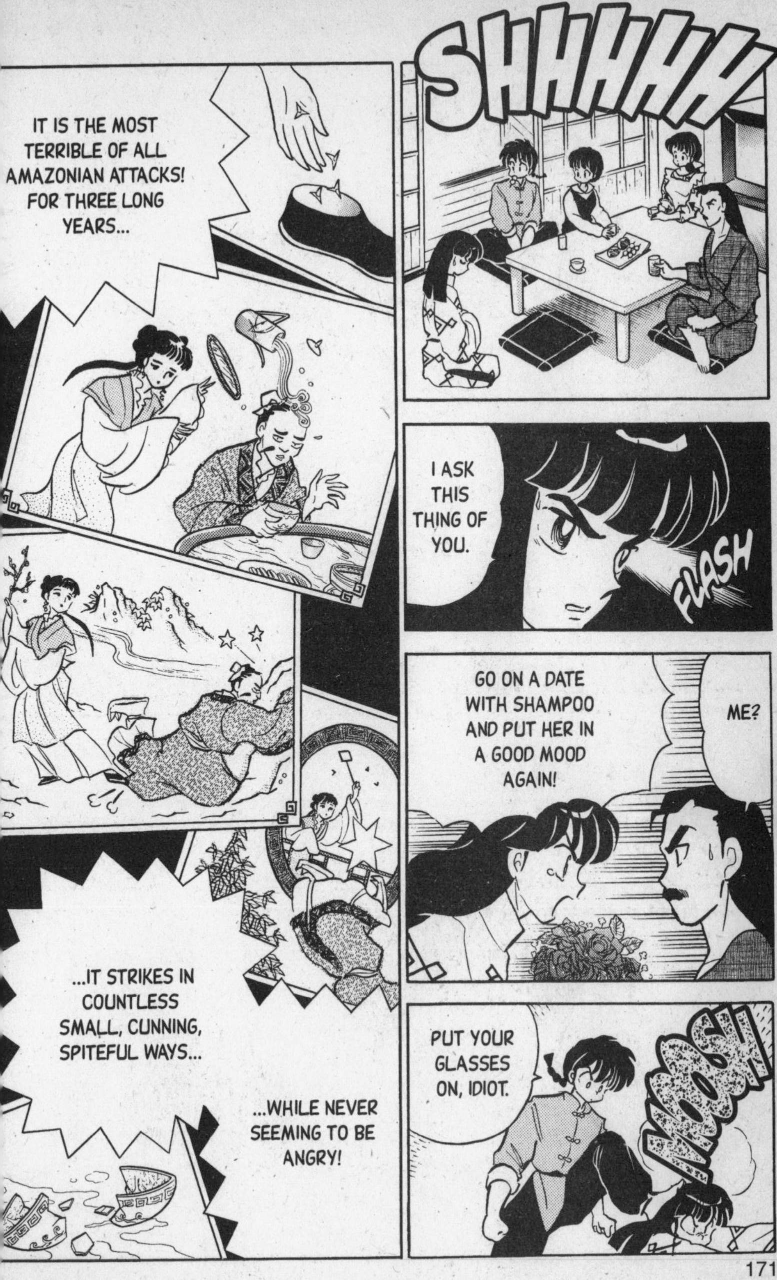
IT IS THE MOST TERRIBLE OF ALL AMAZONIAN ATTACKS! FOR THREE LONG YEARS...
...IT STRIKES IN COUNTLESS SMALL, CUNNING, SPITEFUL WAYS...
...WHILE NEVER SEEMING TO BE ANGRY!
SHHHHH
I ASK THIS THING OF YOU.
FLASH
GO ON A DATE WITH SHAMPOO AND PUT HER IN A GOOD MOOD AGAIN!
ME?
PUT YOUR GLASSES ON, IDIOT.
WOOSH!

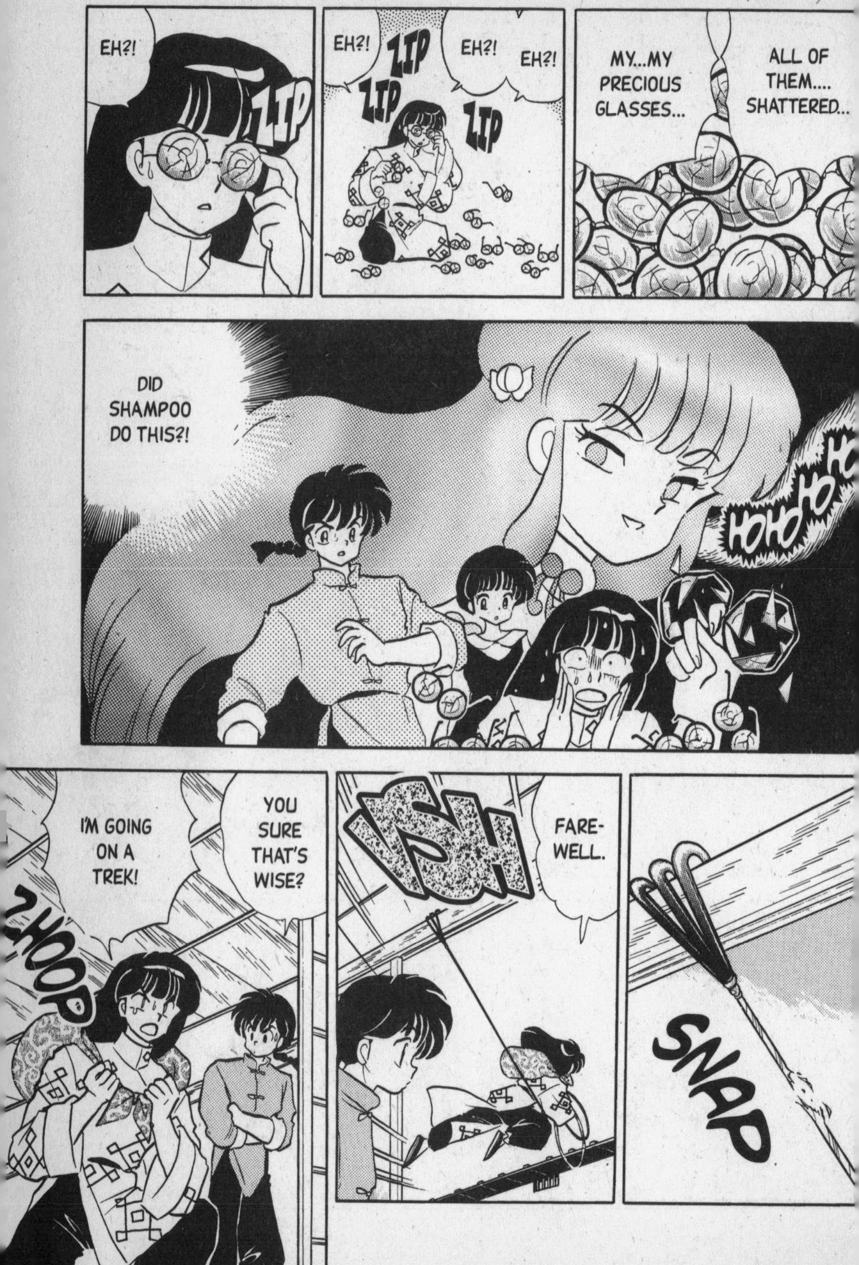
EH?!
ZIP
EH?!
ZIP
ZIP
EH?!
EH?!
ZIP
MY...MY PRECIOUS GLASSES...
ALL OF THEM.... SHATTERED...
DID SHAMPOO DO THIS?!
HOHOHOHO
I'M GOING ON A TREK!
YOU SURE THAT'S WISE?
ZHOOP
FARE-WELL.
SNAP

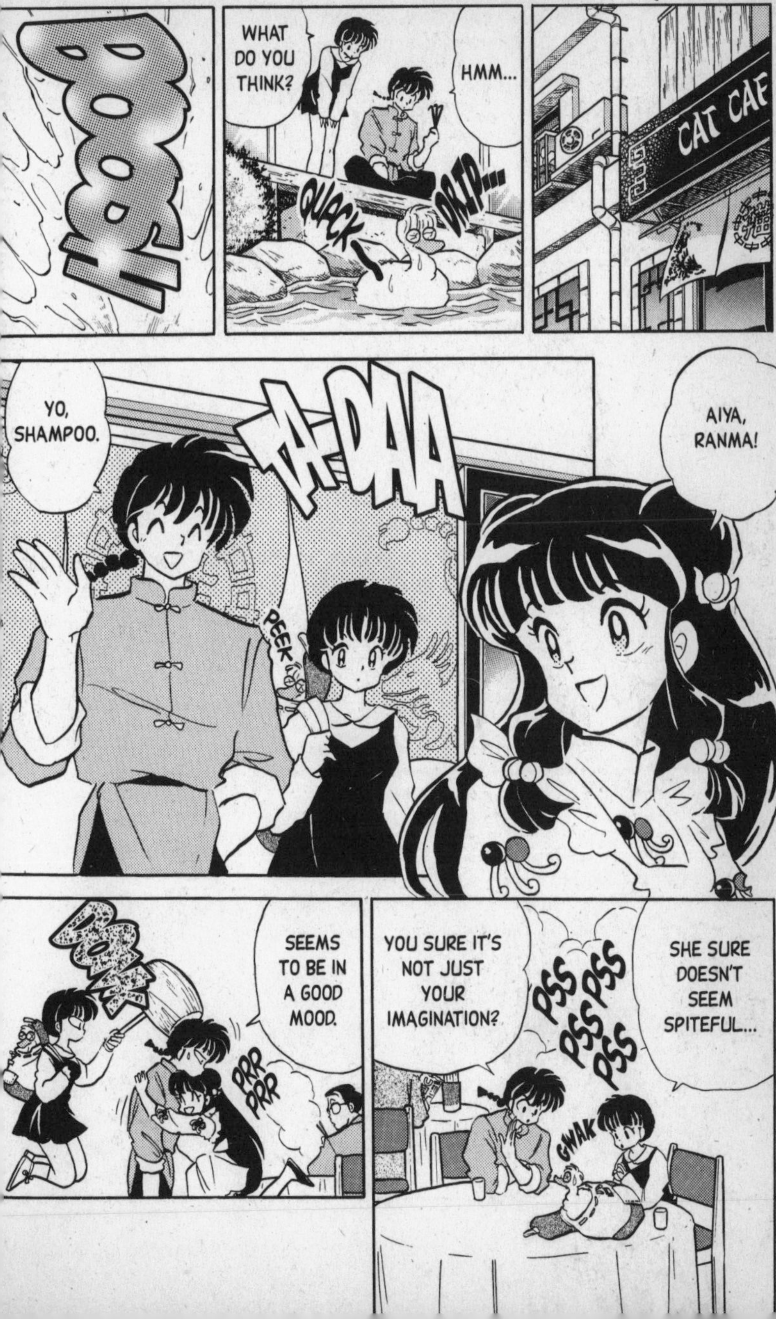
WHAT DO YOU THINK?
QUACK
HMM...
DRIP...
CAT CAF
YO, SHAMPOO.
TA-DAA
PEEK
AIYA, RANMA!
PRR PRR
SEEMS TO BE IN A GOOD MOOD.
YOU SURE IT'S NOT JUST YOUR IMAGINATION?
PSS PSS PSS PSS PSS PSS
GWAK
SHE SURE DOESN'T SEEM SPITEFUL...

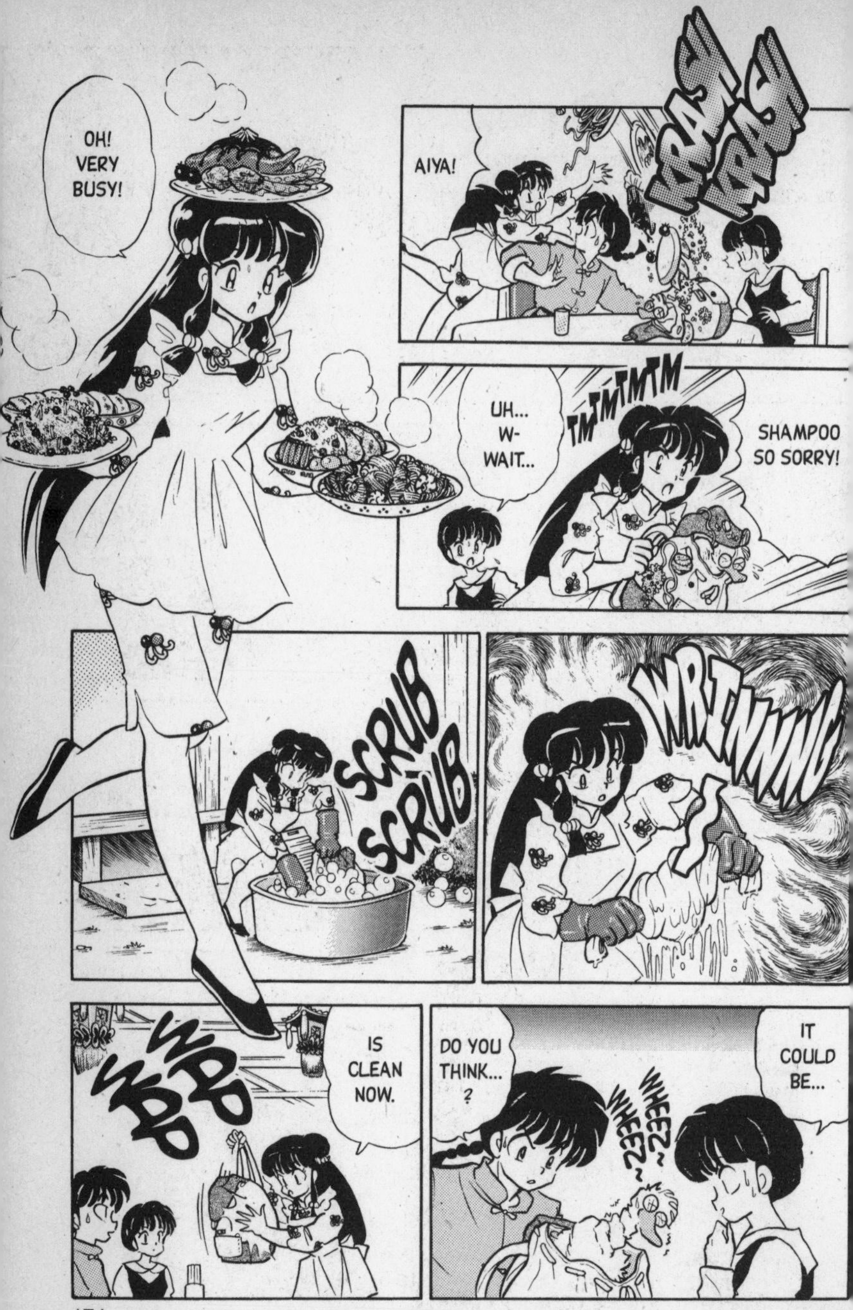
OH! VERY BUSY!
KRASH KRASH
AIYA!
UH... W-WAIT...
TMTMTMTMTM
SHAMPOO SO SORRY!
SCRUB SCRUB
WRINNNNG
WOP WOP
IS CLEAN NOW.
DO YOU THINK...?
WHEEZ~ WHEEZ~
IT COULD BE...

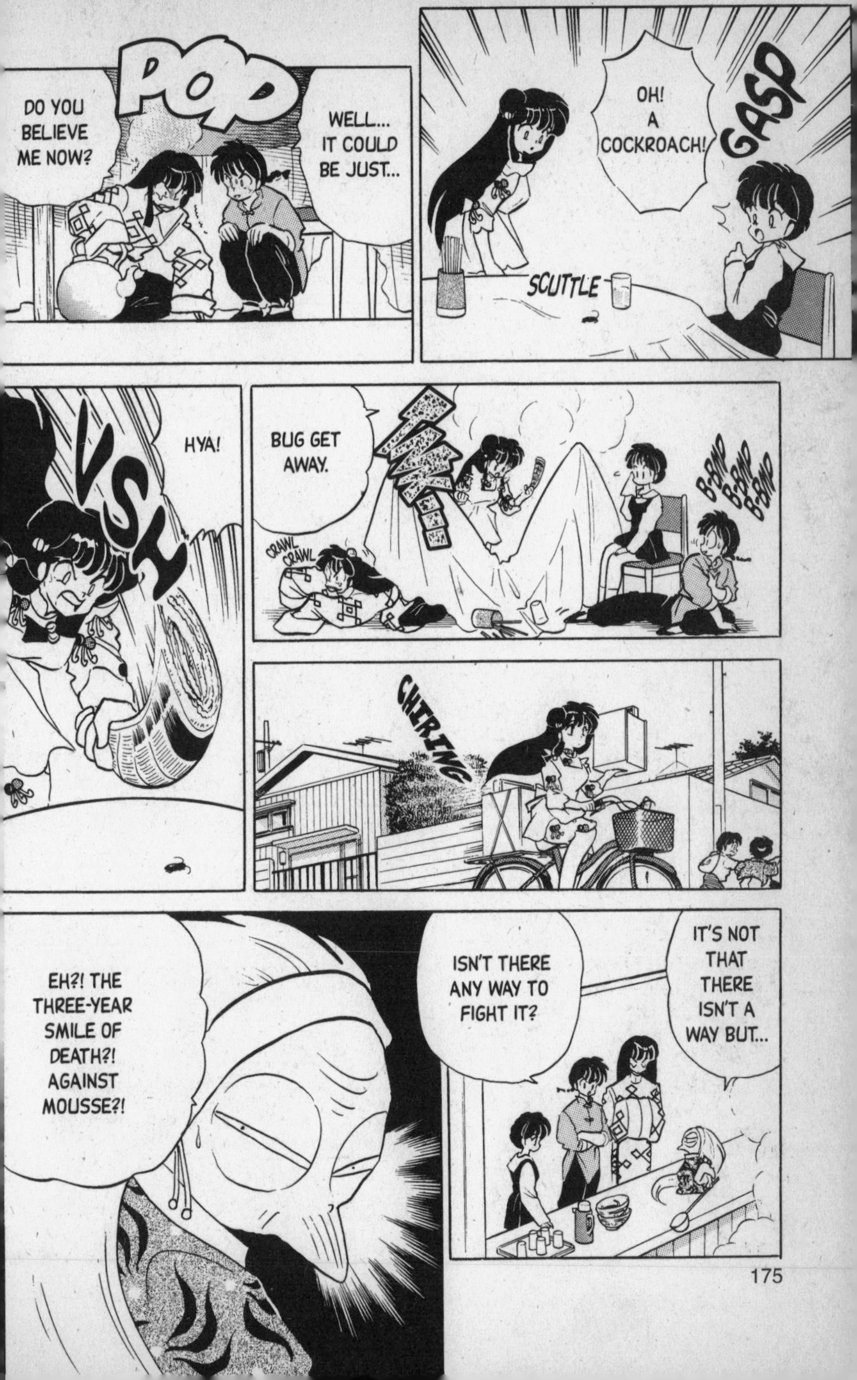
DO YOU BELIEVE ME NOW?
POP
WELL... IT COULD BE JUST...
OH! A COCKROACH!
GASP
SCUTTLE
VSH
HYA!
BUG GET AWAY.
CRAWL CRAWL
B-BMP B-BMP B-BMP
CHIRING
EH?! THE THREE-YEAR SMILE OF DEATH?! AGAINST MOUSSE?!
ISN'T THERE ANY WAY TO FIGHT IT?
IT'S NOT THAT THERE ISN'T A WAY BUT...

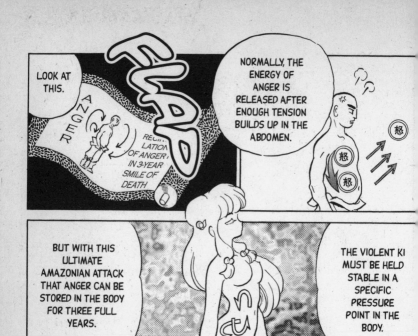

LOOK AT THIS.

ANGER

REGULATION OF ANGER IN 3-YEAR SMILE OF DEATH

NORMALLY, THE ENERGY OF ANGER IS RELEASED AFTER ENOUGH TENSION BUILDS UP IN THE ABDOMEN.

BUT WITH THIS ULTIMATE AMAZONIAN ATTACK THAT ANGER CAN BE STORED IN THE BODY FOR THREE FULL YEARS.

THE VIOLENT KI MUST BE HELD STABLE IN A SPECIFIC PRESSURE POINT IN THE BODY.

SO IF THAT POINT IS PRESSED...

IF YOU CAN PRESS IT.

THIS IS A SPECIALIZED AND DANGEROUS ATTACK, MOUSSE.

WITH YOUR MODEST SKILL, YOU MIGHT LOSE YOUR LIFE.

BUT WITH YOUR SKILL, FUTURE SON-IN-LAW...

OH?

GRRR

WHAT?!

WELP. GUESS IT CAN'T BE HELPED.

THERE ARE JUST TIMES YOU NEED A MASTER LIKE ME.

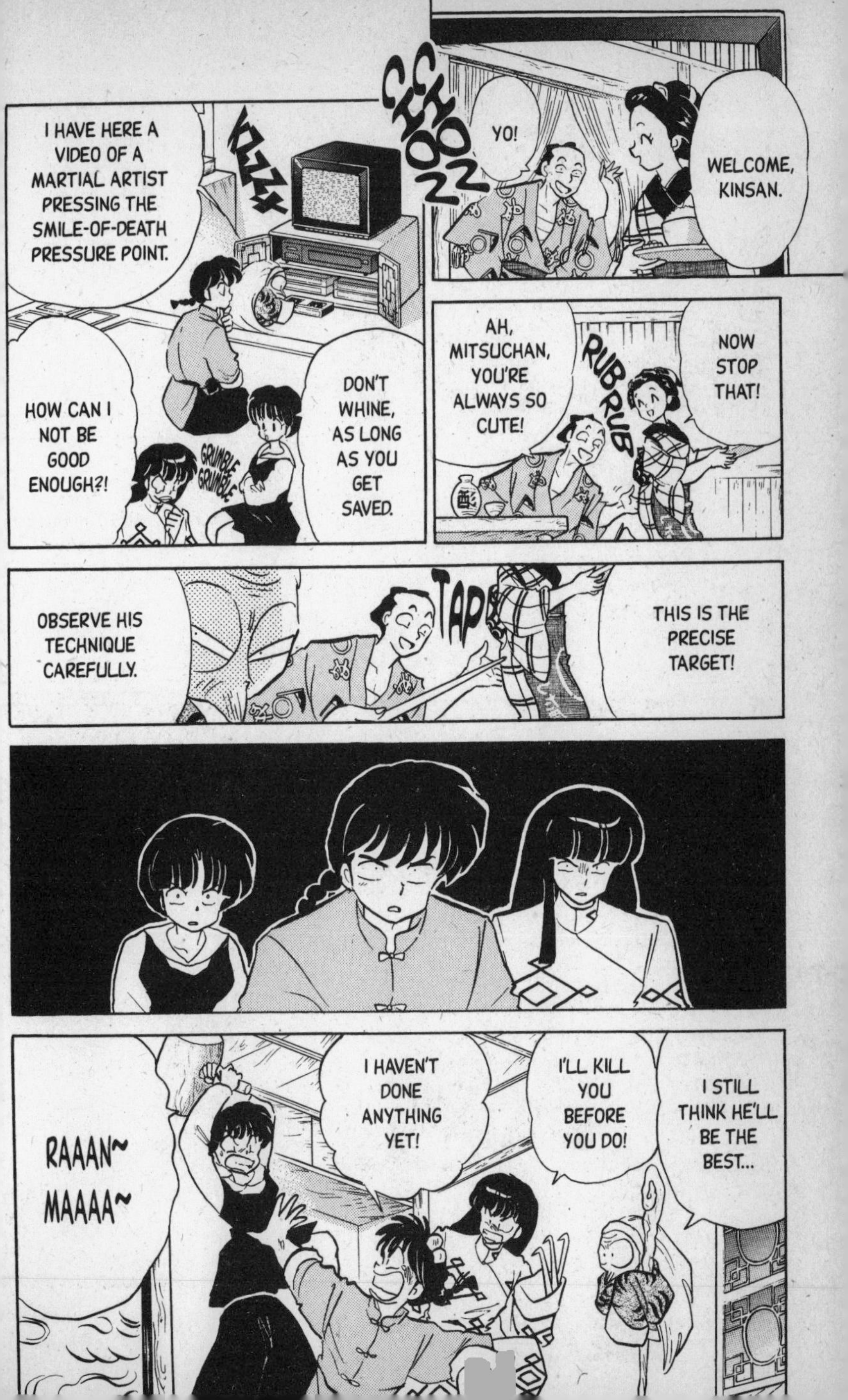
I HAVE HERE A VIDEO OF A MARTIAL ARTIST PRESSING THE SMILE-OF-DEATH PRESSURE POINT.
HOW CAN I NOT BE GOOD ENOUGH?!
GRUMBLE GRUMBLE
DON'T WHINE, AS LONG AS YOU GET SAVED.
YO!
WELCOME, KINSAN.
AH, MITSUCHAN, YOU'RE ALWAYS SO CUTE!
RUB RUB
NOW STOP THAT!
OBSERVE HIS TECHNIQUE CAREFULLY.
TAP
THIS IS THE PRECISE TARGET!
RAAAN~ MAAAA~
I HAVEN'T DONE ANYTHING YET!
I'LL KILL YOU BEFORE YOU DO!
I STILL THINK HE'LL BE THE BEST...

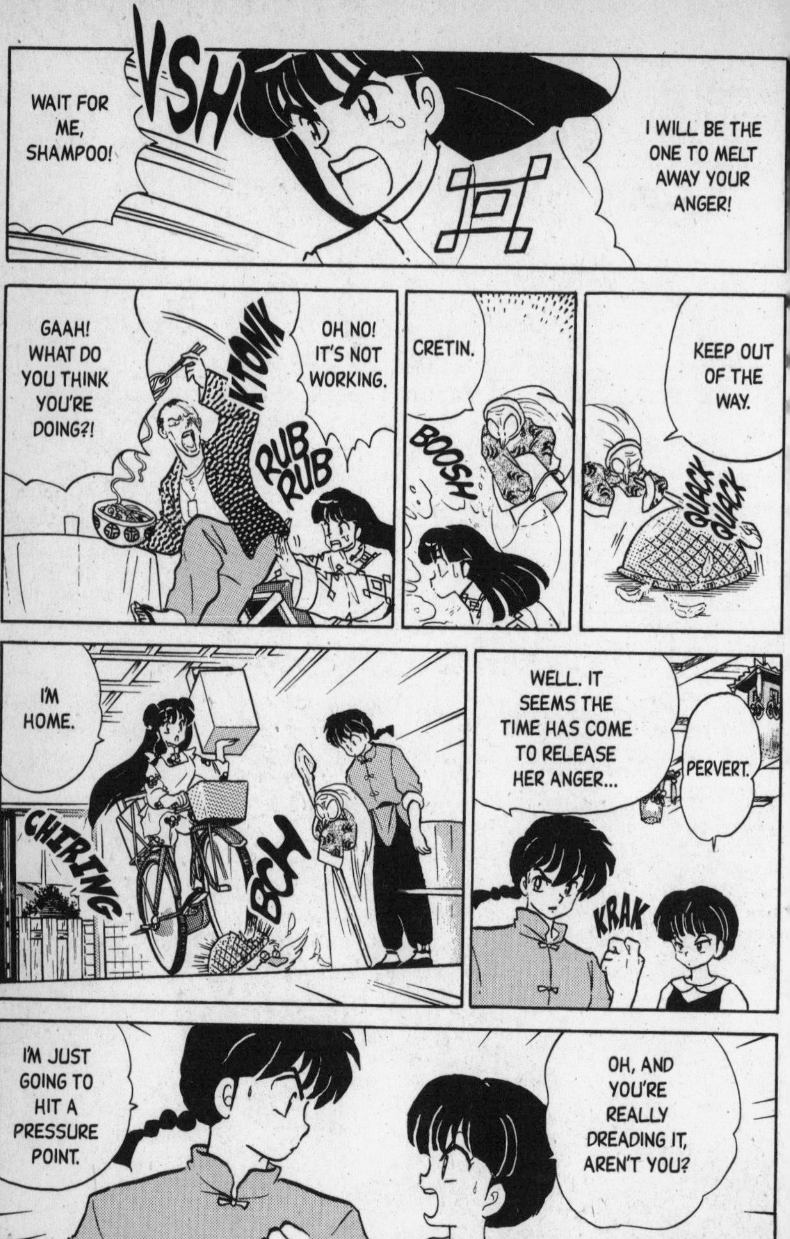
WAIT FOR ME, SHAMPOO!
VSH
I WILL BE THE ONE TO MELT AWAY YOUR ANGER!
GAAH! WHAT DO YOU THINK YOU'RE DOING?!
KTONK
OH NO! IT'S NOT WORKING.
RUB RUB
CRETIN.
BOOSH
KEEP OUT OF THE WAY.
QUACK QUACK
I'M HOME.
CHIRING
BCH
WELL. IT SEEMS THE TIME HAS COME TO RELEASE HER ANGER...
PERVERT.
KRAK
I'M JUST GOING TO HIT A PRESSURE POINT.
OH, AND YOU'RE REALLY DREADING IT, AREN'T YOU?

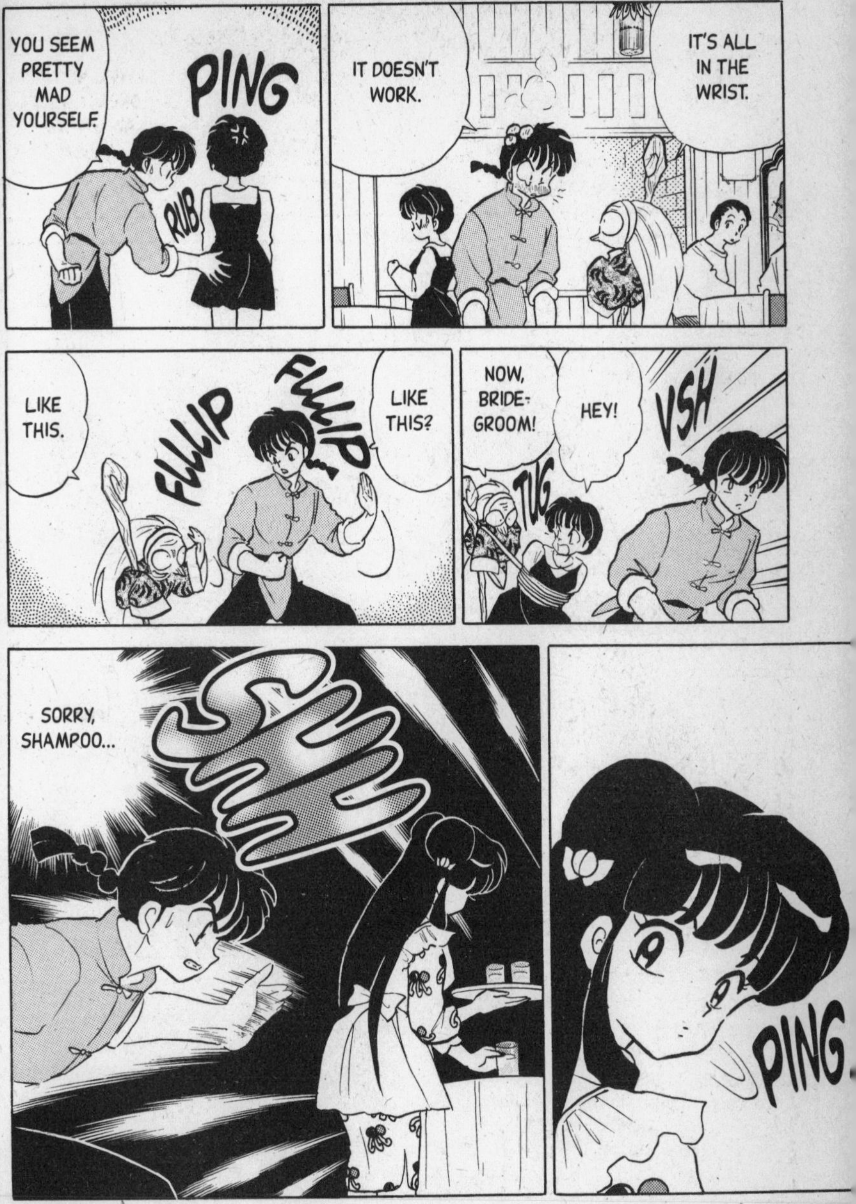
YOU SEEM PRETTY MAD YOURSELF.
PING
RUB
IT DOESN'T WORK.
IT'S ALL IN THE WRIST.
LIKE THIS.
FWLLIP
FWLLIP
LIKE THIS?
NOW, BRIDE-GROOM!
HEY!
VSH
TUG
SORRY, SHAMPOO...
PING

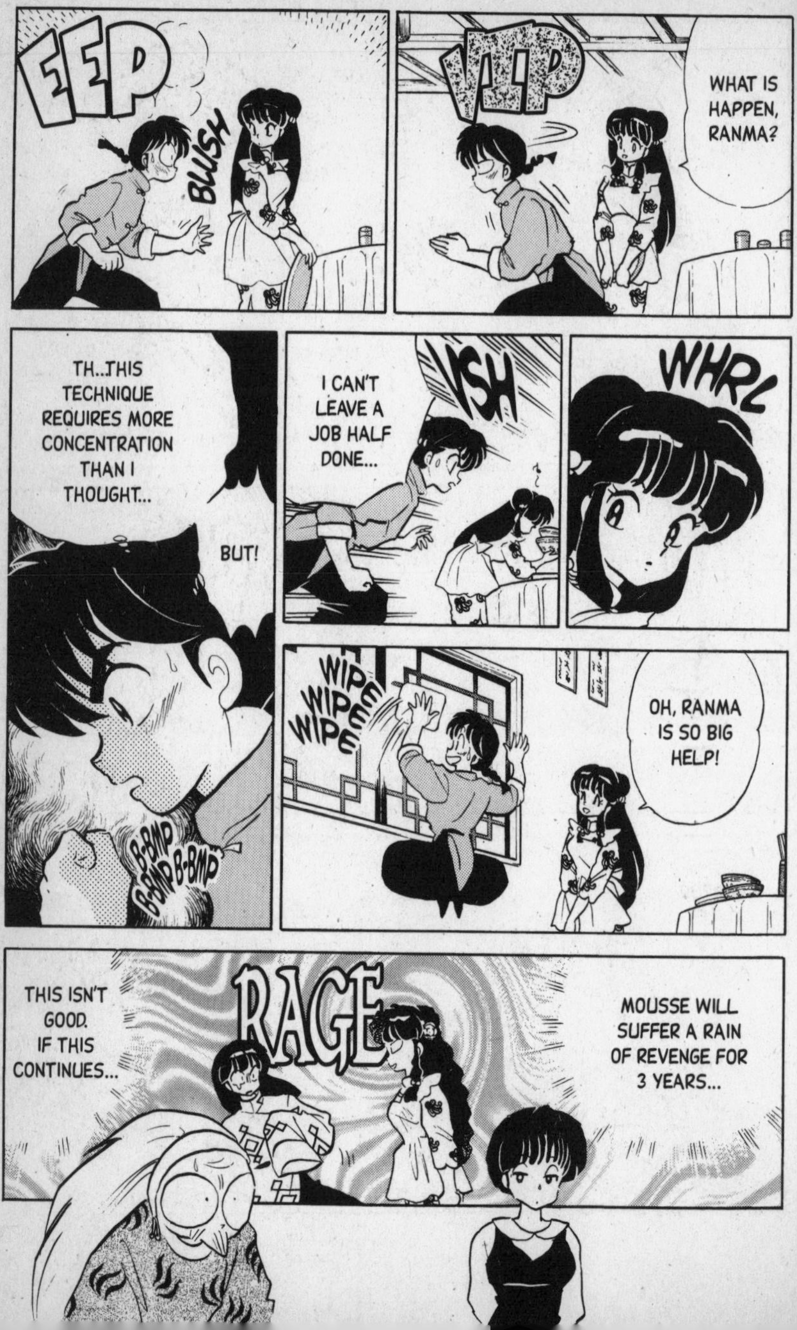
EEP
BLUSH
VIP
WHAT IS HAPPEN, RANMA?
TH...THIS TECHNIQUE REQUIRES MORE CONCENTRATION THAN I THOUGHT...
BUT!
B-BMP B-BMP B-BMP
I CAN'T LEAVE A JOB HALF DONE...
VSH
WHRL
WIPE WIPE WIPE
OH, RANMA IS SO BIG HELP!
THIS ISN'T GOOD. IF THIS CONTINUES...
RAGE
MOUSSE WILL SUFFER A RAIN OF REVENGE FOR 3 YEARS...

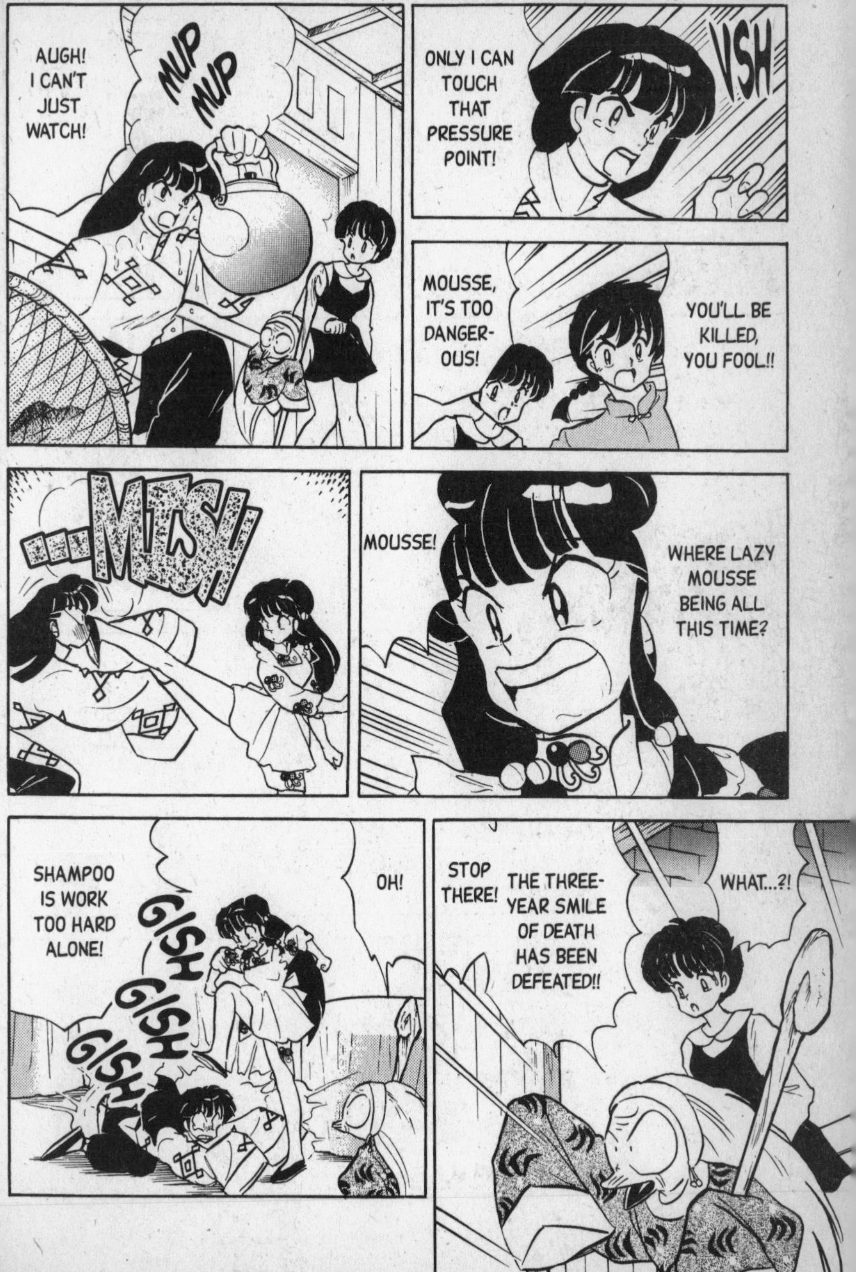
AUGH! I CAN'T JUST WATCH!
MUP MUP
ONLY I CAN TOUCH THAT PRESSURE POINT!
VSH
MOUSSE, IT'S TOO DANGER-OUS!
YOU'LL BE KILLED, YOU FOOL!!
...MISH!
MOUSSE!
WHERE LAZY MOUSSE BEING ALL THIS TIME?
SHAMPOO IS WORK TOO HARD ALONE!
OH!
GISH
GISH
GISH
STOP THERE!
THE THREE-YEAR SMILE OF DEATH HAS BEEN DEFEATED!!
WHAT...?!

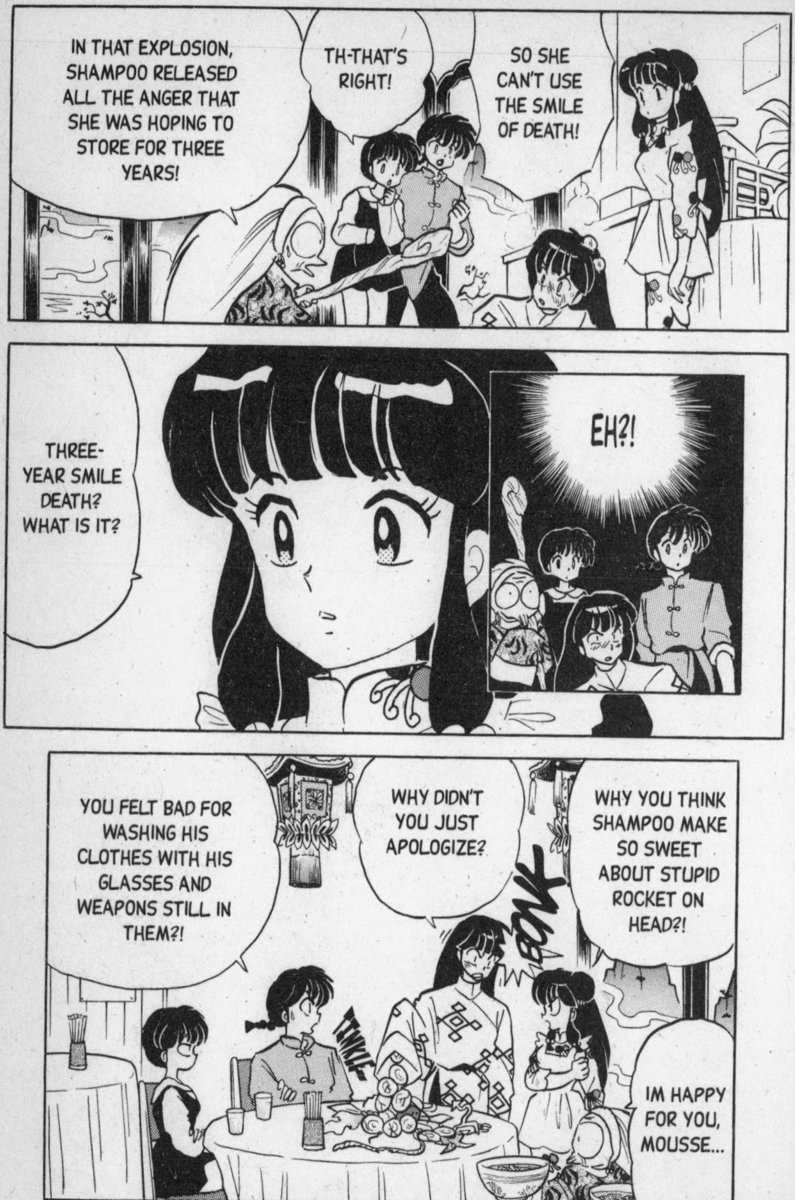
IN THAT EXPLOSION, SHAMPOO RELEASED ALL THE ANGER THAT SHE WAS HOPING TO STORE FOR THREE YEARS!
TH-THAT'S RIGHT!
SO SHE CAN'T USE THE SMILE OF DEATH!
THREE-YEAR SMILE DEATH? WHAT IS IT?
EH?!
YOU FELT BAD FOR WASHING HIS CLOTHES WITH HIS GLASSES AND WEAPONS STILL IN THEM?!
WHY DIDN'T YOU JUST APOLOGIZE?
WHY YOU THINK SHAMPOO MAKE SO SWEET ABOUT STUPID ROCKET ON HEAD?!
BONK
TINKLE
IM HAPPY FOR YOU, MOUSSE...

EDITOR'S RECOMMENDATIONS

If you enjoyed this volume of Ranma 1/2, then here is some more manga you might be interested in:

Here is Greenwood
story and art by Yukie Nasu vol.1

HERE IS GREENWOOD

Perhaps written for a slightly older audience than most of Rumiko Takahashi's work, Yukie Nasu's ***Here is Greenwood*** is exactly like ***Ranma 1/2***, except for the martial arts (none), the wacky hijinks (almost none), and the occasional depiction of the adult relationships among its students. Okay, aside from the fact that they both have male high school students in them, they have nothing in common. But they're both cool!

BOYS over FLOWERS
Hana Yori Dango
1
STORY AND ART BY YOKO KAMIO

BOYS OVER FLOWERS (HANA YORI DANGO)

Another tale of high-school life in Japan, ***Boys Over Flowers*** (or "HanaDan" to most of its fans) is not without its serious side, but overall tends to fall into in the "rabu-kome" or "love-comedy" genre.

Ceres
Celestial Legend
12 Tōya
Yuu Watase

CERES CELESTIAL LEGEND

Aya Mikage is a trendy Tokyo teen with not much else on her mind but fashion, karaoke, and boys. But a terrible family secret involving an ancient family "curse" is about to make things a lot more difficult.

About Rumiko Takahashi

Born in 1957 in Niigata, Japan, Rumiko Takahashi attended women's college in Tokyo, where she began studying comics with Kazuo Koike, author of CRYING FREEMAN. She later became an assistant to horror-manga artist Kazuo Umezu (OROCHI). In 1978, she won a prize in Shogakukan's annual "New Comic Artist Contest," and in that same year her boy-meets-alien comedy series URUSEI YATSURA began appearing in the weekly manga magazine SHÔNEN SUNDAY. This phenomenally successful series ran for nine years and sold over 22 million copies. Takahashi's later RANMA 1/2 series enjoyed even greater popularity.

Takahashi is considered by many to be one of the world's most popular manga artists. With the publication of Volume 34 of her RANMA 1/2 series in Japan, Takahashi's total sales passed one hundred million copies of her compiled works.

Takahashi's serial titles include URUSEI YATSURA, RANMA 1/2, ONE-POUND GOSPEL, MAISON IKKOKU and INUYASHA. Additionally, Takahashi has drawn many short stories which have been published in America under the title "Rumic Theater," and several installments of a saga known as her "Mermaid" series. Most of Takahashi's major stories have also been animated and are widely available in translation worldwide. INUYASHA is her most recent serial story, first published in SHÔNEN SUNDAY in 1996.

Your Favorite Rumiko Takahashi Titles...Now Available From VIZ Media!

Complete your collection with these Takahashi anime and manga classics!

Get yours today!

www.viz.com

INUYASHA © 1997 Rumiko TAKAHASHI/Shogakukan Inc. MAISON IKKOKU © 1984 Rumiko TAKAHASHI/Shogakukan Inc. RANMA 1/2 © 1988 Rumiko TAKAHASHI/Shogakukan

INUYASHA ™

Rated #1 on Cartoon
Network's Adult
Swim!

In its
original,
unedited
form!

maison ikkoku ™

The beloved
romantic comedy
of errors–a fan
favorite!

Ranma ½ ™

The zany, wacky study
of martial arts at its
best!

INUYASHA © Rumiko Takahashi/Shogakukan • Yomiuri TV • Sunrise 2000.
RANMA 1/2 © 2003 Rumiko Takahashi/Shogakukan • Kitty Film • Fuji TV. MAISON IKKOKU © 1986 Rumiko Takahashi/Shogakukan • Kitty Film • Fuji TV.

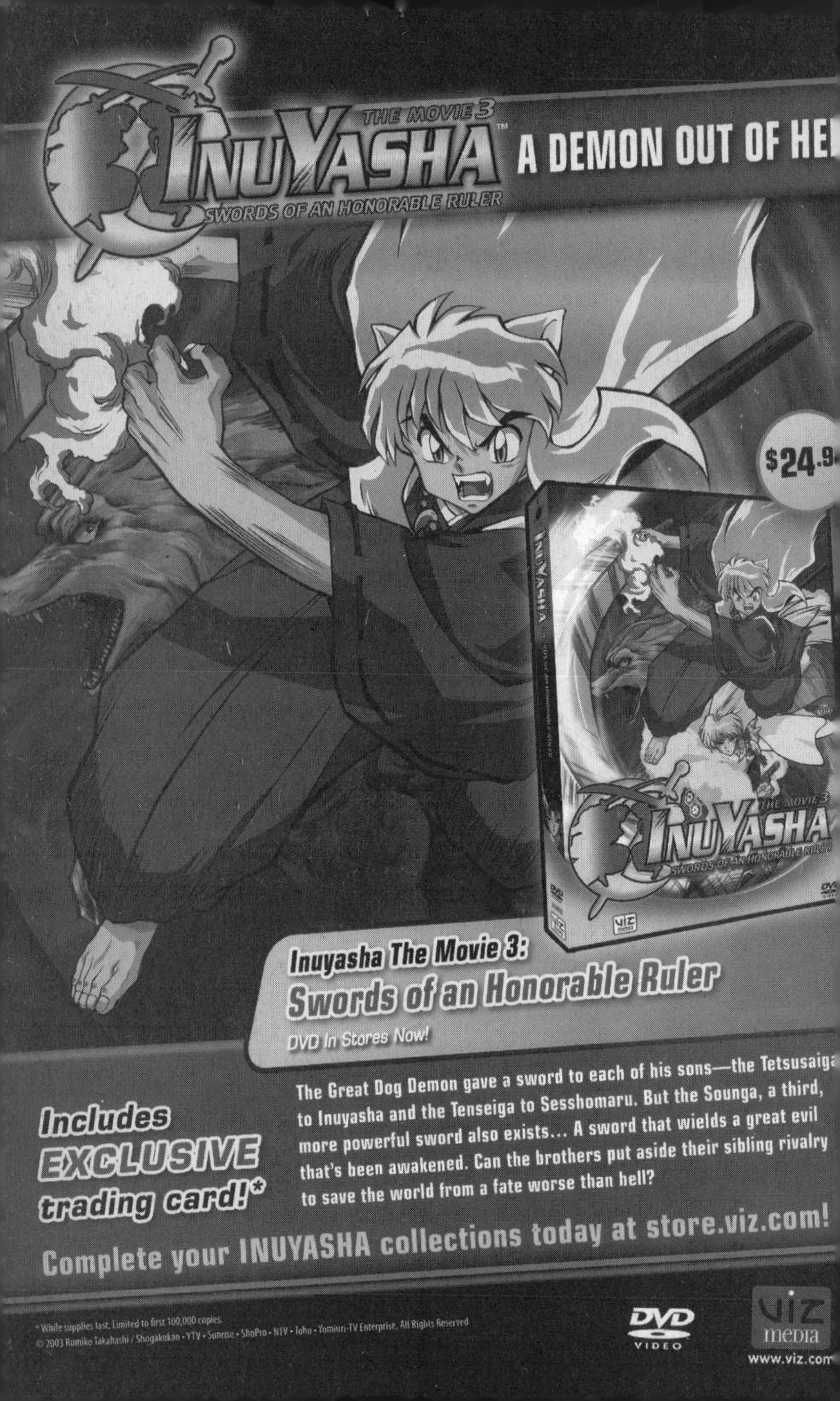
THE MOVIE 3
INUYASHA
SWORDS OF AN HONORABLE RULER
A DEMON OUT OF HEL
$24.9
Inuyasha The Movie 3:
Swords of an Honorable Ruler
DVD In Stores Now!
The Great Dog Demon gave a sword to each of his sons—the Tetsusaiga to Inuyasha and the Tenseiga to Sesshomaru. But the Sounga, a third, more powerful sword also exists... A sword that wields a great evil that's been awakened. Can the brothers put aside their sibling rivalry to save the world from a fate worse than hell?
Includes EXCLUSIVE trading card!*
Complete your INUYASHA collections today at store.viz.com!
* While supplies last. Limited to first 100,000 copies.
© 2003 Rumiko Takahashi / Shogakukan • YTV • Sunrise • ShoPro • NTV • Toho • Yomiuri-TV Enterprise. All Rights Reserved
DVD VIDEO
viz media
www.viz.com

CATCH A MANGA SPELL!

ZATCHBELL!™

Kiyo doesn't have many friends and his too-smart-for-his-own-good attitude doesn't help. So his dad sends him a little boy named Zatch. But Zatch isn't exactly human… When Kiyo reads from Zatch's spell book, not having friends becomes the least of his problems!

ZATCHBELL!
STORY AND ART BY
MAKOTO RAIKU

ONLY $9.99!

VIZ media

START YOUR
GRAPHIC NOVEL
COLLECTION
TODAY—NOW
AVAILABLE AT
STORE.VIZ.COM!

action

All New ACTION Graphic Novels!

www.viz.com

Starting at $8.95!

The latest volumes now available at store.viz.com:

Battle Angel Alita: Last Order, Vol. 6
Case Closed, Vol. 8
Cheeky Angel, Vol. 9
Fullmetal Alchemist, Vol. 4
Kekkaishi, Vol. 3
MÄR, Vol. 4
No Need for Tenchi, Vol. 5 (2nd ed.)
The All-New Tenchi Muyo!, Vol. 7
Ranma 1/2, Vol. 21 (2nd ed.)
Ranma 1/2, Vol. 32

* Also available on DVD from VIZ

ALL-NEW TENCHI MUYO! © 2001 HITOSHI OKUDA © AIC/VAP • NTV. GUNNM LAST ORDER © 2000 by Yukito Kishiro/SHUEISHA Inc. CASE CLOSED © 1994 Gosho AOYAMA/Shogakukan Inc. CHEEKY ANGEL © 1999 Hiroyuki NISHIMORI/Shogakukan Inc. FULLMETAL ALCHEMIST © Hiromu Arakawa/SQUARE ENIX KEKKAISHI © 2004 Yellow TANABE/Shogakukan Inc. MAR © 2003 Nobuyuki ANZAI/Shogakukan Inc. NO NEED for TENCHI! © HITOSHI OKUDA 1996 © AIC/VAP • NTV. RANMA1/2 © 1988 Rumiko TAKAHASHI/Shogakukan Inc.

LOVE MANGA? LET US KNOW!

☐ Please do NOT send me information about VIZ Media products, news and events, special offers, or other information.

☐ Please do NOT send me information from VIZ Media's trusted business partners.

Name: _____

Address: _____

City: _____ **State:** _____ **Zip:** _____

E-mail: _____

☐ Male ☐ Female **Date of Birth** (mm/dd/yyyy): ___/___/_____ (Under 13? Parental consent required)

What race/ethnicity do you consider yourself? (check all that apply)

☐ White/Caucasian ☐ Black/African American ☐ Hispanic/Latino

☐ Asian/Pacific Islander ☐ Native American/Alaskan Native ☐ Other: _____

What VIZ Media title(s) did you purchase? (indicate title(s) purchased) _____

_____

What other VIZ Media titles do you own? _____

_____

Reason for purchase: (check all that apply)

☐ Special offer ☐ Favorite title / author / artist / genre

☐ Gift ☐ Recommendation ☐ Collection

☐ Read excerpt in VIZ Media manga sampler ☐ Other _____

Where did you make your purchase? (please check one)

☐ Comic store ☐ Bookstore ☐ Grocery Store

☐ Convention ☐ Newsstand ☐ Video Game Store

☐ Online (site:_____) ☐ Other _____

How many manga titles have you purchased in the last year? How many were VIZ Media titles?
(please check one from each column)

MANGA
- ☐ None
- ☐ 1 – 4
- ☐ 5 – 10
- ☐ 11+

VIZ Media
- ☐ None
- ☐ 1 – 4
- ☐ 5 – 10
- ☐ 11+

How much influence do special promotions and gifts-with-purchase have on the titles you buy?
(please circle, with 5 being great influence and 1 being none)

1   2   3   4   5

Do you purchase every volume of your favorite series?
- ☐ Yes! Gotta have 'em as my own
- ☐ No. Please explain: _____

What kind of manga storylines do you most enjoy? (check all that apply)

- ☐ Action / Adventure
- ☐ Comedy
- ☐ Fighting
- ☐ Artistic / Alternative
- ☐ Science Fiction
- ☐ Romance (shojo)
- ☐ Sports
- ☐ Other _____
- ☐ Horror
- ☐ Fantasy (shojo)
- ☐ Historical

If you watch the anime or play a video or TCG game from a series, how likely are you to buy the manga? (please circle, with 5 being very likely and 1 being unlikely)

1   2   3   4   5

If unlikely, please explain: _____

Who are your favorite authors / artists? _____

_____

What titles would like you translated and sold in English? _____

_____

THANK YOU! Please send the completed form to:

NJW Research
42 Catharine Street
Poughkeepsie, NY 12601

Your privacy is very important to us. All information provided will be used for internal purposes only and will not be sold or otherwise divulged.

NO PURCHASE NECESSARY. Requests not in compliance with all terms of this form will not be acknowledged or returned. All submissions are subject to verification and become the property of VIZ Media. Fraudulent submission, including use of multiple addresses or P.O. boxes to obtain additional VIZ Media information or offers may result in prosecution. VIZ Media reserves the right to withdraw or modify any terms of this form. Void where prohibited, taxed, or restricted by law. VIZ Media will not be liable for lost, misdirected, mutilated, illegible, incomplete or postage-due mail. © 2005 VIZ Media. All Rights Reserved. VIZ Media, property titles, characters, names and plots therein under license to VIZ Media. All Rights Reserved.